Brain, Body, and Mind

Brain, Body, and Mind
Neuroethics with a Human Face

Walter Glannon

OXFORD
UNIVERSITY PRESS

Oxford University Press is a department of the University of Oxford.
It furthers the University's objective of excellence in research,
scholarship, and education by publishing worldwide.

Oxford   New York

Auckland   Cape Town   Dar es Salaam   Hong Kong   Karachi
Kuala Lumpur   Madrid   Melbourne   Mexico City   Nairobi
New Delhi   Shanghai   Taipei   Toronto

With offices in

Argentina   Austria   Brazil   Chile   Czech Republic   France   Greece
Guatemala   Hungary   Italy   Japan   Poland   Portugal   Singapore
South Korea   Switzerland   Thailand   Turkey   Ukraine   Vietnam

Oxford is a registered trade mark of Oxford University Press
in the UK and certain other countries.

Published in the United States of America by
Oxford University Press
198 Madison Avenue, New York, NY 10016

© Oxford University Press 2011

First issued as an Oxford University Press paperback, 2013.

Library of Congress Cataloging-in-Publication Data
Glannon, Walter.
Brain, body, and mind: neuroethics with a human face/by Walter Glannon.
p. cm.
Includes bibliographical references (p.) and index.
ISBN 978-0-19-973409-2 (hardcover); 978-0-19-931579-6 (paperback)
1. Neurosciences–Moral and ethical aspects.   2. Bioethics.   3. Medical ethics.   I. Title.
RC343.G533 2011
174'.957–dc22   2010028196

Printed in the United States of America
on acid-free paper

For Yee-Wah

Acknowledgments

I thank my editor at Oxford University Press, Peter Ohlin, for his advice and support of this project since I first proposed it to him. The three referees commissioned by OUP, Grant Gillett, Judy Illes, and Neil Levy, gave me very helpful comments on earlier versions of the book's chapters, and I thank them as well. I am grateful to Smitha Raj Kini for skillfully guiding the production process and to Ken Hassman for compiling the index.

I presented many of the ideas in this book to audiences at a number of conferences and workshops. These include the 2007 Pacific and Eastern Division Meetings of the American Philosophical Association in San Francisco and Baltimore; the 2007 Canadian Bioethics Society Meeting in Toronto; a workshop on vision at York University in Toronto in August 2007; the 2007 meeting of the American Society for Bioethics and Humanities in Washington, D.C.; the Crosley Lecture at the University of New England in March 2008; the Disorders of Body and Mind Research Group in Heidelberg in June 2008; the David Thomasma Bioethics Retreat in Paris in June 2008; a workshop sponsored by the Canadian Institutes of Health Research on deep-brain stimulation in Halifax in September 2008; a lecture at the Center for the Study of Religion and Conflict at Arizona State University in October 2008; two Mellon lectures on philosophical psychology at Bates College in March 2009; a conference on law and neuroscience at University College London in July 2009; a neuroscience summer school on metabolic aspects of neurodegenerative diseases in Reisensburg, Germany, in July 2009; the "Brain Matters" conference in Halifax in September 2009; the December 2009 meeting of the North American Neuromodulation Society in Las Vegas, and a workshop sponsored by the Canadian Institutes of Health Research on the neurobiology and ethics of decision-making in Jackson's Point, Ontario, in September 2010. I thank all of these audiences for their comments.

Parts of this book have been published as journal articles and chapters in three edited volumes. These include "Neurostimulation and the Minimally Conscious State" *Bioethics* 22 (2008): 337–345, and "Our Brains Are not Us,"

Bioethics 23 (2009): 321–329, with permission from Wiley-Blackwell Publishing Ltd; "Psychopharmacological Enhancement," *Neuroethics* 1(1) (2008): 45–54, "Moral Responsibility and the Psychopath," *Neuroethics* 1(3) (2008): 158–166, "Deep-Brain Stimulation for Depression," *HEC Forum* 20 (2008): 325–335, and "Decelerating and Arresting Human Aging," in B. Gordijn and R. Chadwick, eds., *Medical Enhancement and Posthumanity* (Berlin & London: Springer, 2008), 175–189, with kind permission from Springer Science & Business Media; "Stimulating Brains, Altering Minds," *Journal of Medical Ethics* 35 (2009): 289–292, with permission from the BMJ Group; "The Blessing and Burden of Biological Psychiatry," *Journal of Ethics in Mental Health* 3(2) (2008) e1–3, and "Neuroscience, Free Will, and Responsibility," *Journal of Ethics in Mental Health* 4(2) (2009): e1–6, with permission from the editor of the Journal; "Consent to Deep-Brain Stimulation for Neurological and Psychiatric Disorders," *Journal of Clinical Ethics* 21 (2010): 104–111, with permission from the *Journal of Clinical Ethics*; "The Neuroethics of Memory," in S. Nalbantian, P. Matthews, and J. L. McClelland, eds., *The Memory Process: Neuroscientific and Humanistic Perspectives* (Cambridge, MA: MIT Press, 2010), 233–251, with permission from the MIT Press; and "What Neuroscience Can (and Cannot) Tell Us about Criminal Responsibility," in M. Freeman, ed., *Law and Neuroscience: Current Legal Issues 2010*, Volume 13 (Oxford: Oxford University Press, 2010), 13–28, with permission from Oxford University Press.

I thank the referees and editors of these journals and books for their thoughtful and constructive reviews. Among the editors, I especially would like to thank Emily Bell, Ruth Chadwick, Paul Ford, Bert Gordijn, Suzanne Nalbantian, Neil Levy, Eric Racine, and Walter Sinnott-Armstrong. I am also grateful to Stephen Morse for his comments on the Introduction and to Adam Zeman for his comments on Chapter 1. Some of the work on this book was supported by the Canada Research Chairs program and the Canadian Institutes of Health Research, NNF 80045, States of Mind: Emerging Issues in Neuroethics. I have benefited greatly from being a co-investigator on the States of Mind project, led by principal investigator Françoise Baylis. While I have learned from all the people on this project, I am particularly grateful to Mary Pat McAndrews and Nir Lipsman for teaching me so much about clinical neuroscience.

Contents

Brain, Body, and Mind

Introduction

In a landmark paper published in 2002, philosopher and neuroscientist Adina Roskies divided neuroethics into two branches: the ethics of neuroscience, and the neuroscience of ethics.[1] The first branch examines practical ethical issues arising from measuring and intervening in the brain. These issues include informed consent and benefit–risk assessments regarding the use of brain imaging, psychotropic drugs, functional neurosurgery such as deep-brain stimulation, and neural stem-cell transplantation. They pertain to standard, experimental, and innovative forms of these interventions. The second branch examines the neural mechanisms that underlie decision making and how these mechanisms bear on questions about free will, moral and legal responsibility, and moral judgment. Roskies claimed that each of these divisions "can be pursued independently to a large extent, but perhaps most intriguing is to contemplate how progress in each will affect the other."[2]

The ethics of neuroscience and the neuroscience of ethics overlap in some respects. Thanks mainly to functional neuroimaging, we have a better understanding of the neural correlates of the cognitive and affective processes behind our practical and moral reasoning. This understanding can help to establish whether a person has enough mental capacity to consider the potential benefits and risks of an intervention in his or her brain and consent to it. Yet the two branches are distinct in that the neuroscience of ethics involves more theoretical issues, while the ethics of neuroscience involves more practical issues. I treat the branches as generally separable, beginning with the theoretical side and then addressing the practical side. The structure of the book reflects this methodology. In the first chapter, I present a particular conception of the brain-mind relation that frames and guides the discussion in the rest of the book. In Chapters 2, 3, and 4, I discuss the neuro-biological basis of free will, moral and legal responsibility, and moral reasoning.

---

1. "Neuroethics for the New Millennium," *Neuron* 35 (2002): 21–23.
2. *Ibid.*, 21.

In Chapters 5, 6, 7, and 8, I discuss cognitive enhancement, severe brain injury, deep-brain stimulation, and neural stem-cell and molecular replacement therapy.

The majority of people writing on this general topic focus on either the theoretical or practical dimension of neuroethics.[3] By addressing both dimensions, I offer a more well-rounded discussion of the current state of the field. I discussed some of these issues in *Bioethics and the Brain*. While that book was more comprehensive in the number of topics it covered, this book offers a more sustained and thorough discussion of the topics that have figured most prominently in debates about neuroethics in the last 5 years and will continue to spark debate in the future. It is aimed at an interdisciplinary audience, including philosophers, clinical and cognitive neuroscientists, legal theorists, psychologists, sociologists, and anthropologists. I have tried not to assume any technical knowledge of philosophy or neuroscience, emphasizing commonalities rather than differences and viewing the disciplines encompassed by neuroethics as complementary rather than competing. The book is written in the spirit of E. O. Wilson's idea of consilience, the synthesis of knowledge from different specialized fields to create a common groundwork for explanation.[4]

While I defend a holistic conception of the brain–mind relation and a compatibilist conception of free will and moral responsibility, I do not adopt a single overarching theory to motivate the discussion of the ethical issues. Doing this in a book that covers a number of issues runs the risk of artificially forcing them to fit the theory. The chapter on neuroscience and moral reasoning could be described as a meta-ethical analysis of our deontological and utilitarian intuitions and judgments, but it does not defend one of these theories against the other. In the last four chapters, I defend a position that combines a libertarian view of individual autonomy with a consequentialist view of promoting benefit and preventing harm.

The title of the book expresses the idea that the mind is the product of interaction between the brain and factors internal and external to the body. I use the same basic conception of the mind as I did in *Bioethics and the Brain*. I describe the mind as a set of unconscious and conscious properties that emerge from the brain when it reaches a certain level of complexity. These emergent properties are necessary for a human organism or subject to adapt to and survive in the environment. Mental states in general are caused or mediated not by localized regions of the brain but by distributed neural networks. These positions have been defended by others. But they are at odds with a number of philosophers who claim that emergent mental states are epiphenomenal and that particular mental states map directly onto particular brain states.[5]

Regarding the first issue, emergent mental states are epiphenomenal only if the causal pathway from brain to mind is bottom-up and linear, moving in only one

---

3. Notable exceptions are E. Racine, *Pragmatic Neuroethics: Improving Treatment and Understanding of the Mind-Brain* (Cambridge, MA: MIT Press, 2010), M. Farah, and G. Gillett. I cite and discuss the work of Farah and Gillett in this introduction as well as in Chapters 2, 5, and 6.
4. *Consilience: The Unity of Knowledge* (New York: Alfred A. Knopf, 1998).
5. See, for example, J. Kim, "Emergence: Core Ideas and Issues," *Synthese* 151 (2006): 547–559.

direction. The facts that chronic psychological stress can cause neural dysfunction in psychiatric disorders such as major depression and generalized anxiety, and that psychotherapies can modulate this dysfunction, suggest a circular causal model in which brain and mind influence each other. This occurs through the mediation of the body and environment in a nested series of feedforward and feedback loops. Not all mental states are epiphenomenal; some can have positive or negative effects on the brain.

Regarding the second issue, depression and anxiety develop from dysfunction in pathways between the cerebral cortex and the limbic system. The symptoms of these psychiatric disorders can be ameliorated by modulating these pathways through psychotherapy or drugs, or a combination of the two. The effects of these therapies indicate that the neural networks underlying the symptoms associated with these disorders are not circumscribed in specific regions of the brain. Deep-brain stimulation confirms this point. Electrical stimulation of an overactive subgenual cingulate can modulate one of the neural circuits implicated in depression and improve some symptoms in some patients. Stimulation of an underactive nucleus accumbens in the reward system can modulate a different circuit and improve other symptoms in this same disorder. These results show that the neural basis of depression is not located in one circuit or region of the brain but involves neural circuits in different regions that project to and from each other. In addition, deep-brain stimulation may generate a greater degree of consciousness in some individuals in a minimally conscious state. It does this by activating neural networks in the cerebral cortex. Yet it is not the cortex that is stimulated but the central thalamus. The projections from the thalamus to the cortex enable the activation associated with an increase in awareness. The ascending reticular activating system in the brainstem also plays an important role in consciousness through its projections to the thalamus and cortex. So it is misleading to say that the cerebral cortex is the seat of consciousness and that conscious states are realized in this region of the brain. Certain regions of the brain play a critical role in mediating certain mental functions. But this does not imply that we can identify a single neural source of every function.

The subtitle of this book captures its antireductionist theme. I argue that persons are more than sets of neurons, synapses, and neurotransmitters, and that our actions and normative practices are more than a function of neural mechanisms. In the clinical neurosciences of neurosurgery, psychiatry, and neurology, the success of any intervention in the brain depends not only on whether it modulates brain function but also on whether it benefits a person and improves his or her quality of life. Neuroscience will not offer a very helpful explanation of persons and how they benefit from or are harmed by psychotropic drugs, functional neurosurgery, or neural stem-cell transplantation if it describes them entirely in terms of brain processes rather than as agents with desires, beliefs, emotions, interests, and intentions. I cite a number of actual cases of people from clinical, experimental, and innovative neuroscience as well as anecdotes to bring the ethical issues to life.

Many reductionist claims about the mind's relation to the brain have been generated by findings from functional neuroimaging in cognitive neuroscience. The conviction that neuroimaging shows that mental states are realized in particular brain states fails to appreciate the limitations of imaging as a measure of brain and mental function. For example, the blood-oxygen-level-dependent (BOLD) signal in functional magnetic resonance imaging (fMRI) is at best an indirect measure of what actually occurs at the neural level. If neuroimaging does not provide direct access to the brain, and if the mind is not reducible to the brain, then neuroimaging does not provide direct access to the mind. In a cautionary note, neurologist Marcus Raichle writes: "If we are not careful, functional brain imaging could be viewed as no more than a modern and extraordinarily expensive version of 19th-century phrenology, which associated certain mental faculties and character with parts of the skull. In this regard, it is worth noting that functional imaging researchers themselves have occasionally unwittingly perpetuated this notion."[6] Raichle cites the admonition of neurologist Korbinian Brodmann (1868–1918) against the idea of localization: "Indeed, recently theories have abounded which, like phrenology, attempt to localize complex mental activity such as memory, will, fantasy, intelligence or spatial qualities such as appreciation of shape and position to circumscribed cortical zones."[7] Further, "these mental faculties are notions used to designate extraordinarily involved complexes of mental functions... One cannot think of their taking place in any other way than through an infinitely complex and involved interaction and cooperation of numerous elementary activities..."[8]

Social neuroscientist John Cacioppo and coauthors also reject the idea of localization: "A fundamental assumption underlying many brain-imaging studies in the cognitive and social neurosciences is that there is... a localization of information-processing components that bear on social cognition and behavior."[9] Highlighting what they call a category error in cognitive neuroscience, Cacioppo et al. point out that "memories, emotions, and beliefs, for instance, were each once thought to be localized in a single site in the brain. Current evidence, however, now suggests that most complex psychological or behavioral concepts do not map into a single center in the brain."[10] Even vision, which has always been considered one of the most localized brain functions, involves activity not just in the occipital lobes but in the parietal, temporal, and frontal lobes as well.

The fact that functional neuroimaging is limited in terms of what it can reveal about the brain and mind should make us question the idea that imaging can read minds. Imaging may reveal some mental content, but only in a very limited and

6. "Neuroimaging," *Cerebrum* 9, January 2006; http://www.dana.org/printerfriendly.aspx?id=4224

7. *Localization in the Cerebral Cortex*, trans. L. Garey (London: Smith-Gordon, 1994) 254–255.

8. *Ibid.* Similarly, W. Penfield states: "To suppose that consciousness or the mind has localization is a failure to understand neurophysiology." In *The Mystery of the Mind: A Critical Study of Consciousness and the Human Brain* (Princeton: Princeton University Press, 1975), 109. See also D. Weisberg et al., "The Seductive Allure of Neuroscience Explanations," *Journal of Cognitive Neuroscience* 20 (2008): 470–477,

9. "Just Because You're Imaging the Brain Doesn't Mean that You Can Stop Using Your Head: A Primer and Set of First Principles," *Journal of Personality and Social Psychology* 85 (2003): 650–661, at 653.

10. *Ibid.*, 654.

indirect way.[11] When one deliberately raises one's arm while in an fMRI scanner, the intention to raise the arm can be inferred, or "read," from images of activity in the pre-motor and motor cortices just before and during the action. Photos of people from different racial groups shown to subjects undergoing a scan can activate limbic regions in a way that might suggest racial bias. In addition, neuromarketing using functional brain imaging may detect preferences for consumer products on the basis of activation of brain regions believed to regulate these preferences.

Brain imaging cannot capture or duplicate the content of most of our thought because this content is outside of the brain. A scan cannot reproduce the external states of affairs that are the objects of one's conscious mental states. Except for a few examples of the type I have given, a brain scan cannot tell a third party what a person is thinking of. Images from a PET or fMRI scan could not tell a radiologist that I was thinking of a real or imagined mountain landscape while undergoing a diagnostic test of my brain. They could not reveal what Woody Allen and Diane Keaton were thinking in the scene from *Annie Hall* when they are conversing and their actual thoughts are described in subtitles. If they were conversing through an intercom while in separate scanners, we could not draw a valid inference about what they were thinking from any images of their brains. Nor could images from repeated scans capture the subjective aspect of James Joyce's thought when he was writing *Ulysses*, much less the stream of consciousness of his character Leopold Bloom in the course of one day in June 1904. In most cases, the content of one's thought is beyond what a scan or series of scans can show. In all cases, the subjective quality of one's thought, or what it is like to have a particular desire, belief, or emotion, eludes even the most sophisticated imaging techniques. Brain imaging would be a literal and not just a figurative and indirect form of mind reading only if it could capture the full content and quality of our thought.

Functional neuroimaging has also been used as form of lie detection. Yet it has many flaws. Brain fingerprinting, or "No Lie fMRI," may not be able to distinguish between spontaneous and rehearsed lies because the activation patterns in the relevant brain regions would be similar in either case. The artificial setting of the scanner could facilitate extensive rehearsal of a lie and be a cognitive countermeasure to the technique. Activation of the ventrolateral prefrontal cortex and anterior cingulate cortex is associated with lying. In response to certain questions, one or both of these regions may become activated in people with schizophrenia who are experiencing delusions. But it is not clear that this would be a sign of lying or deception if they have false beliefs to begin with. For this and similar reasons, people with other cognitive disorders such as dementia, somatoform disorder, and confabulation would not be good candidates for the technique either. False memory can unintentionally produce inaccurate accounts of past events. This would further limit any practical

---

11. Analyzing data from 16 imaging studies, M. Farah et al. state that "the use of imaging to gather information about an individual's psychological traits is already possible, but to an extremely limited extent." "Brain Imaging and Brain Privacy: A Realistic Concern?" *Journal of Cognitive Neuroscience* 21 (2008): 119–127, at 119. Farah says that "the potential of brain imaging for mind reading is uncertain but cannot be dismissed *a priori.*" In Farah, ed., *Neuroethics: An Introduction with Readings* (Cambridge, MA: MIT Press, 2010), 137.

applications of this technique. The privilege against compulsory self-incrimination by defendants and witnesses is yet another obstacle that may prevent fMRI from meeting legal standards of admissibility in court proceedings. It is difficult to imagine any situation in which we could justify scanning people's brains against their will.

Although the term 'mind' appears in the title, this book is not an essay on the philosophy of mind. Instead, my discussion of the psychological, metaphysical, and ethical issues is based on what the clinical neurosciences have revealed about the brain–mind relation. Philosophy of mind predates neuroscience. Yet philosophers have contributed comparatively little to our understanding that conscious and unconscious mental states are generated and sustained by brain states, and that the first can influence and be influenced by the second. This is at least partly because many hypotheses in the philosophy of mind are motivated by thought experiments about fictional people in imagined situations. In contrast, clinical neuroscientists have taught us much more about the brain and mind through observation of actual patients with neuropsychiatric disorders or injuries to brain regions regulating different aspects of thought and behavior. This observation has resulted in a better understanding of normal brain and mental function.

In addition to Brodmann's work, studies of brain-injured patients by neuropsychologist A. R. Luria (1902–1977) reinforced the view that the bases of complex behavioral processes are not localized but distributed across broad areas of the brain. Luria also showed how the brain and culture interact in generating our psychology. Neurologist Norman Geschwind (1926–1984) further explained cognitive and behavioral disorders resulting from brain lesions and neurological dysfunction in his patients. He is probably best known for the "Geschwind syndrome," a personality disorder consisting of hypergraphia, excessive verbal output, hyposexuality, and hyperreligiosity in some patients with temporal lobe epilepsy. From studies of patients who had undergone commissurotomies, or "split-brain" operations, neuropsychologist Roger Sperry (1913–1994) demonstrated that each of the two brain hemispheres is a conscious system in its own right. In addition, neuroanatomist James Papez (1883–1953) outlined the "Papez circuit," a major pathway of the limbic system regulating emotion. This view has been revised by neuroscientists emphasizing that some regions of the Papez circuit involve functions that are not limited to emotion, and that different types of emotion may have their own circuits. Neurosurgeon Wilder Penfield (1891–1976) also made a major discovery about the neurobiological basis of cognition, memory, and sensation while performing "awake" neurosurgery on patients with epilepsy. And contemporary behavioral neurologist Antonio Damasio has shown from studies of patients with lesions in prefrontal brain regions that cognition and emotion are interacting processes mediated by interacting cortical and subcortical systems in the brain.

This is just a partial list of clinical neuroscientists who have made significant contributions to our knowledge that the brain generates and sustains the mind. Nevertheless, neuroscience does not tell us how the brain enables mental processes. Knowing *that* certain regions of the brain mediate certain cognitive and affective functions does not mean that we know *how* the brain makes these functions possible. Neuroscience does not offer a complete explanation of enabling mechanisms in the brain-mind relation.

Here is a brief summary of the eight chapters. In Chapter 1, I argue that persons are constituted by their brains but are not identical to them. By showing that the mind is the product of interaction between and among the brain, body, and environment, I reject the reductionist view that all of our psychological properties can be explained entirely in terms of brain function. The conception of the brain–mind relation that I develop in this chapter motivates the discussion of psychological, metaphysical, and ethical issues in the chapters that follow.

In Chapter 2, I argue that the findings from cognitive neuroscience do not show that free will is an illusion and point out flaws in the argument from illusion. The fact that a mental state or event has a physical cause in the brain does not imply that it is not among the causes of an action. Nor does it imply that our choices and actions are coerced, compelled, or constrained by normal brain processes. We have enough control of our conscious mental states to be the authors of the actions in which they issue. I also discuss the neurobiological basis of moral responsibility and maintain that brain dysfunction impairs or undermines responsibility when it impairs or undermines the mental capacity necessary for responsibility. I focus on psychopathy to test this position. I continue the discussion of responsibility in Chapter 3, arguing that neuroscience, in the form of neuroimaging, can inform but not determine whether an individual has the requisite mental capacity to be responsible for criminal behavior. I point out that brain dysfunction can be a matter of degree, and that this may influence judgments of responsibility, mitigation, and excuse in the criminal law. In analyzing these judgments, I distinguish lacking mental capacity, having partial mental capacity, and having full mental capacity but failing to exercise it. Chapter 4 examines claims by some philosophers and psychologists conducting functional neuroimaging experiments about the neural basis of moral intuitions and judgments. I question the idea that there are distinct cognitive and emotional subsystems in the brain driving utilitarian and deontological judgments. I appeal to neuroscientific research showing that cognition and emotion are interacting processes mediated by interacting neural systems distributed throughout the brain. Still, the reasons we adduce to justify actions depend not only on brain systems but also on social and environmental factors external to the brain.

Chapter 5 is a discussion of the ethical aspects of cognitive enhancement. I consider the use of psychotropic drugs to improve attention and focus and whether this gives some people an unfair advantage over others. I also consider the potential positive and negative effects of enhancing memory and argue that enhancement does not necessarily undermine authenticity or alienate us from our true selves. My general position is that competent adults should be allowed to take cognition-enhancing drugs but should also be responsible for any resulting personal and medical costs. I explore the metaphysical and ethical implications of severe brain injury in Chapter 6, discussing the respects in which individuals with these injuries survive or fail to survive them. Even when they survive, they may or may not benefit from medical interventions that keep them alive and restore a greater degree of consciousness. Survival and consciousness by themselves have no value. What matters is which physical and cognitive functions are restored, the degree to which they are restored, and how they compare with the functions the individual had before the injury. In some cases, recovering a greater degree of consciousness can be worse for a person and result in significant harm. Chapter 7 considers the use of deep-brain stimulation as a treatment for neurological and psychiatric disorders. I address the question of whether a person with a disease of the mind can consent to stimulation of the brain, and how patients and medical teams weigh the potential benefits and risks of the treatment. The medical and moral justification of this technique depends not only on whether it modulates brain function but also on how it affects all the psychological properties of the patient. Chapter 8 examines neural stem-cell and molecular replacement therapy for neurodegenerative diseases and spinal cord injury. While these interventions have the potential to regenerate the brain and spinal cord, results from clinical trials testing them over the last 25 years have not been very promising. The goal of decelerating neural degeneration and restoring brain function is still an unrealized possibility. I point out that the underlying pathophysiology of neurodegenerative diseases may limit or preclude the regenerative potential of transplanting or injecting cells into the brain. I then explore some of the possible social and psychological consequences of two hypothetical scenarios: one in which regeneration of the brain does not keep pace with regeneration of the body; and one in which it does.

1

Our Brains Are not Us

In *The Astonishing Hypothesis*, Francis Crick confidently asserts that "you, your joys and sorrows, your memories and ambitions, your sense of personal identity and free will, are in fact no more than the behavior of a vast assembly of nerve cells and their associated molecules."[1] This idea is traceable to Hippocrates, who states that "from the brain, and from the brain only, arise our pleasures, joys, laughter and jests, as well as our sorrows, pains, grief, and tears."[2] Similarly, Jean-Pierre Changeux states in *Neuronal Man* that "all forms of behavior mobilize distinct sets of nerve cells, and it is at their level that the final explanation of behavior must be sought."[3] Further, Joseph LeDoux states that the underlying theme of his book, *Synaptic Self*, is that "you are your synapses."[4] These and similar claims made by other neuroscientists and philosophers suggest that our thought and behavior can be explained completely in terms of neurons, synapses, and neurotransmitters, and how they regulate brain function.[5] Our conative, cognitive, and affective states, and the

---

1. *The Astonishing Hypothesis: The Scientific Search for the Soul* (New York: Scribner's, 1994), 3. J. Greene and J. Cohen present a similar view in claiming that our mental lives are the by-product of a mass of neuronal instrumentation, in "For the Law, Neuroscience Changes Nothing and Everything," *Philosophical Transactions of the Royal Society of London* 359 (2004): 1775–1785.
2. *On the Sacred Disease* (epilepsy), cited by J. D. Spillane in *The Doctrine of the Nerves* (Oxford: Oxford University Press, 1981), 8.
3. *Neuronal Man: The Biology of Mind*, trans. L. Garey (Princeton: Princeton University Press, 1997), 97.
4. *Synaptic Self: How Our Brains Become Who We Are* (New York: Viking, 2002), ix.
5. Philosophers who defend different versions of neuroreductionism and locate the mind in the brain include D. Dennett, *Consciousness Explained* (Boston: Little Brown, 1991); P. Churchland, *The Engine of Reason, the Seat of the Soul* (Cambridge, MA: MIT Press, 1995); P. S. Churchland, *Brain-Wise; Studies in Neurophilosophy* (Cambridge, MA: MIT Press, 2002); and J. Bickle, *Philosophy and Neuroscience: A Ruthlessly Reductive Account*

actions in which they issue, can be fully accounted for by structural and functional features of the brain and its connections with the rest of the central nervous system (CNS). This explanatory reductionism informs the ontological reductionist claim that our minds are entirely a function of our brains. Mental states just are brain states. We are essentially our brains.

In this chapter, I challenge and reject neuroreductionism by showing that the mind emerges from and is shaped by interaction among the brain, body, and environment. The mind is not located in the brain but is distributed among these three entities as the organism engages with and constructs meaning from its surroundings. As persons, our capacity for unconscious and conscious states of mind, and to deliberate, choose, and act, is a function of the fact that we are embodied and embedded minds. We are embodied minds in the sense that our mental states are generated and sustained by the brain and its interaction with external and internal features of our bodies. We are also embedded minds in the sense that the content and quality of our mental states is shaped by how we act within the social and natural environment. We are constituted by our brains but are not identical to them. The brain is the most important but not the only factor in shaping personhood, identity, and agency. It is necessary but not sufficient to account for the physical and psychological properties that make each of us a unique individual. The brain is most plausibly conceived of as an organ that mediates interaction between the organism, or human subject, and the environment. It is not an isolated, self-sustaining organ but an enabling or relational organ that shapes and is shaped by this interaction. The mind is not based solely on brain structure and function, but on the continuous interaction of the brain with the body and the external world.

After describing the different respects in which our minds are embodied and embedded, I explore some of the implications of this view for neuroethics. Conceiving of the mind as embodied and embedded shows that neuroethical discussions have been too narrowly focused on the brain. Whether psychopharmacology, functional neurosurgery, and other interventions in the brain benefit or harm us depends on how they affect our minds. Yet if our minds are not located in and not reducible to our brains, then we need a broader framework to adequately assess the potential benefit and harm. Specifically, we need to consider how interventions that do not directly target the brain and CNS but other bodily systems and the environment can have salutary or deleterious effects on the brain and the mind.

Embodied Minds

The mind can be described as a set of unconscious and conscious states that emerge from the brain and its interaction with the body and environment. These include

---

(Amsterdam: Kluwer, 2003). In his book, Dennett says that he "will explain the various phenomena that compose what we call consciousness, showing how they are all physical effects of the brain's activities..." (16). Cognitive scientist M. Minsky gives the most straightforward version of this position in claiming that minds are simply what brains do in *The Society of Mind* (New York: Simon and Schuster, 1986).

beliefs, desires, emotions, feelings, and intentions. The mind emerges from a higher level of brain function in order to promote the adaptability and survival of the organism. This cannot be done at a lower level by neurons alone. Neurons cannot fully represent the environment to the organism because they lack the property of intentionality, or directedness toward states of affairs in the external world.[6] Mental states such as beliefs and emotions are intentional and their content includes these states of affairs. Nor can neural activity alone explain what it is like to have experience, or what may be called phenomenal consciousness. These intentional and phenomenological properties are necessary for the subject to accurately perceive and engage with the environment. Although the brain generates and sustains mental states, it is not an agent that can have interests and plan and execute intentions in actions. It is not the brain but the person constituted by the brain, body, and mind that acts and interacts with others in the world.

Agency operates at interacting unconscious and conscious levels. As one component of agency, the emotional state of fear enables us to develop a memory of and an unconscious learned response to external threats. It gives us the capacity for the fight-or-flight response necessary to successfully confront or avoid these threats. Although the reaction of fear is mediated by the amygdala and projections to it from the sensory thalamus and sensory cortex, the stimuli triggering this reaction are not located in the brain. Conscious beliefs enable us to discriminate between threatening and benign stimuli and respond appropriately to them. They enable us to avoid a chronic stress response that puts our bodies and brains on a constant state of alert that fails to align with the actual nature of these stimuli. When unconscious arousal and stress systems of the brain and mind become stuck in the "on" position and dysregulated, we can develop maladaptive and pathological conditions such as anxiety and depression. Beliefs and their intentional content provide the subject with a map and compass necessary to navigate in the natural world. I will not attempt to give a causal explanation of how consciousness arises from gray and white matter in the brain.But a brief functional explanation may help to understand the emergence of conscious mental states from the brain. As neurologist Adam Zeman puts it, the function of consciousness "is to free the organism from control by its immediate environment."[7] In positive terms, consciousness enables the organism to control its environment.

Most, if not all, cognitive neuroscientists reject Platonic and Cartesian substance dualism between mind and body. Yet claims by cognitive neuroscientists that who we are is essentially a function of neurons and synapses suggest that the

---

6. The concept of intentionality derives from F. Brentano, *Psychology from an Empirical Standpoint*, trans. T. Rancurello, D. Terrell, and L. McAllister (Atlantic Highlands, NJ: Humanities Press, 1973). E. Husserl developed Brentano's concept further in *Logical Investigations*, trans. J. Findlay (London: Routledge, 1970), and *The Phenomenology of Internal Time Consciousness*, trans. J. Churchill (Bloomington, IN: Indiana University Press, 1966).

7. "Does Consciousness Spring from the Brain? Dilemmas of Awareness in Practice and in Theory," in L. Weiskrantz and M. Davies, eds. *Frontiers of Consciousness* (Oxford: Oxford University Press, 2008), 289–321, at 312.

brain is only contingently related to the body. This introduces another version of dualism: brain–body dualism. Neuroreductionism can be described as a contemporary version of dualism in the sense that it locates the mind in the brain and either ignores or fails to appreciate the effects of the body on the brain and mind. An example of the extreme view that the brain could operate in a disembodied state was the brain-in-a-vat thought experiment that figured prominently in philosophical debates about the mind in the 1980s.[8] This experiment was based on a functionalist-computational theory of mind. According to this theory, mental states can be explained entirely in terms of their functional role, or their causal relations to other mental states, sensory inputs, and behavioral outputs. Because these states are multiply realizable, what matters is not *what* their source is or *how* they come about, but only *that* their source performs the appropriate functions. Cognitive and affective processes, as well as their neural basis, can be understood independently of their physical embodiment. In the thought experiment, a disembodied brain is sustained in a chemical bath. Neurons are connected by wires to a computer that provides them with the same electrical impulses the brain would ordinarily receive. The brain is capable of cognitive and other mental functions associated with our conscious experience provided that the neurons are stimulated in the right way. Stimulation of neurons and their connections to the computer can account for all of our experience. Neither a body nor an environment external to the brain and the vat is required. The experiment presumably showed that we do not need to go outside of the brain to account for the content and quality of mental states. Mental states are identical to and thus nothing more than brain states.

Antonio Damasio was one of the first neuroscientists to question neuroreductionism and the idea of a disembodied brain by proposing his somatic marker hypothesis.[9] This hypothesis emphasizes the role of bodily signals in emotion, and how these signals make emotion integral to reasoning and decision making. These signals, or markers, enable one to unconsciously or consciously monitor one's own body while perceiving external events and making sense of them. Changes in bodily states are translated into particular mental images mediated by different brain regions. Feeling an emotion, for example, is the experience of these bodily changes juxtaposed to mental images. By representing bodily states to the brain and the organism as a whole, somatic markers form a link between memory of previous experiences stored throughout the cortex and the feeling of these experiences mediated by the amygdala, hippocampus, and other limbic structures. Feelings, then, are not reducible to neural processes. Since the mind is constituted in part by feelings, the mind is not reducible to these processes. The body is a necessary frame

---

8. There is a large philosophical literature on this topic. H. Putnam offers the clearest description of this thought experiment in *Reason, Truth, and History* (New York: Cambridge University Press, 1981), Chapter 1. Putnam discussed the idea of a brain in a vat, not to defend embodiment, but to raise questions about our conceptual schemes.

9. *Descartes' Error: Emotion, Reason, and the Human Brain* (New York: Grosset/Putnam, 1994), and *The Feeling of What Happens: Body and Emotion in the Making of Consciousness* (Orlando, FL: Harcourt Brace, 1999), 40, 41–42.

of reference for our thought and its content. Discussing the constellation of physical and psychological states that constitute the self, Damasio says:

> ... numerous brain systems must be in full swing, as must numerous body-proper systems. If you were to cut *all* the nerves that bring brain signals to the body proper, your body state would change radically, and so consequently would your mind. Were you to cut *only* the signals from the body proper to the brain, your mind would change too. Even partial blocking of brain-body traffic, as happens in patients with spinal cord injury, causes changes in mind state.[10]

Damasio summarizes his position thus: "the mind is embodied, in the full sense of the term, not just embrained."[11]

Philosopher Shaun Gallagher's discussion of proprioception is in many respects an extension of Damasio's emphasis on the importance of the body for the mind.[12] Proprioception refers to the way in which the somatosensory system in the brain mediates perceptual processes related to the skin and body. It involves the position of the limbs in space as computed by receptors in the muscles and joints. These receptors are distributed throughout the body and convey information about the body to the brain. Gallagher distinguishes *body image*, which consists of a system of perceptions, attitudes, and beliefs pertaining to one's own body, from *body schema*, which consists of sensory-motor capacities that function without awareness or the necessity of perceptual monitoring. These unconscious physiological processes constitute what Gallagher calls "prenoetic constraint," which refers to how the body shapes and limits our perception of the world.[13] These processes "condition, constrain, and color perception. They involve the attunement of the body to the environment, as well as the homeostasis of the body itself. If that tuning were upset, if a certain process connected with respiration, for example, failed, then one's perception of the world would be different in some way."[14]

Gallagher's account of perception is influenced by Maurice Merleau-Ponty's analysis of the phenomenology of perception. For Merleau-Ponty, the perceiving subject is not a disembodied conscious entity disengaged from the world who perceives it as a detached observer. Rather, the subject is situated through the lived body in space and time. This embodiment of the subject is not separable from but an integral part of perception and the experiential quality of what the subject perceives.[15] Philosophers Alva Noe and Evan Thompson defend a similar position in their theories of embodied consciousness. The biological realization of consciousness includes not just the brain but also the body beyond the brain. Consciousness is not strictly a brain phenomenon but an organism phenomenon, and the physical substrate of consciousness includes features of the organism that are not limited to the brain. It is not a state that obtains inside the head but something we do as we

---

10. *Descartes' Error*, 227.
11. *Ibid.*, 118.
12. *How the Body Shapes the Mind* (Oxford: Clarendon Press, 2005), 1–7, 24.
13. *Ibid.*, 149–152.
14. *Ibid.*, 150.
15. *Phenomenology of Perception*, trans. C. Smith (London: Routledge, 2002).

interact with the world around us.[16] As one aspect of consciousness, cognition is a process that runs from the brain through the body, to the world, and then back again. Noe's and Thompson's views are consistent with Zeman's proposal that the function of consciousness is to enable the organism to control its immediate environment.

In addition to external properties of the body pertaining to perception, properties of systems internal to the body can affect the content and quality of our mental states. Depletion of endogenous estrogen correlates with some degree of neural loss in the hippocampus and prefrontal cortex and cognitive decline in some postmenopausal women.[17] Although estrogen is produced primarily by the ovaries, it can influence brain mechanisms regulating short-term, working memory. This consists in the capacity to hold and process information in an active state for brief periods. Working memory is mediated by the prefrontal cortex and is necessary for executive functions such as decision-making. The impairing effect of lower estrogen levels on this type of memory is more pronounced in younger women who have had their ovaries removed. Another example of endocrine effects on the brain and mind involves glucocorticoids, specifically cortisol. Stress-induced chronic hypersecretion of this hormone from the adrenal cortex can result in neurodegenerative changes in the hippocampus, prefrontal cortex, and amygdala and the progression of symptoms associated with dementia.[18] Low levels of estrogen and high levels of cortisol can both impair working memory.

The parathyroid gland is another component of the endocrine system that can influence the mind. Hyperparathyroidism causes elevated levels of blood calcium and parathyroid hormone, which can cause or exacerbate symptoms of major depressive disorder. These can include low mood, anhedonia (inability to experience pleasure from previously pleasurable activities), avolition (lack of motivation to pursue meaningful goals), and in some cases paranoia and psychosis. Restoring normal parathyroid function through surgery or drugs can restore normal levels of calcium and parathyroid hormone and in turn normalize mood, desire, and volition.

Adrenaline (epinephrine) and noradrenaline (norepinephrine) are catecholamines secreted by the adrenal medulla and have a range of critical functions in the body. High levels of these hormones can adversely affect the brain and mind.

---

16. Noe, *Out of Our Heads: Why You Are not Your Brain, and Other Lessons from the Biology of Consciousness* (New York: Hill and Wang, 2009). Thompson, *Mind in Life: Biology, Phenomenology, and the Sciences of Mind* (Cambridge, MA: Harvard University Press, 2007). See also A. Clark, *Being There: Putting Brain, Body, and World Together Again* (Cambridge, MA: MIT Press, 1997), and *Supersizing the Mind: Embodiment, Action, and Cognitive Extension* (Oxford: Oxford University Press, 2008).

17. B. Sherwin, "Estrogen and Cognitive Aging in Women," *Neuroscience* 138 (2006): 1021–1026.

18. R. Sapolsky, *Stress, the Aging Brain, and the Mechanisms of Neuron Death* (Cambridge, MA: MIT Press, 1992). Also, J. Csernansky et al., "Plasma Cortisol and Progression of Dementia in Subjects with Alzheimer-Type Dementia," *American Journal of Psychiatry* 163 (2006): 2164–2169.

Pheochromocytomas, which are neuroendocrine tumors of the adrenal medulla, can cause release of excess adrenaline and elevate blood pressure to dangerous levels. In rare cases, this process can result in mania and psychosis. The release of adrenaline into the bloodstream also activates noradrenergic mechanisms in the amygdala, which promote the formation, consolidation, and reconsolidation of unconscious memories of fearful and other emotionally charged events. This is different from the effects of hormones on working memory. Release of hormones to form and strengthen a memory of a threatening event is adaptive when it enables us to avoid similar threats in the future. But hypersecretion of adrenaline and noradrenaline in response to a traumatic event can consolidate an unconscious memory of that event so strongly that it results in a pathological condition. It can contribute to the uncontrolled traumatic flashbacks of the stressful and emotionally charged experience characteristic of posttraumatic stress disorder (PTSD).

These same hormones also contribute to the formation and consolidation of episodic memory in the hippocampus and reconsolidation of this same type of memory in regions of the cerebral cortex. Episodic memory is often autobiographical, involving first-person recall of actions we have performed or events that have happened to us. It is a critical component of the psychological continuity in virtue of which we experience ourselves persisting through time. Psychological continuity consists of links between our past and present desires, beliefs, intentions, and emotions, the realization of these mental states in actions, the recall of these actions in memory, and anticipation of the future.[19] In addition to its role in connecting the present to the past, episodic memory provides a link between the present and future by enabling us to imagine and project ourselves into the future as a mirror image of our past. Episodic memory is thus the basis of prospective memory. It is also essential for narrative identity, the unified set of characteristics and experiences that constitute the distinctive autobiography of a person.[20]

There are receptors in the brain for all of these hormones. The activation of these receptors can influence a range of brain functions and how they generate and sustain our mental states. Significantly, however, in each case the source of these hormones is outside the brain. There would be no such effects on the brain and the mind if the relevant hormones acting on the relevant receptors were not produced by other organs in other systems in the body.

Cytokines are perhaps the best example of interaction between the immune and central nervous systems and its effects on the mind. These are messenger proteins secreted by lymphoid cells in response to stress or viruses. Cytokines are generally immunomodulatory, in the sense that they amplify some immune responses and inhibit others. Pro-inflammatory cytokines such as interleukin-1, interleukin-6,

---

19. The psychological continuity account of persistence through time is often associated with D. Parfit, *Reasons and Persons* (Oxford: Clarendon Press, 1984), Part III. J. Locke first developed this account in *An Essay Concerning Human Understanding*, ed. P. H. Nidditch (Oxford: Clarendon Press, 1975), Book II, Chapter xxvii.
20. Narrative identity has been discussed and defended principally by M. Schechtman in *The Constitution of Selves* (Ithaca: Cornell University Press, 1996), and D. DeGrazia in *Human Identity and Bioethics* (New York: Cambridge University Press, 2005).

and tumor necrosis factor-alpha secreted in response to stress, infection, or tumors can penetrate the blood–brain barrier. They can also be released by microglia and astrocytes in the brain. Cytokine release from any of these triggers can activate and cause dysregulation of the hypothalamus and the hypothalamic-pituitary-adrenal (HPA) axis, which can alter neurotransmitter levels. Some studies have shown a correlation between high levels of pro-inflammatory cytokines and abnormal metabolism of serotonin, dopamine, and norepinephrine in the brain. The studies suggest that cytokines can be psychoactive and can induce abnormal affective states and behavioral changes characteristic of anxiety and depression.[21] Cytokines activated in response to infection can result in psychopathological symptoms similar to those associated with cytokines activated in response to stress-related psychiatric disorders. They include anhedonia, fatigue, disruption of sleep–wake cycles, and cognitive impairment.[22] By blunting desires and the cognitive ability to form and execute plans in actions, cytokines can impair some of the mental capacities necessary for human agency.

The integrity of the endocrine and immune systems is necessary for the integrity of the brain and mind, and vice versa. As illustrated in the example of the association between chronic high levels of glucocorticoids and dementia, an overactive endocrine system can adversely affect mental states. An overactive immune response can result in mental disorders in addition to anxiety and depression. In the autoimmune disease systemic lupus erythematosus, immune dysfunction can lead to such neuropsychiatric manifestations as schizophreniform disorder in some individuals. These include psychological symptoms such as delusions, hallucinations, flattened affect, and avolition. In a reverse process, psychological dysfunction can adversely affect the brain and in turn cause immune dysfunction. Chronic psychological stress can suppress T-cell and other functions of the immune system and make us more susceptible to infection.

The external and internal properties of the body that I have described show the implausibility of the neuroreductionist view that the mind is located in and can be explained entirely in terms of the brain. Because the content and subjective quality of our mental states are influenced by bodily systems outside the brain, mental states are not just brain states. This refutes the claim that the mind is identical to the brain. Embodiment in all its forms influences brain function and shapes cognition, mood, agency, and personal identity. Nevertheless, embodiment alone cannot completely account for the content of our mental states and how they represent features of the environment. Our brains and minds are not only shaped by our bodies but also by the natural, social, and cultural contexts in which we are embedded. Brain states function not only by obeying internal constraints of the central nervous system but also by their dynamic interaction with other bodily systems and the external world.

---

21. C. L. Raison et al., "Cytokines and the Blues: Inflammation and the Pathogenesis of Depression," *Trends in Immunology* 27 (2006): 24–31, and E. Bell, "Neuroimmunology: Finding a Way into the Brain," *Nature Reviews Immunology* 9 (2009): 386.
22. R. Dantzer et al., "From Inflammation to Sickness and Depression: When the Immune System Subjugates the Brain," *Nature Reviews Neuroscience* 9 (2008): 46–56.

Embedded Minds

In the 1930s and 1940s, neurosurgeon Wilder Penfield would place a stimulating electrode on the exposed temporal lobes of some patients on whom he was operating to relieve symptoms of severe epilepsy. The patients were awake during the surgery, and when Penfield stimulated a particular area with the probe, some of them reported recalling experiences from their past.[23] Among other aspects of consciousness, Penfield's procedure and his patients' reports suggested that structures in the temporal lobes were associated with episodic memory. This was significant in two respects: it appeared to be evidence for a physical basis of memory, and it suggested that certain memories have a particular physical location in the brain. Although brain imaging was not available at the time of Penfield's procedure, functional magnetic resonance imaging (fMRI) and positron emission tomography (PET) scans would have shown activation in the hippocampus, parahippocampal gyrus, and areas of the prefrontal cortex in the form of increased blood flow and glucose metabolism while the patients were engaged in memory retrieval. Neurosurgery of the type performed by Penfield would not be necessary to produce these effects. Memory retrieval could be triggered by photos of events associated with an individual's past experience while he or she was in the scanner. What could the images that a radiologist, neurologist, psychiatrist, or neurosurgeon saw from the brain scan tell them about the meaning of the experience for that individual?

Suppose that I volunteer for an fMRI study of the brain regions and mechanisms mediating episodic memory. I have photos of the Andalusian landscape and cities in southern Spain taken when I visited the region many years ago and give them to the investigator conducting the study. While in the scanner, I am shown the photos, and they elicit a vivid recall of my Andalusian experience. The photos cause activation in the hippocampus. There is also activation in the parahippocampal gyrus, prefrontal cortex, and amygdala, all of which mediate the emotional aspects of episodic memory and its retrieval. In addition, there is activation in the parietal cortex, which mediates our orientation in space and time and enables us to construct a holistic representation of the environmental setting in which we experience and recall events. My brain's olfactory system is activated as well. Still, the images showing increased activity in these brain regions could not capture the content or meaning of my experience. This is because the scanner cannot reproduce the landscape, sunlight, and temperature of that particular place and time. It cannot reproduce how these geographical and climatic features affected my mood and the qualitative aspects of my interactions with other people. The scanner cannot replicate the phenomenological feel of the sights, smells, and sounds of my sojourn in Andalusia. Scents of olive oil, garlic, and espresso wafting from restaurants, the strong odor of black tobacco from people smoking in cafes and on sidewalks, and diesel fuel from motor vehicles similar to what I experienced while walking through the streets during my travels can trigger a memory of that experience. Yet even if the fMRI investigator provided the relevant sensory stimuli to me in the scanner, and all of the

---

23. "Memory Mechanisms," *Archives of Neurology and Psychiatry* 67 (1952): 178–191, and *The Mystery of the Mind*, 21–27.

brain regions that I have mentioned were activated, this would not tell him or her what it was like for me to be in Andalusia or to recall it. The images from the scanner would not give the investigator access to my experience in that place and at that time.

The experiential *content* of my memory—what I saw, heard, and smelled—cannot be divorced from the social and physical *context* in which the remembered events occurred. The source of these events is essential to my cognitive and emotional recording of and response to the events when experiencing and recalling them. These processes constitute the autobiographical aspect of my episodic memory and contribute to the larger narrative identity of my life as a whole. They involve first-person experience of events, not simply third-person objective accounts of them. I do not recall an isolated set of events that I perceived as a detached observer, but a unified set of events within which I am an agent and from which I construct meaning in line with my values and interests. My autobiographical past, present awareness, and anticipation of the future collectively constitute my experience as a subject persisting through time. My state of mind at the time I was in Andalusia and my present recall of it are influenced by the particular spatial and temporal framework in which I travelled. How my brain records these memories at a lower level, and how my mind constructs meaning from them at a higher level, is a function of unique contextual features. Our brains and minds are not only embodied but also embedded in the social and physical environment with which we engage and which influences how we think, feel, and act.

The hippocampus in the medial temporal lobe, the parahippocampal gyrus, and anterior regions of the prefrontal cortex are all necessary to form and retain episodic memories. But these brain regions are not sufficient to account for how factors external to the brain shape the emotional content of our memories and enable us to make sense of our experience. Thus it is misleading to ask questions such as, "Where in the brain is the memory of one's past?"[24] Even within the brain, the question of *where* the episodic memory system is located can be misleading. This system is not localized but consists of a distributed network of circuits regulating the process of consolidation, reconsolidation, storage, and retrieval of recorded events.

---

24. E. Tulving and M. Lepage discuss the idea of a locus for episodic memory in "Where in the Brain Is the Awareness of One's Past?" in D. Schacter and E. Scarry, eds., *Memory, Brain, and Belief* (Cambridge, MA: Harvard University Press, 2000), 208–228. Recall Brodmann's comment, cited in the Introduction, on the phrenology-like attempt to localize complex mental activity such as memory in a particular region of the brain. A team led by J. Rissman conducted two experiments to investigate whether neural signatures of recognition memory could be decoded reliably from fMRI data. They concluded that "although subjective memory states can be decoded quite accurately under controlled conditions, fMRI has uncertain utility for objectively detecting an individual's past experience." J. Rissman, H. Greely, and A. Wagner, "Detecting Individual Memories through the Neural Decoding of Memory States and Past Experience," *Proceedings of the National Academy of Sciences*, published online April 12, 2010. It is unclear what the authors mean by 'decode', Their conclusion suggests that, whatever the scan can detect, it does not include the content of one's memory.

Cognitive functions are regulated mainly by the frontal lobes as part of the organism's need to adapt to the surrounding natural and social context. This region of the brain plays a major role in generating and sustaining the beliefs, intentions, and choices that are components of human agency and enable this adaptation and control. At the same time, the occipital, parietal, and temporal lobes regulate the spatial and temporal orientation necessary for the organism to act. These brain regions also develop in response to the environment as the organism interacts with it. Yet the frontal lobes play a more important role than the other lobes in this adaptation because of the importance of executive functions in navigating the environment. An example of the significance of this role is the effects of frontotemporal dementia. This is a degenerative disease affecting primarily the frontal and anterior temporal lobes. It is marked by dramatic changes in personality, behavior, and judgment. Some patients with this type of dementia develop artistic or other creative capacities. One explanation for this is that the degenerating frontal lobes, which ordinarily constrain the parietal and temporal lobes, allow these areas of the brain to become more active and unleash creative potential. Yet these same patients often become so cognitively dysfunctional and so poor at reasoning and decision making that they can no longer effectively interact with the social and physical world.[25] The shift in activity from anterior to posterior regions of the brain inhibits rather than promotes adaptability to one's surroundings.

Neural connections form and function as they do not because of properties intrinsic to themselves but because of their role in mediating interaction between a human organism and the environment. This is analogous to the relation between genes and epigenetic factors regulating how genes are expressed in phenotypic traits. Epigenetics refers to heritable changes in gene structure or expression not involving changes in the genetic code. Just as gene expression is shaped not only by nucleotide sequences but also by other internal biological and external environmental factors, so too brain development and function is shaped not only by neurons, synapses, and neurotransmitters but also by many of the same internal and external factors. The idea that we are our genes is as implausible as the idea that we are our brains.[26]

The claim that the content of our mental states need not extend beyond the brain cannot explain differences in people's ability or inability to adapt to different environments. It also ignores the extent to which sensory stimulation from the environment shapes brain structure and function. The ability of the brain to alter its circuits and functions is not a property of the brain operating independently of external factors but of dynamic interaction between the brain and these factors. Psychiatrist Bruce Wexler explains: "There is a neurobiological imperative that an individual's internal neuropsychological structures match key features of his or her external environment, a principle of internal–external consonance. This principle

---

25. B. Miller and C. Hou, "Portraits of Artists: Emergence of Visual Creativity in Dementia," *Archives of Neurology* 61 (2004): 841–844.
26. R. Lewontin refutes genetic reductionism in *The Triple Helix: Gene, Organism, and Environment* (Cambridge, MA: Harvard University Press, 2000). For present purposes, the relevant triple helix consists of brain, organism, and environment.

is of great importance, since people are linked to their environments by obligatory, continuous, multimodal sensory stimulation."[27] Neuroplasticity, the ability of nerve cells to modify their activity in response to change, occurs to a greater degree earlier in life and diminishes later in life. Further, Wexler writes:

> During the first part of life, the brain and mind are highly plastic, require sensory input to grow and develop, and shape themselves to the major recurring features of their environments. During these years, individuals have little ability to act on or alter the environment, but are easily altered by it. By early adulthood, the mind and brain have elaborately developed structures and a diminished ability to change those structures. The individual is now able to act on and alter the environment, and much of that activity is devoted to making the environment conform to the established structures.[28]

Wexler points out that dissonance between internal and external worlds is more common among older people because external changes no longer match established internal structures. The brain of an older person does not adjust so easily to a new environment, and this can result in negative psychological symptoms. Wexler gives examples of immigration and bereavement to illustrate dissonance between internal neuropsychological processes and external social processes. For people in these situations, adjustment to social change and personal loss is difficult. The time and effort required to modify internal structures so that they match the altered environment often result in distress and psychological dysfunction.

Some who endorse neuroreductionism might claim that functional brain imaging eventually will establish causal connections between brain states and mental states. These connections might suggest that mental states are just brain states. Yet the most refined imaging techniques provide only an indirect measure of what actually occurs in the brain. Images of blood flow and glucose metabolism produced by fMRI and PET scans are not identical to events and processes occurring at the neural level. They are visualizations of statistical analyses based on a large number of images and are more accurately described as scientific constructs than actual pictures of the brain. Even if the temporal and spatial resolution of neuroimaging improved to the point where we had a more accurate picture of neural activity, this could not capture the full content of one's mental life. This content is external to what brain scans measure. Nor could a scan reproduce the phenomenology of what it is like for a subject to experience events and interact with others in the world. This property is a function of the context in which one has the experience. Imaging can display brain dysfunction correlating with psychiatric disorders; but it cannot capture how it feels to be depressed or anxious. The experience of having a psychiatric disorder cannot be "seen" on a functional brain scan. This is because imaging cannot explain how the external body, internal bodily systems, and the environment influence the brain and generate the psychological properties associated with these disorders. There will always be an explanatory gap between the

---

27. *Brain and Culture: Neurobiology, Ideology, and Social Change* (Cambridge, MA: MIT Press, 2008), 5.
28. *Ibid.*, 5.

objectivity of the brain and the subjectivity of experience. Neuroimaging cannot read minds in any substantive sense because the mind is not located in the brain.

To support the claim that we can read minds through images of the brain, one would have to show that these images capture brain states, and that particular brain states cause particular mental states. Yet most brain states and mental states are linked not by a one–one relation but many–many relations. These relations resist linear causal explanations. Multiple interacting regions of the brain can mediate a particular mental state. Anxiety, for example, involves a cognitive component of belief mediated by the prefrontal cortex and an affective component of fear mediated by the amygdala. Other cortical and subcortical regions may be involved in generating anxiety, and the functions of these regions are influenced by how the subject responds to the external world. We could not infer the mental state of anxiety from activation of a particular brain region. Nor could we infer the mental process of decision making solely from activation of the frontal lobes, given the role of the parietal and temporal lobes and subcortical regions such as the cerebellum in agency. Projections to and from the different brain structures that mediate mental states and processes cannot be visualized on brain scans. Because neuroimaging does not provide direct evidence of what actually occurs in the brain, and because brain states cannot completely account for the content and quality of mental states, neuroimaging will always come up short in describing and explaining the mind. This discredits neuroreductionism, since functional brain imaging is the best available technique to support this theory.

Given the ways in which the body shapes perception, a different body would mean that a person's perception of the world would be different. Given the ways in which the environment shapes experience, a different environment would mean that the content of a person's experience would be different. This is why a brain transplant from one body into another—if it ever became feasible—would not preserve the identity of the person whose brain was transplanted. A different body of a different organism would result in a developmentally and functionally different brain. It would also result in a different set of psychological properties conditioned by the brain and the organism's interaction with the natural and social environment. Whether one's narrative identity was preserved would depend not just on one's brain but also on the context in which one lived and acted over time.

It will be helpful to give some additional examples of environmental influences on our brains and minds. The placebo effect depends on the person's belief that a biochemically inert pill or infusion is biochemically active and will cause physiological changes in one's body and brain. The belief that a sham surgical procedure is an active intervention can produce the same effect. This outcome may also be due to a belief that an active drug or procedure that is effective for some conditions will be effective for others. This belief is a function of the expectation of efficacy, which is strongly shaped by the person's previous experience with effective interventions similar to the new pill or infusion. If a physiological change occurs, it is because the belief informs the brain that the intervention is effective. Such a belief may be part of a larger belief system that is grounded in a patient's trust in the physician as a healer and as someone who always acts in the patient's best interests. It is shaped by social expectations of what physicians can and should do for patients. The belief that a pill or substance will be effective is influenced by the belief in the physician as an advocate for the patient, and this second type of belief is influenced by psychosocial factors.

Many brain–environment interactions involve harmful effects on the mind. Schizophrenia is a complex psychiatric disorder involving dysregulation of dopamine, glutamate, and possibly other neurotransmitters. It has a diffuse pathology resulting from dysfunction in multiple interacting neural pathways in cortical and subcortical regions of the brain. This disorder may consist of "positive" symptoms, such as psychosis, paranoia, and delusions, or "negative" symptoms, such as avolition, anhedonia, and flat affect. The variation in cognitive and affective symptoms among those with schizophrenia is likely the result of how the genes implicated in the disorder express themselves in response to epigenetic factors such as methylation in brain tissue, viruses, and other factors outside the body and brain. From a phenomenological perspective, schizophrenia is a psychiatric disorder where embodiment and embeddedness are interrelated. In both positive and negative symptoms, the individual may experience the loss of embodied contact with reality. The experience of disembodiment results in a self that is alien to rather than immersed in the world.[29]

In other psychiatric disorders, some individuals may develop a chronic fear response to environmental stimuli because of a perception of these stimuli as fearful or threatening. A chronic cognitive and emotional response that is out of proportion to external events can lead to dysregulation in serotonergic, dopaminergic, and adrenergic systems in cortical-limbic pathways and result in major depressive disorder or generalized anxiety disorder. The relevant brain regions mediating beliefs and emotions become dysfunctional. Importantly, the brain dysfunction is at least partly the consequence of the subject's inability to have the beliefs and emotions necessary to adapt to the environment. Appeal to events in the brain alone cannot account for all of the factors contributing to dysfunction at neural and mental levels in these cases.

Some psychiatrists consider mild to moderate forms of depression as an adaptive mechanism that may have developed as a response to situations in which a desired goal is unattainable.[30] Depression may alert us to avoid projects that require considerable effort and generate high expectations but through which we achieve nothing. It may be part of a defense mechanism that protects us from harming ourselves by forcing us to align our desires and expectations with what social and natural circumstances allow us to do. Mild depression may be a warning to disengage from unattainable goals. A study of adolescent females suggests that failure to disengage from these goals may put one at risk of developing major depressive disorder.[31]

---

29. T. Fuchs and J. Schlimme, "Embodiment and Psychopathology: A Phenomenological Perspective," *Current Opinion in Psychiatry* 22 (2009): 570–575.
30. R. Nesse, "Is Depression an Adaptation?" *Archives of General Psychiatry* 57 (2000): 14–20.
31. C. Wrosch and G. Miller, "Depressive Symptoms Can Be Useful: Self-Regulatory and Emotional Benefits of Dysphoric Mood in Adolescence," *Journal of Personality and Social Psychology* 96 (2009): 1181–1190. Nesse defends a similar position in, "Explaining

These views on the etiology of depression underscore the importance of the individual's attunement to the environment. One does not become depressed solely because of dysfunctional circuits in the brain. The disconnection between one's goals and the world is one cause of the neural dysfunction. There are other conditions that fall within the explanatory framework of evolutionary psychiatry. Alleles of genes that predispose children and adults to attention-deficit/hyperactivity disorder may have been adaptive during most of our evolutionary history. Sitting still for hours focused on a specific cognitive task was probably not advantageous in hunter-gatherer societies. Alleles predisposing people to anxiety and obsessive-compulsive disorder might have been advantageous when people were constantly under the threat of predators. Whether these conditions were adaptive or maladaptive was a function of the particular geography where they lived.

Another example of the role of the environment in shaping brain function or dysfunction and adaptive or maladaptive mental states is PTSD. As noted, PTSD is characterized by flashbacks and nightmares of traumatic events that one cannot eliminate from one's emotionally charged unconscious memory. The flashbacks often occur when a stimulus triggers a recall that makes the brain and mind believe that one has returned to the environment where one experienced the traumatic event. The emotional intensity of the event and repeated exposure to stimuli reminding one of it result in a learned pathological response to these stimuli. It is as though the subject were in a constant fight-or-flight relation to his or her surroundings.

Environment also plays a role in drug addiction. Addictions develop when the reward circuit in the mesolimbic dopamine system becomes overactivated from repeatedly taking a drug like nicotine or heroin. This results in a cascade of events that cause dysregulation in a number of limbic and cortical circuits. Drug addiction is characterized by compulsion to seek and take the drug, loss of control in limiting intake, and a negative emotional state when access to the drug is prevented.[32] The compulsion and loss of control are reinforced by environmental cues reminding the addict that the drug is available to him or her. This belief and its content activate neural circuits in a way that maintains addictive behavior.

All of the examples I have presented illustrate that the brain and the mental states it generates and sustains do not develop and do not become disordered solely because of processes internal to the brain. The content of our beliefs and other mental states is a representation of distinct environments to which we adapt or fail to adapt. The brain alone cannot represent these external features to the organism or human subject and can only interpret them with the aid of the mind. Looking into a person's brain directly through an intracranial surgical procedure or indirectly through a PET or fMRI scan would not provide access to what that

---

Depression: Neuroscience Is not Enough, Evolution Is Essential," in C. Pariante et al., eds. *Understanding Depression: A Translational Approach* (Oxford: Oxford University Press. 2009), 17–36.

32. P. Kalivas and N. Volkow, "The Neural Basis of Addiction," *American Journal of Psychiatry* 162 (2005): 1403–1413, and G. Koob and N. Volkow, "Neurocircuitry of Addiction," *Neuropsychopharmacology* 35 (2010): 217–238.

person was thinking.[33] Yet this is what neuroreductionism suggests, which provides a compelling reason to reject this theory of the brain and mind. The brain is one part of a holistic system that also includes the mind and body of a subject interacting with the world. No two people, and no two people's brains, respond to the environment in the same way. Each person's brain functions and mental states are unique to him or her.

Gallagher emphasizes the importance of the interdependence of embodiment and embeddedness for the mind:

> The conscious processes that we associate with the mind are not fully explainable in terms of what happens in the brain, or even in the whole nervous system. The neurophysiological components of such embodied processes are part of a larger system that involves the entire body interacting with its environment. How I experience the world depends, in some degree, on how hot or cold it is in my part of the world. How I experience the world depends, to some extent, on how much food I have in my stomach, and on certain hormonal levels existing in different parts of my body, and so forth. These are not only objective, physical facts, they are facticities to which my body reacts and with which it copes. Much of the reacting and coping may be describable in terms of neurophysiological functions, but neither the fact of the matter, nor the facticity of embodiment, is fully reducible to or identical with the firing of neurons.[34]

Psychiatrist and philosopher Thomas Fuchs further supports the view of the mind as a distributed set of psychological properties emerging from and shaped by interaction between the embodied subject and the environment. He says:

> Neuroreductionist claims such as "you are but a pack of neurons" or "you are just your brain" are both a category error and biologically unsound. On the contrary, you are a living bodily subject of experience in relation to others. Whatever we may conjecture about a fictitious brain-in-a-vat, the most reasonable would be that in order to create the illusion of a self and a world, the device would need to duplicate not only homeostatic regulation but all brain-body-environment interactions, and thus it would require a vat that is nothing else than a living body engaged in the world. The brain is only an organ, and it is not the brain, but the organism or the living person that has conscious access to the world.[35]

The brain is not the sole cause of or influence on the mind but a relational organ that shapes the mind by mediating interaction between the organism and the

---

33. Compare this point with L. Wittgenstein: "If God had looked into our minds, he would not have been able to see there whom we were speaking of." *Philosophical Investigations*, 3rd edition, trans. and ed. by G. E. M. Anscombe (Cambridge, MA: Blackwell, 1997), 217. We can substitute 'brains' for 'minds.' Wittgenstein's point is that mental content is not internal but external to the subject.

34. *How the Body Shapes the Mind*, 151.

35. "Mind, Brain, and Life; A Phenomenological View on Embodied Cognitive Neuroscience," unpublished paper presented at a neurophilosophy symposium in Munich, September 20, 2007. See also Fuchs, "The Challenge of Neuroscience: Psychiatry and Phenomenology Today," *Psychopathology* 35 (2003): 319–326.

external world.[36] Zeman says that we should not view the brain as a "magic lamp" that produces immaterial mind events. Instead, "we should regard the brain as an enabler—an instrument that brings us into contact with the world."[37] This view, as well as the conception of embodied consciousness and cognition defended by Noe and Thompson, is similar in some respects to what Andy Clark and David Chalmers have called the "extended mind."[38] They employ thought experiments to show that the content of beliefs and other mental states is not confined to the head but can extend into the environment.

Luria's work predates this contemporary conception of the brain-mind relation. For Luria, the environment that shapes the brain and mind is not just physical but also cultural and historical. Cognition is a culturally constituted phenomenon.[39] Rejecting a localized and modular view of the brain, Luria theorized that the brain is part of a functional system that extends into the cultural-historical world. This extracortical organization is dynamically intertwined with the neural organization of the working brain. All of these externalist views reject the internalist view that everything about the mind can be explained in terms of its relation to the brain. To insist on the internalist view is to commit the "mereological fallacy" in neuroscience, attributing properties to an organ that can only be attributed to the organism or person as a whole.[40] Because the brain is influenced by the environment, interventions designed to affect the brain and mind should not be directed exclusively at the brain but should involve the subject's relation to the environment as well.

Environmental Interventions

Psychotropic drugs, neurosurgery, and electrical and magnetic neurostimulation can directly affect the brain and can have positive or negative effects on the mind.

---

36. This idea is from Fuchs and is captured in the title of his book, *Das Gehirn—Ein Beziehungsorgan* (Berlin: Springer, 2008).
37. "Does Consciousness Arise from the Brain?" 316.
38. "The Extended Mind," *Analysis* 58 (1998): 7–19.See also R. Menary, ed. *The Extended Mind* (Cambridge, MA: MIT Press, 2010); and N. Levy, "Rethinking Neuroethics in the Light of the Extended Mind Thesis," *American Journal of Bioethics—AJOB Neuroscience* 7(9) (2007): 3–11, and *Neuroethics: Challenges for the 21st Century* (Cambridge: Cambridge University Press, 2007), 44–63.
39. *The Working Brain: An Introduction to Neuropsychology*, trans. B. Haigh (Cambridge, MA: Harvard University Press, 1973). See also the chapters in A.-L. Christensen, E. Goldberg, and D. Bougakov, eds., *Luria's Legacy in the 21st Century* (New York: Oxford University Press, 2009).
40. M. R. Bennett and P. M. S. Hacker coin the term "mereological fallacy" in neuroscience in *Philosophical Foundations of Neuroscience* (Malden, MA: Blackwell, 2003), 15, 29.'Mereology' derives from the Greek and refers to the logic of part–whole relations. Bennett and Hacker claim that "neuroscience can… discover the neural preconditions for the possibility of the distinctively human power of thought and reasoning… What it cannot do is replace the wide range of ordinary psychological explanations of human activities in terms of reasons, intentions, purposes, goals, values, and conventions by neurological explanations" (3).

Interventions in bodily systems other than the CNS can also have significant effects on the brain and mind. I have mentioned some of these interventions in the body and will now discuss interventions that manipulate the environment and an individual's perception of it. These interventions can help to modulate brain and mental functions in neuropsychiatric disorders and benefit those who have them. In moderate forms of disorders of the brain and mind, the salutary effects of these therapies indicate that too much emphasis has been put particularly on psychopharmacology in treating them. We need to move beyond the idea of the brain as an isolated, independent organ and make more use of other treatment modalities.

The hypothesis that a maladaptive response to stimuli plays a key role in the pathogenesis of major depressive and generalized anxiety/panic disorders motivates therapies that aim to alter the individual's relation to the environment. This may be achieved in part by removing or altering the stimuli causing or exacerbating the brain dysregulation underlying these disorders. Cognitive-behavioral therapy (CBT) helps individuals to reframe their beliefs so that the content of these beliefs aligns with the states of affairs to which they are directed. This and other forms of psychotherapy can correct one's misinterpretation of external stimuli. CBT can help to block or attenuate the force of stimuli prompting a conditioned response involving an unconscious memory that can generate conscious fear or anxiety that is out of proportion to the issues at hand. Studies have convincingly shown that combined pharmacological treatment and psychotherapy is generally more effective in treating major depression among adults and adolescents than drug therapy alone.[41] In at least one study, psychotherapy was shown to significantly reduce the risk of suicidal thinking in adolescents with moderate to severe depression.[42] It was also shown to help make drug treatment safer and prevent relapse within this age group. Another study showed that combined antidepressant (selective serotonin reuptake inhibitor [SSRI]) therapy and CBT resulted in a highly positive response rate in children with anxiety.[43] All of this underscores the importance of beliefs and their relation to the environment in both the development and treatment of some psychiatric disorders.

Repeated exposure to a fearful situation in a controlled setting may also enable one to reframe one's beliefs so that they realign with external events. This can reduce anxiety and some phobias. It may involve being placed in a particular social or physical setting or in a virtual reality program that mimics these settings. In constructive avoidance, patients are taught to develop appropriate responses to stimuli by working through harmless to gradually more difficult stimuli until they become manageable. Extinction training consists in the introduction and withdrawal of stimuli that reinforce certain behavior. It can be used to attenuate the emotional content of traumatic memories. Patients may be exposed to two stimuli that trigger

41. S. Pampallona et al., "Combined Pharmacotherapy and Psychological Treatment for Depression: A Systematic Review," *Archives of General Psychiatry* 61 (2004): 714–719.

42. J. March et al., "The Treatment of Adolescents with Depression Study (TADS)," *Archives of General Psychiatry* 64 (2007): 1132–1143.

43. J. T. Walkup et al., "Cognitive Behavioral Therapy, Sertraline, or a Combination in Childhood Anxiety," *New England Journal of Medicine* 359 (2008): 2753–2766.

recall of these memories. One stimulus is withdrawn, while the patient is repeatedly exposed to the other. The emotional response to a memory or memories gradually weakens as a result. Memories that have been consolidated need to be reconsolidated, or updated, for long-term storage. This is an adaptive mechanism that allows new information to be integrated into the representation of an initial memory. Extinction training is most effective when memories are in the labile process of updating.[44] In obsessive-compulsive disorder, CBT can help some individuals to reshape their beliefs and modulate hyperactivity in the anterior cingulate gyrus, rostral caudate nucleus, and internal capsule that has been associated with the condition. Habit-reversal training, a form of CBT, instructs people with Tourette syndrome to be aware of the characteristic motor and vocal tics so that they can anticipate and suppress them.

Imaging studies indicate that psychotherapy can modulate cortical-limbic pathways and rewire the brain in a manner different from the effects of psychopharmacology.[45] It can have positive top-down effects on brain regions mediating some of the symptoms associated with some mental disorders. Psychotherapy can complement positive bottom-up effects of drugs in subcortical regions implicated in these disorders. More recent imaging studies have replicated these results.[46] They suggest that the mind is not simply the product of a linear, bottom-up, causal process emanating from the brain. Neither a bottom-up nor top-down model of the brain–mind or mind–brain relation is accurate. Our mental states are products of circular causation consisting of neurophysiological and environmental influences continuously interacting with each other in a nested series of positive feedforward and negative feedback loops.[47] Mental states such as beliefs about the environment influence this interaction. Mental disorders result when something goes awry in this process. The causal pathway goes from the mind, or the subjective experience of the situation, to the brain and body, and then back to the mind.

Negative symptoms at the mental level can be attenuated or corrected by intervening in a critical part of this pathway and altering the subject's beliefs about the environment. Psychotherapy is one way of doing this; neurofeedback is another. Subjects in chronic pain, for example, may undergo functional imaging revealing activity in brain regions mediating pain. By showing this activity to subjects and explaining the correlations between it and their pain, researchers and clinicians

44. D. Schiller et al., "Preventing the Return of Fear in Humans Using Reconsolidation Update Mechanisms," *Nature* 463 (2010): 49–53.
45. K. Goldapple et al., "Modulation of Cortical-Limbic Pathways in Major Depression: Treatment-Specific Effects of Cognitive Behavior Therapy," *Archives of General Psychiatry* 61 (2004): 34–41.
46. M. Beauregard, "Mind Does Really Matter: Evidence from Neuroimaging Studies of Emotional Self-Regulation, Psychotherapy, and Placebo Effect," *Progress in Neurobiology* 81 (2007): 218–236.
47. See Fuchs, "Neurobiology and Psychotherapy: An Emerging Dialogue," *Current Opinion in Psychiatry* 17 (2004): 479–485. G. Gillett defends this same position in *Subjectivity and Being Somebody: Human Identity and Neuroethics* (Exeter, UK: Imprint Academic, 2008).

may enable subjects to modulate their experience of pain while undergoing imaging. The success of this technique depends on the subjects' beliefs about the relation between the images of their active brain regions and their pain. It also depends on the way in which the researcher conducting the technique explains this relation to the subject.

The effectiveness of psychotherapies that manipulate environmental influences on the mind supports the circular causation model for understanding and treating at least some mental disorders. Therapies that enable one to reframe beliefs do not just have positive effects on cognition. More importantly, these effects can change the subject's behavior so that he or she can once again engage in interpersonal interaction and experience positive relations with others. Drug therapy targeting the relevant neural pathways and neurotransmitter systems treats only one dimension of these disorders. Antidepressants and anxiolytics can influence brain function and cognitive and affective states mediated by the brain. But the effects of drugs are different from the circular causation model of psychotherapy, whereby mental states both influence and are influenced by brain function. In anxiety disorders, altering the cognitive state of belief about certain stimuli can modulate activity in brain regions mediating one's affective response to these stimuli so that they are no longer perceived as fearful or threatening. Nonpharmacological therapies that focus on altering one's thought and behavior operate on the recognition that beliefs, emotions, and other mental states are inseparable from the world that circumscribes them.

Some may claim that the effects of psychotherapy are largely placebo effects. It may be difficult to tease apart brain changes associated with psychotherapy from changes associated with these effects.[48] A patient's trust in a psychotherapist and the expectation that he or she will experience symptom relief can induce these changes. Trust and expectation are functions of the context of the patient–physician encounter. This includes psychosocial factors that the patient brings to the encounter and the behavior of the physician in manipulating these factors for the benefit of the patient. Placebos can induce changes in both prefrontal cortical and subcortical regions, where they match changes associated with active drugs. The neural effects of psychotherapy may be limited to prefrontal cortical areas, though they may not be as transient as the effects from placebos. Nevertheless, the idea that there may be placebo effects from psychotherapy confirms rather than discredits the claim that factors external to the brain can induce changes in the brain and mind.

Addiction is another neuropsychiatric disorder where environmental intervention can be effective. Newer dopamine antagonists have shown promise in controlling some addictions, or at least physical dependence on certain substances. Vaccines are also being developed to treat a number of addictions. Depending on availability and access, individuals addicted to heroin may go to clinics dispensing methadone or prescribed heroin to control physical craving. I mentioned that compulsive drug-seeking is influenced by social and physical cues reminding the addict of the drug to which he or she is addicted. Ways of treating the condition

---

48. F. Benedetti discusses this in *Placebo Effects: Understanding the Mechanisms in Health and Disease* (Oxford: Oxford University Press, 2009), 142–143.

include removing the individual from settings where these cues are present, or else altering the settings so that the cues are no longer present. This and other aspects of neighborhood dynamics can play an important role in controlling addictions. Here again, the subject's interaction with the environment can be critical to both the development and treatment of a psychiatric disorder.

Unfortunately, CBT and virtual reality programs have had limited efficacy in treating PTSD. In this disorder, the problem is not one of retaining a positive memory. Rather, the problem is not being able to rid oneself of a pathological memory whose triggers are outside of one's conscious awareness and cognitive control. Emotionally charged memories are better remembered than memories that are emotionally neutral, and recall of traumatic experiences is more emotionally charged than recall of pleasant experiences.[49] As noted, unconscious memories of the type associated with PTSD are formed, consolidated, and reconsolidated in the amygdala through the action of adrenaline and noradrenaline. The beta-adrenergic receptor antagonist propranolol has been used in a number of studies to treat PTSD by blocking the release of these hormones and their effects on the amygdala. Given the role of these hormones in memory formation, blocking their release theoretically could prevent or dampen emotionally charged memories. In some experiments, propranolol and similarly acting drugs modulated people's emotional response to traumatic memories. Other experiments using these drugs suggest that the fear response to these memories might even be extinguished.[50]

These experimental interventions separate the emotionally charged content of a memory from the memory itself. One could recall an event without re-experiencing it as traumatic or fearful.[51] One would become emotionally disengaged from the context in which one experienced the event. Yet we need to be careful in trying to manipulate memory, even pathological memory, in this way. Pharmacological interventions that separate the emotional content of a memory of an event from the context in which we experienced it might alleviate the pathological state of mind in PTSD. But there are projections from the amygdala to the hippocampus, and vice versa, and considerable overlap between the memory functions they mediate. Both of these limbic structures influence how we recall the events in our lives. It is possible that dampening the content of unconscious emotionally charged memories

49. J. McGaugh, "The Amygdala Modulates the Consolidation of Memories of Emotionally Arousing Experiences," *Annual Review of Neuroscience* 27 (2004): 1–28. Also, McGaugh, "Make Mild Moments Memorable: Add a Little Arousal," *Trends in Cognitive Sciences* 10 (2006): 345–347. For more recent findings, see B. Roozendaal et al., "Adrenal Stress Hormones, Amygdala Activation, and Memory for Emotionally Arousing Experiences," *Progress in Brain Research* 167 (2008): 79–97.

50. For a study showing a modulated fear response, see R. Pitman et al., "Pilot Study of Secondary Prevention of Posttraumatic Stress Disorder with Propranolol," *Biological Psychiatry* 51 (2002): 189–192. For a study suggesting that the fear response could be weakened and possibly erased, see M. Kindt et al., "Beyond Extinction: Erasing Human Fear Responses and Preventing the Return of Fear," *Nature Neuroscience* 12 (2009): 256–258.

51. N. Medford et al., "Emotional Memory: Separating Content and Context," *Psychiatric Research: Neuroimaging* 138 (2005): 247–258.

might also dampen the emotional content of conscious autobiographical episodic memories.

Recent advances in cognitive neuroscience have shown that recollection of personal episodes from the past depends on activation and reactivation of latent emotional associations with these episodes.[52] Well-documented cases of severe retrograde and anterograde amnesia following brain injury have shown that memory systems can operate independently of each other.[53] Yet the emotional associations with episodic memory suggest that distinct but interacting memory systems are involved in this process. If the amygdala and hippocampus function interdependently in enabling these associations, then weakening the heightened emotional response to unconscious pathological memory might also weaken the moderate emotional response to conscious episodic memory. Studies have indicated that an amygdalar-hippocampal network supports emotional arousal, while a prefrontal-hippocampal network supports emotional valence. But because the hippocampus is active in both networks and both types of emotion, it is possible that altering one circuit could alter the other and that altering emotional arousal could alter emotional valence.

Even if our ability to recall events were intact, neutralizing the emotional content of our episodic memories could impair our ability to make sense of our past. It could impair our ability to place experienced events within a unified and meaningful narrative. We might be left with the capacity to recall particular events without being able to understand how they relate to each other or how they affect us and shape our autobiographies. Experiences such as my travels in Andalusia would have no subjective first-person significance for me. I would only recall them in objective third-person terms as a nonintegrated set of events. My autobiographical episodic memory would function like semantic memory of impersonal concepts and facts. Losing some of the content of one's autobiographical memory may be an acceptable price to pay for modulating an emotionally charged memory, but only if it has a significant negative impact on one's quality of life.

The physical and social context in which one experiences an event is a critical component of the emotional content of one's memory of that event. This emotional content is in turn a critical component of our experience of recalling it. The connection between context and content in episodic memory is part of the spatial and temporal structure of our mental life consisting of integrated past, present, and future experiences. We project ourselves into the future on the basis of the meaning we construct from where and when we experienced events in our past. Removing the emotional content of memory from the context in which one experienced the recalled event might disrupt this structure and the integrity of one's autobiography. Pharmacological therapies targeting memory systems need to be sensitive to the fact that emotion imbues the content of both nondeclarative and declarative

---

52. K. LaBar and R. Cabeza, "Cognitive Neuroscience of Emotional Memory," *Nature Reviews Neuroscience* 7 (2006): 54–64.
53. D. Schacter, *Searching for Memory: The Brain, the Mind, and the Past* (New York: Basic Books, 1996), Chapter 1, and Schacter and E. Tulving, eds., *Memory Systems* (Cambridge, MA: MIT Press, 1994). I discuss two of these cases in Chapter 6.

memory. They also need to be sensitive to how spatial and temporal features of the environments in which we act shape the content and meaning of memory for us. Adverse effects of emotion-blunting drugs could be avoided by the use of nonpharmacological therapies. The most promising of these is extinction training. This and other psychological interventions may enable people to weaken traumatic memories and retain positive episodic memories.

The Blessing and Burden of Biological Psychiatry

Depression, anxiety, schizophrenia, and other disorders of the brain and mind have never been treated on a par with bodily diseases such as heart disease and cancer. This inequality has persisted despite the fact that psychiatric disorders affect millions of people and often involve severe mental and physical disability, lost productivity, and impaired quality over much of their lives. One recent report estimated that severe mental illness is associated with an annual loss of earnings totaling $193.2 billion in the United States alone.[54] Depression is projected to be the leading cause of the burden of disease in developed countries by the year 2030.[55] For years, many believed that psychiatric disorders did not warrant being classified as illnesses. Diseases of the body were taken seriously. Disorders of the mind were often dismissed as imagined or feigned, presumably because there was no biological basis of their etiology and symptomatology. According to a national survey commissioned by the Canadian Medical Association and released in August 2008, a significant number of people still hold this view: nearly half of one thousand Canadians surveyed said that mental illness is not always real but an excuse for bad behavior and personal weakness.[56]

People with these conditions suffered from a double curse. There were few effective treatments to control their physiological and psychological symptoms. And rather than elicit sympathy, they became objects of discrimination and had to endure the social stigma attached to deeply misunderstood conditions. People with neurological disorders such as epilepsy have also suffered from a similar misunderstanding, though not to the same degree as those with psychiatric disorders. This may be due to the fact that for many years electroencephalography (EEG) has been able to detect seizures, and some neurosurgeons have been able to initiate seizures by stimulating the temporal lobes of some patients. More effective treatments for seizure disorders have helped as well. Misunderstanding of mental disorders is partly responsible for the inadequate funding of treatments for these conditions by health care systems in many countries. As a result, millions of people have continued to

---

54. R. Kessler et al., "Individual and Societal Effects of Mental Disorders on Earnings in the United States: Results from the National Comorbidity Survey Replication," *American Journal of Psychiatry* 165 (2008): 703–711.
55. C. Mathers and D. Loncar, "Projection of Global Mortality and Burden of Disease from 2002 to 2030," *PLoS Medicine* 3(2) (2006): e442.
56. Canadian Medical Association, 8th Annual National Report Card on Health Care, August 2008. http://www.cma.ca/report-card/august2008.html.

suffer from untreated or undertreated psychiatric disorders. This has been the most unfortunate legacy of mind–body dualism in medicine.

In an influential paper published in 1998, psychiatrist Eric Kandel outlined the beginning of a new conceptual framework for psychiatry that emphasized the neurobiological basis of the brain–mind relation.[57] Together with an understanding of how gene expression shapes neural circuits, this framework helped to establish biological psychiatry as the model for diagnosing and treating mental illness. Thanks largely to advances in functional neurosurgery and functional brain imaging, the neurobiological model of the brain–mind relation has done much to discredit mind–body dualism in medicine and reduce the harmful effects it has had on people with psychiatric disorders. Neuroimaging can establish correlations between structural and functional brain abnormalities and symptoms of these disorders. Combined with behavioral criteria, imaging may confirm a diagnosis of a particular condition. PET and the newer perfusion MRI can also enable researchers and clinicians to monitor the neurophysiological effects of psychotropic drugs in treating these conditions. By modulating the neural circuitry underlying some psychiatric disorders, deep-brain stimulation has further validated the neurobiological basis of mind and behavior. In addition, some epidemiological studies of psychiatric disorders indicate that their symptoms are strikingly similar across cultures. They are more deeply embedded in common neurobiology than in cultural differences.[58]

These empirical findings have confirmed that psychiatric disorders do indeed have a neurobiological basis. Biological psychiatry has done much to dispel the view that these conditions are "all in the mind" and as such not illnesses at all. Once it became clear that the brain was the organ that generates and sustains our mental states, and that brain dysfunction can result in mental dysfunction, it also became clear that what was inside the head played an important role in shaping the mind. A new initiative from the National Institute of Mental Health (NIMH) will reinforce this view. Instead of relying on the *Diagnostic and Statistical Manual of Mental Disorders*, which even in its revised fifth edition (2013) focuses on symptoms rather than causes, the NIMH's Research Domain Criteria (RDoC) will classify psychiatric disorders based on identifiable neural circuits.[59] This shift may help to further weaken the stigma and discrimination experienced by people with mental illness. It will do this by emphasizing that the problem is not with people but their brains. Focusing on neural circuits should lead to more public funding for mental health programs so that people with these conditions will receive the treatment they need and to which they are entitled.

---

57. "A New Intellectual Framework for Psychiatry," *American Journal of Psychiatry* 155 (1998): 457–469. T. Insel and P. Wang affirm Kandel's position in stating that mental disorders "are disorders of brain circuits likely caused by developmental processes shaped by a complex interplay of genetics and experience." "Rethinking Mental Illness," *Journal of the American Medical Association* 303 (2010): 1970–1971, at 1971.
58. S. Pallanti, "Transcultural Observations of Obsessive-Compulsive Disorder," *American Journal of Psychiatry* 165 (2008): 169–170.
59. G. Miller, "Beyond *DSM*: Seeking a Brain-Based Classification of Mental Illness," *Science* 327 (2010): 1437.

Together with his emphasis on the neurobiological and genetic basis of mind and behavior, Kandel pointed out how social factors modulate the biological structure of the brain. The framework for psychiatry he proposes and defends includes biological as well as social determinants. The examples I have cited in this chapter show that the symptoms of psychiatric disorders have a neurobiological underpinning; but they are not *just* neurobiological. The reductionist claim that psychiatric disorders can be explained entirely in neurobiological terms may give us destigmatization at the cost of depersonalization. Emphasis on impersonal brain mechanisms may eliminate feelings of guilt or shame associated with psychiatric disorders, as well as the tendency of others to blame individuals for having them. Yet biological psychiatry may be a mixed blessing. By focusing on the brain rather than the person, it may lose sight of the fact that we are agents whose minds are shaped by interaction with our natural and social surroundings. Although some studies show general similarities in psychiatric symptoms across cultures, they ignore how different cultures can influence how individuals experience diseases of the mind.

A neuroreductionist model that explains disorders of the mind entirely in terms of brain mechanisms strips persons of their autonomy and agency. It weakens the conviction that persons have the capacity to regulate and guide their mental states and actions and be the authors of their behavior. Such a model can undermine the belief in self-determination by reinforcing a learned helplessness in those who have mental disorders and the idea that all of our thought and behavior is controlled by the brain. As Fuchs points out, "a reductionist biological concept of mental life may lead to a self-alienation: in the wake of a popularized neurobiology, we are beginning to regard ourselves not as persons having wishes, motives, or reasons, but as agents of our genes, hormones, and neurons."[60] Rather than supporting the idea that persons can be effective agents in the world, biological psychiatry risks leaving us with the idea that everything we do is at the will of the brain. Yet my discussion of the effects of psychotherapy on cortical function suggests that our ability to consciously alter our mental states gives us some control of our thought and behavior. A complementary model that bases mental disorders on neurobiology and acknowledges the importance of beliefs, environment, and culture in the etiology and treatment of these disorders can both reduce the stigma associated with them and preserve a robust sense of personhood and agency.

One example of how persons are not just a function of neurobiology is the autobiography of the Russian soldier Lyova Zazetsky, written in collaboration with Luria.[61] During the Battle of Smolensk in the Second World War, Zazetsky sustained a severe head injury that caused extensive damage to the left occipital-parietal region of his brain. This caused his memory, visual field, and bodily perception to

---

60. "Neurobiology and Psychotherapy," 483. Psychiatrist J. Sadler asserts that "stigma requires much more moral, social, educational, and political attention than neurobiological attention" in "Stigma, Conscience, and Science in Psychiatry: Past, Present, and Future," *Academic Medicine* 84 (2009): 413–417, at 414.
61. *The Man with a Shattered World: The History of a Brain Wound*, trans. L. Solotaroff (Cambridge, MA: Harvard University Press, 1987). Luria writes that Zazetsky "fought with the tenacity of the damned to recover the use of his shattered brain," xx.

become fragmented. It left him with the experience of a constantly shifting and unstable self in what for him had become a shattered world. The injury did not destroy his agency, however, because enough of his brain was intact for him to try to make sense of his experience. He retained his imagination and capacity for fantasy and empathy. To cope with his experience of fragmentation, he kept a journal for 20 years, recording his thoughts and memories as they occurred on a daily basis. While this required excruciating effort, he wrote thousands of pages. Because of his mental impairment, Zazetsky was not able to completely re-establish psychological connectedness and continuity with his pre-injury state. But his efforts enabled him to retain a minimal sense of identity and autobiography in adjusting its later chapters to his post-injury state.

Zazetsky's determination in trying to reshape his identity and construct a meaningful narrative of his life after his brain injury illustrates how one can retain and exercise the will in spite of significant neurological and psychological impairment. It is an example of the human capacity to recognize, invent, and realize possibilities of action despite being constrained to some degree by a damaged brain. This Russian soldier's efforts suggest that there is more to a person and the will than a set of neural processes. Personhood and agency also involve a subjective, authorial conception of oneself in making sense of one's experience. This does not suggest dualism but affirms the view that persons are constituted by but not identical to their brains.

Brain, Behavior, and Knowledge

It is important to emphasize that while the brain alone cannot account for all the features of the mind, the brain is necessary to explain our thought and behavior. In a recent article, legal theorists Michael Pardo and Dennis Patterson offer a welcome antidote to the explanatory reductionism in much of neuroscience and neuroethics.[62] They acknowledge that the properties associated with the mind depend on a properly functioning brain. At the same time, they claim that the idea that persons are their brains leaves too much out of our understanding of human action for this idea to be plausible.

While I am generally sympathetic to their position, they leave too little of the brain in their account of different types of knowledge and behavior. As a result, they do not offer an adequate explanation of such activities as rule-following, understanding, and interpretation. The examples that Pardo and Patterson use support the view that what we think and do cannot be explained entirely in terms of brain function. Yet persons know how to do such things as follow rules because normal brain functions enable these practices by generating and sustaining the mental capacities associated with them. Pardo and Patterson are concerned more with conceptual questions involving the proper application of this knowledge than with empirical questions regarding the brain and its functions. Given their acknowledgment that the mind depends on the brain, I do not take them to mean that empirical questions can be excluded from an account of behavior. Instead, they

---

62. "Minds, Brains, and Norms," *Neuroethics*, published online June 19, 2010.

suggest that the empirical does less work than the conceptual in such an account. But they underemphasize the extent of the brain's role in behavior. A satisfactory account of behavior requires equal emphasis on conceptual and empirical aspects of the relation between the brain and behavior. Our thought and action cannot be separated from their neurobiological underpinning. Empirical explanations of practical and moral knowledge may not make any sense in and of themselves; nor do purely conceptual explanations. The empirical correctness of how the brain enables behavior is necessary to make sense of how we think and act. The brain does not understand concepts or follow rules—persons do. But it is because of their brains that persons can do these things.

Pardo and Patterson claim that particular neurological states *may* be a necessary condition for various mental activities. Failure to state that neurological states *are* necessary (though not sufficient) for mental life and behavior underlies the limitations of their account. The mental states associated with behavior are not reducible to brain states. This does not imply that the dependence relation of the mind to the brain is only contingent, however. These authors note the influence of the later Wittgenstein in their discussion of rule-following. This activity, together with the associated activities of interpretation and understanding, are all part of what Wittgenstein calls "mastering a technique."[63] They are not simply functions of neurological or mental states but also of human subjects acting and interacting in social and cultural contexts. We know that a person understands a concept or correctly applies a rule not by having access to some process in his or her brain or mind, but by observing that person in action. Nevertheless, while brains alone cannot account for how we follow rules, we could not engage in this activity without a normally functioning brain.

Pardo and Patterson question the idea of unconscious rule-following. One would have to be aware of a rule in order to follow it. This is puzzling because many forms of rule-following occur at the unconscious level. We can distinguish following a rule from conforming to a rule. It is not surprising to say that one can conform to rules unconsciously. But my claim here is the stronger one that following a rule can be an unconscious activity. Many of our beliefs obtain outside of our conscious awareness; they are not before the mind. One need not be consciously aware of rules in order to know how to follow them. There is not just one but two epistemic components—conscious and unconscious—to this activity. Although these components operate at the mental level, both are grounded in neurobiological functions. Our use of linguistic rules when we speak is one example of rule-following that occurs outside of our conscious awareness. The capacity to follow these rules depends on the proper function of the cortical brain regions mediating language. Damage to these regions can impair the capacity to use words and construct sentences. Individuals with Broca's aphasia are impaired in their ability to produce language. This is caused by lesions in the inferior frontal cortex. Those with Wernike's aphasia retain fluent speech but have impaired language comprehension. This is caused by lesions in the superior temporal cortex. Behavior alone will not explain why these individuals are compromised in their ability to use language.

---

63. *Philosophical Investigations*, 208.

Behavior based on procedural memory is another example of unconscious rule-following. Unlike the declarative forms of semantic and episodic memory, which involve knowing *that* something is the case and knowing *when* something occurred, procedural memory involves knowing *how* to do things, such as ride a bicycle or drive a car. As nondeclarative memory, procedural memory is a form of tacit knowledge. In some countries, we are taught to drive on the right side of the road; in others, the rule is to drive on the left. This is a rule of which we are consciously aware in the initial stages of driving. It becomes an unconscious mental state or process, a conditioned response to driving, after we have performed it countless times. My staying on the right side of the road when I drive is a form of rule-following, and I do it without consciously thinking about doing it. I do not have to be consciously aware of the rule or of the fact that I am following it in order to follow it correctly. This form of procedural memory is not a purely psychological state but one that is regulated by neurobiological processes in the brain.[64] The subcortical cerebellum and striatum regulate procedural memory. Damage to these regions could make one lose this type of memory and the capacity to follow certain rules. Behavioral evidence is necessary to know that one can or cannot follow rules involving procedural memory. We also need to know why one retains or loses this capacity. Failure to know how to perform a motor activity likely has an organic cause requiring a neurobiological explanation.

Pardo and Patterson say that the criterion of remembering an event is not a particular neurological state. Memory is the retention of knowledge, an epistemic ability. The criterion of this ability is how it is manifested in behavior. This is correct as far as it goes—but it does not go far enough. One's actions indicate whether one knows how to do certain things. Yet this knowledge and action necessarily depend on normal functions in the brain regions that enable them.

Many would agree with Wittgenstein's claim that "an inner process stands in need of outward criteria."[65] In addition to confirming an inner psychological process through its manifestation in behavior, though, we must know about the neural underpinning of that process in order to know *why* an agent can or cannot engage in the relevant behavior. We must also know about the neural underpinning in order to know *that* an agent has or lacks the relevant capacity. Consider locked-in syndrome. I will discuss this condition in the context of brain injury in Chapter 6. For present purposes, it is important to point out that locked-in individuals are unable to move but retain full consciousness. Functional neuroimaging is one technique that can establish whether one is in such a state. This cannot be confirmed on the basis of outward behavior. A similar situation occurs when patients are given insufficient general anesthesia and awaken during surgery. Because they are also given a paralyzing drug to prevent movement, they are unable to indicate that they are awake and can feel pain. Here too behavioral criteria fail to establish that an individual is conscious and thinking certain thoughts. Pardo and Patterson say that, as a conceptual matter, neural states of the brain do not fit the criteria for

---

64. See S. A. Bunge and J. D. Wallis, eds., *Neuroscience of Rule-Guided Behavior* (Oxford: Oxford University Press, 2008).

65. *Philosophical Investigations*, sec. 580.

ascriptions of knowledge. Yet these criteria presuppose normal functioning of the neural states that ground the capacity for knowledge. The intelligibility of a conceptual explanation of knowledge and behavior rests on an empirical explanation of it. These should not be seen as competing but complementary explanations. The point here is not that a neural explanation can be added to a conceptual explanation to strengthen the latter, but that a neural explanation is necessary for a complete account of knowledge and behavior. Persons are more than their brains. Still, persons would not have the mental capacity to understand and know how to do things without their brains. We should not overstate the role of the brain in our lives; but we should not understate it either.

Conclusion

Responding to Crick's claim that we are nothing but a bunch of neurons, neurobiologist Steven Rose endorses the same nonreductionist model of the brain–mind relation that I have defended. Rose states:

> 'We' are a bunch of neurons, and other cells. We are also, in part by virtue
> of possessing those neurons, humans with agency. It is precisely because
> we are biosocial organisms, because we have minds constituted through the
> evolutionary, developmental, and historical interaction of our bodies and brains
> (the bunch of neurons) with the social and natural worlds that surround us, that
> we retain responsibility for our actions, that we, as humans, possess the agency
> to create and re-create our worlds.[66]

Zeman expresses a similar view: "We may come to acknowledge that the richness of experience derives as much from the physical world we inhabit, the cultural world we inherit, and the processes of development through which we become experts in navigating both, as from the intricacies of the workings of the brain."[67] So does physician and philosopher Raymond Tallis: "When scientists are tempted like Crick (echoing Hippocrates) to assert that 'you... are no more than a vast assembly of nerve cells and their associated molecules,' they should recall that brains are meaningless without bodies, that bodies cannot function without environments, and environed human bodies are not human beings without societies."[68]

We are not just our brains but subjects whose ordered and disordered states of mind are the products of interaction between us and the social and natural environment. The mind is not located in the brain but is distributed among the brain, body, and world in which the subject is situated. This distributed model of the mind can be helpful in understanding the etiology of many psychiatric disorders and providing effective therapies for them. Exclusive emphasis on neurobiology fails to appreciate the extent to which the mind is shaped by what occurs outside the brain.

---

66. *The Future of the Brain: The Promise and Perils of Tomorrow's Neuroscience* (Oxford: Oxford University Press, 2005), 305.
67. "Does Consciousness Spring from the Brain?" 318.
68. "Trying to Find Consciousness in the Brain," *Brain* 127 (2004): 2558–2563, at 2562.

A holistic model that conceives of the brain as a relational and enabling organ mediating interaction between the embodied subject and the environment provides the best model to guide interventions in the brain that will have the most salutary effects on the mind. There is more to us than can be dreamed of in our neuroscience.[69]

---

69. Gillett makes a similar point in *Subjectivity and Being Somebody*, 220.

2

Neuroscience, Free Will, and Moral Responsibility

Cognitive and affective neuroscience have yielded important insights into the neurobiological underpinning of our capacity for practical and moral reasoning. Experiments involving human subjects undergoing functional magnetic resonance imaging (fMRI) scans while engaged in cognitive tasks have established correlations between brain states and the mental states that figure in our deliberation and decision making. Neuroimaging has shown that the desires, beliefs, emotions, and intentions that issue in actions are mediated by interacting cortical and subcortical networks in the brain. This has resulted in a better understanding of some aspects of the brain-mind relation.

Some cognitive neuroscientists and psychologists claim that our understanding of the relation between the brain and behavior implies that mental functions can be completely explained in terms of unconscious mechanistic processes in the brain. This suggests that the source of our actions is not within our conscious control and that our mental states have no causal role in producing them. Free will consists in the capacity to initiate and execute plans of action. This involves the capacity to respond to reasons and to choose in accord with our mental states by controlling how they issue in our actions. It also implies that our actions have an impact on events in the world. But if we are not the source of our actions and our mental states are causally inert, then our idea of conscious free will is an illusion. Furthermore, if free will is an illusion, then no one can be responsible for his or her actions or omissions, since responsibility usually rests on the assumption that we have free will.

This chapter is divided into two general parts. In the first part, I argue that neuroscience does not undermine free will because it does not show that deterministic or mechanistic processes in the brain completely explain human behavior. Any plausible conception of free will is consistent with the idea that some mental states can causally influence actions while having physical causes in the brain.

Because the brain generates and sustains the mind, and the mind in turn can influence the brain, a satisfactory account of human agency must include both unconscious physical and conscious mental states and events as the causes of our actions. My aim is not to argue on practical grounds that, even if our belief in free will were an illusion, we would still praise, blame, and hold people responsible for their behavior. Rather, my aim is to show that the argument from illusion is misguided and flawed on theoretical grounds.[1] Neuroscience does not threaten free will and moral responsibility because nothing about normal brain function suggests that we lack the capacity to choose and act freely.

In the second part of the chapter, I consider the idea that brain dysfunction may undermine the mental capacities necessary for one to act freely and responsibly. I define the capacity to be responsible in terms of the capacity to respond to reasons for or against certain actions. On the basis of this definition, I challenge the view that brain dysfunction undermines this capacity by discussing psychopathy and whether or to what extent psychopaths can be responsible for their behavior. Brain and mental dysfunction come in degrees, and individuals with psychopathy and other mental disorders may be responsible to varying degrees. Specifically, I argue that the psychopath is at least partly responsible for his actions.

Free Will as an Illusion

Philosopher and psychologist Joshua Greene and psychologist Jonathan Cohen claim that neuroscientific evidence may show that "every decision is a thoroughly mechanical process, the outcome of which is completely determined by the results of prior mechanical processes."[2] They argue that the "new neuroscience will undermine people's common sense, libertarian conception of free will…"[3] Among other things, they hold that this argument should move us to reject our retributive model of punishment and replace it with a consequentialist one. Although Greene and Cohen mainly discuss the implications of neuroscience for the criminal law, their claims challenge common assumptions about free will. From a slightly different perspective, cognitive neuroscientist Martha Farah states that "all behavior is 100% determined by brain function, which is in turn determined by the interplay

---

1. A. Roskies argues that claims about neuroscience threatening free will are misguided in "Neuroscientific Challenges to Free Will and Responsibility," *Trends in Cognitive Sciences* 10 (2006): 419–423, and "Why Libet's Studies Don't Pose a Threat to Free Will," in W. Sinnott-Armstrong and L. Nadel, eds., *Conscious Will and Responsibility: A Tribute to Benjamin Libet* (New York: Oxford University Press, 2010), Chapter 2. Some surveys show that a significant majority of people believe that living in a deterministic world does not negate the intuition of free will. See, for example, E. Nahmias et al., "Surveying Freedom: Folk Intuitions about Free Will and Moral Responsibility," *Philosophical Psychology* 18 (2005): 561–584. Of course, the intuition that we have free will does not prove that we in fact have it.
2. "For the Law, Neuroscience Changes Nothing and Everything," 1781.
3. *Ibid.*, 1776.

of genes and experience."[4] Expressing a third perspective, psychologist Daniel Wegner maintains that "the real causal mechanisms underlying behavior are never present in consciousness."[5] The most confident assertion of this third position is made by psychologist Henry Roediger and coauthors: "Clearly conscious intentions cannot cause an action if a neural event that precedes and correlates with the action comes before conscious intentions."[6]

These claims present three distinct worries from neuroscience about free and effective action. One worry concerns determinism: if the brain is a deterministic system, then we cannot be free because free will is incompatible with determinism. A second worry concerns mechanism: if the brain is just a mechanism, then we cannot be free because free will is incompatible with the idea that all natural phenomena can be explained by natural causes and mechanistic principles A third worry concerns epiphenomenalism: if our conscious mental states and events are physically caused but have no physical effects or causal role in our actions, then none of our actions results from them. Although these are distinct claims, together they appear to threaten two basic assumptions about free will: (1) that as conscious agents we are the authors of our actions, and (2) that we have a causal impact on events in the world. Determinism and mechanism appear to undermine (1), while epiphenomenalism appears to undermine (2). If these cognitive psychologists and neuroscientists are correct about the implications of neuroscience, then our idea of conscious free will is an illusion. Determinism, mechanism, and epiphenomenalism together form the argument from illusion.

The first neuroscientist to question the idea of conscious will and the presumed efficacy of our conscious mental states on the basis of empirical evidence was Benjamin Libet. In a series of experiments he conducted in the early 1980s involving subjects who were asked to flex their wrist or finger, Libet noted that unconscious brain events preceded the conscious intention to flex by 300 to 500 milliseconds.[7] These events are readiness potentials measuring activity in the motor cortex that precedes voluntary muscle movement. The activity was recorded by electrodes placed on the scalp as part of an electroencephalogram. The brain formed the state associated with the intention before the subjects became aware of it. From his experiments, Libet concluded that "the discovery that the brain unconsciously initiates the volitional process well before the person becomes aware of an intention or wish to act voluntarily... clearly has a profound impact on how we view the

---

4. "Neuroethics: The Practical and the Philosophical," *Trends in Cognitive Sciences* 9 (2005): 34–40, at 38.
5. *The Illusion of Conscious Will* (Cambridge, MA: MIT Press, 2002), 97.
6. "Free Will and the Control of Action," in J. Baer, J. Kaufman, and R. Baumeister, eds., *Are We Free? Psychology and Free Will* (Oxford: Oxford University Press, 2008), 205–225, at 208.
7. "Unconscious Cerebral Initiative and the Role of Conscious Will in Voluntary Action," *Behavioral and Brain Sciences* 8 (1985): 529–566. Also, Libet, "Consciousness, Free Action, and the Brain," *Journal of Consciousness Studies* 8 (2001): 59–65, *Mind Time: The Temporal Factor in Consciousness* (Cambridge, MA: Harvard University Press, 2004), and "Do We Have Free Will?" in Sinnott-Armstrong and Nadel, Chapter 1.

nature of free will."[8] For most neuroscientists, the impact is negative. Specifically, on the basis of the data from Libet's experiments, neuropsychologist Patrick Haggard claims that because "conscious intention occurs after the onset of preparatory brain activity" it "cannot... cause our actions."[9] Contrary to what many of us believe, the processes preceding action appear to take place entirely at the unconscious level. If our actions are the result of unconscious deterministic or mechanistic processes in the brain, then we do not have free will and cannot be responsible for what we do.

To assess the argument from illusion, it will be helpful to place it within the historical philosophical debate on free will. For philosophers, the main threat to free will has come from causal determinism. This says that natural laws and events in the past jointly determine a unique future. More precisely, causal determinism says that a complete description of the state of the world at a particular time, in conjunction with a complete formulation of the natural laws, entails the truth about the physical state of the world at later times. This means that any action one performs at a particular time is the only action one could have performed at that time. Causal determinism rules out alternative possibilities (APs) to do otherwise than what one actually does. Incompatibilists hold that APs are necessary for free will and that causal determinism is incompatible with APs. Hard incompatibilists believe that causal determinism is true and that we do not have free will. Libertarian incompatibilists hold that we have free will and that causal determinism is false. Compatibilists claim that we choose and act freely when we are not coerced, compelled, or constrained. We have the mental capacity to respond to reasons for or against certain actions and the physcial capacity to act or refrain from acting in line with these reasons. Because causal determinism does not entail coercion, compulsion, or constraint, free will is compatible with causal determinism.

Philosopher Robert Kane insists that the AP condition is too thin a basis on which to rest the case for libertarianism. Kane says that, in addition to the forward-looking AP condition, a backward-looking condition of ultimate responsibility (UR) is necessary for libertarian free will. UR consists in "the power of agents to be the ultimate creators (or originators) and sustainers of their own ends and purposes."[10] Kane emphasizes that this condition "puts the emphasis for being up to us not in the power to do otherwise, but on the *source* or *explanation* of the action that is actually performed: that source must be in us." We must be the "ultimate, buck-stopping originators of our actions."[11] But we cannot be the originators of our actions if the mental states issuing in them are causally determined by antecedent events. I take Greene and Cohen to be referring to a version of the UR condition when mentioning "people's common sense libertarian conception of free will." On their view, the threat to libertarian free will is not from natural laws and events in the past and the idea that they rule out alternative possibilities. Rather, the threat is from neural processes and the idea that they, not our conscious mental states, are the ultimate

---

8. *Mind Time*, 201.
9. "Conscious Intention and Motor Cognition," *Trends in Cognitive Sciences* 9 (2005): 290–295, at 291.
10. *The Significance of Free Will* (New York: Oxford University Press, 1996), 4.
11. *Ibid.*, 34.

and only effective source of our choices and actions. Neuroscience suggests that the UR condition cannot be met. Insofar as neuroscience implies that brain processes do all of the work in the causal pathway leading to action, we cannot be ultimately responsible for our choices and actions because we are neither the source nor the authors of them.

Kane is an event-causal libertarian. He holds that the decisions and actions of human agents are physically caused. Free will requires only that these events are caused in an undetermined way. If decisions and actions are caused but not determined by antecedent conditions, then this may be enough for us to be the authors of at least some of our actions. Many agent-causal libertarians claim that agents can initiate causal processes without any antecedent causes. Some events are caused, not by other events, but solely by agents.[12] According to compatibilist versions of free will, at least some mental states and events can be within our conscious control and causally efficacious in action even if they are causally determined. The question is whether the idea that something is caused in a deterministic or mechanistic way implies that it has no causal influence of its own.

For a causal explanation of a voluntary action, we need to account for all of the steps in the causal sequence resulting in that action. At the mental level, this would include desires to act, beliefs about the circumstances surrounding the action, the intention or plan to act, and the execution of that intention in the choice or decision to act. At the neural level, this would include all the cortical and subcortical regions that mediate thought and behavior. What occurs at the mental level depends on what occurs at the neural level. Although some philosophers identify intentions with decisions, I distinguish them as separate components of the mental process leading to action. An intention is a plan to do something.[13] A decision or choice is the execution of that plan in action. One can change one's mind, alter one's plan, and execute a different plan in an action different from what one initially intended. The pathway from desire to action involves an extended process consisting of both unconscious brain events and conscious mental events. But the cognitive neuroscientists and psychologists I have cited claim that brain events are doing all of the causal work. In that case, our conscious decisions and actions are not really up to us and have no impact on any events internal or external to us.

Defusing the Threat

Libet's experiments to measure intention focus on a narrow time frame, the proximal urge or intention to act now and the wrist- or finger-flexing that immediately follows it. As philosopher Alfred Mele points out, Libet confuses proximal urges or desires to act with proximal intentions to act: "Failing to distinguish intending from wanting can lead to serious errors."[14] There could be an unconscious desire to flex,

12. R. Clarke discusses agent-causation in *Libertarian Accounts of Free Will* (New York: Oxford University Press, 2003).
13. As defined by M. Bratman, *Intention, Plans, and Practical Reason* (Cambridge, MA: Harvard University Press, 1987).
14. *Free Will and Luck* (New York: Oxford University Press, 2006), 31.

which could be followed by a conscious intention to flex. This suggests that the mental events of forming and executing the intention to flex causally influence the act of flexing. Or as a distal intention, a person could plan to perform a particular action not now but at a later time.[15] Even if the "act now" event were an unconscious brain event, it would not rule out long-range planning leading up to the action as at least partly a conscious process. Also, Libet noted from his experiments that although the intention to flex was unconscious, his subjects could "veto" this intention, suggesting that a conscious intention and decision not to flex would result in their not flexing.[16] This seems to open a window of opportunity for free will. Still, Libet's notion of a veto only suggests that we can consciously refrain from performing some actions that would have issued from unconscious urges or intentions. It does not satisfactorily explain how or why one would translate a different conscious intention into a different action. Even if one accepts the notion of a conscious veto, it offers only an incomplete account of free will.

Mele takes issue with a different aspect of Libet's idea of a veto, asking how an agent simultaneously can be settled on A-ing at t and settled on not A-ing at t.[17] This may not be a problem for Libet if we distinguish between forming intentions and making decisions as separate mental acts. For example, I may form an intention to take a certain route to the airport. Just before turning onto that route, I notice that the traffic is heavy and quickly form a different intention to take a different route instead. I can form but veto one intention and form and decide to act on a different intention, in which case I was not settled on the first. What *is* a problem for Libet is that this process does not only occur at the unconscious level. The fact that taking a different route is motivated by my conscious awareness of the traffic and by a more general conscious distal intention to go to the airport suggests that an important part of the process occurs within my conscious control. When I start to drive, my intention to go to the airport as quickly as possible is a conscious distal intention that influences the proximal intention about the best route to take now. One cannot draw general conclusions about willing and acting from Libet's experiments because wrist- and finger-flexing are not representative of most of the actions we perform in our lives. Many of these actions involve at least some conscious deliberation and formation and execution of conscious intentions, a process that extends over time.

The claims by Greene and Cohen and Farah that mechanistic processes in the brain determine behavior seem to imply that they completely explain my behavior. But consider the following example. Suppose that I have distinct desires to begin an essay and exercise at the same time. Each of these desires corresponds to a proximal urge in my brain. Whether I form and execute an intention to do one thing rather than the other cannot be explained satisfactorily in terms of unconscious neural

15. *Ibid.*, 32. Also, Mele, "Recent Work on Free Will and Science," *American Philosophical Quarterly* 45 (2008): 107–130, at 109; *Effective Intentions: The Power of Conscious Will* (New York: Oxford University Press, 2009), especially Chapters 2–4; and "Libet on Free Will, Readiness Potentials, Decisions, and Awareness," in Sinnott-Armstrong and Nadel, Chapter 3.
16. *Mind Time*, 137–149.
17. "Recent Work on Free Will and Science," 115.

urges. Each of these competing desires is influenced by distinct long-range plans of mine to be healthy and more productive in my scholarship. My decision to write or exercise at a particular time depends on how I respond to the reasons for performing these actions. My response to these reasons will be influenced by my conscious response to factors external to the brain, such as the weather, the volume of noise in my home, and the deadline for submitting the essay. These reasons involve more than proximal urges in my brain. They also involve conscious beliefs whose content reflects features of the external environment. As part of this environment, the reasons for performing either action reflect the fact that I live in a culture that values health and scholarship. Appeal to the brain alone cannot explain why I perform one action rather than the other. In a different situation, my brain does not determine my decision to keep or return a lost wallet to its owner.

Unconscious mechanistic processes in the brain are part of the pathway leading to my decision and action. But one must not mistakenly infer from the fact that a decision has an unconscious cause that the decision itself is unconscious. Unconscious brain states may initiate an action. But this does not imply that conscious mental states play no causal role when an agent forms and executes a proximal intention in that action. An unconscious urge to act may itself be influenced by a conscious distal intention involving long-range planning. The brain does not do all of the causal work in the process leading up to and resulting in action, but causally *under*determines it. At least some mental states are doing some of the causal work. In the examples I have given, the fact that events in the external environment influence my plan of action shows that more than just the brain is involved in what I choose and do. Like the brain, though, the environment influences but does not determine which action I perform. Given the same environmental conditions, I may choose to perform a different action.

Wegner offers the most extreme version of the view that conscious intentions play no causal role in our actions. He claims that "conscious will is an illusion... in the sense that the experience of consciously willing an action is not a direct indication that the conscious thought has caused the action."[18] The intentions and other mental states we associate with conscious will are epiphenomenal. Wegner admits that we do have conscious intentions. If they are causally inert, then why would he claim that we have them? His reply is that conscious intentions give us a sense of responsibility for some of the things we do, albeit in a magical or supernatural sense. "Seeing one's own causal influence as supernatural is part of being human."[19] Free will is part of what Wegner calls a "magic self." In using this term, he appears to associate the self and free will with substance dualism and the idea of an immaterial mind or soul causally independent of physical events in the brain. Biologist Anthony Cashmore is more explicit in saying that "if we no longer entertain the luxury of a belief in the 'magic of the soul,' then there is little else to offer in support of the concept of free will."[20] Yet if conscious will is not real but magical, then we cannot

---

18. *The Illusion of Conscious Will*, 2.
19. "Self Is Magic," in Baer, Kaufman, and Baumeister, 226–247, at 228.
20. "The Lucretian Swerve: The Biological Basis of Human Behavior and the Criminal Justice System," *Proceedings of the National Academy of Sciences* 107 (2010): 4499–4504,

attribute the property of agency to ourselves. Wegner posits a mysterious conception of agency based on an implausibly strong assumption about the extent of unconscious processes in the production of actions. Responding to Wegner's position, Mele notes that "if one sets the bar for free will (that is, for the power or ability to act freely) ridiculously high, the thesis that people sometimes act freely should strike one as ridiculous."[21] Mele adds that "if the bar for the existence or efficacy of 'conscious will' is set so high that we have to be supernatural beings for conscious will to exist or be efficacious in us, then, of course, conscious will should be lumped together with ghosts, fairies, and the like."[22]

Most cognitive psychologists and neuroscientists give more weight to libertarianism than it has in philosophical debates on free will. They also ignore the fact that there are different (agent-causal and event-causal) versions of libertarianism. More importantly, some erroneously assume that free will presupposes substance dualism and the idea that mental states can operate independently of physical states and events in the brain. Libertarians are a minority among philosophers writing about free will. A very small number of these are substance dualists. The majority of philosophers working on free will are compatibilists. For most compatibilists, causal determinism just means that our mental states and actions are the products of antecedent physical events, such that if it were not for the latter, the former would not occur. Mental states are necessarily generated and sustained by brain states. But this does not mean that the choices and actions that issue from mental states are coerced, compelled, or constrained. This is consistent with what David Hume calls "liberty of spontaneity," which involves freedom from force or constraint. He argues that since the existence of causal laws governing our actions does not undermine this type of liberty, there is no conflict between causal determinism and moral responsibility.[23] John Locke holds a similar view and presents the example of a man who finds himself in a room from which he cannot leave because the door is locked. Since this fact does not affect his choice to remain in the room at that moment, he chooses freely even though he could not have done otherwise.[24] This is a negative default conception of free will. Many compatibilists offer a positive conception as well.

Philosopher Harry Frankfurt has developed one of the most influential positive compatibilist accounts of free will. He defines persons as individuals with the capacity to form first-order desires to perform certain actions. They also have the capacity to form second-order desires to have certain first-order desires. The will is the effective first-order desire that moves or would move a person all the way to action. One wills and acts freely when one's effective first-order desires align with one's second-order desires, and one identifies with both. There is a mesh between valuational and motivational mental states. Identification follows from a process of critical self-reflection after which the relevant desires become part of the set of a person's motivational states. The agent forms an unopposed second-order desire to make

---

21. "Recent Work on Free Will and Science," 124.
22. *Ibid.*, 124, and *Effective Intentions*, 111–112.
23. *A Treatise of Human Nature*, ed. P. H. Nidditch (Oxford: Clarendon Press, 1978), 407 ff.
24. *An Essay Concerning Human Understanding*, Book II, Chapter XXI.

a particular first-order desire his will. In addition, the agent judges that no further consultation with even higher-order desires would result in a reversal of that judgment. This process of reflective self-control enables one to make the mental springs of action one's own.[25] Reflection on the springs of our actions is what makes them self-generated and makes us autonomous agents. Still, the challenge to free will from cognitive neuroscience is not that brain processes interfere with identification, or that they coerce or compel us to act. Rather, the challenge from Wegner and others is that brain processes alone account for all the events in the pathway leading to action. If so, then these processes render mental states epiphenomenal.

Our first-order desires may very well be causally determined in the sense that they are necessarily generated and sustained by events in the brain. But this does not put all of these and other motivational states beyond our conscious control. Nor does it render all of them causally inert. Our capacity to make these desires conform to second-order desires, to identify with them, and to translate them into actions may provide us with enough conscious control of our motivational states to be the authors of them and to make them play a causal role in our actions. As discussed in Chapter 1, psychotherapies that reframe beliefs can modulate cortical brain function and influence the behavior of people with depression and anxiety disorders. There is both brain–mind and mind–brain causal interaction. The underlying brain circuits are re-entrant loops in which information is constantly recycled. The causal trajectories are best described as neither top-down nor bottom-up but circular.[26] Cognitive-behavioral therapy is just one example of how some mental states can be causally efficacious in altering brain states and influencing actions that issue from them. Reframing our beliefs about the world can have modulating effects on cortical and even limbic regions of the brain. These effects occur because of the intentionality of beliefs, a property that neurons lack.

If the lower- and higher-level capacities in Frankfurt's model are intentional and part of circular causal trajectories involving the brain and the mind, then these capacities may be sufficient for us to be ultimate, buck-stopping originators of some of our actions. They may be sufficient for some of our conscious mental states to be causally efficacious in producing these actions. In these respects, Frankfurt's version of compatibilism can satisfy a condition analogous to UR. We do not need to endorse a libertarian rejection of causal determinism to satisfy it. If neuroscience threatens only libertarianism and not also compatibilism, then the threat to free will might not be so great after all.

Unlike libertarian incompatibilists such as Kane, for Frankfurt and other compatibilists what matters in having or lacking free will is not so much whether external *sources* influence the mental states issuing in our action; indeed, they do. What matters more is whether we have the internal *resources* to identify with our desires,

25. "Freedom of the Will and the Concept of a Person" and "Identification and Externality" in *The Importance of What We Care About* (New York: Cambridge University Press, 1988), 11–25, 58–68.

26. S. Spence emphasizes this in *The Actor's Brain: Exploring the Cognitive Neuroscience of Free Will* (Oxford: Oxford University Press, 2009), 154. It reiterates my description in Chapter 1 of the brain–mind relation as involving a circular causal process.

beliefs, and intentions, and execute them in actions. Just because these resources have physical causes does not mean that we cannot consciously identify with or act on them. Some would claim that social factors beyond our control have such a strong influence on our thought and behavior that what we think and do are not up to us. These external sources play such a significant role in the causal history of our choices and actions that they preclude free and responsible agency.[27] This may be a legitimate challenge to free will and responsibility for a compatibilist. Some may question whether the process of identification can minimize the force of these external factors on one's motivational states. They may question whether one can integrate these factors into the autonomous springs of one's actions, or whether they are alien to these springs and thus not one's own. Yet this is not part of the challenge to free will from neuroscience, which is not concerned with social factors but only events in the brain.

In Libet's model, unconscious brain events associated with urges or intentions to act occur at discrete, measurable times. But it is difficult to see how a mechanistic model of the brain–behavior relation based on readiness potentials can account for the extended temporal process involved in deliberation and decision making leading to action. There is a similar weakness in Frankfurt's account, which fails to acknowledge that the process of identification extends into the past. Philosopher Michael Bratman defends a historical theory of practical reasoning and intention. An agent may reason and act in a nondeliberative and nonreflective way at a certain time; yet there is often a rational link to prior deliberation. "It seems quite plausible to suppose that the relevant process is the *extended deliberation* that begins at t0 [some time in the past] and continues through to t1 [the present time of action]."[28] Further, "assessments of the rationality of agents are sensitive to how in fact the agent comes to have the intentions he has, not to how he might have come to have them."[29] Bratman's historical theory of intentions supports the idea of distal intentions and how these can influence the proximal intentions that directly issue in actions.

If an intention is part of a deliberative process that extends into the past, then this casts doubt on Libet's claim that forming an intention occurs at a particular time or within a very narrow temporal interval. It also calls into question the claim that events and processes in the brain occurring at specific times determine the formation of an intention and its execution in action. By focusing on the current time-slice relation of a brain event to a mental event such as forming an intention, many neuroscientists ignore the critical role of the history behind this mental event.

---

27. This claim has been made by "source incompatibilists" such as G. Strawson and D. Pereboom. See Strawson, "The Impossibility of Moral Responsibility," *Philosophical Studies* 75 (1994): 5–24, and Pereboom, *Living Without Free Will* (New York: Cambridge University Press, 2001). This position has also been called "constitutive luck," reflecting the idea that one's character and other mental traits are constituted by factors beyond one's control.

28. *Intention, Plans, and Practical Reason*, 80.

29. Ibid., 82.

In a study published in 2007, neuroscientist John-Dylan Haynes and colleagues used fMRI to monitor patterns of activity in the prefrontal cortex as subjects concentrated on choosing between two future actions.[30] The researchers reported that the cortical activity patterns corresponded to the subjects' different plans. This study seemed to show that the process of deliberating and decision making could be measured by brain imaging. It seemed to display brain activity corresponding not only to proximal intentions but distal intentions as well. While this study was an improvement over Libet's experiments, it had limitations of its own. The duration of the patterns of brain activity was relatively short. They did not correspond to plans that extended over many hours, days, or months. So, one can question whether the imaging could accurately measure distal intentions and their influence on proximal intentions. Moreover, the correspondence between the cortical activity and the plans did not rule out the possibility that conscious mental states influenced the plans and the execution of one plan rather than the other in action. Even if imaging could display the neural mechanisms underlying the choice between two future actions in the experiment, it could not explain why a subject entertains different plans of action in actual life. Nor could it explain why a subject forms and executes one plan rather than another. Satisfactory answers to these questions require consideration of factors in addition to the brain.

There are seven main problems with the argument from illusion. This is by no means an exhaustive list. But these problems are enough to show that the argument is weak.

First, claims about neuroscientific determinism or mechanism presumably are based on empirical evidence. Most of this evidence is in the form of neuroimaging. Functional brain imaging can show correlations between brain activity and behavior. Correlation is not causation. Yet the claim that every decision is a mechanistic process completely determined by prior mechanistic processes in the brain is a causal claim. Some correlations may be strong enough to suggest causation, especially if one can eliminate other factors in explaining the relation between anatomical and functional brain features and behavior. If a person loses control of impulses, a brain scan shows a tumor in the person's prefrontal cortex, and he or she regains impulse control with the removal of the tumor, then this could indicate a causal connection between the brain abnormality and the behavior. But this is an example of brain dysfunction. It does not support the claim that imaging establishes a causal connection between normal brain function and a particular action or pattern of behavior. Correlations between normal brain activity and behavior are not strong enough to support the claim that brain processes completely determine behavior. In the absence of a causal connection, the claim that brain processes completely determine behavior is an assumption lacking the necessary empirical evidence. Correlations between brain processes and behavior may leave room for some of our conscious mental states to play a causal role in our actions.

---

30. "Reading Hidden Intentions in the Human Brain," *Current Biology* 17 (2007): 323–328. Also, Haynes, "Beyond Libet: Long-Term Prediction of Free Choices from Neuroimaging Signals," in Sinnott-Armstrong and Nadel, Chapter 8.

Second, claims about a causal connection between brain events and decisions are usually based on images of localized brain activity. They tend to focus on executive functions in the prefrontal, premotor, and motor cortices. Yet the neural activity that underlies decisions and actions is distributed throughout the brain. The anterior cingulate cortex also plays a critical role in behavior control by mediating cognitive and affective processing and the capacity to monitor and select plans of action. In subcortical regions, the basal ganglia and cerebellum not only enable voluntary movement but also influence such cognitive functions as planning, working memory, and attention. Psychiatrist Sean Spence explains that the neural circuits mediating action involve mainly basal ganglia-thalamic-cortical loops. These run from the cerebral cortex, to the basal ganglia, to specific thalamic nuclei, and then project back to the cortex.[31] Functional brain scans may show activation in these regions when a person performs cognitive tasks in a scanner. But they do not show how these regions project to and from each other, or how these projections enable the coordinated brain functions that are necessary to form and execute intentions in actions.

Third, many experimental settings using functional brain imaging and similar techniques involve artificial scenarios that cannot replicate real-world situations in which people choose and act. The techniques cannot diagnose post hoc what one was thinking when one performed a particular action and thus cannot explain why one performed that action. With the exception of some motor functions, imaging cannot predict how one would act in a given situation. When one gets into the driver's seat of a car or mounts a bicycle, the actions that follow are to some extent predictable. But their predictability and the fact that they are performed unconsciously does not mean that there is nothing voluntary about them or that they are beyond our conscious control. This further calls into question claims about determinism and mechanism based on neuroimaging. There was nothing artificial about Libet's experiments. Still, finger- and wrist-flexing are not the sorts of actions that make us candidates for attributions of praise, blame, and responsibility.

Fourth, the argument from illusion involves an invalid inference about causation. The fact that a mental state or event has a physical cause in the brain does not imply that it is not among the causes of an action. Just because an action is preceded by unconscious brain events does not mean that no conscious mental states and events have a causal role in the pathway leading to that action. As Mele points out, "not only is there no rule against causes themselves having causes, it is also the *norm* for causes to have causes (How many causal processes start with uncaused causes?)."[32] Libet, Haggard, Roediger et al., and Wegner all make this faulty inference. It is symptomatic of the view held by some neuroscientists and psychologists that free will presupposes substance dualism and the idea that the soul or mind can function independently of physical states and events in the brain. Very few philosophers

---

31. *The Actor's Brain*, 154.
32. *Effective Intentions*, 72. This position is consistent with what Mele calls "psychological causalism," the thesis that "all psychological events, including overt and nonovert intentional actions, are caused, either deterministically or indeterministically (probabilistically)," 151–152.

writing on free will hold this view. Greene and Cohen associate compatibilism with a materialist account of the mind. They say: "However, in our estimation, even people who do or would readily endorse a thoroughly material account of human action and its causes have dualist, libertarian intuitions."[33] Compatibilists would strongly disagree with this claim, and their writings would support them.

Fifth, the idea that conscious mental states and events play no causal role in action and are epiphenomenal offers an impoverished account of human agency. It implies that we never do anything on the basis of our desires, beliefs, emotions, intentions, and decisions. All of our behavior is the product of unconscious mechanistic processes. It seems to explain away practical and moral reasoning and decision making. Indeed, if we define persons as essentially agents who act on the basis of conscious mental states, then on this account persons do not exist. In addition to conscious desires and beliefs, interests are an important component of human agency in the way they shape the distal and proximal intentions that lead to our actions. Neither neurons nor unconscious urges have interests; only persons do.

Sixth, the idea from Libet and other neuroscientists that we can explain how brain events cause mental events in a current time-slice ignores the history of our intentions and choices. Proximal intentions may be influenced by distal intentions. These in turn may be shaped by the cultivation of values and dispositions over a period of time. Because values, dispositions, and some intentions extend into the past, the neuroscientific time-slice view leaves out an important historical component of planning and acting.

Seventh, if an explanation of our behavior just consists of neurons up and down, then the motivation for the claim that we should relinquish our belief in free will and revise our ethical and legal practices is unclear. This is a normative claim, and normative claims involve an assumption of agency. Appeal to neurons alone cannot support this assumption because human agents are more than clusters of neurons. This appears to be pulling a normative rabbit out of an empirical hat. There is a need to explain how to derive a normative "ought" from an empirical "is."[34] Empirical facts about the brain may explain why we have certain intuitions about cases of moral conflict. These may involve intuitive responses to questions such as whether we can harm some people in order to save others. But the judgment that a person has or lacks free will and is or is not responsible for his or her actions involves more than intuitions generated by neural processes. It requires justification based on reasons reflecting principles and rules of behavior constructed by human agents in a social setting. While information about the brain can inform moral judgments, the social construction of these principles and rules forms the basis of these judgments.

Every human agent enlists unconscious and conscious mental states when he or she interacts with the environment. These are not discrete, isolated events occurring at specific times in the brain or mind. They are part of a broader process of agency that extends over time and involves the brain, body, and external world.

---

33. "For the Law, Neuroscience Changes Nothing and Everything," 1779.
34. See Greene, "From Neural `Is' to Moral `Ought': What Are the Moral Implications of Neuroscientific Moral Psychology?" *Nature Reviews Neuroscience* 4 (2003): 847–850.

Against Libet's view, neurosurgeon and philosopher Grant Gillett asserts that "a decision is... not a circumscribed event in neuro-time that could be thought of as an output, and an intention is not a causal event preceding that output, but both are much more holistically interwoven with the lived and experienced fabric of one's life."[35] Further, "the dynamic structure of normal human action makes such a posit look mistaken, an artificial construct bolstered not only by bad philosophy but also by an experimental situation in which the actions are of a staccato and discrete kind."[36] Decisions, intentions, and actions are more than just a function of events in the brain. The interaction of the organism, or subject, with the environment influences the activity of billions of neurons and can change the morphology and function of the brain. Since the subject's actions influence brain function, this discredits the idea that particular brain states can predict or determine particular choices and actions. Organism–environment interaction undermines neurobiological determinism, which assumes that there is only one causal direction in explaining action—from the brain to action. It ignores the fact that there is a second causal direction at work—from the environment to the brain.

Some who endorse a mechanistic view of personhood employ a particular strategy to defend ontological reductionism and epiphenomenalism about the brain–mind relation. In a position similar to that of Wegner and Cashmore, Farah and theologian Nancey Murphy state that "brain processes... are not mere correlates but are the physical bases of the central aspects of our personhood. If these aspects of the person are all features of the machine, why have a ghost at all?"[37] The suggestion is that we are either machines identical to our brains or ghosts identical to mental properties that are independent of the brain. We can explain away the ghost by accepting the presumed fact that we are just machines. But from the fact that the mental aspects of personhood have physical bases in the brain, it does not follow that mental properties are nothing more than physical properties. We are neither machines nor ghosts defined essentially in terms of either physical or psychological properties. This is a mistaken picture because we are essentially constituted by the embodied brain and mind. Brain and mind are interacting components of a person. They mutually influence each other in enabling human agency. Neither the brain nor the mind can account for agency on its own.

As noted, in his earlier work replicating results from Libet's experiments, Haggard makes a faulty inference about brain processes alone causing action. In a recent article, Haggard notes that networks in the presupplementary motor cortex, anterior prefrontal cortex, and parietal cortex underlie voluntary action and responsibility. Yet Haggard suggests that mental states may causally influence the brain in saying that: "Responsibility might depend on the reason that triggered a neural process culminating in action, and on whether a final check should have stopped the action."[38] Reasons can be either external or internal to human agents. An external

---

35. "Intention, Autonomy and Brain Events," *Bioethics* 23 (2009): 330–339, at 333.
36. *Subjectivity and Being Somebody*, 115.
37. "Neuroscience and the Soul," *Science* 323 (2009): 1168.
38. "Human Volition: Towards a Neuroscience of Will," *Nature Reviews Neuroscience* 9 (2008): 934–946, at 944.

reason is associated with rules or norms recognizable by any rational person as a member of a social community. External reasons ground contractualist moral theories, where agents interacting in a social context agree on rules and principles to guide behavior. These reasons obtain independently of particular agents and provide objective grounds for the permissibility or impermissibility of any given action. An internal reason consists of a combined desire and belief of a particular agent.[39] Internal and external practical and moral reasons motivate persons to perform some actions rather than others. Haggard appears to be using 'reason' in both senses. One can plausibly assume that internal reasons are emergent mental states that are dependent on but not reducible to neural processes. Insofar as these reasons can function as a check on our action, they can influence processes at the neural level. If so, then we have at least some control of our behavior because of processes operating at the mental level.

Haggard notes that our ability to respond to external reasons for or against actions can influence processes at the neural level: "Interestingly, both decisions [to act or not to act] have a strong normative element; although a person's brain decides the actions that they carry out, culture and education teach people what are acceptable reasons for action, what are not, and when a final predictive check should recommend withholding action. Culture and education therefore represent powerful learning signals for the brain's cognitive-motor circuits."[40] He adds: "Although neuroscientific descriptions of the brain circuits that generate action and conscious awareness can contribute an evidence-based theory of responsibility, it is unclear whether they can capture all the nuances of our social and legal concepts of responsibility."[41] Given the role that Haggard attributes to external reasons and associated normative practices in actions, neuroscience cannot capture these nuances.

There are three points that are worth making in light of Haggard's claims. First, they suggest that the social environment can influence the brain and the way it mediates the mental states associated with voluntary action. Second, they suggest that mental states associated with internal reasons and one's response to external reasons can influence events in the brain. Third, the upshot of the first two points is that neural networks alone cannot satisfactorily explain human behavior. The brain does not decide what we do. Spence says that "ventral and medial brain systems seem to function `as if' biology `recognizes' valence, value, moral checks

39. The literature on reasons is large. The seminal article is B. Williams, "Internal and External Reasons," in *Moral Luck* (Cambridge: Cambridge University Press, 1981), 101–113. See also T. Scanlon, *What We Owe to Each Other* (Cambridge, MA: Harvard University Press, 1998).

40. "Human Volition," 944.

41. *Ibid.*, 944. Compare A. Damasio: "I am not reducing ethics to a simple matter of evolution, or of gene transmission or expression, or of brain structures alone. As conscious, intelligent, and creative creatures inhabiting a cultural environment, we humans have been able to shape the rules of ethics, shape their codification into law, and shape the application of the law into what we call justice." From "The Neural Basis of Social Behavior," in S. Marcus, ed. *Neuroethics: Mapping the Field* (New York: Dana Press, 2002), 18–22, at 22.

and balances. It doesn't necessarily 'do the right thing,' but it does seem to 'represent' what is right and what is wrong. It is the agent who 'chooses' what 'to do' next."[42] This is because there is an essential subjective element in human agency that cannot be explained in terms of brain function. A description of cognitive-motor circuits cannot capture the first-person experience of deliberating and choosing what to do. Spence continues: "We might conclude that no account of human action (and therefore human moral responsibility) is ever complete in the absence of a subjective report, a 'view from within,' provided by the agent... So, when we wish to apportion responsibility, we are not merely identifying an organism... we are saying something important about 'its' underlying volitional processes: the symmetry pertaining between desires and deeds, intentions and actions"[43] A satisfactory explanation of behavior must include internal and external reasons, which reflect the subjectivity of the agent and the social and cultural environment in which the agent lives and acts.

These points indicate that free will and moral responsibility are not just empirically grounded metaphysical notions involving causation, possibility, and necessity. They are also normative notions reflecting the fact that we are social beings with expectations about what we can and should do. Some philosophers argue that free will should be construed even more broadly to include a political dimension. David Schmidtz and Jason Brennan argue thus:

> Freedom of the will is not an on/off switch, something you either have or not. Instead, real-world freedom of the will is an ongoing achievement. It is achieved in degrees, and not everyone achieves it to the same degree. Moreover, our wills can be freer in some circumstances than in others. Because our culture and system of government affect people's inclinations and ability to make up their own minds, the most interesting views of the free will problem today are personal, social, and political, not metaphysical.[44]

The most defensible model of voluntary action is one that includes complementary empirical and normative dimensions reflecting causal interaction between the embodied brain and mind of a human subject acting in the world. It is worth noting that, in contrast to Wegner, Haggard does not attribute anything magical to the normative dimension of human behavior. This dimension is a real function of our activity as social beings. This makes it difficult to understand how we could retain the normative concept of responsibility without the idea that willing and acting are at least partly within our conscious control. Otherwise, it would be magical.

Nothing about the normal structure and function of the brain, or how it generates and sustains the mind, implies that we are mistaken in believing that we have the capacity to form intentions and execute them in choices and actions. Neuroscience does not show that our conscious mental states have no causal role in our behavior. Nor does it imply that an action is coerced, compelled, or constrained

---

42. *The Actor's Brain*, 306.
43. *Ibid.*, 236. See also Gillett, *Subjectivity and Being Somebody*.
44. *A Brief History of Liberty* (Malden, MA: Wiley-Blackwell, 2010), 208.

if it is causally determined by brain events. It is possible that future advances in neuroscience will call into question our conviction that we have free will and can be responsible for our behavior. If it does, then it will still be unclear how empirical findings about the brain–mind relation will influence our normative judgments about moral and legal responsibility. In particular, even with advances in brain imaging, there will always be a need for behavioral criteria in making judgments about guilt or innocence in the criminal law. This will require debate about the meaning of information about the brain, which will not be limited to neuroscientists but will include philosophers, legal theorists, social scientists, and indeed society as a whole. As matters now stand, neuroscience is not in a position to seriously challenge our belief in conscious free will.

Moral responsibility requires the capacity to control how our mental states issue in our actions. This includes the capacity to execute voluntary bodily movements. It also includes the capacity to respond to reasons when acting and to have beliefs about the probable consequences of our actions. Brain dysfunction diminishes or undermines responsibility when it diminishes or undermines the physical and mental capacities necessary for responsibility. Neuropsychiatric disorders or brain injuries resulting in paralysis, tremors, psychosis, and compulsions are some examples. But a dysfunctional brain alone does not necessarily mean that one cannot be responsible. We need to address two main questions: What are the conditions of moral responsibility? What degree of brain dysfunction and associated mental incapacity in reasoning is enough to claim that a person cannot be morally responsible for his or her actions and their consequences? After providing an account of moral responsibility, I discuss psychopathy as a test case for addressing these specific questions and the more general question of the significance of neuroscience for responsibility.

Reasons-Responsiveness and Moral Responsibility

Moral responsibility presupposes causal responsibility. One is causally responsible for an action if it is causally sensitive to one's voluntary bodily movements and the conative, cognitive, and affective states that issue in the action. The action must link up with these mental states in the appropriate causal way, such that one would not have performed the action in the absence of these states. One is morally responsible for an action when one is causally responsible for it and is capable of responding to reasons for why the action should or should not be performed. Reasons-responsiveness provides us with what philosophers John Martin Fischer and Mark Ravizza call "guidance control" of our behavior.[45] They argue that this type of control grounds moral responsibility for our behavior. Guidance control forms the core of Fischer and Ravizza's compatibilist account of moral responsibility. They distinguish it from the "regulative control" in libertarian accounts requiring forward-looking alternative possibilities external to the agent and backward-looking ultimate responsibility.

---

45. *Responsibility and Control: A Theory of Moral Responsibility* (New York: Cambridge University Press, 1998), 31, 230–236.

Fischer and Ravizza state that an agent exhibits guidance control when the agent's actions issue from his or her own reasons-responsive mechanism.[46] As they use the term, 'mechanism' does not imply anything about natural principles of explanation; it refers to a deliberative or reflective process. For the mechanism leading to action to be one's own, one must take responsibility for it.[47] One takes responsibility for the mental states issuing in action when one has the capacity to critically reflect on and evaluate them. In this way, one comes to identify them as one's own. There may be a nonreflective aspect to this process, though conscious evaluation is required. This account is similar in many respects to Frankfurt's compatibilist account of free will. Unlike Frankfurt, however, Fischer and Ravizza claim that identification is not a brief process or a "snapshot" event occurring at a particular slice of time.[48] Instead, it requires an account of the history of how an agent comes to have a particular motivational state or set of these states. Like Bratman, they argue that the mental resources necessary to make intentions and other mental states leading to action one's own cannot be understood without an account of how one develops them over time.

Some of our actions reflect dispositions to behave in a certain way in certain circumstances. As dispositions, they are acquired through a process of education, cultivation, and habituation that needs to be traced to some extent to the past. If one performs a compassionate act, then one's compassionate disposition may partly explain the act. This is not to say that a person's set of character traits determines which act the person will perform in every case. Capacity is not the same as character; one may act out of character yet have the capacity to respond to reasons against that action. The point here is that any action for which one is responsible requires some sense of the history of the mental states that issue in that action. If a driver of a motor vehicle is charged with criminal negligence for injuring a pedestrian while driving under the influence of alcohol, then the charge presupposes that the driver had the capacity to foresee the likely consequence of driving after drinking. The impaired mental and physical states at the time of the accident must be traced back to the earlier time when the agent started drinking. In both compassionate and criminally negligent acts, if the agent is capable of critically reflecting on the motivational states that issue in his or her actions, then the agent is capable of identifying with these states and taking responsibility for them. The mechanism issuing in the action is the agent's own. It is not just factors obtaining at the time when the agent performs the action that ground the attribution of responsibility, but also the process that extends back to a time before the action. Thus, responsibility is an essentially historical notion. Neither Libet's experiments nor other experiments that have replicated his results capture the historical dimension of the conscious mental states that issue in our actions.

As the second component of guidance control, Fischer and Ravizza claim that the agent must be appropriately responsive to reasons. An agent is morally responsible for an action when it issues from his or her moderately reasons-responsive

---

46. *Ibid*, 170.
47. *Ibid.*, Chapter 8.
48. *Ibid.*, Chapter 7.

mechanism. Moderate reasons-responsiveness consists of two capacities: regular receptivity, and at least weak reactivity.[49] Regular receptivity consists in the capacity to recognize moral reasons for or against certain actions. It implies a general pattern of recognizing these reasons and an understanding of how they fit together and connect with different sets of values, beliefs, and desires. Reactivity is the capacity to translate reasons into actions. An agent is strongly reasons-reactive when he or she always acts on the strongest reason for a particular action. An agent is at least weakly reasons-reactive when there is a sufficient reason to do otherwise than what the agent is inclined to do, the agent recognizes this reason, and is capable of doing otherwise for this same reason. He or she may exhibit weakness of will and act on a weaker reason for one action rather than a stronger reason for a different action. A student may act on a weaker reason to see a movie rather than a stronger reason to study for an exam. But provided that the student displays regular receptivity to reasons, he or she may display weak reactivity and be responsible for failing to study.

Moderate reasons-responsiveness is a necessary and sufficient condition of moral responsibility. Insofar as it depends on the capacity to respond to different reasons for and against different actions, not just the reasons to which one actually responds, moral responsibility is based on a capacity-theoretic model of responsiveness. Being morally responsible requires that one be morally respons*able*. Consistent with the clinical findings of Damasio and other neuroscientists, responsiveness is not just a cognitive capacity but a capacity involving interacting cognitive and affective processes.

Using reasons-responsiveness as a conceptual framework, let us now examine psychopathy to test the claims I have made about moral responsibility. Specifically, we need to consider whether or to what extent brain abnormalities in psychopathy could mitigate attributions of responsibility or provide grounds for excusing psychopaths from responsibility. The discussion of psychopathy and moral responsibility here will set the stage for the discussion of psychopathy and criminal responsibility in Chapter 3.

Psychopathy I

Psychopathy is described as a personality disorder involving impaired capacity for empathy and remorse, as well as impaired responsiveness to fear-inducing stimuli and poor behavior control.[50] The combination of these features explains the difficulty

---

49. *Ibid.*, 62–91, 230–236, 243–244. G. Watson distinguishes two aspects of moral responsibility: attributability and accountability. The first concerns the connection between the agent and his or her action. The second concerns the interaction of the agent with his or her moral community. I take attributability and accountability to be intertwined because an agent cannot be judged responsible independently of the moral community to which he or she belongs. See Watson, "Two Faces of Responsibility," in *Agency and Answerability* (New York: Oxford University Press, 2004), Chapter 9.

50. H. Cleckley, *The Mask of Sanity*, 2nd ed. (St. Louis: Mosby, 1967). Cleckley distinguishes between primary and secondary psychopaths. Primary psychopaths are often socially skilled, intelligent, even charming individuals. Despite being impulsive, they display

psychopaths have in considering the rights, interests, and needs of others, in deliberating, planning and choosing rationally, and conforming to social norms. They are deficient in both prudential and moral reasoning. However, these features do not constitute the excusing conditions typically invoked in discussions of moral responsibility. Although psychopaths may act impulsively and without empathy or remorse, they are not coerced or compelled to act by their mental states and are not ignorant of the circumstances in which they act.

Brain imaging of individuals diagnosed with psychopathy and sociopathy has revealed structural and functional abnormalities in the prefrontal cortex, anterior cingulate cortex, and amygdala. The normal integrated functions of these cortical and limbic areas of the brain mediate the cognitive and affective processing necessary for practical and moral reasoning. The correlation between the brain abnormalities and the behavior of psychopaths suggests that they lack the requisite control of their motivational states and actions to be morally responsible for them. The characteristic features of psychopathy are often associated with those of antisocial personality disorder. There is some overlap between this disorder and psychopathy, since both conditions involve a lack of regard for others and failure to abide by social rules.[51] A complicating factor is that, in many psychiatric disorders, one does not have complete control or lack control of behavior but has or lacks it to varying degrees. This raises three related questions: Do psychopaths have a sufficient degree of control of their behavior to be at least partly responsible for it? Do they lack this control and thus should be excused? Where does psychopathy lie on the spectrum of control and moral responsibility?

Studies conducted by Antonio Damasio have shown that abnormalities in the orbitofrontal cortex (OFC) correlate with impulsive and antisocial behavior.[52] Despite seeming cognitively intact, individuals with damage to this brain region are unable to conform to social norms when they act. Cognitive neuroscientist James Blair has observed similar behavioral traits in patients with structural damage to and dysfunction in the ventromedial prefrontal cortex (VMPFC).[53] This is another

---

no anxiety in their behavior. Secondary psychopaths are socially inept and withdrawn individuals with high levels of anxiety in their behavior. Both types are impulsive and impaired in the capacity for empathy. See also R. Hare, *The Hare Psychopathy Checklist*, 2nd ed. (Toronto: Multi-Health Systems, 2003); *Without Empathy: The Strange World of the Psychopaths Among Us* (New York: Pocket Books, 1993); and "Psychopaths and their Nature," in T. Millon et al., eds., *Psychopathy: Antisocial, Criminal, and Violent Behavior* (New York: Guilford Press, 1998), 188–212.

51. *Diagnostic and Statistical Manual of Mental Disorders*, fourth edition, text revision (*DSM-IV-TR*) (Washington, DC: American Psychiatric Association, 2000), 702–703.

52. "A Neural Basis for Sociopathy," *Archives of General Psychiatry* 57 (2000): 128–129.

53. R. J. R. Blair, "Neurobiological Basis of Psychopathy," *British Journal of Psychiatry* 182 (2003): 5–7; "Aggression, Psychopathy and Free Will from a Cognitive Neuroscience Perspective," *Behavioral Sciences & the Law* 25 (2007): 321–331; "The Cognitive Neuroscience of Psychopathy and Implications for Judgments of Responsibility," *Neuroethics* 1 (3) (2008): 149–157; and Blair, D. Mitchell, and K. Blair, *The Psychopath: Emotion and the Brain* (Malden, MA: Blackwell, 2005). Also, A. Damasio, "Neuroscience and Ethics: Intersections," *American Journal of Bioethics—AJOB Neuroscience* 7 (1) (2007): 3–7,

frontal brain region that mediates the cognitive and affective processing necessary for deliberation and decision making. The VMPFC was the main brain region damaged in the famous case of Phineas Gage. In 1848, Gage sustained a severe injury to this region from an explosion on a railway construction project in Vermont that sent an iron rod through his skull. He lost his capacity to restrain his impulses, reason about the future, and regulate his behavior according to social norms.[54] Gage effectively lost his capacity for moral agency. This is an example of a condition caused by brain damage that would appear to excuse one from responsibility for one's actions.

The OFC and the ventromedial and ventrolateral prefrontal cortex receive projections from and send projections to the amygdala. The OFC mediates the emotion of regret, which is critical to counterfactual reasoning in choosing between different courses of action. The amygdala mediates the capacity for normal responses to fear-inducing stimuli, and the anterior cingulate cortex mediates the capacity for empathy. This enables us to recognize that others have needs and interests and to recognize wrongful and harmful actions. A normal empathic response to others and a normal fear response to threatening situations inhibit the performance of these actions. These responses enable persons to internalize moral norms and feel guilt and remorse for what they do or fail to do. The psychopath's impaired capacity for these responses adversely affects his rational and moral capacities and increases the likelihood of overt antisocial behavior. James Blair, Derek Mitchell, and Karina Blair note that "there are strong reasons to believe that individuals with psychopathy present with orbital/ventrolateral frontal cortex dysfunction as well as amygdala dysfunction."[55] These brain abnormalities desensitize the psychopath to normal emotional responses. In the conclusion to their study of a neurocognitive model for psychopathy, Blair, Mitchell, and Blair state: "At the core of the model is the suggestion of amygdala dysfunction in individuals with the disorder. This amygdala dysfunction gives rise to impairments in aversive conditions for instrumental learning, and the processing of fearful and sad expressions. These impairments interfere with socialization such that the individual does not learn to avoid actions that cause harm to other individuals."[56]

Given the critical role of the amygdala in emotional processing and the interconnecting cortical-limbic pathways in decision making, dysfunction in these regions of psychopaths' brains suggests that they have impaired cognitive and affective control of their behavior. Although orbitofrontal and ventromedial/ventrolateral pathology may be present with or develop independently of amygdala pathology, the connections between these regions suggest that pathology and dysfunction in one or more of them can impair the capacity for practical and moral reasoning.

---

and A. Bechara and M. Vander Linden, "Decision-Making and Impulse Control after Frontal Lobe Injuries," *Current Opinion in Neurology* 18 (2005): 784–790.
54. This well-known case is discussed by A. Damasio, *Descartes' Error*, Chapter 1, and H. Damasio et al., "The Return of Phineas Gage: the Skull of a Famous Patient Yields Clues about the Brain," *Science* 264 (1994): 1102–1108.
55. *The Psychopath*, 139.
56. *Ibid.*, 139.

Evidence of this dysfunction in psychopaths seems to provide a strong reason for claiming that they cannot be responsible for their actions. But let us examine the empirical evidence more closely.

Imaging studies of dysfunctional cortical-limbic pathways in individuals displaying psychopathic behavior provide correlations between the dysfunction and the behavior. But structural or functional features of the brain alone do not determine the extent of one's cognitive and affective capacities. There is a gradual reduction in the volume of the cerebral cortex as we age. This does not always correlate with cognitive decline, or the same rate of decline, for all people. Also, some people sustain injuries to localized regions of the brain associated with reasoning and decision making. Yet only in cases where there are marked structural and functional brain abnormalities can inferences of impaired mental capacity be drawn from them. In the absence of a causal connection between a brain abnormality and psychopathic behavior, one cannot claim that the first determines the second. Even if the correlations are strong enough to suggest that brain dysfunction goes some way toward explaining psychopathic behavior, we are left with one general question: How extensive must brain dysfunction be to significantly impair or undermine the cognitive and affective processing necessary for responsibility?

Severe brain dysfunction and severe impairment in the relevant cognitive and affective capacities might be enough for excuse. If trauma or an infection damaged the anterior cingulate cortex to the point where it was rendered completely dysfunctional, then a person displaying psychopathic behavior might be excused from responsibility for it. Since this brain region mediates the capacity for empathy, the damage might undermine this capacity and thus the ability to recognize the interests, needs, and rights of others. An individual with this damage may have lost the capacity to distinguish between right and wrong and on this basis may not be responsible for his or her actions. Yet the claim that the brain abnormality caused the behavior can be upheld only when all other factors that could explain it have been eliminated. The cases where this occurs are rare. It is more likely that the brain dysfunction underlying psychopathic behavior is moderate, which might not be enough to make one incapable of internalizing moral norms. It is also unclear whether the social environment might modulate or exacerbate brain dysfunction over time and have an inhibitory or excitatory effect on the psychopath's behavior. This idea recalls Haggard's claim that culture and education can influence the brain's cognitive-motor circuit and our capacity to understand how social rules prohibit harmful behavior. How we evaluate the psychopath's behavior would also depend on whether or to what extent he could manipulate or adjust to the environment. There is little, if any, data on whether the incidence of psychopathy is higher in developed than in developing countries, which could shed light on the question of behavior control in people with this condition.

To say that one is impaired with respect to a particular capacity is not equivalent to saying that one lacks that capacity altogether. In the absence of evidence showing that the psychopath lacks the capacity to recognize and respond to reasons, and in the absence of a causal connection between cortical-amygdala dysfunction and his behavior, at most one could argue that psychopathy warrants mitigated responsibility. It does not warrant exoneration. This is not only because the empirical findings are not compelling enough to demonstrate that the psychopath completely lacks the capacity for moral reasoning. It is also because any consensus on what degree of brain dysfunction is enough for mitigation or excuse could not be reached on empirical grounds alone. It would also rely on normative considerations and reflect social factors to a considerable extent.

We are now in a position to assess the psychopath's behavior by using a reasons-responsive model. One possible explanation of his behavior is that he can *recognize* moral reasons for or against actions but lacks the capacity to *react* to these reasons. In that case, the psychopath's receptivity to reasons would be intact. The problem would be one of reactivity, of difficulty in translating reasons into actions. It might be due to some mental obstacle in the pathway between intentions and choices. Yet given that the psychopath's emotional impairment makes it difficult for him to consider the interests and needs of others and to conform to social rules, the problem might have less to do with impaired reactivity and more to do with impaired receptivity. Difficulty with receptivity to reasons would entail difficulty with reactivity to reasons.

The psychopath's capacity to recognize or be receptive to moral reasons for or against certain actions may be too weak to have much motivational force and issue in morally appropriate behavior. What may weaken receptivity further is that the psychopath's impaired capacity for empathy and remorse appears to make him incapable of critically reflecting on his motivational states and taking responsibility for them. This same emotional impairment may make it difficult for the psychopath to engage in counterfactual reasoning and choose between different courses of action. He may be incapable of considering reasons to do otherwise and of refraining from acting, or incapable of acting differently than he does. If so, then he would fail the test for both receptivity and reactivity. Assuming that he fails this test, one could argue that the psychopath lacks the requisite guidance control of his motivational states and actions and therefore cannot be responsible for them to any degree. But this is too quick.

Citing earlier work by social psychologist Leonard Berkowitz, Blair, Mitchell, and Blair. distinguish *reactive* from *instrumental* aggression:

> In reactive aggression (also referred to as affective or impulsive aggression), a frustrating or threatening event triggers the aggressive act and frequently also induces anger. Importantly, the aggression is initiated without regard for any potential goal (for example, gaining the victim's possessions or increasing status within the hierarchy). In contrast, instrumental aggression (also referred to as proactive aggression) is purposeful and goal-directed. The aggression is used instrumentally to a specific desired goal.[57]

---

57. *The Psychopath*, 12; L. Berkowitz, *Aggression: Its Causes, Consequences, and Control* (Philadelphia: Temple University Press, 1993).

They note that psychopaths present with highly elevated levels of both instrumental and reactive aggression.[58] Their discussion of goals suggests a key role for intentions in instrumental aggression. If psychopaths are capable of goal-directed and purposeful behavior in this type of aggression, then they are capable of forming and executing intentions in actions. Psychopaths are capable of recognizing and reacting to instrumental reasons in using others as means for their own ends. Although they can be impulsive, their ability to act on instrumental reasons gives them some control of their behavior. Failure to control one's impulses does not imply an inability to control them. In addition, although psychopaths are impaired in the capacity for empathy, they can fake emotions in order to appear charming and persuasive to others. This is not the mark of an inability to control one's behavior. These considerations suggest that psychopaths may have enough cognitive control of their behavior to be responsible for it to some degree.

Damasio's studies have indicated a strong connection between cognition and emotion in practical and moral reasoning. An emotional deficiency, such as lack of empathy, remorse, or regret, can impair both types of reasoning. This is the negative aspect of the cognitive–affective connection in psychopathy. There may also be a positive aspect to this connection. The fact that the psychopath is capable of recognizing and reacting to instrumental reasons indicates that he is capable of at least one form of practical reasoning. If practical and moral reasoning are interconnected, and if the psychopath is capable of practical reasoning, then one can ask whether he is capable of some degree of moral reasoning. One can ask whether the psychopath has some capacity to recognize and react to reasons for refraining from performing actions that harm others. This would include some capacity to critically reflect on and take responsibility for at least some of his mental states issuing in his actions. The fact that the psychopath performs harmful acts is not by itself sufficient to show that he lacks this capacity; he may have but fail to exercise it. To reject this possibility, one would have to show that practical and moral reasoning are interconnected when they are both impaired but may be disconnected when some type of practical reasoning is intact. It is not obvious that we can separate practical and moral reasoning in some types of decision making and not others.

One can plausibly argue that the rational agency the psychopath displays (albeit imperfectly) in his instrumental aggression involves some degree of moral agency. We need to distinguish moral from conventional transgressions. In the first type of transgression, the transgressor identifies the person he harms as a victim and knows that the victim suffers from the action. In the second type of transgression, there is no identifiable victim who suffers from the action. When he engages in instrumental aggression, the psychopath clearly identifies the individual to whom the aggression is directed as a victim. Insofar as instrumental aggression is deliberate and the psychopath knows that an individual will be victimized and harmed by his actions, he is capable of knowing to some degree that this is a moral transgression. He is capable of responding at least weakly to a moral reason against the aggression.

---

58. *The Psychopath*, 13.

The psychopath is impaired in his reasoning, but not so impaired that he cannot plan to direct his aggression to particular individuals and know that this is wrong.

This argument rejects the claim that the psychopath and his actions do not merit the degree of wrongfulness and blame that attaches to moral transgressions.[59] The psychopath's capacity to recognize and react to moral reasons may very well be too weak to always translate into morally appropriate behavior; but it may not be so weak that it has no moral motivational force at all. He may have enough capacity to respond to reasons recommending that he refrain from acting. If so, then the psychopath may be morally responsible to some degree for his behavior because he has some degree of control of it. Results of one study indicate that psychopaths have normal understanding of right and wrong but diminished regulation of morally appropriate behavior. In exploiting others and disregarding their rights and interests, psychopaths know that their actions are wrong; but they do not care.[60] If psychopaths have normal moral understanding, then their diminished regulation of morally appropriate behavior may be due to a failure rather than an inability to regulate it. They may have enough of this understanding to refrain from performing morally wrong actions and be responsible for performing them.

The plausibility of the argument that psychopaths have some degree of moral understanding hinges on the question of the interaction between practical and moral reasoning. If they are separable forms of reasoning mediated by separable regions and functions in the brain, then the case for claiming that the psychopath is capable of responding to moral reasons is weak. But if practical and moral reasoning and the brain regions mediating them are not separable, then the case for claiming that the psychopath is capable of responding to moral reasons to some degree may not be so weak after all. In that case, the problem would not be one of lacking but of failing to exercise the relevant capacity.

Some have reframed the diagnosis of psychopathy as resting on the distinction between legal and moral recognition of wrongdoing. Psychologist Cordelia Fine and philosopher Jeanette Kennett propose that although psychopaths may know that their transgressions are *legally* wrong, they do not know that they are *morally* wrong.[61] They draw this distinction on the basis of research on moral development, which points to "the importance of affect in early moral cognition and in the development of moral concepts."[62] Presumably, this epistemic asymmetry is due to the psychopath's inability to distinguish between moral and conventional transgressions, with legal transgressions being a type of conventional transgression. Fine and

---

59. N. Levy, "The Responsibility of the Psychopath Revisited," *Philosophy, Psychiatry & Psychology* 14 (2007): 129–138.

60. M. Cima, F. Tonnaer, and M. Hauser, "Psychopaths Know Right from Wrong but Don't Care," *Social Cognitive and Affective Neuroscience* 5 (2010): 59-67. Also, I. Haji, "Psychopathy, Ethical Perception, and Moral Culpability," *Neuroethics* 3(2) (2010): 135–150.

61. "Mental Impairment, Moral Understanding, and Criminal Responsibility: Psychopathy and the Purposes of Punishment," *International Journal of Law and Psychiatry* 27 (2004): 425–443. The authors argue that psychopathy should be an exculpating rather than aggravating condition.

62. *Ibid.*, 428.

Kennett claim that without the capacity to recognize morally wrong actions, psychopaths "lack the essential prerequisites of moral life."[63] Yet they do not offer a persuasive argument for the claim that psychopaths completely lack the relevant moral capacity and thus cannot be described as moral agents. Insofar as psychopaths' instrumental aggression involves the capacity to know that this is a moral transgression, they are capable of responding to moral reasons to some degree and are at least minimal moral agents.

Contrary to my claim at the beginning of this section, philosopher Lennart Nordenfelt argues that psychopaths act compulsively and cannot be morally responsible for this reason. Nordenfelt defines compulsion as the inability to consider alternative actions from those one performs. He claims that "the psychopath is unable to weigh alternative actions and consider which among the alternatives is the most appropriate to perform."[64] Further, he claims that "given the psychopath's desires, there is, in a particular situation, only one course of action—namely, the most desire-fulfilling one—available to him or her. Thus the actions of the psychopath fulfill my criteria for compulsion."[65]

This does not show that the psychopath acts compulsively. The fact that the psychopath is impaired and has difficulty in considering alternative courses of action does not mean that he lacks the capacity to consider them at all. Nordenfelt fails to distinguish impairment from incapacity. While the psychopath's instrumental reasoning may be strongly linked to a particular desire to harm another, it does not mean that it is the *only* desire on which he can act. The very idea of instrumental reasoning suggests at least some competing desires for alternative actions. Alternative desires may not be the most salient of his motivational states, but they may have some influence on his instrumental reasoning in attaining his short-term goals. The desire not to be caught for wrongdoing may be enough for him to at least briefly reconsider his intended action and provide him with a reason not to act. If the desire not to be caught is a contrary desire that can influence his instrumental reasoning, then it suggests that he can recognize an alternative reason not to act and refrain from acting. Although it may be a weaker desire and reason than the desire and reason to perform a harmful act of instrumental aggression, it is enough to show that there is more than one desire among the psychopath's motivational states. Just because the reason to refrain from performing a harmful action is not the most salient of his mental states does not mean that it is beyond his cognitive awareness. Because of his tendency to act impulsively, he does not give sufficient prudential or moral weight to the alternative desire and reason. But impulsivity is not equivalent to compulsion: unlike compulsion, impulsive action is not necessarily involuntary. A compulsion is an irresistible urge to a form of behavior against one's wishes, an urge that cannot be checked or overridden by reason. An impulse is a sudden tendency to act without reflection. Not all impulses are irresistible. Some can be resisted with mental effort in making oneself aware of them and recognizing a

---

63. *Ibid.*, 427.
64. *Rationality and Compulsion: Applying Action Theory to Psychiatry* (Oxford: Oxford University Press, 2007), 182.
65. *Ibid.*, 183.

reason for not acting on them. The availability of an alternative desire and reason is sufficient to show that the psychopath is not compelled to act. This gives him enough cognitive control of his actions to be partly responsible for them.

I have noted that a defining feature of psychopathy is impaired prudential reasoning. At first blush this may seem inconsistent with the research indicating that the psychopath is able to engage in reasoning to carry out his instrumental aggression. But in fact these two points are consistent. While the psychopath is capable of effective instrumental reasoning in attaining short-term goals, he is not very capable of effective rational planning for long-term goals. Although impulsivity is not equivalent to compulsion, it can limit the range of one's instrumental reasoning. Consider the following confession from the American psychopathic killer Gary Mark Gilmore:

> I ain't a great thief. I'm impulsive. Don't plan, don't think. You don't
> have to be super intelligent to get away with that…You just have to think.
> But I don't. I'm impatient. Not greedy enough. I could have gotten away with
> lots of things that I got caught for.[66]

This raises the issue of the relation between actions and consequences. One is responsible for a consequence of an action when (1) one is responsible for the action, (2) the consequence would not have occurred but for the action, and (3) one has the capacity to foresee the consequence as a probable outcome of the action. The consequence need only be foreseeable, not foreseen, for one to be responsible for it. This occurs in cases of criminal negligence. Foreseeability gives one the requisite cognitive control of the sequence of events leading to the consequence. One can exercise this control by deciding not to act and thereby prevent the consequence from obtaining. The psychopath's cognitive impairment makes it difficult for him to foresee the consequences of his actions.[67] Recent research shows that psychopaths have a hyperactive reward circuit in the mesolimbic dopamine system of the brain.[68] Like those with addictions, this could impair prefrontal inhibitory mechanisms and cause psychopaths to strongly discount the long-term effects of their actions. They appear to lack the cognitive control to duly consider the outcomes of their behavior. As with addictions, there are questions about the degree to which brain dysfunction influences temporal discounting and impairs the capacity to consider the consequences of one's choices. If an individual's practical reasoning about long-term goals or outcomes is limited, then the individual may lack the necessary degree of foresight to be responsible for the consequences of his actions. Recall the earlier point that a dysfunctional OFC can impair the capacity for regret and with it the capacity for counterfactual reasoning about possible courses of action. This dysfunction could significantly impair one's capacity to foresee and be responsible for the consequences of one's behavior.

---

66. Cited in Hare, *Without Empathy*, 88.
67. A. Bechara et al., "Insensitivity to Future Consequences Following Damage to Human Prefrontal Cortex," *Cognition* 50 (1994): 7–15.
68. J. Buckholtz et al., "Mesolimbic Dopamine Reward System Hypersensitivity in Individuals with Psychopathic Traits," *Nature Neuroscience* 13 (2010): 419–421.

We must not confuse difficulty in long-term planning with an inability to plan. Psychologist J. P. Newman notes that "whereas most people automatically anticipate the consequences of their actions... psychopaths may only be aware of such factors with effort"[69] As Blair, Mitchell, and Blair point out, Newman is *not* claiming that individuals with psychopathy are incapable of regulating this and other aspects of their behavior, only that it requires more effort for them to do so.[70] Again, we need to distinguish having a capacity from exercising it. It is not obvious that the psychopath is so impaired in considering the consequences of his actions that he should be excused from responsibility for all of them. He may be responsible for the consequences of his actions that fall within the limited temporal scope of his instrumental reasoning. But the impairment may excuse him from responsibility for consequences occurring at later times. In addition to a dysfunctional OFC, a dysfunctional ventromedial prefrontal cortex can make it difficult for the psychopath to represent outcomes of actions in his reasoning. This may support the claim of excuse from responsibility for long-term consequences of his actions. In addition, although the psychopath may have enough cognitive and affective capacity to foresee that his actions can harm others, he may not be able to foresee the magnitude of this harm.

How one responds to the question of moral responsibility in psychopathy depends to a great extent on whether one adopts positive or negative criteria of responsibility. It depends on whether one insists on demonstrating that individuals have the relevant cognitive and affective capacities, or whether one takes the default position of assuming that one has these capacities and acts responsibly barring evidence of coercion, compulsion, constraint, or ignorance of the circumstances of action.[71] I take the negative default position and assume that people can be at least partly responsible for their actions unless they lack the necessary mental capacities altogether. If psychopaths can be excused from responsibility, then there must be decisive evidence that they lack these capacities. Empirical studies have not provided this evidence. Therefore, psychopaths cannot be excused from responsibility. For those who defend the positive view and claim that the psychopath does not meet the criteria of responsibility, the onus is on them to demonstrate that the cognitive and affective impairment of the psychopath is of such a degree that it completely undermines his capacity to respond to moral reasons. By my lights, this has not been demonstrated. There may be cases where brain dysfunction in psychopathy is severe enough to undermine the cognitive and affective capacities necessary for moral responsibility. But these cases are likely the exception rather than the rule.

Moral responsibility requires control of the mental states that issue in actions. This control is not an all-or-nothing mental capacity but can come in degrees.

---

69. "Psychopathic Behavior: An Information Processing Perspective," in D. Cooks, A. Forth, and R. Hare, eds., *Psychopathy: Theory, Research, and Implications for Society* (Dordrecht: Kluwer, 1998), 81–104, at 84.

70. *The Psychopath*, 68.

71. This position is traceable to Aristotle, *Nicomachean Ethics*, J. Barnes, trans. and ed. (Princeton: Princeton University Press, 1984), Book III, Chapter V.

So, moral responsibility can be a matter of degree. There is a spectrum of control based on a spectrum of mental capacities. Given that most psychopaths have both impaired and intact capacities, it is not clear where each lies on the spectrum. It seems plausible to say that among psychopaths there are varying degrees of cognitive and affective impairment. It also seems plausible to say that not all psychopaths lack these capacities altogether and that at least some fall on the part of the control spectrum where attributions of moral responsibility are justified.

It is possible that more refined brain imaging, genetic analysis, and behavioral assessment will show that psychopaths lack the capacity to recognize and react to moral reasons. Still, judgments about responsibility will reflect not only empirical data but also professional and public consensus about the normative significance of this data. Currently, the empirical research shows only that psychopaths are impaired in certain moral capacities. It does not tell us that this impairment means that they are incapable of responding to moral reasons. Given what we now know from neuroscience, genetics, and behavioral criteria, the evidence of neurobiological and mental dysfunction in psychopaths is not compelling enough for excuse. Psychopathy may involve enough cognitive and affective impairment to rule out full responsibility, but not partial responsibility.

Conclusion

Neuroscience does not threaten free will because it does not show that we are not the originators of our actions and that our conscious mental states play no causal role in these actions. While neuroscience has elucidated many aspects of the brain–mind relation, it is mistaken to infer that just because a conscious desire, belief, or intention has a physical cause in the brain, these and other mental states do not causally influence our actions. Causation is not equivalent to coercion, compulsion, or constraint and as such does not imply that we have no conscious control of what we do or fail to do. The argument that free will is an illusion is not persuasive because it rests on a misconception about the relation between the brain and the mind. Nothing about normal brain function implies that we cannot act freely and responsibly. We are not victims of neural circumstances. I considered whether any abnormalities in brain regions mediating cognitive and affective capacities can justify mitigation or excuse in judgments of moral responsibility. I used psychopathy as a test case for this question and argued that, despite some brain abnormalities, psychopaths have enough mental capacity to be at least partly responsible for their actions.

The real threat to free will is from brain dysfunction that impairs the capacity for self-control. Examples include seizure disorders, loss of motor control in advanced Parkinson's and Huntington's disease, and extensive damage to the prefrontal cortex making one unable to control violent urges. It also includes the psychosis in schizophrenia that makes one unable to accurately perceive or engage with the world, the anhedonia and avolition in schizophrenia and major depression making it difficult to motivate oneself to act, and the overwhelming desires and beliefs in obsessive-compulsive disorder. These conditions undermine free will when they undermine a person's physical and mental ability to voluntarily perform certain actions and refrain from performing others.[72] Some would include addictions in this group, though there is disagreement about whether they should be included. There is no empirical data decisively showing that a hyperactive reward system in the brain completely disables inhibitory mechanisms in the prefrontal cortex and the ability to make voluntary choices at least some of the time. Some people temporarily abstain from taking addictive drugs or permanently stop taking them. Addiction as such does not necessarily compromise free will.

Brain dysfunction does not always undermine self-control. How much freedom of will one retains depends on the extent to which the dysfunction impairs one's physical and mental capacities. People with brain injuries and neuropsychiatric disorders may retain some degree of free will in initiating and completing actions. The post-injury life of the Russian soldier Zazetsky is one instance of this. Obsessive-compulsive disorder involves pathological desires and beliefs. Yet most people with this disorder retain the cognitive capacity to be aware of their condition and seek and consent to treatment for it. They retain some control of their behavior and in this respect retain some degree of free will. Therapies such as CBT can restore a greater degree of behavior control in moderate forms of this and other neuropsychiatric disorders. Pharmacological and neurosurgical interventions can have this effect in more severe forms. Antipsychotic medications for schizophrenia and deep-brain stimulation for Parkinson's and treatment–resistant depression and obsessive-compulsive disorder are some examples.

In some psychiatric disorders, it may not be clear whether the symptoms associated with brain dysfunction undermine free will. In depression, anhedonia and avolition may prevent one from committing suicide by preventing the capacity to form an intention to kill oneself. A reduction in these symptoms may release internal mental constraints and enable suicidal ideation, a plan to kill oneself, and the execution of that plan in suicide. Despite the persistence of some depressive symptoms, the decision may be rational and thus free if the person has enough cognitive and affective capacity to reflect on the reasons for and against suicide. Alternatively, the intended action may be strongly driven by a disordered affective state that undermines the capacity to reason and would compel one to take one's life. In that case, one would not be acting freely, and there would be justification for third-party intervention to prevent suicide. A large number of suicides are the result of an impulsive or sudden decision with only a brief period of reflection beforehand. They may be associated with symptoms of chronic or acute depression. Suicide in these instances may appear to be driven by something other than the person's responsiveness to reasons for doing it. Still, the suddenness of the decision by itself does not imply that it is due to dysregulated neural circuits that put the person's thought and behavior

---

72. Years ago, I taught Spanish at Smith College. A student in one of my courses uncharacteristically began missing classes. After two weeks, she appeared in my office and said that she had a history of major depression, experienced a relapse, and was committed to the psychiatric ward of the local hospital. She said that her depression prevented her from getting out of bed for several days and felt that she did not have any free will. Significantly, she did not mention causal determinism or mechanism but that something that had gone awry in her brain was the cause of her loss of free will.

beyond his or her control. Giving little thought to an action does not necessarily mean that it is not performed freely. These considerations suggest that suicide in a depressed person is an expression of a will that may or may not be free. They suggest that there can be gray area in this and other psychiatric disorders where the question of whether one has or lacks free will does not have a definitive answer.

Some individuals with neurological and psychiatric disorders may use their own psychological techniques to maintain control of their behaviour and exercise free will. With the onset of an aura, some individuals with epilepsy may avoid seizures by focusing their attention in listening intently to music or to other people's conversations. Zeman points out that, "while specific experiences sometimes engender seizures, attacks can also be resisted by an act of will."[73] As I pointed out in Chapter 1, habit-reversal training may enable some people with Tourette syndrome to anticipate and suppress seemingly uncontrollable motor and vocal tics. These are mental acts that are preceded by the event or process of trying to perform them, which has a phenomenological aspect that cannot be captured by appeal to brain processes alone. Although their effects may be limited, by these acts of will some people can expand the space of agency beyond what neurobiology has given them.

Brain abnormalities may interfere with the mental capacities necessary for one to be responsible for one's behavior. In some of these cases, this interference may be severe enough to rule out responsibility. In most cases, people have sufficient control of their behavior to be at least partly responsible for it. Depending on the extent of brain dysfunction and how it affects the relevant capacities, persons may exercise them to varying degrees along a spectrum of control. Brain imaging may help to identify persons with diminished control. But it cannot determine how much or how little control one has, or how much is necessary and sufficient for responsibility. Imaging can only approximate an answer to these questions and only as a supplement to behavioral criteria. The discussion of psychopathy shows that there are cases of brain dysfunction where one's capacity for free and responsible agency may be impaired but not undermined.

---

73. *Consciousness: A User's Guide* (New Haven: Yale University Press, 2004), 121.

3

What Neuroscience Can (and Cannot) Tell Us about Criminal Responsibility

Criminal responsibility presupposes the capacity to respond to reasons against actions that make one liable to punishment.[1] It is in virtue of this rational capacity that we can control which actions we perform. Until recently, whether or to what extent one had this capacity was inferred entirely from one's behavior. The neurobiological basis of our actions remained elusive, making it difficult to draw valid inferences from brain to mind to action. The increasing use of structural and especially functional neuroimaging in the criminal law has revealed an association between some types of criminal behavior and dysfunction in brain regions mediating practical and moral reasoning and decision making. By showing correlations between brain dysfunction and impaired cognitive and affective processing, neuroimaging might support claims of mitigation or excuse from criminal responsibility for certain actions.

There are, however, limitations in what neuroimaging can tell us about brain function and its relation to mental states and behavior. Because of these limitations, the interpretation of brain images and their legal significance are fraught with uncertainty. What further contributes to this uncertainty is that empirical data from brain scans are assessed against a background of normative considerations regarding how persons are expected to control their behavior. There is disagreement about the extent to which persons have and exercise this control.

---

1. H. L. A. Hart defines this capacity as "the ability to understand what conduct legal rules or morality require, to deliberate and reach decisions concerning those requirements, and to conform to decisions when made." *Punishment and Responsibility* (Oxford: Clarendon Press, 1968), 227.

In this chapter, I present ten cases to frame and discuss the general question of how neuroscience, in the form of neuroimaging, can inform evaluations of people's actions in the criminal law. The first two cases address the question of criminal intent. In the first case, imaging is used to argue for exoneration from the charge of sexual assault, while in the second case it is used to argue for a lighter sentence for a person convicted of first-degree murder. The next four cases involve the issue of whether underactive cortical and overactive limbic regions make one incapable of controlling impulses. If these brain features impair or undermine this control, then they could constitute a mitigating or excusing condition for the actions that result from them. The seventh, eighth, and ninth cases raise the question of whether dysfunction in the brain regions mediating the capacity for empathy and emotional responses to other people demonstrates that those with psychopathic and similar traits are not responsible for their behavior. Continuing the discussion from Chapter 2, I also consider whether abnormal cortical-limbic pathways in the psychopath's brain make him unable to control his aggressive impulses. The tenth case considers whether appeals to neuroimaging can elucidate the role of memory in behavior and resolve questions about criminal negligence. Discussion of these actual and hypothetical cases will support the view that neuroscience can inform but not determine judgments of criminal responsibility. Even when scans show significant dysfunction in regions of the brain associated with reasoning and decision making, they at most will supplement and not supplant behavioral evidence in legal judgments of responsibility, mitigation, and excuse.

Criminal Intent

For one to be criminally responsible for sexual assault or first-degree murder, one must have formed and executed an intention to perform the criminal act. The act must be causally related to a particular state of mind.[2] In legal parlance, the *actus reus* ("bad act") must be appropriately linked to the *mens rea* ("guilty mind"). The *mens rea* condition has subjective and objective tests. According to the subjective test, criminal responsibility for killing or otherwise harming a person requires that the accused intended to perform the harmful action and that the intention issued in that action. According to the objective test, although the accused lacked the intention to perform a particular harmful action, *mens rea* may be imputed to him or her on the basis of the state of mind a reasonable person would have had in the same circumstances. The objective test is pertinent to cases of criminal negligence.

In a 2007 case in the United States, defendant Peter Braunstein was charged with kidnapping, sexual abuse, burglary, robbery, and arson for a series of actions committed on Halloween in 2005. A Positron emission tomography (PET) scan of the defendant's brain was introduced by the defense in an attempt to show that he

---

2. M. Moore offers the most comprehensive account of the role of causation in judgments of criminal responsibility in *Causation and Responsibility* (New York: Oxford University Press, 2009).

was unable to plan the sexual assault of a former co-worker.[3] The defendant's not-guilty plea was not based on the insanity defense. He did not claim that he was suffering from a mental disorder making him unable to reason and appreciate the wrongfulness of his conduct. Instead, the not-guilty plea was based on the claim that a brain abnormality made him incapable of forming an intention or plan to commit the crime.[4] He lacked the necessary *mens rea* to be criminally responsible and liable for it. The PET scan was introduced as evidence that the defendant had dysfunctional frontal lobes, the executive part of the brain regulating personality, planning, decision making, and moral judgment. A psychiatrist testifying for the defense stated: "If I saw this scan without knowing anything else… I would say this person has changes in personality, will have difficulty planning, making executive judgments, and thinking ahead." Under cross-examination, the psychiatrist responded affirmatively to the question: "Was the defendant completely unable to plan?"[5]

Presumably, the PET scan explained the change in the psychiatrist's assessment from the weaker claim that the defendant had "difficulty planning" to the stronger claim that he was "completely unable to plan." But this ignores the many limitations of functional neuroimaging that I spelled out in the Introduction and Chapters 1 and 2. There are additional problems with using brain scans to argue that one lacked a criminal state of mind at the time of action. Data linking underactive or overactive brain regions to impaired cognition are based on correlations between aggregate data and outcome measures. This can obscure differences between individuals in the level of activity in their brains associated with cognitive and affective functions. The claim that levels of brain activation can tell us that an individual had or lacked the relevant neural and mental capacities is problematic as well. Activation is measured by subtracting resting levels from levels when the brain is performing a specific task. As psychiatrist Paul Appelbaum points out in his analysis of the Braunstein case: "When a bright patch of color fails to appear in a brain region of interest, the finding does not signify that the region was inactive, only that it was not

3. A. Hartocollis, "Attack not Disputed at Trial, Just Intent of the Attacker," *New York Times*, May 23, 2007. http://www.nytimes.com/2007/05/23/nyregion/23fake.html
4. P. S. Appelbaum, "Through a Glass Darkly: Functional Neuroimaging Evidence Enters the Courtroom," *Psychiatric Services* 60 (2009): 21–23, and "Insanity, Guilty Minds, and Psychiatric Testimony," *Psychiatric Services* 57 (2006): 1370–1372. See also E. C. Aharoni et al., "Can Neurological Evidence Help Courts Assess Criminal Responsibility? Lessons from Law and Neuroscience," *Annals of the New York Academy of Sciences* 1124 (2008): 145–160, N. Eastman and C. Campbell, "Neuroscience and Legal Determination of Criminal Responsibility," *Nature Reviews Neuroscience* 7 (2006): 311–318, and B. Garland and P. Glimcher, "Cognitive Neuroscience and the Law," *Current Opinion in Neurobiology* 16 (2006): 130–134. For discussion of the role of intention in law, see R. A. Duff, *Intention, Agency, and Criminal Liability: Philosophy of Action and the Criminal Law* (Oxford: Blackwell, 1990).
5. Hartocollis, "In Support of Sex Attacker's Insanity Plea, A Look at his Brain," *New York Times*, May 11, 2007. http://www.nytimes.com/2007/05/11/nyregion/11fake.html Contrary to the headline of this article, neither the defendant nor his defense attorney invoked a plea of insanity. Appelbaum points this out in "Through a Glass Darkly," citing the two comments by the psychiatrist testifying for the defense.

significantly more active in response to the stimulus than in its absence. In theory, a person who is more efficient than the average subject at performing a particular task may show results that falsely suggest a failure to activate the relevant regions... dramatic contrasts on a scan can reflect relatively minor differences in actual levels of brain activity."[6]

Brain abnormalities detected by functional brain imaging do not always imply significant impairment in rational or moral thought. Whether one is capable of such thought also needs to be assessed on the basis of one's behavior. Except perhaps in cases of severe brain dysfunction, PET or fMRI scans of the frontal lobes alone cannot determine whether an individual lacked the capacity to plan a crime, had less than full capacity to plan it and difficulty forming and executing his intention, or had full capacity to plan it and executed his intention straightaway. A variant of this distinction may be more pertinent to the issue of impulse control, and I will return to it in the next section. In the present case, neither the stronger claim that the defendant lacked the capacity to plan the assault nor the weaker claim that he had difficulty planning it withstands scrutiny. The elaborate scheme he devised to assault the victim, which consisted in not one but a series of actions, and the duration of the assault, clearly showed that he had full capacity to plan and execute his criminal behavior. The defendant dressed as a firefighter and set off a smoke bomb in the lobby of his victim's apartment building. To gain access to her apartment, Braunstein knocked on her door and claimed that he had come to inspect the smoke damage. After she let him into her apartment, he used chloroform to render her unconscious and then committed the sexual assault over a period of 13 hours. His behavior demonstrated that any brain abnormality displayed on the PET scan did not interfere with his cognitive capacity to plan and act. It played no role in his behavior and thus provided no grounds for reversing the charge and conviction that his criminal course of action was intentional. This case illustrates that "without knowing anything else," faulty inferences can be drawn from brain scans to explanations of actions.

In most cases, the claim that one was unable to plan a criminal act that one performed is not defensible. It would have to be consistent with a pattern of behavior symptomatic of an inability to plan or difficulty planning. One would have difficulty performing many cognitive tasks in everyday life. Holding a job and managing one's finances would be a challenge. The defense claimed that Braunstein was a paranoid schizophrenic and had recently walked away from a successful career in journalism. Abandoning his journalistic career may have been an irrational decision, but it is not necessarily a symptom of paranoid schizophrenia or a general inability to plan. Just because a decision is irrational does not mean that it was caused by a dysfunctional brain and that the individual making the decision had no control of the motivational states that led to it. It is possible that dysfunction in the frontal-parietal network could cause an acute episode of psychosis, in which case one would not know what one was doing and would not have cognitive control of one's actions. This might constitute an excusing condition from responsibility for sexual assault. But this type of dysfunction and behavior is not consistent with the behavior of the

---

6. "Through a Glass Darkly," 22.

defendant in committing the assault. Given the elaborate nature of the interconnected set of his actions, any claim that his behavior was caused by acute psychosis would be implausible. Braunstein's behavior undermined the defense attorney's claim that his actions were performed in a "vague, improvisational haze," and that he did not know "what he was going to do from one moment to the next."[7]

It is surprising that Braunstein's attorney did not argue explicitly for the insanity defense. The characterization of his actions conceivably could meet the cognitive criterion of the defense according to the M'Naghten Rules and the Model Penal Code.[8] "Vague, improvisational haze" suggests that Braunstein had a defect of reason preventing him from appreciating the wrongfulness of his actions. This could rule out criminal intent. Nevertheless, the defendant's behavior indicated that he had no difficulty planning the crime. His actions leading up to and including the assault were evidence of the fact that considerable planning went into it. The PET scan introduced to support the defense's claim that Braunstein was unable to form an intention to commit the crime was refuted by his behavior, and the assault charge and conviction were upheld. The testifying psychiatrist's initial weaker claim that the PET scan indicated difficulty planning was not sustainable in court either. Braunstein was sentenced to 18 years to life for his crime. Even if the scan displayed frontal lobe dysfunction correlating with cognitive impairment involving difficulty in planning, this by itself would not be evidence that Braunstein lacked criminal intent. One may have difficulty planning and performing a criminal act and still perform it. What matters for criminal responsibility is that one executed the relevant intention, regardless of whether one did it with ease or difficulty.

Imaging was used in the Braunstein case to argue for an excuse from the charge of sexual assault. In a 2000 Florida case, imaging was used to argue that brain dysfunction was a mitigating factor that should influence the sentencing of a person convicted of first-degree murder. At a sentencing hearing, a psychologist presented functional brain images suggesting that the defendant, Eddie Lee Sexton, had a diminished level of self-control due to dysfunction in his prefrontal cortex.[9] This evidence was introduced to support the defendant's claim that he was suffering from extreme mental disturbance when he committed the crime. Sexton and the defense claimed that this disturbance prevented him from forming and executing an intention to kill his victim. They argued that this should be a mitigating factor against the

---

7. Cited by Hartocollis in her two 2007 *New York Times* articles.
8. M'Naghten's Case, 8 Eng. Rep. 718, 722 (1843), cited in the Report of the Committee on Mentally Abnormal Offenders (London: Her Majesty's Stationery Office, 1975), 217, and the Model Penal Code, Official Draft and Commentaries (Philadelphia: American Law Institute, 1985), 4.01. The not guilty by reason of insanity defense consists of cognitive and control criteria. The first criterion says that a person is not guilty of a criminal act if he or she suffered from a mental disorder causing him or her to lack substantial capacity to appreciate the wrongfulness of that conduct. The second says that a person is not guilty if he or she was unable to control his or her conduct so that it conformed to the requirements of the law. One can question the separation of these criteria, since any sense of behavior control presupposes a cognitive component.
9. *Sexton v. State.* 775 So. 2d. 923 (Fla. 2000).

death sentence. Yet the trial court imposed the death penalty on the grounds that aggravating factors outweighed any evidence of diminished self-control. The defendant's behavior displayed a carefully planned course of action in which he manipulated his mentally disabled son to kill his son-in-law, who knew of Sexton's involvement in another homicide. The behavioral evidence that the crime was "cold, calculating, and premeditated" discredited the neuroscientific evidence suggesting diminished responsibility. The Florida Supreme Court upheld the death sentence, noting that "nothing in the expert testimony presented [including the brain scans] suggests that Sexton was incapable of planning [the] murder and manipulating his children to assist with the murder."[10] Imaging indicating brain dysfunction might be used to support the claim that an individual lacked the capacity to intend to kill. This might change a conviction from first-degree murder to second-degree murder or manslaughter. But behavioral evidence manifesting one's ability or inability to respond to reasons for or against certain actions would be needed to confirm the neuroscientific findings.

Violent Impulses

Suppose that a couple is having an argument. One partner criticizes and blames the other for everything that has gone wrong in their disintegrating relationship. The one who is blamed becomes violently angry and strangles and kills the other. Charged with second-degree murder, the defense for the accused claims that his action was an instance of a general inability to control violent impulses. He undergoes PET and fMRI scans showing abnormally high activity in the amygdala, which regulates emotions such as fear and anger. The imaging also shows abnormally low activity in the prefrontal cortex, which regulates the inhibition of impulses. The particular findings are consistent with general findings from studies conducted by a number of neuroscientists. They have shown that many impulsive murderers have reduced activity in the prefrontal cortex and increased activity in the amygdala.[11] Since normal activity in these brain regions is necessary to control impulses, the images in this hypothetical case might suggest that the accused had significantly impaired impulse control. This might be a mitigating, if not an excusing, condition that could absolve him from responsibility for killing his partner.

Some would argue that impulse control is one area where neuroimaging could be helpful in evaluating criminal behavior. But the limitations of imaging are most obvious on this issue. Brain scans may establish correlations between brain abnormalities and criminal behavior. Yet because correlation is not causation, generally one cannot claim that a neurobiological abnormality caused a criminal act. In some cases, the correlation between a brain abnormality and criminal behavior may be strong enough to establish a causal connection between them and excuse a person from responsibility for that behavior. If loss of the capacity for impulse control resulting in criminal behavior correlated with the presence of a tumor in the prefrontal

---

10. *Ibid.*, 934.
11. R. Davidson et al., "Dysfunction in the Neural Circuitry of Emotion Regulation—a Possible Prelude to Violence," *Science* 289 (2000): 591–594.

region of the brain, and this capacity was restored upon removal of the tumor, then this would suggest a causal connection between the tumor and the behavior. The tumor and the associated brain dysfunction could explain why a person was unable to control his impulses. This occurred in the case of an American teacher in Virginia who began displaying pedophilia. His uncharacteristic behavior was associated with a tumor pressing on his right orbitofrontal cortex. The pedophilia resolved when the tumor was removed. But the behavior returned with the growth of a new tumor in the same brain region and resolved again when the second tumor was removed.[12] In most cases, there are only correlations between brain abnormalities and criminal behavior. The correlations are based not on individual but group data, which makes claims about a link between brain features and behavior probabilistic rather than deterministic. Not everyone with a brain abnormality in the prefrontal region commits criminal offenses. The evidence is not strong enough to claim that a particular brain abnormality caused a particular action or series of actions.

Given the emotionally cool artificial setting of a PET or fMRI scanner, brain regions activated when one was asked to perform a cognitive task would not be as active as they were when one performed a criminal act. This setting would be very different from the emotionally heightened state that issued in the earlier impulsive act. Attempts to elicit an emotional reaction in the scanner with photos or verbal cues could not replicate the emotional reaction that led to the crime because the scanner could not replicate the neurobiological, environmental, and psychological factors that obtained at that time. Moreover, knowing ahead of time that one's brain would be scanned could facilitate rehearsal of imagined action and be a cognitive countermeasure to the technique.

A brain scan would not be able to determine whether the individual lacked the capacity to inhibit the impulse to strangle and kill his partner, had some capacity to inhibit it but had difficulty doing so, or had the capacity to inhibit the impulse but simply failed to at the time of his action. Legal theorist Bernadette McSherry argues that "there is no objectively verifiable test determining that an accused individual could not control him or herself or that he or she would not."[13] Neurobiologist Robert Sapolsky further notes difficulties associated with "distinguishing between an irresistible impulse and one that is to any extent resistible but which was not resisted."[14]

12. J. Burns and R. Swerdlow, "Right Orbitofrontal Tumor with Pedophilia Symptom and Constructional Apraxia Sign," *Archives of Neurology* 62 (2003): 437–440. See also S. Batts, "Brain Lesions and their Implications for Criminal Responsibility," *Behavioral Sciences & the Law* 27 (2009): 261–272, and J. Knabb et al., "Neuroscience, Moral Reasoning, and the Law," *Behavioral Sciences & the Law* 27 (2009): 219–236.
13. "Criminal Responsibility, Fleeting States of Mental Impairment, and the Power of Self-Control," *International Journal of Law and Psychiatry* 27 (2004): 224–257.
14. "The Frontal Cortex and the Criminal Justice System," *Philosophical Transactions of the Royal Society of London* 359 (2004): 1787–1796 at 1790. See also N. Vincent, "Responsibility, Dysfunction, and Capacity," *Neuroethics* 1(3) (2008): 199–204.

Consider the case of Spyder Cystkopf.[15] He suffocated his wife in a violent reactive response to her scratching his face during an argument. CT and MRI brain scans showed that he had a large arachnoid cyst between his left frontal and left temporal lobes. A PET scan showed reduced metabolism in these brain regions. The question arose as to whether his brain abnormality caused him to lose control of his cognitive inhibitory mechanisms when he impulsively killed his wife. If he did lose it, then he could have met the control criterion of the not guilty by reason of insanity defense and have been judged not criminally responsible. This question was never answered because be declined surgical excision of the cyst and plea-bargained to accept a conviction of manslaughter. It is possible that Cystkopf lost cognitive control when he acted. But since he declined the surgery, there was no way of comparing his actions with and without the cyst and thus no way of establishing a causal connection between the cyst and the act of killing his wife. If the cyst caused dysfunction in brain regions regulating his impulses, and if he could not control them on this occasion, then he likely would not have been able to control them on other occasions either. Whether or to what extent one has or lacks the capacity to control one's behavior must be assessed by observing that behavior over a period of time. Brain images may be necessary to confirm this assessment, though it cannot be confirmed on the basis of brain imaging alone.

A structural or functional abnormality in a circumscribed area of the brain associated with impulse control does not imply the loss of the ability to control impulses. This and other functions are mediated by distributed and interacting neural networks. Some networks involving regions of the frontal lobes not affected by a cyst or other malformation might be enough to sustain the ability to control impulses and make rational decisions. This does not suggest that there are substitutable components of these functions in the brain, only that an abnormality in one part of a distributed neural network would not necessarily disable that network. The fact that multiple brain regions mediate decision making should make us cautious in drawing inferences about mental capacity or incapacity from localized deficits in the brain. Given that the brain becomes less plastic as we age, rewiring or bypassing dysfunctional circuits in frontal regions may be more probable in a younger person and less probable in an older one. This might suggest that the first individual would have a greater degree of control of his impulses than the second and be held to a greater degree of responsibility. His behavior might be more in line with the law's reasonable person standard. Admittedly, this is speculative. It also involves making a questionable inference from groups to individuals, which neglects the fact that no two people's brains respond in the same way to pathology or injury. In any case, a judgment of greater or lesser control on the basis of age would require observation of the individual's behavior.

Brain dysfunction and mental impairment come in degrees. There is no empirical measure that could establish a threshold at or over which one who has these features is criminally responsible and under which one is not responsible. As an

---

15. N. Relkin et al., "Impulsive Homicide Associated with an Arachnoid Cyst and Unilateral Frontotemporal Cerebral Dysfunction," *Seminars in Clinical Neuropsychiatry* 1 (1996): 172–183. Spence discusses this case in *The Actor's Brain*, 326–331.

imperfect empirical measure of brain function and its relation to behavior, imaging cannot tell us what degree of brain dysfunction can excuse one from criminal responsibility for an action. There will be disagreement within the legal community about how much brain dysfunction is enough to impair or undermine responsibility-relevant mental capacities and support mitigation or excuse. Empirical considerations regarding information about the brain cannot be isolated from normative considerations regarding the behavioral and legal significance of that information. What degree of control of one's mental states is necessary and sufficient for responsibility will be influenced by social expectations about how individuals should act in conforming their conduct to social rules and the requirements of the law.

A significant degree of prefrontal damage and dysfunction might suggest that one could not control one's impulses. Even here, though, a general pattern of impulsive behavior would be needed to support this claim. The execution of the violent impulse that resulted in the death of the partner would be one manifestation of this behavior. If the individual's inability to control his impulse on this occasion was caused by a dysfunctional prefrontal cortex, then this dysfunction would probably manifest in other incidents of violent impulsive action. Other than perhaps an acute psychotic episode, brain dysfunction disrupting cognitive and affective processing would likely not manifest in mental impairment and uncontrollable behavior in only one incident. In addition, there would have to be consensus within the neuroscientific and legal community in interpreting imaging data and evaluating the significance of the correlation between the brain damage and behavior to argue that the individual was not responsible. Nevertheless, a certain degree of dysfunction in cortical-limbic pathways could make it difficult for an individual to fully engage his cognitive capacity and control his behavior. Neuroimaging displaying this dysfunction might support a claim of impairment in restraining impulses and thus might be a mitigating factor in judgments of criminal responsibility for harmful impulsive acts. But imaging alone would not be able to establish this; behavioral evidence would be needed as well.

The fact that neuroimaging data may be open to different interpretations presents a number of challenges for the use of imaging in criminal cases. If brain scans cannot objectively determine that an individual has or lacks the requisite degree of control of his or her behavior, then scans have minimal probative value for criminal responsibility. The data from these scans allow only rebuttable and not conclusive inferences to be drawn from the brain to behavior.[16] Any probative value they might have is outweighed by the potential for misinterpretation and prejudice in determining the facts of the case.[17] Prosecution and defense could present ambiguous imaging data to insufficiently cautious judges and juries in biased ways. Moreover, in countering a claim from the defense that brain dysfunction impaired the cognitive processing of the accused, the prosecution could appeal to neuroplasticity and argue that dysfunction in a particular region of the brain would not necessarily undermine this processing. Appeals to age could complicate matters further.

---

16. I thank Stephen Morse for this point.
17. W. Sinnott-Armstrong et al., "Brain Images as Legal Evidence," *Episteme* 5(3) (2009): 359–373.

The prosecution could argue that a 40-year-old with some damage to frontal regions may have recovered some cognitive inhibitory functions. In a different case, the defense could exploit the fact that the frontal lobes are not fully developed until early adulthood in arguing that a 17-year-old could not be fully responsible for a criminal act because he lacked the inhibitory mechanisms in the brain necessary for responsibility.

This was one of the arguments presented in the 2005 U.S. case of *Roper v. Simmons*.[18] At issue was whether Christopher Simmons, who 12 years earlier had murdered a woman when he was 17, should receive the death penalty for his crime. The American Medical Association filed an *amicus curiae* brief based on imaging studies of adolescent brains. Drawing from these studies, the Association stated: "To a degree never before understood, scans can now determine that adolescents are immature not only to the observer's naked eye, but in the very fibers of their brains."[19] The U.S. Supreme Court ruled 5-to-4 that the death penalty was unconstitutional as punishment for murder by a juvenile and upheld the sentence of life imprisonment. The imaging studies did not influence but confirmed the Supreme Court majority opinion by Justice Anthony Kennedy, which was based largely on accepted views of developmental psychology. The ruling in this case underscores the following point. Just because brain scans confirm that adolescents are comparatively less mature in their reasoning and decision making and have less developed frontal lobes than adults does not imply that they cannot be responsible to any degree for their actions.

In contrast to cases involving the question of criminal intent, brain imaging data may play a greater role in cases where responsibility hinges on the question of impulse control. This is because the correlations between images of brain dysfunction and behavior may be stronger in the latter than they are in the former. Still, the combination of imaging data with behavioral evidence and normative evaluations of behavior is more significant than imaging data alone. As the cases I have presented show, a functional brain scan revealing an underactive prefrontal cortex or overactive amygdala by itself will not be diagnostic of a loss of control of one's behavior.

Psychopathy II

A man has been bullying a younger co-worker with verbal taunts for several weeks. He lures his colleague to his apartment, claiming that he is having a party with friends. As soon as the younger person arrives, the bully kills him by stabbing him with a knife and then disposes of his body. After he is charged with first-degree

---

18. *Roper v. Simmons* 543 U. S. 551 (2005).

19. *Ibid.*, No. 03-633. In a more recent case, the U.S Supreme Court cited the Eighth Amendment in ruling 6-to-3 that life imprisonment without the possibility of parole for juveniles convicted of non-homicide offenses is unconstitutional. In *Graham v. Florida* 560 U.S. (2010), the justices reasoned that these individuals need to be given a chance to show that they have matured enough while in prison to be ruled "fit to rejoin society." Among other things, the ruling in this case suggests that the fate of an offender depends on more than his or her brain at the time of a crime.

murder, a psychologist interviewing the defendant notices that he has a number of psychopathic traits. The defendant undergoes PET and fMRI scans, which show that he has abnormal activity in pathways between the prefrontal cortex and amygdala. During the trial, his defense attorney presents data from neuroimaging studies showing that this brain abnormality is common among psychopaths. He then presents images from the brain of the defendant to argue that his psychopathy constitutes an excusing condition and that he could not be criminally responsible for killing the co-worker.

In the previous chapter, I argued that psychopaths are at least partly morally responsible for their actions. I cited a number of imaging studies showing that psychopaths have brain abnormalities. Yet I argued that these abnormalities alone cannot demonstrate that psychopaths are unable to respond to reasons against performing harmful actions. It will be helpful to extend this argument to the criminal law. A recent imaging study conducted by neuroscientists Andrea Glenn, Adrian Raine, and Robert Schug has shown that psychopaths have reduced activity in all of the regions making up the moral neural circuit.[20] This includes the amygdala, medial prefrontal cortex, anterior and posterior cingulate cortex, and angular gyrus. Such reduced activity can interfere with the capacity for the social interactions that are central to moral behavior. Insofar as this capacity is necessary for one to be criminally responsible for one's behavior, and the psychopath lacks this capacity, it seems to follow that he is not responsible for any criminal acts he commits. Or, if he does not lack but is impaired in this capacity, then the impairment constitutes a mitigating factor and thus he can be only partly responsible.

This type of argument was used recently by the defense of a convicted killer in Illinois. In July 2009, 53-year-old Brian Dugan pleaded guilty to raping and killing a 10-year-old girl after kidnapping her from her home in 1983. He was already serving life sentences for two other murders, and the prosecution sought the death penalty for the third. The defense introduced fMRI images from Dugan's brain showing abnormalities consistent with psychopathy. They argued that Dugan was born with these abnormalities and that they were indicative of this mental disorder, which should have been a mitigating factor because it impaired his ability to control his behavior.[21] Psychopathy may warrant life in prison, but not the death penalty. In spite of this, the jury sentenced Dugan to death. They deliberated for 10 hours before reaching a decision. This was considerably longer than what many had expected, which some attributed to the brain images. The jury's prolonged deliberation may have been due more to the seductive allure of the images of the brain than to their role in an argument for a link between the brain abnormalities and the defendant's behavior. In fact, the jury initially planned to sentence Dugan to life in prison. The harsher sentence of the death penalty suggests that the scans were not so seductive after all.

20. "The Neural Correlates of Moral Decision-Making in Psychopathy," *Molecular Psychiatry* 14 (2009): 5–6. See also K. Kiehl et al., "Limbic Abnormalities in Affective Processing by Criminal Psychopaths as Revealed by Functional Magnetic Resonance Imaging," *Biological Psychiatry* 50 (2001): 677–684.
21. G. Miller, "fMRI Evidence Used in Murder Sentencing," *ScienceInsider*, November 23, 2009, http://blogs.sciencemag.org/scienceinsider/2009/11/fmri-evidence-u.html. In March 2011, Illinois Governor Pat Quinn signed legislation repealing the death penalty in that state.

In the end, the jury was not convinced that the brain abnormalities and the psycho-pathic traits were mitigating factors.

Perhaps the jury would have reached a different decision in sentencing Dugan if the imaging evidence had been combined with data from behavioral genetics. Results from a study conducted by cognitive neuroscientist Essi Viding and colleagues appear to support the claim that psychopaths cannot be criminally responsible for their actions.[22] The researchers note that psychopathic traits are present in childhood. Antisocial psychopathic individuals start offending from a young age and continue to offend over the course of their lives. Their offenses are often predatory, reflecting a lack of empathy. Viding et al. claim that their results indicate that "exhibiting high levels of callous-unemotional traits at 7 years, as assessed by teachers at the end of the first year of school, is under strong genetic influence."[23] They further claim that "anti-social behavior for children who are high on the callous-unemotional (CU) scale (i.e., children with psychopathic tendencies) is highly heritable."[24] If the phenotypic traits of psychopaths are highly heritable, then one might be inclined to say that their antisocial, immoral, and criminal behavior is determined by genetic factors beyond their control. In that case, they could not be responsible for their actions.

But how strong must the genetic influence in psychopathy be to constitute a mitigating or excusing condition? With the exception of Mendelian, single-gene conditions expressing in neurodevelopmental or neurodegenerative disorders, genes influence a broad range of behavior. Genetic influence is not genetic determinism. How genes are expressed in phenotypic traits depends on epigenetic factors, which are a function of interaction between and among our genes, our bodies, and the environment. This suggests that psychopathy is not a purely genetic disorder but a multifactorial one. We need to ask what degree of genetic influence is necessary to claim that a psychopathic child or adult lacks control of his or her behavior. Behavioral criteria of the sort used by Viding et al. do not tell us what degree of genetic influence impairs or undermines the capacity to recognize that others might be harmed by one's behavior. Nor do these criteria help us to distinguish between having some of this capacity but failing to exercise it, on the one hand, and lacking this capacity, on the other. They do not help us to know when one has or lacks the relevant sort of control of one's behavior. It is doubtful that a more scientifically informed jury in the Dugan case would have decided on a lighter sentence if they were given this type of genetic information about Dugan.

A similar controversy in behavioral genetics has involved the role of the gene encoding the neurotransmitter-metabolizing enzyme monoamine oxidase A (MAOA). A study published in 2002 found an association between low levels of MAOA expression and aggressiveness and criminal conduct of young boys raised in abusive environments.[25] In 2009, an Italian court reduced the sentence given to a

22. "Evidence for Substantial Genetic Risk for Psychopathy in 7-Year-Olds," *Journal of Child Psychology and Psychiatry* 46 (2005): 592–597.
23. *Ibid.,* 595.
24. *Ibid,* 596.
25. A. Caspi et al., "Role of Genotype in the Cycle of Violence in Maltreated Children," *Science* 297 (2002): 851–854.

convicted killer by a year because he had low levels of MAOA in his brain.[26] The reduced sentence was based on the belief that genetics and environmental factors predisposed him to criminal behavior. But it is not clear what "predispose" means in terms of the likelihood of committing a criminal act. Does it mean that an individual with low levels of MAOA in his or her brain has a 60 percent probability of committing such an act? Would this be significantly different from a 30 percent probability? What degree would be enough for mitigation or excuse? The main problem here is that behavioral genetics is based on population statistics, and one cannot draw a valid inference from the behavior of a population or group to individual behavior. Not everyone with low levels of MAOA in their brains commits criminal acts or is inclined to commit them. So, one could not claim that a person could not control his or her behavior solely on the basis of low levels of this enzyme. Similarly, one could not claim that a person could not control his or her behavior solely on the basis of brain abnormalities associated with psychopathy.

Psychologist Robert Hare argues that psychopathy should be an aggravating rather than a mitigating factor in determining criminal responsibility and sentencing.[27] Although Hare has been involved in imaging studies showing limbic abnormalities in psychopaths, his argument in support of aggravation is based mainly on behavioral traits. As noted in Chapter 2 and earlier in this chapter, studies by Blair and others have shown that psychopaths have some brain dysfunction. But it has not been established that this dysfunction causes their criminal behavior. Within the legal community, there is no consensus on what degree of dysfunction is enough for the psychopath to lack the cognitive and affective capacity necessary to respond to reasons against harmful actions and be criminally responsible for them. Here, too, normative considerations involving evaluation of the psychopath's behavior and how scans of his brain are interpreted will influence judgments of responsibility. Imaging data alone will not determine that the psychopath is not receptive and cannot react to reasons. Being impaired in a mental capacity is not equivalent to lacking that capacity altogether.

An underactive amygdala or anterior cingulate might impair the psychopath's cognitive and affective processing to such a degree that he would not be able to internalize and respond to reasons against performing criminal acts. Damage to the anterior cingulate could make him lose his capacity for empathy and result in desensitized responses to other persons. Furthermore, a hyperactive reward system in his brain could make the psychopath discount or be unaware of the consequences of his actions. These types of brain dysfunction could deprive the psychopath of the capacity to conform to social rules and the requirements of the law. Lacking this capacity would be grounds for excuse from criminal responsibility.[28] Curiously, like

26. E. Feresin, "Lighter Sentence for Murderer with 'Bad Genes,'" *Nature*, published online October 30, 2009. http://www.nature.com/new/2009/091030/full/news.2009.1050.html. See also W. Bernet et al., "Bad Nature, Bad Nurture, and Testimony Regarding MAOA and SLC6A4 Genotyping at Murder Trials," *Journal of Forensic Science* 52 (2007): 1362–1371.

27. *The Hare Psychopathy Checklist*, and "Psychopaths and their Nature." Hare was a co-author with Kiehl in the paper cited in note 20.

28. S. Morse analyzes this argument in "Psychopathy and Criminal Responsibility," *Neuroethics* 1(3) (2008): 205–212.

psychopaths, individuals with autism spectrum disorders are impaired in the capacity for empathy.[29] One hypothesis for this impairment is that individuals with autism have dysfunctional mirror neuron systems in cortical and limbic regions. Unlike psychopaths, those with autism do not deliberately harm others. Perhaps differences in the structure and function of the anterior cingulate between these two groups might go some way toward explaining why one group deliberately commits harmful acts while the other does not. I cannot adequately address this issue here. But the fact that both psychopaths and persons with autism have impaired capacity for empathy, and that their behavior is very different, suggests that this type of impairment alone is not enough to excuse psychopaths from responsibility for their actions. There would have to be agreement within the legal community that severe dysfunction in the anterior cingulate or other brain regions clearly deprives the psychopath of an empathic capacity. In these cases, and even more so in cases of moderate brain dysfunction, imaging would not be a sufficient basis on which to conclude that psychopaths could not be responsible for their behavior.

Recall from Blair's studies the association between a dysfunctional amygdala and the psychopath's impaired response to fear-inducing stimuli. Because the amygdala mediates primitive emotions such as fear, it may not play as great a role as the anterior cingulate in mediating cognitive-affective processing and responsiveness to moral reasons. But the function of the amygdala in mediating fearful responses probably plays as important a role as the anterior cingulate in influencing the prefrontal inhibitory mechanisms that enable one to refrain from performing harmful actions. This is because of the projections from the amygdala to the prefrontal cortex. Appeals to neuroplasticity might not be helpful in arguing for the responsibility of the psychopath despite a dysfunctional amygdala. Through its regulation of fear and its role in the fight-or-flight response to external threats, this brain region is critical to survival. This function might not be taken over so readily by other regions. More primitive hard-wired functions in the brain and the unconscious mental states they generate and sustain might not be so amenable to transfer from one region to another. Still, imaging studies of psychopaths do not always show severe dysfunction in cortical-limbic pathways.

The results of a study published by Raine and colleagues 13 years ago were quite different from those of Blair's studies. Raine's group used PET scans to examine the brains of impulsive murderers and predatory psychopaths.[30] Compared to normal controls, the impulsive murderers showed reduced activity in the bilateral prefrontal cortex and increased activity in limbic areas such as the amygdala. The predatory psychopaths had relatively normal prefrontal function and increased activity in the amygdala and hippocampus. Neuroscientist Dean Mobbs and coauthors state that "these results suggest that predatory psychopaths are able to regulate their impulses,

29. See, for example, S. Baron-Cohen, "Autism — 'Autos': Literally, A Total Focus on the Self?," in T. Feinberg and J. Keenan, eds., *The Lost Self: Pathologies of the Brain and Identity* (Oxford: Oxford University Press, 2005), 166–180.
30. A. Raine et al., "Reduced Prefrontal and Increased Subcortical Brain Functioning Assessed Using Positron Emission Tomography in Predatory and Affective Murderers," *Behavioral Sciences & the Law* 16 (1998): 319–332.

in contrast to impulsive murderers, who lack the prefrontal 'inhibitory' machinery that stops them from committing violent transgressions."[31] While I have emphasized the limitations of imaging to support claims of mitigation or excuse, if anything Raine's study supports the claim that psychopaths have enough control of their behavior to be responsible for it. It is also noteworthy that Glenn, Raine, and Schug did not conclude from their imaging study that dysfunction in brain regions mediating moral decision making decisively shows that psychopaths cannot control their behavior or conform to social norms. Instead, they concluded that this dysfunction "may *partly* explain a complex social problem—the psychopath."[32]

The characterization of psychopaths as "predatory" is significant because it suggests that they are not as deficient in instrumental and moral reasoning as some might think. Again, psychopaths present with highly elevated levels of both instrumental and reactive aggression.[33] Instrumental aggression is purposeful and aimed at a specific goal. Bullying is an example of instrumental aggression. When he engages in this type of behavior, the psychopath identifies the person to whom it is directed as a vulnerable individual he desires and intends to manipulate for his selfish ends. Given that his instrumental aggression is deliberate and he knows that a particular individual will be victimized and harmed by his actions, the psychopath is capable of knowing to some degree that this is a criminally liable transgression. Insofar as the psychopath is capable of knowing that his instrumental aggression is a legal transgression, he can be criminally responsible for it.

If the psychopath is criminally responsible for his legal transgressions, then the question arises as to whether he deserves some form of retributive punishment. Greene and Cohen argue that retributive punishment for criminal acts could only be justified by a libertarian account of responsibility.[34] Since libertarianism is probably false, we should reject retributivism and "shift towards a consequentialist approach to punishment, i.e., one aimed at promoting future welfare rather than meting out just deserts."[35] The sort of control that libertarian theories require for responsibility is regulative control. This consists of nondeterministic forward-looking alternative possibilities (AP) and backward-looking ultimate responsibility (UR). But I have argued that compatibilist guidance control is sufficient for moral responsibility. This type of control is also sufficient for criminal responsibility and retributive punishment. There is no need for libertarian AP or UR conditions. Nothing in the law's reasonable person standard suggests that libertarian freedom is necessary for a person to be liable to punishment. Liability requires the capacity to respond to reasons and guide one's intentions to actions. Coercion, compulsion, and constraint are excusing conditions when they interfere with this capacity. Causal determinism does not preclude responsiveness to reasons because it does not imply

---

31. "Law, Responsibility, and the Brain," *PLoS Biology* 5(4) (2007): e103.
32. "The Neural Correlates of Moral Decision-Making in Psychopathy,"6. Emphasis added.
33. Blair, Mitchell, and Blair., *The Psychopath*, 12–13. See also A. Glenn and A. Raine, "Psychopathy and Instrumental Aggression: Evolutionary, Neurobiological, and Legal Perspectives," *International Journal of Law and Psychiatry*, 32 (2009): 253–258.
34. "For the Law, Neuroscience Changes Nothing and Everything," 1776.
35. *Ibid.*, 1776.

any of these types of interference in our thought and behavior. So, the idea that one's actions are causally determined does not rule out liability.

There have been no convincing arguments from philosophers, cognitive psychologists, or neuroscientists to support the claim that the indeterminism presupposed by libertarianism is necessary to ground any sense of retributive punishment. Insofar as the psychopath has some capacity to respond to reasons against legal transgressions, he deserves some form of retributive punishment for his transgressions. This is based not only on the harmful effects of his actions but also on his state of mind in performing them. His instrumental aggression in performing these actions indicates that he has enough of a *mens rea* to justify at least a limited term of incarceration.

The probability that a psychopath who has harmed others will continue to harm could also justify incarceration, even if he were deemed not criminally responsible for his behavior because of cognitive and affective impairment. This is a plausible deterrence-based consequentialist argument for punishment, given the high rate of recidivism among psychopaths. It is distinct from the argument for retributive punishment based on responsibility for harmful actions and consequences that have already occurred. It is unlikely that incarceration for reasons of retribution or deterrence would have any positive effects on the psychopath's thought and behavior and thus would not rehabilitate him. There is an alternative, however. At least one study has been conducted to test a pharmacological intervention as a treatment for psychopathy. The alpha 2-adrenergic receptor agonist guanfacine (Tenex) was used to manipulate the noradrenergic system in subjects. But it was not effective in modulating the dysfunctional cortical-limbic pathways implicated in the disorder.[36] Still, conceivably similar drugs might modulate dysfunctional neural networks in children and adolescents with psychopathic traits because their brains are still developing and may be amenable to therapy.

This raises the ethical questions of whether parents could consent to the use of a drug on behalf of a child and whether it could be forced on a child without his or her assent. How one responds to these questions may depend on the severity of the child's psychopathic traits, the harmful behavior the child has already displayed, the probability of harmful behavior in the future, and the safety and efficacy of using the drug for this purpose. Adult psychopaths might benefit from the drug as well if it had modulating effects on pathways between the prefrontal cortex and amygdala. It is possible that their brains are so hard-wired that no pharmacological intervention would have any therapeutic effect. Yet it is also possible that their brains are plastic enough for certain drugs to correct dysfunctional circuits. Assuming that adult psychopaths convicted of crimes retained enough decisional capacity, they could consent to the treatment if it were offered to them. If the choice were between incarceration and a drug with a favorable benefit–risk ratio, then it would not be a coercive offer or a form of forced treatment. The drug would be preferable to incarceration and might have positive effects on the psychopath's mental states. It would be a form of therapy rather than enhancement because its purpose would be to generate or increase the psychopath's capacity for empathy and moral sensitivity to the normal level possessed by the general population. It could be used to influence

---

36. James Blair has informed me of this in personal communication.

his future conduct, helping him to become more humane by making him more responsive to moral reasons and the rule of law.[37]

Whether this therapy could provide the psychopath with the capacity to be fully responsive to reasons and not just partly but completely responsible for his actions is an open question. But by modulating dysfunctional cortical-limbic pathways and improving the capacity for reasons-responsiveness, certain drugs could minimize the likelihood of harm to others. On these grounds, psychopharmacological intervention would be permissible. Indeed, an interdisciplinary group of neuroscientists, philosophers, and legal theorists make a stronger claim. They argue that if brain-invasive treatments for severe psychopathy became available, then the relevant professionals would not only be permitted but obligated to offer them to psychopaths as alternatives to life-long incarceration.[38] These might include drugs as well as deep-brain stimulation to modulate an underactive amygdala or anterior cingulate. Altering psychopathic traits from an early age could benefit these individuals and reduce the harm to others resulting from this pervasive psychological, social, and legal problem.

Criminal Negligence

I have argued that neuroimaging displaying brain abnormalities by itself cannot determine that an individual is so mentally impaired that he or she cannot be criminally responsible for certain behavior. I have noted that, in some cases, there may be a causal connection between a brain abnormality and criminal actions. Such a connection could excuse a person from responsibility for these actions. Another type of case where imaging may support an excuse is when it shows a brain abnormality correlating with an unintentional omission of a person resulting in the death of another. Damage to brain regions mediating the formation of episodic memories of recent events may significantly impair a person's capacity for short-term working memory, reasoning, and decision-making. It raises the question of whether such a person could rightfully be charged with criminal negligence.

Suppose that a single-parent father leaves his young son unattended at the edge of an outdoor swimming pool when he goes inside his house to answer a phone call. The conversation lasts about an hour, and during this time he is unaware of where he left his son. As soon as he completes the call, he goes outside and sees him floating in the pool. He tries to resuscitate him to no avail because he is already dead. The father is charged with criminal negligence causing death for the consequence of his child drowning. Although he did not intend and did not foresee the drowning as a consequence of his actions, a reasonable person in these same circumstances would have foreseen this as a probable consequence and would have acted to prevent it from occurring. His omission in forgetting where he left the child plays a critical causal role in the sequence of events leading to the outcome. The criminal

---

37. Spence defends a similar position in "Can Pharmacology Help Enhance Human Morality?," *British Journal of Psychiatry* 193 (2008): 179–180.

38. R. Merkel et al, *Intervening in the Brain: Changing Psyche and Society* (Berlin and Heidelberg: Springer, 2007), 200.

negligence charge is made on the grounds that his behavior meets the objective test for *mens rea*. Nevertheless, he claims that he could not recall leaving his child by the pool and that this is one instance of a recent pattern of forgetful behavior. After explaining that he had a herpes encephalitis infection several months ago, his defense attorney suspects that his memory impairment may not be just psychogenic but have an organic cause beyond his cognitive control.[39] What is critical in this case is not the defendant's physical capacity to perform certain actions, but whether he had the mental capacity to have beliefs about the probability of certain events resulting from his actions.

Structural CT and MRI scans of his brain show significant bilateral damage to his hippocampi and adjacent structures in his medial temporal lobes. These structures are necessary for declarative memory, which includes episodic memories of events one has experienced. Damage to these regions of the brain can result in anterograde amnesia, the inability to form and retain new memories.[40] It is unlikely that other regions of the brain could compensate for this condition because different brain regions and systems mediate different types of memory. Although some memory systems may overlap to some degree, there is no evidence that other brain regions could take over the functions of the hippocampus in the formation and retention of episodic memory. It is highly probable that the earlier viral infection caused the hippocampal damage in the accused and severely impaired his capacity to develop new memories.

In this hypothetical case, if the hippocampal damage of the accused was extensive, then it could support the claim that the father was not responsible for his son's drowning. His amnesia made him unable to have a memory of leaving his son unattended by the pool. This in turn undermined his capacity to reason that leaving a young child unattended by a swimming pool entailed a high probability of the child drowning. Ordinarily, he would have been able to draw this inference and not leave his son out of his sight for so long. This would have prevented the tragic consequence. Yet he was unable to do this because he had no memory of where he left his son. Given his damaged and dysfunctional hippocampi and anterograde amnesia, he was not responsible for the consequence of the drowning because he was not responsible for failing to recall where he left his child. The first state of affairs is causally connected to the second. In fact, it is inaccurate to describe this case as one of omission, since the father could not have failed to recall something of which he had no memory.

The neurobiological argument for excuse is more persuasive than the psychological argument that he was experiencing information overload, with too many cognitive tasks to plan and execute within a compressed period of time. This could have led to a temporary retrieval block of his episodic memory of leaving his son unattended. Yet unless the memory block was strongly correlated with a detectable brain dysfunction, a purely psychological explanation of it would not have much force as an excusing condition. Although one may have difficulty recalling

---

39. I discuss an actual case where this type of brain injury occurred in Chapter 6.
40. See Schacter, *Searching for Memory*, Schacter and Scarry, *Memory, Brain, and Belief*, and Schacter and Tulving, *Memory Systems*.

an event, one may be able to recall it with some effort. Unlike procedural memory, episodic memory is not involuntary but within one's capacity for conscious recall. However, anterograde amnesia that severely impaired his episodic memory could have put his son's whereabouts outside of the father's set of beliefs and thus beyond his cognitive control. Episodic memory and its retrieval in prefrontal-mediated working memory would be critical to the reasoning necessary for the father to foresee the drowning as the probable outcome of his actions. Individuals with anterograde amnesia at best are able to retain any newly formed episodic memories for a very brief period of time. This does not always impair working memory, where information need only be held for a few seconds. Crucially, the event of leaving his son unattended was outside the narrow temporal limit of the father's working memory. This would deny him the cognitive control necessary to prevent the harmful consequence from occurring. Some might claim that the father's awareness of his condition should have led him to take steps that would have prevented the sequence of events resulting in the drowning. These would have included having a phone with him at all times. He could have been responsible for failing to do this and thus also responsible for his son's death. Yet if his amnesia severely impaired his capacity to reason, then he might have been aware of his condition but unable to draw inferences from his actions to their probable consequences. If so, then one could uphold the claim that he was not responsible for the drowning.

Still, the evidence of hippocampal damage from the brain scans as an explanation for his behavior would be only one part of the argument for excuse. By itself, it would not be sufficient to absolve the father of responsibility. His inability to recall leaving his child beside the pool would have to be one instance in a consistent pattern of forgetful behavior over a period of time. It is only within this pattern that the information from his brain CT and MRI scans would be legally significant. As in the cases discussed earlier, imaging showing structural and functional brain abnormalities would have to be evaluated together with behavioral evidence to suitably inform legal judgments of responsibility for actions, omissions, and their consequences.

Conclusion

What can neuroscience, mainly in the form of neuroimaging, tell us about criminal responsibility? Structural and functional imaging can reveal abnormalities in regions of the brain mediating cognitive and affective processing. These abnormalities may establish a neurobiological basis of mental impairment resulting in criminal behavior. In this respect, neuroimaging may inform judgments of criminal responsibility. Yet this technology alone cannot determine whether one has enough mental capacity to form and execute criminal intentions, to respond to reasons against harmful actions, to restrain one's impulses, and to foresee the consequences of one's actions. Even in cases where there is a causal connection between brain dysfunction and criminal behavior, whether one has the requisite mental capacity will be based primarily on behavioral evidence and only secondarily on imaging data.

Neuroimaging should not supplant but supplement behavior as the basis of these judgments. In most cases, brain scans do not establish causal connections between brain states and behavior but only correlations between them. Brain scans cannot determine that a person lacks the capacity to control his or her behavior, has limited capacity to do this, or has full capacity but fails to exercise it. Also, there will be differences in the interpretation of the psychological and legal significance of brain imaging data between and among different individuals and groups. This will be decided not just by appeal to empirical considerations but also to normative considerations regarding how individuals can be expected to respond to reasons in conforming to social rules and the requirements of the law. The cases I have presented suggest that brain imaging may be more useful in assessing judgments of criminal negligence, less useful in judgments of impulsivity and psychopathy, and least useful in judgments of criminal intent.

To claim that neuroimaging alone can tell us that a person has or lacks the necessary cognitive control to be criminally responsible for an action and its consequences is to fall prey to what legal theorist Stephen Morse calls "brain overclaim syndrome."[41] Morse points out that this could undermine the integrity of the process of determining responsibility for criminal acts. It is symptomatic of an oversimplified view of the relation between the brain and the mind, and between the brain and one's actions. Appelbaum expresses this same concern in saying that, in the courtroom setting, "perhaps the most important limitation on the current use of functional imaging evidence is the discrepancy between the inferences that can be drawn and the legal standards to be met."[42] He also states that "although neuroscientists talk in general terms about brain regions associated with moral reasoning and behavioral control, at this point there are no data identifying a given degree of impairment in a particular locus of the brain that corresponds to substantial impairment in either of the capacities at issue."[43] Further refinement of neuroimaging may result in it having a greater supplementary role in elucidating the processes through which a person's mental states issue in actions. But it will not obviate the need for behavioral evidence in shaping and justifying judgments of criminal responsibility. Morse argues: "In principle, no amount of increased causal understanding of behavior, from any form of science, threatens the law's notion of responsibility unless it shows definitively that we humans (or some subset of us) are not intentional, minimally rational actors. And no information about biological or social causes can show this directly. It would have to be demonstrated behaviorally."[44] Another legal theorist, Rebecca Dresser, expresses this same sentiment in a way that captures the gist of my discussion: "Proof that a biological (or environmental) condition influenced someone's behavior does not necessarily defeat the legal presumption that most people are sufficiently rational to be held accountable for their actions."[45]

---

41. "Brain Overclaim Syndrome and Criminal Responsibility: A Diagnostic Note," *Ohio State Journal of Criminal Law* 3 (2006): 397–412.
42. "Through a Glass Darkly," 22.
43. *Ibid.*, 22.
44. "New Neuroscience, Old Problems," in B. Garland, ed., *Neuroscience and the Law: Brain, Mind, and the Scales of Justice* (New York: Dana Press, 2004), 157–198.
45. "Neuroscience's Uncertain Threat to Criminal Law," *Hastings Center Report* 38 (6) (2008): 9–10.

Neuroimaging enables us to identify mechanisms in the brain associated with cognitive and affective control of our actions. It may lead to a better understanding of the role of these mechanisms in our behavior; but they are only one component of this control. A complete account of our capacity to regulate our behavior consists not only of neural processes but also mental states, actions, and objective assessments of these actions. Neuroimaging may help us to refine the normative concepts we use to make individuated judgments of criminal responsibility. It may aid us in clarifying the criteria of legal insanity and establishing when individuals meet these criteria. But legal insanity and related concepts will not be explained away by descriptive neuroscience and empirical data about the brain. The standards of the criminal law are different from the standards of neuroscience, and it would be mistaken to insist that the second should drive the first. If neuroscientific techniques reveal dysfunction in brain regions that mediate the mental capacity to respond to reasons, then there will be questions about whether or to what extent a person retains this capacity and can be criminally responsible. Given the limitations of brain imaging, however, neuroscience alone will not resolve these questions.

4

Neuroscience and Moral Reasoning

Normative ethics addresses the general question of how we ought to act. It is traceable to Plato's *Republic* and Socrates' question of how we ought to live. Unlike descriptive ethics, which employs empirical measures to account for why we behave as we do or why we have certain moral intuitions, normative ethics specifies principles and reasons to justify actions. When deciding which is the right or most defensible action in a case of moral conflict, the justification for that action depends on the reasons one gives for it. Reasons and justifications are part of a deliberative process that is over and above our immediate intuitive responses to these cases.

Psychologist Jonathan Haidt and Joshua Greene have called this way of thinking into question. For Haidt, moral judgments are post hoc rationalizations of our intuitive responses to conflict cases.[1] These judgments are driven primarily by automatic emotional processes. Greene and coauthors have used results from functional magnetic resonance imaging (fMRI) experiments involving subjects presented with hypothetical cases to argue that our perception of moral conflict is a function of warring emotional and cognitive subsystems grounded in different regions of the brain.[2] The emotional subsystem favors deontological intuitions, which focus on rights, duties, and giving equal weight to individual claims. The cognitive subsystem favors utilitarian, or consequentialist, intuitions, which focus on acting to bring about the best outcome. Our intuitive responses to moral dilemmas depend on which subsystem has more force at any given time. Greene et al. favor cognition and

---

1. "The Emotional Dog and Its Rational Tail: A Social Intuitionist Approach to Moral Judgment," *Psychological Review* 108 (2001): 814–834.
2. "An fMRI Investigation of Emotional Engagement in Moral Judgment," *Science* 293 (2001): 2105–2108. See also Greene and Haidt, "How (and Where) Does Moral Judgment Work?," *Trends in Cognitive Sciences* 6 (2002): 517–523; Greene, "From Neural 'Is' to Moral 'Ought,'" and Greene et al., "The Neural Bases of Cognitive Conflict and Control in Moral Judgment," *Neuron* 44 (2004): 389–400.

consequentialism over emotion and deontology.[3] They maintain that those who give the "correct" response in these cases allow the cognitive subsystem to override the emotional one. Unlike consequentialist judgments, deontological judgments have no moral force because they depend on morally irrelevant factors. For the deontologist, the emotional dog is wagging its rational tail.

In this chapter, I argue that Haidt and Greene et al. do not show that deontological judgments have no normative significance, and that we should always favor consequentialist judgments over deontological ones. They oversimplify the neurobiological and psychological factors involved in moral reasoning. Their claims are not supported by empirical facts about how the brain enables this reasoning. Cognition and emotion are not distinct subsystems but overlapping processes generated and sustained by interacting neural circuits distributed throughout the brain. Moral justification based on deontological reasons is not simply a post hoc rationalization of an emotional response to morally irrelevant factors. Nor is moral justification just a function of neural activity. The reasons we adduce to justify a particular action are also shaped by causal and situational factors external to the brain. Two people can cite different reasons to justify the same action. The brain activity associated with these reasons would likely be similar because this activity is necessary for one to engage in practical and moral reasoning in the first place. If a deontologist and a consequentialist give different reasons to justify the same action, and if the brain activity underlying these reasons is relevantly similar between them, then moral reasoning involves more than just the brain.

The hypothetical cases that Greene and colleagues use in their experiments are artificial and not representative of the conflict cases we encounter in our actual lives. They are thus limited in explaining our moral psychology. A description of the way we think about moral questions does not obviate the need for normative theories to analyze and justify our actions. Descriptive ethics is no substitute for and does not explain away normative ethics. Nor does anything about brain function suggest that it does.

Trolleys

Greene et al. conducted experiments in which subjects were asked to respond to a large number of dilemmas by pushing either an "appropriate" or an "inappropriate" button while undergoing fMRI scans.[4] These consisted of personal moral

3. "Cognitive Load Selectively Interferes with Utilitarian Moral Judgment," *Cognition* 107 (2008): 1144–1154. Also, Greene, "The Secret Joke of Kant's Soul," in *Moral Psychology, Volume 3: The Neuroscience of Morality: Emotion, Brain Disorders, and Development*, W. Sinnott-Armstrong, ed. (Cambridge, MA: MIT Press, 2008), 35–79. Noting that an outcome may affect people differently, consequentialists are more concerned with the greatest good than the good of the greatest number, as utilitarians generally are. Nevertheless, the differences are not significant and thus I use "consequentialist" and "utilitarian" interchangeably.

4. "An fMRI Investigation." In the first experiment on which this article is based, nine subjects responded to fourteen personal moral dilemmas, nineteen impersonal moral dilemmas,

dilemmas, impersonal moral dilemmas, and nonmoral dilemmas presented in random order. The most relevant for our purposes involved the following hypothetical case. You are the driver of a runaway trolley approaching a fork in the track. On the track to the left is a group of five railway workers; on the track to the right is one worker. If you do nothing, the trolley will go to the left, causing the death of the five. You can flip a switch on the dashboard of the trolley and make it go to the right. This will save the five but will kill the one worker on that track. Is it appropriate, or permissible, for you to redirect the trolley, thereby killing one to save the five? To test our moral intuitions further, consider a variant of this example. The same trolley is headed toward the five. You are not able to flip the switch because you are not driving the trolley but instead are on a footbridge over the track. You notice a man on the bridge who is large enough to stop the trolley, if you were to push him over the bridge and onto the track. This act would save the five but would kill the man you pushed. Is it permissible to push him? Is there a morally significant different between flipping the switch and pushing the man?

Philosopher Philippa Foot introduced what has come to be known as the Trolley Problem as a thought experiment to examine the doctrine of double effect (DDE).[5] This doctrine is traceable to Aquinas' discussion of killing in self-defense. It states that there is a morally significant difference between intending a bad outcome and foreseeing it as an unintended consequence of a good action. Foot's aim was to determine whether the DDE could help to resolve the Trolley Problem. She concluded that this doctrine was not a plausible response to it. Instead, Foot distinguished between what we owe to people in the form of aid and what we owe to them in the form of non-interference. Aiding others is a positive duty. Not interfering with others is a negative duty. Foot argued that negative duties outweigh positive duties. In her original example, the agent is the driver of a runaway trolley headed toward five workers on the track. The driver can prevent their deaths by turning the trolley onto a different track on which there is one worker. Appealing to negative duties, she argued that, since at least one person will die no matter what the driver does, he should redirect the trolley and kill the one person. Philosopher Judith Jarvis Thomson developed this problem further by replacing the driver with a bystander and the choice of doing nothing or flipping a switch to send the trolley onto a second track.[6] Thomson also introduced variants such as the Footbridge Case

---

and twenty nonmoral dilemmas. In the second experiment reported in this same article, nine subjects responded to twenty-two personal moral dilemmas, nineteen impersonal moral dilemmas, and twenty nonmoral dilemmas. The study reported in "Neural Bases" involved thirty-two new subjects who responded to twenty-two personal moral dilemmas, eighteen impersonal moral dilemmas, and twenty nonmoral dilemmas.

5. "The Problem of Abortion and the Doctrine of Double Effect," in *Virtues and Vices: And Other Essays in Moral Philosophy* (Oxford: Oxford University Press, 2002), Chapter 2.

6. "Killing, Letting Die, and the Trolley Problem," *The Monist* 59 (1976): 204–217, "The Trolley Problem," *Yale Law Journal* 94 (1985): 1395–1415, and "Turning the Trolley," *Philosophy & Public Affairs* 36 (2008): 359–374. In this last article, Thomson argues that, while it is permissible to divert the trolley if one is the driver, it is impermissible to divert it if one is the bystander. Although Foot introduced this hypothetical moral dilemma,

(or what she calls "Fat Man") and the Loop Case. In the second variant, the trolley is headed toward the five. It can be redirected to the other track on which the one person sits. However, the track loops back toward the five. The trolley will either kill the five if the bystander does not redirect it, or it will kill the one person by looping, grinding to a halt after hitting him and thereby avoiding the five. Thomson argued that it would be permissible for the bystander to flip a switch so that the trolley loops in this way. Since the agent would be doing this with the intention of killing the one, she also concluded that the DDE could not explain or justify the moral judgment in this case.

Since the papers by Foot and Thomson, the literature on the Trolley Problem has evolved from a primary focus on intention to analyses combining intention and causation regarding how the bystander might act to stop the trolley from killing the five. It has proliferated to the point where it now constitutes a distinct subcategory of normative ethics. Some of the variants of the original example have become even more fanciful, with increasingly baroque details. But the purpose of these hypothetical cases is to determine what grounds our different judgments about certain moral dilemmas. In discussing the reasons for the permissibility or impermissibility of different actions in these dilemmas, we need to establish how these reasons correlate with neural processes. We need to ascertain whether normative justification is nothing more than a function of these processes. In addition, we need to determine whether brain activity underlying the different reasons we give to justify the same action varies according to these reasons.

The Dual-Process Hypothesis

Most of the subjects in Greene et al.'s experiments judged that it would be permissible to flip the switch and redirect the trolley. But there was disagreement about what to do with the man on the footbridge. Greene and coauthors state that "the thought of pushing someone to his death is, we propose, more emotionally salient than the thought of hitting a switch that will cause a trolley to produce similar consequences, and it is this emotional response that accounts for people's tendency to treat these cases differently."[7] Brain activity corresponding to the different responses to the two cases seemed to confirm this proposal. In their experiments, regions of the brain associated with instinctive emotional responses to personal moral dilemmas were more active in the subjects who said that it was not permissible to push the man. These regions included the medial prefrontal cortex, posterior cingulate cortex, and angular gyrus/superior temporal sulcus. Regions associated with cognitive responses to impersonal moral dilemmas, such as the dorsolateral prefrontal cortex and parietal lobe, were initially less active but became more active in subjects who had a delayed response in judging that it was permissible to push the man. It appears that their longer response time resulted from their cognitive subsystem overriding the intuitive response driven by their emotional subsystem. They had an initial emotion-laden response and then reasoned their way out of it. This explains

---

Thomson coined it the "Trolley Problem."

7. "An fMRI Investigation of Emotional Engagement in Moral Judgment," 2106.

why those who chose the "appropriate" option in the Footbridge Case had a longer response time than those who chose the "inappropriate" option. Greene et al. use "emotional processing" to refer to information processing involving behaviorally valenced representations that trigger behavioral responses with direct motivational force. They use "cognitive processing" to refer to information processing involving inherently neutral representations that do not trigger behavioral responses. Emotional processes provide quick responses and tend to be domain-specific, while cognitive processes tend to be slow, flexible, and domain-neutral.[8]

Greene et al. distinguish three types of moral dilemmas: (1) dilemmas that engage emotional processing versus dilemmas that engage cognitive processing, (2) dilemmas that elicit deontological judgments versus dilemmas that elicit consequentialist judgments, and (3) dilemmas that are emotionally salient and personal versus dilemmas that are emotionally neutral and impersonal. Emotional processing aligns with deontological judgments and personal dilemmas, while cognitive processing aligns with consequentialist judgments and impersonal dilemmas. This yields the dual-process hypothesis:

> Deontological judgments are characteristically driven by emotional processes, whereas consequentialist judgments are characteristically driven by cognitive processes. These processes compete for one's overall moral judgment about a given case.[9]

Greene says that since our ancestors evolved in an environment in which they lived in close proximity to each other, "it makes sense that we would have evolved altruistic instincts that direct us to help others in dire need, but mostly when the ones in need are presented in an 'up-close-and-personal' way."[10] In the Footbridge Case, presumably the deontological constraint against pushing the man is just a by-product of our evolutionary past; there is no good reason to attribute any moral significance to it. This also grounds the claim and argument for the lack of a morally significant difference between the Trolley Problem and the Footbridge Case. Of the subjects who judged that it was permissible to push the man in front of the trolley, philosopher Peter Singer writes: "The answer these subjects gave is, surely, the rational answer. The death of one person is a lesser tragedy than the death of five people. That reasoning leads us to throw the switch in the standard trolley case, and it should also lead us to push the stranger on the footbridge, for there are no morally relevant differences between the two situations."[11] He adds that even if this more reasoned response is based on an intuition, "it is different from the intuitions to which Haidt and Greene refer. It does not seem to be one that is the outcome of our evolutionary past."[12] Like Greene, Singer takes the longer response time of the

8. "The Neural Bases of Cognitive Conflict."

9. *Ibid.*, 398; "Cognitive Load," 1145; and "The Secret Joke of Kant's Soul," 40–41.

10. "From Neural 'Is' to Moral 'Ought,'" 849.

11. "Ethics and Intuitions," *The Journal of Ethics* 9 (2005): 331–352, at 350.

12. *Ibid.*, 350.

subjects who thought that it was permissible to push the man as evidence of the cognitive subsystem overriding the emotional one.

The rational response and the cognitive subsystem that drives it are not an extension of our evolutionary past, since we no longer find ourselves in environments where we are constantly in close contact with other people. If deontological responses are an emotionally driven by-product of this history, and if this history is not relevant to our moral judgments, then it seems to follow that deontological responses have no moral relevance. Accordingly, with Singer, Greene et al. favor cognitive processing and consequentialist principles over emotional processing and deontological principles. The permissibility of pushing the man could be sustained despite the emotional salience of his death. Without this override, the subjects would have retained their initial intuitive response that it was not permissible to push him. For Singer and Greene, there is no morally significant difference between the two cases because killing one to save five is the correct, consequentialist, response driven solely by the cognitive subsystem. This reasoning applies to both the Trolley Problem and the Footbridge Case.

This suggests the following argument from the moral irrelevance of deontological intuitions:

> The emotional processing that gives rise to deontological intuitions responds to factors that make a dilemma personal rather than impersonal.
> The cognitive processing that gives rise to consequentialist intuitions responds to factors that make a dilemma impersonal rather than personal.
> The factors that make a dilemma personal rather than impersonal are morally irrelevant.
> So, the emotional processing that gives rise to deontological intuitions responds to factors that are morally irrelevant.
> So, deontological intuitions (unlike consequentialist intuitions) are morally irrelevant.[13]

Greene states that "there are good reasons to think that our distinctively deontological moral intuitions… reflect the influence of morally irrelevant factors that are therefore unlikely to track the moral truth."[14] Deontological moral judgments about the impermissibility of actions are just emotionally based intuitive responses to conflict situations. Further, he says; "I have… argued that these judgments can be explained in terms of patterns of emotional response and that these patterns reflect the influence

---

13. Here I follow S. Berker's formulation in "The Normative Insignificance of Neuroscience," *Philosophy & Public Affairs* 37 (2009): 293–325, at 321. Berker calls it the "argument from morally irrelevant factors."

14. "The Secret Joke of Kant's Soul," 69–70. Unlike philosophers, who take 'deontology' to refer to a moral theory focusing on duties and rights, in this same article Greene takes "deontology" to refer to a psychological natural kind (37–38). This and other differences in the meanings that philosophers and psychologists attribute to terms can generate confusion in raising and discussing questions in moral psychology. I use 'deontology,' 'non-consequentialism,' 'utilitarianism,' and 'consequentialism' as terms referring to moral theories in the philosophical sense.

of morally irrelevant factors."[15] Cognitive responses, especially those involving a longer response time, are not by-products of our evolutionary past. This seems to be behind the claim that we can privilege cognitive responses and associated consequentialist judgments over emotional responses and associated deontological judgments.

This argument is weak because it is based on a questionable neurobiological model of moral reasoning. It is based on what appears to be an artificial separation of cognitive and affective processing in this reasoning. The argument is also weak because deontological judgments are more than emotional responses to personal dilemmas. Deontology is more nuanced than the way it is presented in Greene's argument. Some philosophers labeled "deontologists" call themselves "nonconsequentialists." They do not deny the moral significance of consequences, but argue that consequences are not the only morally relevant consideration when we act. The rights of the people on the second track and the footbridge not to be harmed would be one nonconsequentialist consideration that would have to be factored into the moral calculus. Fairness requires giving equal weight to the claims of all those who would be harmed. In this regard, nonconsequentialists can evaluate these states of affairs from an impartial rather than a personal point of view. Thus, the claim that deontological,or nonconsequentialist, judgments are nothing more than emotional responses to "up-close-and-personal" cases is an oversimplification at best and false at worst. The strict correspondence between deontological judgments and emotional responses collapses, as does the correspondence between emotional responses and personal conflicts. As a result, the argument from the moral irrelevance of deontology fails.

The Neurobiological Basis of Moral Judgment

One of the brain regions critical to moral reasoning and decision making is the ventromedial prefrontal cortex (VMPFC). We associate this region with cognition, but it projects to other cortical and subcortical regions mediating emotions, which in turn project to the VMPFC. Interaction between these brain pathways mediates the cognitive and affective processes necessary to deliberate and make rational and moral decisions. Curiously, the VMPFC was not one of the brain regions mentioned in Greene et al.'s imaging experiments. Perhaps this is because it does not support a strictly cognitive subsystem. The fact that interacting distributed neural networks underlie moral reasoning casts doubt on the dual-process hypothesis. One of the limitations of functional neuroimaging such as fMRI or PET is that it cannot capture how these networks project to and from each other and interact to enable rational and moral capacities.

Damasio has noted from studies of patients that damage to and dysfunction in the VMPFC impairs both cognitive and affective processing. This is because of its projections to regions extending beyond the prefrontal area. His comments on acquired sociopathy are instructive:

> ... it is reasonable to suggest that the brain systems that support decision-making (general, social and moral), and those that support emotion *overlap* within the

---

15. *Ibid.*, 75.

territories of the prefrontal cortex, in which damage yields the syndrome of acquired sociopathy. In other words, the systems are made up of many other sites, elsewhere in the prefrontal cortex, and elsewhere in the brain, besides the mostly VMPFC first identified by the syndrome. For example, the system that supports decision-making includes the dorsolateral prefrontal regions as well as higher-order association cortices in the temporal and parietal regions, the early sensory cortices, and numerous regions of the motor system, cortically and subcortically (e.g., basal ganglia, cerebellum), as well as other cortical sites (e.g., insular cortex). However, the decision-making and emotional systems overlap and interact within the VMPFC.[16]

Given that the VMPFC is critical for decision making, and that cognitive and emotional systems are active within the VMPFC, decision making is both a cognitive and emotional process. Damasio and other clinical and cognitive neuroscientists have shown that emotional impairment in psychopaths and sociopaths often correlates with irrational choices. This indicates that interacting cognitive and affective processes ground our capacity to engage in practical and moral reasoning. Both processes are necessary to make considered moral judgments about conflict cases.[17]

Unlike spontaneous intuitive moral responses, considered moral judgments involve reflection and formulation of reasons for or against an action.[18] One limitation of Greene et al.'s experiments is that subjects were not asked to give reasons for their intuitive responses while they were in the fMRI scanner. These considered judgments would involve more than immediate or slightly delayed responses. They would require some degree of critical reflective thought, where the subjects would take longer to justify pushing the man. In the first study, the nine subjects were given a maximum of 46 seconds to read through the screens describing the cases and press the "appropriate" or "inappropriate" button.[19] This may explain why they did not give reasons for their responses, since this is not the sort of thing that most people can do in less than a minute.

Had they been asked to justify their responses and given adequate time to do so, it is likely that the VMPFC and other cortical and subcortical regions would have been activated to roughly the same degree in all the subjects. Given the overlap of cognitive and affective processing within the VMPFC, greater activity in this region would suggest that both types of processing would have been active when subjects gave their reasons for their judgments. There may have been some differences in the activity of the VMPFC between those who gave a deontological reason for not

---

16. "Neuroscience and Ethics: Intersections," 4.

17. See, for example, P. Appelbaum, "Ought We to Require Emotional Capacity as Part of Decisional Competence?" *Kennedy Institute of Ethics Journal* 8 (1998): 371–387.

18. Psychologists tend to define 'intuition' as a spontaneous "gut feeling" about an issue or situation, which is how Greene et al. seem to use the term. Like some philosophers, I take an intuition to be a type of judgment made without any explicit reasoning. See D. Meyers, *Intuition: Its Powers and Perils* (New Haven: Yale University Press, 2002), and Berker, "The Normative Insignificance of Neuroscience," 299, n. 11.

19. "An fMRI Investigation," 2108.

pushing the man from the footbridge and those who gave a consequentialist reason for pushing him. But the different reasons would not necessarily correspond to *significant* differences in activity throughout the brain, since a certain level of activity in distributed neural networks is required for a subject to reason at all. It may not have been feasible to keep subjects in the scanner for too long. Nevertheless, scanning brains during a relatively brief period that allows for a delayed intuitive response but not enough time for reasons to justify the response could reflect an experimental bias. This could skew the results in favor of the normative irrelevance of deontological moral judgments. This is one flaw in the design of the experiments.

A better designed and more recent study was conducted by a group of cognitive neuroscientists led by Carla Harenski. They used functional brain imaging to compare the neural correlates of moral deliberation with those of moral intuition by presenting subjects with moral pictures. This type of study could provide a clearer view of the differences between intuitive and considered judgments. The responses of the subjects suggested that activity in the VMPFC may contribute more to moral deliberation, while activity in the temporal–parietal junction may contribute more to moral intuition.[20] The study did not test whether or to what extent subcortical regions were active in the subjects. More importantly, the study did not reveal whether there were significant differences in VMPFC activity between subjects who were consequentialists and those who were nonconsequentialists as they engaged in moral deliberation.

Greene suspects that activity in the anterior cingulate cortex (ACC) is evidence of conflict between cognitive and emotional subsystems in the brain when persons are faced with a moral dilemma.[21] Presumably, the ACC is a neutral arbiter in this conflict, part of neither the cognitive nor the emotional subsystem. The dorsal part of the ACC plays a critical role in mediating conflict resolution. It is also critical for monitoring and selecting action plans. More significant for the issue at hand, the ventral part of the ACC plays a role in mediating the capacity for empathy. This mental state has both cognitive and affective components. The cognitive component consists in understanding others' feelings and seeing things from their perspective. The affective component consists in an observer's emotional response to the emotional state of another person.[22] Sympathy is perhaps the most common type of this affective state. It involves both feeling an emotional response to someone else's distress or suffering and a desire to alleviate that suffering. Because empathy involves both cognitive and emotional aspects, activation of the ACC would be evidence that there are both cognitive and emotional processes underlying deliberation and justification of a particular action in moral conflict. Different immediate intuitive responses ("gut reactions") to these conflicts might suggest a separation of cognition and emotion. But in fact both of these processes are at work in giving reasons to justify these responses. Activation of the ACC would not be evidence of a conflict

20. "A Functional Imaging Investigation of Moral Deliberation and Moral Intuition," *NeuroImage* 49 (2010): 2707–2716.
21. "Neural Bases," 395.
22. See the chapters in J. Decety and W. Ickes, eds., *The Social Neuroscience of Empathy* (Cambridge, MA: MIT Press, 2009).

between warring cognitive and emotional subsystems separated by a neutral arbiter acting as a tie-breaker. Rather, the activation would be evidence that the subjects' perception of conflict was enabled by the engagement of the empathy-mediating capacity of the ACC.

Against the claim that the delay in the subjects' response was due to the cognitive subsystem overriding the emotional subsystem, it is more plausible to suppose that the delay was an ACC-mediated empathic response. This enabled them to recognize a reason against harming the man on the footbridge by pushing him to his death. Empathy enables us to recognize that others have rights, interests, and needs. This recognition does not apply only to more salient personal cases but to more distant impersonal cases as well. A psychopath would likely have the same immediate and delayed responses to the footbridge dilemma—push the man. This could be accounted for by an impaired capacity for empathy and fear, which forms an inhibitory mechanism against performing actions that harm others. These responses could not be explained by appeal to a purely cognitive subsystem. They could be explained by the psychopath's pattern of behavior over time, combined with brain imaging showing dysfunction in the ACC and its projections to the amygdala and certain areas of the prefrontal cortex. Singer's utilitarian reason for pushing the man from the footbridge would involve an empathic aspect, since the claim that it is a greater tragedy if five die than if one dies acknowledges that it is bad for the one person to die. Psychopaths and other individuals deficient in the capacity for empathy probably would not be sensitive to this consideration.

Subjects deficient in this capacity would probably not be capable of providing a plausible reason for their decision, if indeed they could provide *any* reason for it. Activation of the ACC indicates that a subject is thinking about a moral conflict and engages both cognitive and emotional processing in doing this. It is not evidence of distinct warring cognitive and emotional subsystems. This brain region may be activated in our intuitive response to a moral conflict. But it would also be activated when we give reasons for why an action that would resolve the conflict is permissible or impermissible.

The thalamic-amygdala circuit is a primitive hard-wired emotional system in the brain that may function independently of cognition. The sensory thalamus can bypass the sensory cortex in sending information about stimuli directly to the amygdala. This allows for a quick response to threats and is thus critical to our survival.[23] Any conscious cognitive delay could interfere with this adaptive response, which is grounded in our capacity to react to fear-inducing stimuli. Our protective response to kin may be another hard-wired behavior that operates outside of conscious reasoning. Immediate gut reactions to moral dilemmas may be a vestige of these primitive emotional responses. The cognitive processes associated with reasoning emerge at a higher level and enable us to select between different courses of action when we are not under an immediate threat. So, it may be correct to say that there are two systems operating at lower and higher levels in the brain. However, this does not mean that only cognitive processes operate in the widely distributed

---

23. As explained by J. LeDoux in *The Emotional Brain* (New York: Simon and Schuster, 1996), 164.

neural networks that enable our considered judgments about moral dilemmas. These judgments are mediated not by the thalamic-amygdala circuit but by more complex circuits involving the amygdala, VMPFC, ACC, and other cortical and subcortical regions. The relevant emotions include not just the more primitive fear but also the more evolved social emotions of compassion, remorse, regret, and empathy.

Greene et al. leave out too many neurobiological and psychological details in their account of moral judgment. Filling in the necessary details yields a model of moral reasoning that raises questions about the dual-process hypothesis and the idea of warring subsystems in the brain. The discussion of the role of the VMPFC, ACC, and related brain structures in moral reasoning shows the artificiality of any rigid separation of cognition and emotion in this reasoning. Greene et al. seem to think that the normative task of using principles to justify responses to Trolley-like cases can be reduced to the descriptive task of listing the neurobiological mechanisms that underlie our responses to these sorts of cases. Yet their account of these processes is not accurate. More precisely, it may accurately describe brain activity corresponding to our immediate or short-term reactions to these cases. But it does not accurately describe the more temporally extended process involved in our considered moral judgments about them.

More than 30 years ago, philosopher Jonathan Glover presented the hypothetical case of a trapped coal miner to illustrate the conflict in decision making between known and statistical lives.[24] Intuitively, some would say that all necessary resources should be used to save the miner. Others would say that we should limit the amount of resources used for this purpose so that there will be enough resources for safety programs that would save the lives of other miners in the future. An immediate emotional response to a known life threatened by death may explain the bias in favor of the trapped miner over the lives of future miners. This reflects the limitations of an intuitive moral judgment about this case. A considered moral judgment would indicate that using unlimited resources to rescue the miner could not be justified and that there should be limits on the use of these resources. The lives of unknown future miners are as valuable as the life of a known miner. Temporal distance does not give less weight to people's moral claims. These claims need to be evaluated not just collectively but individually. Each future miner's claim not to be a victim of an accident has as much weight as the present miner's claim. This gives the argument for limiting the use of present resources as much deontological as consequentialist force. In the absence of clear empirical support for a strict cognitive–emotional distinction, there is no basis for the claim that deontological judgments have no normative force in these cases.

Interestingly, Greene and coauthors state: "Like David Hume... we suspect that all action, whether driven by 'cognitive' judgment or not, must have some affective basis."[25] They say this in light of their experiments showing a correlation between activity in the posterior cingulate, which is associated with emotion, and utilitarian

---

24. Glover discusses this hypothetical case in *Causing Death and Saving Lives* (New York: Penguin, 1977), 210–213.
25. "Neural Bases," 397.

responses to dilemmas like the Footbridge Case. They appear to question their dual-process hypothesis and the strict separation of cognition and emotion in moral judgment. Indeed, they should question it and acknowledge that reasoning and decision making have cognitive and affective aspects. They should jettison this hypothesis because it gives a misleading picture of the neural and psychological underpinning of moral judgment.

It is puzzling that Greene et al. invoke Hume to motivate their question about the role of affect in choice and action. Hume claims that "reason is, and ought only to be, the slave of the passions, and can never pretend to any other office than to serve and obey them."[26] He is not saying that moral judgments are driven only partly by reason and primarily by the passions, but that moral judgments are driven entirely by the passions. Any internal conflict is not between passion and reason but between different passions. This subverts rather than affirms the dual-process hypothesis, since it gives no weight to cognition in moral judgments. In contrast, for Kant morality cannot be based even partly on desires or emotions, but on reason alone. We impose the moral law on ourselves and act in accordance with it in virtue of our capacity for reason.[27] The distinction between reason and emotion seems to leave us at an impasse regarding the neural and psychological grounding of our moral judgments.

Exploring the implications of Trolley-like cases, Singer reasons thus:

> In the light of the best scientific understanding of ethics, we face a choice. We can take the view that our moral intuitions and judgments are and always will be emotionally based intuitive responses, and reason can do no more than build the best possible case for a decision already made on nonrational grounds. That approach leads to a form of moral skepticism… Alternatively, we might attempt the ambitious task of separating those moral judgments that we owe to our evolutionary and cultural history from those that have a rational basis… it is the only way to avoid moral skepticism.[28]

As we have seen, both Singer and Greene argue that we can defend the claim that moral judgments have a rational basis, provided that these judgments are consequentialist and not deontological. This is not a very helpful way of avoiding moral skepticism. It reinforces the spurious distinction between reason and emotion drawn throughout much of the history of philosophy. The choice between reason or emotion as the basis of our moral judgments is misleading because they are interdependent faculties. The best scientific understanding of the neural underpinning of our moral judgments shows that it is mistaken to think that we can base these judgments on reason alone or emotion alone.

Thanks largely to the work of Damasio and other cognitive and clinical neuroscientists, the Platonic, Cartesian, Humean, and Kantian dichotomies of reason versus emotion are part of an outdated model of the mind. The dual-process

---

26. *A Treatise of Human Nature*, 2.3.3.
27. *Groundwork of the Metaphysics of Morals*, trans. and ed. M. Gregor (New York: Cambridge University Press, 1998).
28. "Ethics and Intuitions," 351.

hypothesis is symptomatic of a discredited model that attempts to locate the neural basis of mental capacities such as moral judgment in distinct brain regions. Moral reasoning and other complex thought and behavioral processes are not localized in specific regions but distributed across broad areas of the brain. This distribution mediates the overlapping cognitive and emotional processing that enables moral reasoning. The best way to avoid moral skepticism is to reject the strict cognitive–affective distinction and accept the overlapping hypothesis instead. It is unclear whether pursuing the line of thought suggested by Greene et al. in their comment about Hume would lead them to modify or reject the dual-process hypothesis, the distinctions between emotional–cognitive, deontological–consequentialist, and personal–impersonal responses, and the argument from the normative irrelevance of deontology. But the research on the neural bases of practical and moral reasoning suggests that this is the right direction in which to go.

In a study conducted by neuroscientist Michael Koenigs and colleagues, six subjects with damage to the VMPFC were presented with a version of the Footbridge Case and asked if they would push the man from the bridge to stop the trolley.[29] These subjects were compared with a second group of twelve subjects with brain damage not involving the VMPFC or other regions associated with social emotions (amygdala, insula, and right somatosensory cortex), and a third group of twelve subjects with no brain damage. While a slight minority of the second group and a slight majority of the third group favored what Koenigs et al. called the "utilitarian option" of pushing the man, a clear majority of the first group favored this option. They were more likely to make this choice because damage to the VMPFC impaired their capacity for social emotions, which in turn impaired their capacity for moral reasoning. The findings of the study suggest that, for a select set of moral dilemmas, the VMPFC is critical for normal judgments of right and wrong. They also suggest a critical role for social emotions in the capacity to make these judgments.

The results of this study do not confirm the dual-process hypothesis of warring cognitive and emotional subsystems. If it did, then it might suggest that brain damage enables the cognitive subsystem to override the emotional subsystem! Equally important, the results do not support the idea that utilitarian judgments in moral dilemmas are based entirely on cognition and do not involve any affective component. The prefrontal damage in these subjects likely disrupted the projections between and among the VMPFC, ACC, and amygdala. By impairing their capacity for social emotions like empathy and compassion, the damage likely would have impaired the emotional processing necessary for them to justify their response. While their gut reaction may have favored the utilitarian option, they may have been too cognitively and affectively impaired to give a reason why it was a morally preferable option. If they could give a reason, then it probably would have been based on maximizing the number of lives saved rather than on any consideration regarding the claims of the five outweighing the claim of the one not to be harmed. Because of their impairment, it is unlikely that they would have given Singer's utilitarian justification that the death of the one person on the bridge is a lesser tragedy than the death of the five

---

29. "Damage to the Prefrontal Cortex Increases Utilitarian Moral Judgments," *Nature* 446 (2007): 908–911.

people on the track. We would have to qualify the claim that they selected the "utilitarian" option. An intuition or gut reaction based solely on the number of people involved in a moral dilemma is not enough to defend the permissibility of pushing the man off the footbridge and onto the track. It requires a justification based on a reason or reasons why the death of five is worse than the death of one.

There are important differences between the study conducted by Koenigs' group and the experiments conducted by Greene's group.[30] The first involved brain-damaged patients; the second did not. Also, Greene's group asked their subjects if it would be appropriate to push the man off the footbridge; Koenigs' group asked their subjects if they would push him. We should be careful in drawing any normative conclusions from a study involving only six brain-damaged patients responding to a specific question and without observing their behavior over time. Nevertheless, the results of this study seem to confirm Damasio's findings that the VMPFC mediates both cognitive and affective processing. People with damage to this region are impaired in their capacity for practical and moral reasoning. In fact, Damasio was one of the co-investigators in the Koenigs study. Imaging studies of psychopaths have revealed structural and functional abnormalities in the amygdala and prefrontal cortex. These correlate not only with impairment in moral sensitivity but also impairment in the ability to make rational decisions. Something more than cognition is at work in making and justifying moral judgments based on a consequentialist principle. By the same token, something more than emotion is at work in making and justifying moral judgments based on a nonconsequentialist principle.

Recall Singer's claim that there is no morally significant difference between the Trolley and Footbridge Cases. In contrast, philosopher Frances Kamm argues that, while it would be permissible for the bystander to redirect the trolley, it would not be permissible for him to push the man from the footbridge.[31] One might think that Kamm's judgment about the second case confirms the claims of Haidt and Greene that the deontological constraint against pushing the man is a function of the emotional subsystem driving the intuition that it is wrong to harm a person in an up-close-and-personal way. After all, Kamm is a nonconsequentialist who believes that bringing about the best outcome is not the only morally relevant factor in conflict cases. The fact that Kamm is a nonconsequentialist does explain her judgment in the Footbridge Case. But the intricate causal explanation she offers for the impermissibility of pushing the man indicates that her justification is much more than the product of an emotional subsystem in her brain.

She invokes the principle of permissible harm (PPH) to argue that it is permissible to redirect the trolley in the original case: "The basic idea of the PPH is that an

---

30. J. Moll and R. Oliveira-Souza question the notion that the Koenigs study supports Greene et al.'s dual-process hypothesis in "Moral Judgments, Emotions, and the Utilitarian Brain," *Trends in Cognitive Sciences* 11 (2007): 319–321. Greene replies to Moll and Oliveira-Souza in "Why Are VMPFC Patients More Utilitarian? A Dual-Process Theory of Moral Judgment Explains," *Trends in Cognitive Sciences* 11 (2007): 322–333.

31. *Intricate Ethics: Rights, Responsibilities, and Permissible Harm.* (Oxford: Oxford University Press, 2007), 23–32, 138–146, and "Neuroscience and Moral Reasoning: A Note on Recent Research," *Philosophy & Public Affairs* 37 (2009): 330–345.

act is permissible if (i) a greater good, or (ii) a means that has the greater good as its noncausal flip side, causes a lesser evil."[32] Further, "when harm is a side effect of the achievement of a greater good, we may permissibly do what harms."[33] Kamm combines PPH with what she calls the doctrine of triple effect (DTE), which distinguishes between doing something *because* an effect will occur and doing it *in order* to bring about the effect. Appealing to PPH and DTE, Kamm says that "the trolley moving away, which kills the one person, is a means to saving the five, and this greater good is its noncausal flip side."[34] She also argues that it would be permissible to redirect the trolley in Thomson's Loop Case. Kamm reasons thus: "The judgment… shows that a rational agent can pursue a goal (saving the five) that he knows is achievable only by his causing a certain event, and do so without intending to cause that event. That is—contrary to what is commonly believed—a rational agent can continue to intend something without intending the means to it"[35] Redirecting the trolley in the Loop Case is permissible because the agent who redirects it does not intend that the innocent bystander be hit and killed.

Kamm also considers the Lazy Susan Case. Here the five people toward whom the trolley is headed are seated on a large swivel table. One person is seated opposite the five on the Lazy Susan. If we turn the table to save the five, then the one person will be moved into the path of the trolley and killed. Kamm argues that it would be permissible to turn the table because "means that have the greater good as an aspect may cause, or lead to the cause, of the lesser evil."[36] She then explains why it is impermissible to push the man in the Footbridge Case: "Unlike what is true in the Lazy Susan Case… the one person being hit (which leads to his death) is causally necessary for producing the greater good; it is not the effect of the greater good, or of means that have a non-causal relation to the greater good (as when the greater good is a flip side or aspect of the means)."[37] It is impermissible to treat a person as a causally necessary means and thereby kill him to save other people. Significantly, the fact that the Footbridge Case is an up-close-and-personal case is not decisive in the justification of the constraint against pushing the man. Instead, the justification relies on a causal analysis of harm.

Equally significant is Kamm's defense of the permissibility of turning the table in the Lazy Susan Case. This can be described as a personal dilemma for the agent, given the emotional salience of the one person at the other end of the table. Kamm says that turning the Lazy Susan toward the one person is "something up close and personal."[38] One might expect Kamm to defend a deontological constraint against turning the table because it will harm the one. Yet she argues that turning it is

---

32. *Intricate Ethics*, 24.
33. *Ibid.*, 24.
34. *Ibid.*, 25.
35. *Ibid.*, 25.
36. *Ibid.*, 142.
37. *Ibid.*, 143.
38. "Neuroscience and Moral Reasoning," 334. In a note alluding to one of the principal themes of this chapter, Kamm says: "I omit discussion here of the large issue of whether there is a sensible distinction between cognition and emotion," 332, n. 7.

permissible. Again, the up-close-and-personal nature of this case is not decisive in the justification of turning the table. What is decisive is the causal role of the agent in bringing about the outcome and the soundness of the reasons one gives in explaining the moral significance of this role. This is a nonconsequentialist justification that is not motivated by the idea of saving the greater number. Instead, it is motivated by considering how the one person is used as a causal or noncausal means in the pathway resulting in his death and saving the five. One may or may not agree with Kamm's reasons in her justification of different actions in these cases. But it seems implausible that the appeal to PPH and DTE is nothing more than a post hoc rationalization of an intuitive response generated by morally irrelevant emotions. Her reasoning is much more than an example of the emotional dog wagging its rational tail.

A utilitarian like Singer would say that we should turn the Lazy Suzan because the death of the five is worse than the death of the one. A nonconsequentialist like Kamm would defend the same action, but with a different justification based on causation and independent of any emotional salience of the situation. Since both defend the action with equally plausible justifications, there is no obvious reason to privilege the utilitarian reason over the nonconsequentialist one. This confounds the simple distinction between utilitarian and nonconsequentialist responses and their correspondence with impersonal and personal dilemmas. According to the dual-process hypothesis, different brain regions would be activated depending on whether one says that turning the table is permissible or impermissible. Yet if both the utilitarian and the nonconsequentialist say that turning the table is permissible, then presumably there would be no significant difference in brain activity between the two when they make this judgment. There would not likely be any significant difference in brain activity when they gave their distinct justifications for their responses either. Cortical and subcortical regions mediating overlapping cognitive and affective processes would be activated in order for them to give these justifications. This further discredits the dual-process hypothesis. There *would* be significant differences in brain activity between someone like Kamm or Singer and the patients with VMPFC damage in Koenigs' study. But while this study sheds light on the brain regions enabling moral reasoning, it would not indicate any significant difference in normal brain function between two people defending the same action for distinct reasons.

The delay in the response time of the subjects who said that it would be permissible to push the man from the footbridge was described as a consequentialist response driven by the cognitive subsystem. But surely Kamm's nonconsequentialist defense of why it would be impermissible to push the man involves a very long response time. Response time alone, especially when one is giving reasons for a particular judgment, does not favor one moral principle or theory over another. Besides, the fact that the subjects in the experiment had only 46 seconds to respond to the moral dilemmas should make us question the idea of a "delayed" response. If what Greene et al. and Singer say is supposed to be taken as a general thesis about moral judgment, then Kamm's justifications for different actions in the Footbridge and Lazy Susan cases are exceptions that challenge it.

I have claimed that Greene et al. do not provide an accurate account of the neurobiological underpinning of our moral judgments. I will make an additional claim: If brain activity is relevantly similar between two people when they give distinct reasons to justify the same action, then this suggests that moral justification is grounded in but involves more than neural processes. Which reason or set of reasons one gives to justify an action is not solely a function of what is going on in one's brain. They are also a function of the fact that we are human agents interacting in a social environment, engaged in constructing and defending principles to guide behavior within that environment. Disagreement about which principles we should adopt and how we employ them to argue that an action is permissible or impermissible is a reflection of people's different interests and values. These are at least partly influenced by social and cultural factors. Earlier, I said that our protective response to kin may be a hard-wired feature of our brains. Yet in societies where food has been scarce, some families have practised infanticide to promote their survival. This involves a conscious decision to resolve a moral conflict that is influenced by factors external to the brain. It also involves a utilitarian justification for killing people in an up-close-and-personal way. Unlike the unconscious response that enables us to avoid immediate threats to our survival, infanticide and its moral justification are not hard-wired in the brain. The capacity to reason depends on normal brain function. But the different nonconsequentialist and utilitarian justifications for turning the table in the Lazy Susan Case suggest that the reasons one gives to justify an action are more than just a function of processes in the brain.

Methodological Limitations

There are a number of limitations in the design of Greene et al.'s experiments that further question any general conclusions we can draw from them about the neural basis of moral reasoning. The responses of the subjects were to moral emergencies, where one had to make a decision about the right action in a very short period of time. They would have allowed just enough time for the cognitive subsystem to override the emotional subsystem in responding that it was permissible to push the man from the footbridge. But we are rarely confronted with these cases in real life. Most of the important moral decisions we have to make are not momentary. They require deliberation and reflection on the reasons for and against acting in one way rather than another. Decisions that have to be made quickly are not of the type for which one would expect a moral justification. Nevertheless, the immediate response one gives to these cases may very well be a reflection of a disposition to act in a certain way, a disposition developed through cultivation and habituation over a considerable period of time. This is consistent with the discussion of the role of the history of the values and dispositions behind our choices in Chapter 2. Given the influence of the mind on the brain, these values and dispositions could influence the activation of the relevant brain regions when we give intuitive and deliberative responses to conflict cases.

It is noteworthy that the data from Greene et al.'s fMRI experiments were from subjects responding to hypothetical scenarios. One would have to assess brain activity when subjects were responding to actual scenarios to get a clear sense of which brain regions were behind their moral judgments. Although "Trolley" and "Footbridge" were presented as moral dilemmas, the subjects responded to them in the cognitively and affectively "cool" setting of the scanner. Responses to dilemmas in real-life settings would likely be different. Philosopher Kwame Anthony Appiah articulates the problem:

> It is an interesting and unobvious assumption, which hasn't had the attention it deserves, that our responses to imaginary scenarios mirror our responses to real ones. Joshua Greene's account of these cases presupposes, in other words, that our intuition about what to do in the imaginary case is explained by the activation of the very mechanisms that would lead us to act in a real one. Without this assumption, his explanation of why we do fails. When I think about the footbridge scenario there is, in fact, no 300-pound man around and no one to save. There is no emergency. I'm making a guess about how I'd respond in those circumstances.[39]

Greene would say that imagining oneself to be in this situation would trigger the same or similar activity in the brain and the same cognitive and emotional processes as if it were an actual case. But imagination is not a good predictor of how one would act.[40] The fMRI scanner cannot replicate the actual world. So, intuitive responses to hypothetical moral dilemmas while in the scanner, and the imaging data correlating with these responses, may be of limited value in predicting people's considered judgments about actual moral dilemmas. This critique is not unique to Greene but applies generally to the literature on the Trolley Problem.

In many moral emergencies, the choices we make are often not binary choices. They do not require us to make choices such as "push" or "don't push" but involve more than two options. For example, the parents of a child diagnosed with an aggressive form of leukemia would have to choose within days among chemotherapy alone, radiation alone, combined chemotherapy and radiation, a bone-narrow transplant, or no treatment for the child. Even binary choices can be influenced by multiple factors. Consider the emergency room physician who has to decide which of two hemorrhaging patients should go first to a hospital's only available surgical suite. The decision is based not only on the extent of the bleeding but also on whether the patients have other conditions that would affect the probability of survival. The upshot is that any normative conclusions about human choices and actions that we could derive from neuroscientific data about hypothetical cases such as Trolley and Footbridge would be limited.

Appiah suggests that there may be a reason for the instinctive reluctance to push strangers over bridges: "Suppose that, in fact, one ought to push the heavy stranger off the footbridge. Even so, there might be reasons for wanting to be the kind of person who couldn't do it. Holding onto revulsion against killing people 'up close and personal' is one way to make sure we won't easily be tempted to kill people when it suits our interests."[41] This may be one reason for not wanting to leave our evolutionary past behind us. The emotional salience of up-close-and-personal cases

---

39. *Experiments in Ethics* (Cambridge, MA: Harvard University Press, 2008), 100.

40. Appiah points out problems in drawing moral conclusions about actual cases from hypothetical cases, as does Berker in "The Normative Insignificance of Neuroscience," 306, n. 27.

41. *Experiments in Ethics*, 98.

might be morally relevant after all. Even if one rejects this view, it is doubtful that such a response would be entirely emotional. The revulsion against killing people and the recognition of their right not to be harmed depends in part on the capacity for empathy, which has both cognitive and affective aspects.

Still another problem with Greene et al.'s experiments involves the role of framing, or order, effects. How a problem is described can influence how one responds to it. The order in which moral options are presented to us can influence which option we choose.[42] Again, Appiah: "In the bystander-at-the-switch version of the trolley problem, we are always told first about the five people whose lives are imperiled; we learn about the one person on the side track as a subsequent complication. Having resolved to do whatever you can to stop the train from its destructive course—and having learned about the switch, and the side track—you have already formed a strong resolve: you look to be confirmed in your decision (as confirmation bias might suggest) and view countervailing considerations with a grain of skepticism."[43] Reframing the order in which the options are presented, or reframing the question, could result in a different response from at least some of the subjects in the experiments.

Variations on the Footbridge Case could further complicate the subjects' responses. In a recent article, Greene et al. cite evidence suggesting that what explains people's moral judgments about Footbridge-like cases is whether the agent intentionally harms the man through what they call "personal force."[44] This might provide a constraint against pushing the man. But suppose that he is leaning over the bridge railing and will fall onto the track if the bystander does not pull him back. The bystander is larger and stronger than the man and physically capable of saving him. Yet he knows that letting him fall onto the track will stop the trolley and prevent the death of the five. By refusing to perform an act he is physically capable of performing, the bystander intentionally can harm the man without using any personal force. Would the subjects say that it was permissible for the bystander to let the man fall from the bridge? Is there a morally significant difference between pushing the man and letting him fall onto the track? It is not clear that there would be a difference between doing and allowing if the agent has cognitive control of the sequence of events leading to the same outcome. If there is no difference, then allowing the man to fall from the bridge seems as impermissible (or permissible) as pushing him over it. One important consideration would be the risk of the bystander falling onto the track in trying to pull back the man. This might incline some subjects to judge that it would be permissible to allow the man to fall. These variations on the original example suggest that physical force by the agent might not be the decisive moral factor.

Another factor is whether a greater number of people in the trolley's path would change people's responses. Not everyone is a strict consequentialist or

---

42. See A. Tversky and D. Kahneman, "The Framing of Decisions and the Psychology of Choice," *Science* 211 (1981): 453–458.

43. *Experiments in Ethics*, 92.

44. "Pushing Moral Buttons: The Interaction between Personal Force and Intention in Moral Judgment," *Cognition* 11 (2009): 364–371, at 364.

nonconsequentialist. While many nonconsequentialists would maintain that pushing the man would be impermissible no matter how many lives were at stake,
some who are not committed to any particular moral theory might say that pushing
the man would be permissible if 25 people were on the track. Others might say that,
while pushing the man onto the track would not be permissible, allowing him to fall
onto it would be, given the number of lives involved. Against this view, one could
argue that there is no single individual who suffers the loss of 25 people. Losses do
not sum over people, and therefore the death of 25 is no worse than the death of 1.[45]
Yet many would insist that the claims of 25 individuals not to be killed are significant
enough to outweigh the claim of a single individual not to be killed. A smaller
number on the track might not be enough to justify allowing the man to fall, but a
larger number might be.

The main limitation of Greene et al.'s experiments is something I mentioned
in my earlier discussion of subjects' response times to the Footbridge Case. Any
experiment designed to ascertain the neurobiological basis of moral reasoning
should allow enough time for people to give reasons to justify their moral judgments
of cases. A sound empirical study of how people reason morally would consist of
more than simply asking subjects questions about the permissibility or impermissibility of an action and recording their intuitive responses. It would also consist of
putting subjects through a series of mental tasks involving different actual and hypothetical scenarios, testing their considered judgments and their justification of these
judgments. Comparing the shorter and longer response times between immediate
intuitive responses and deliberative justifications would be a more empirically
robust experiment yielding more illuminating results. Failure to do this could confirm rather than exclude bias in the design of the experiment and interpretation of
the results. I have noted the limitations of neuroimaging in detecting activity
throughout the brain and how different regions project to and from each other.
Even if imaging could detect these projections, a longer period of scanning subjects' brains would not likely reveal a significant difference in brain activity between
one person giving a nonconsequentialist justification for an action and another
person giving a utilitarian justification for the same action. This is because all practical and moral reasoning engages cognitive and affective processing mediated by
the same cortical and subcortical brain regions.

Still, the normative task of justifying actions consists of more than empirical
facts about the brain and people's opinions. Commenting on the method of Greene
et al.'s experiments, philosopher Selim Berker asserts: "It is simply a mistake to think
that by merely surveying people's opinions about the moral permissibility of certain
actions, we can empirically study what sorts of factors elicit characteristically

---

45. This question is a variant of the more general question of the moral relevance of
the number of lives saved when only one of two groups of different size can be saved.
J. Taurek raised this question in "Should the Numbers Count?" *Philosophy & Public
Affairs* 6 (1977): 293–316. There has been a large literature on this topic since Taurek's
seminal article, much of it consisting of articles published in *Philosophy & Public
Affairs*. See Kamm's discussion, "Aggregation and Two Moral Methods," in *Intricate
Ethics*, 48–77.

deontological judgments. All these studies tell us is that these people make certain moral judgments about certain scenarios, and certain other moral judgments about other scenarios; which of these judgments count as characteristically deontological is not something we can just read off from the empirical results."[46] Whether one gives consequentialist or nonconsequentialist reasons for or against an action is not determined solely by empirical facts about the brain. The reasons are influenced by these facts together with psychological, social, and cultural factors constituting norms beyond the brain.

Psychiatrist and philosopher Georg Northoff cites two major problems with identifying moral judgments with activity in specific brain regions:

> First, one confuses the necessary conditions, that is, the neural mechanisms, and what they condition, that is, the moral judgment as the result... Second, one also confuses descriptive and normative components of moral judgments. The neural observations describe facts, the descriptive component, whereas the moral judgment also implicates a normative component that goes beyond the descriptive component by referring to normative dimensions. If one now infers what kind of brain state is morally correct from the empirical findings about moral judgment, one confuses descriptive and normative components and thus facts and norms.[47]

Conclusion

The claim that nonconsequentialist judgments align with emotional responses to personal conflicts, and that consequentialist judgments align with cognitive responses to impersonal conflicts, rests on an oversimplified view of moral reasoning. In some cases, we can justify the impermissibility of killing one to save others without appealing to the emotional salience of the people involved. In other cases, we can justify the permissibility of a similar action with the same outcome in spite of emotional salience. Nonconsequentialist judgments about actions can be motivated by considerations of impartiality, where equal weight is given to the claim of each person not to be harmed. There may be cases where a deontologist and consequentialist will agree that the same action should be performed, though their justifications for it will depend on distinct reasons. This undermines the argument that deontological judgments are morally irrelevant and that we should privilege consequentialist judgments in reasoning about moral conflicts.

The dual-process hypothesis behind Greene et al.'s argument from morally irrelevant factors is questionable because it rests on a questionable view of the neurobiological underpinning of moral reasoning. This view is more reflective of the virtual lab of thought experiments than the actual lab of well-designed empirical studies of the brain–behavior relation and human experience. Our considered moral judgments are more than just post hoc rationalizations of intuitive responses

---

46. "The Normative Insignificance of Neuroscience," 323, n. 73.
47. "What Is Neuroethics? Empirical and Theoretical Neuroethics," *Current Opinion in Psychiatry* 22 (2009): 565–569, at 567.

driven by separate and warring cognitive and emotional subsystems located in distinct regions of the brain. Moral justification consists in a temporally extended process of reasoning grounded in interacting cognitive and affective processing mediated by interacting systems in the brain.

Normative questions of how we should act are not reducible to and cannot be explained away by empirical facts about how our actions correlate with neural processes. To insist otherwise is to conflate normative and descriptive ethics. Neuroscientific accounts of moral reasoning are based primarily on functional neuroimaging. Yet this technology is limited because it cannot detect activity over the entire brain or in pathways between different regions of the brain that project to and from each other. Neuroimaging cannot establish a causal connection between brain states or the mental states associated with the reasons we give to justify actions. Singer points out that "Greene's data alone cannot prove any normative view of right and wrong. Normative argument is needed…"[48] Even if Greene's model of the neurobiological underpinning of moral reasoning were accurate, we would still be left with the normative task of justifying our judgments of how we should act in particular cases. This does not mean that neuroscience has no normative significance. Neuroscience tells us *that* the brain enables moral reasoning; but it does not tell us *why* a person gives a particular reason to justify a particular action. Nor can neuroscience tell us what the right action is in any given situation. Brain function alone does not determine that a person will give a consequentialist or nonconsequentialist reason for or against an action. We should recognize the limits of neuroscience in explaining moral behavior and be cautious in trying to derive any normative conclusions from empirical facts about the brain.

---

48. "Ethics and Intuitions," 347. Neuroscientists L. Young and M. Koenigs state: "The brain may thus constrain the moral mind, but how we decide to deal with such constraints may be best determined in philosophical debate." "Investigating Emotion in Moral Cognition: A Review of Evidence from Functional Neuroimaging and Neuropsychology," *British Medical Bulletin* 84 (2007): 69–79, at 79.

5

Cognitive Enhancement

Many prescription psychotropic drugs have off-label uses for which they were not originally designed. These uses were not part of the approval of the drugs and are not included in their labeling. Some drugs designed to treat neuropsychiatric disorders may enhance normal cognitive functions. Methylphenidate (Ritalin) is prescribed for children and adults with attention-deficit/hyperactivity disorder (ADHD) to enable them to focus attention and carry out cognitive tasks. This drug has also been used by people who do not have this disorder to increase their concentration and improve performance on exams or in their work. Modafinil (Provigil) has been prescribed for narcolepsy, sleep apnea, and shift-work sleep disorder. It has also been used to promote alertness in people with normal sleep–wake cycles. The beta-adrenergic receptor antagonist, or beta-blocker, propranolol (Inderal) has been prescribed as an antihypertensive and anti-arrhythmic drug. It is now taken by some people to prevent or attenuate the anxiety associated with public speaking and musical performance. Other drugs are being developed to improve the storage and retrieval of long-term memory in people without any memory impairment.

"Enhancement" is usually defined as any intervention "designed to improve human form or functioning beyond what is necessary to sustain or restore good health."[1] "Therapy" can be defined as any intervention that sustains or restores good health. For our purposes, the type of health in question is mental health, specifically the cognitive functions of attention, alertness, and memory. In some conditions, the boundary between therapy and enhancement is not always precise. There may be a continuum from treating dysfunction to enhancing function. Philosopher and bioethicist John Harris claims that "treatments or preventive measures which protect humans from things to which they are normally

---

1. E. Juengst, "What Does Enhancement Mean?" in E. Parens, ed., *Enhancing Human Traits: Ethical and Social Implications* (Washington, DC: Georgetown University Press, 1998), 29–47, at 29.

vulnerable, or which prevent harm... are necessarily also enhancements."[2] Immunizations and reading glasses are just two examples. In psychiatry, there is a clear-cut distinction between normal mental function and severe disorders such as schizophrenia. But it is not always clear where mild disorders such as dysthymia, acute anxiety, or seasonal affective disorder fall on the neuropsychiatric spectrum. This has ethical implications for physicians considering whether to prescribe psychotropic drugs for individuals who want to improve their cognitive functions and whether this is consistent with their professional duties of beneficence and nonmaleficence. It raises questions about the ratio of benefits to risks in using these drugs, how much risk is acceptable, and who should take responsibility for any harmful consequences.

In this chapter, I discuss the main ethical issues surrounding the most commonly used cognition-enhancing drugs. I cite empirical evidence showing that the extent to which one can benefit from enhancement depends on one's baseline capacity for working memory. The data provide evidence that the effects of cognition-enhancing drugs are more limited than what many have claimed. There may be trade-offs between different cognitive functions, where enhancing one function may impair another. I also consider the risks of chronic use of these drugs. Differences in benefit among people inform the discussion of whether enhancement will exacerbate social inequality or level the social playing field. Although pharmacological interventions to reduce anxiety and depression involve not only cognition but also emotion, I will not discuss the idea of enhancing mood. This is based on recent meta-analyses showing substantial benefit of antidepressants over a placebo for those with severe depression, but minimal or no benefit for those with mild or moderate depressive symptoms.[3] There is disagreement among psychiatrists and psychologists about the benefit of antidepressants for those with mild to moderate depression. But the meta-analyses cast doubt on claims that those who do not have mood disorders can elevate their mood by taking a selective serotonin reuptake inhibitor (SSRI). Any enhancement of mood is probably due not to any biochemical properties of these drugs but a placebo response to them.

In addition, I argue that trying to enhance long-term memory could result in more burdens than benefits, and I describe a case of hyperthymestic syndrome to illustrate this point. Preventing the formation of or erasing memories that are critical to our emotions of shame, regret, and remorse might be morally objectionable because of their role in inhibiting harmful behavior. Yet preventing or erasing a disturbing memory may be permissible in some cases. I also argue that enhancement would not necessarily make us lose our authenticity or become alienated from our true selves. Overall, I defend a position that strikes a balance between respect for individual autonomy and prevention of harm. Cognitive enhancement should be

---

2. *Enhancing Evolution: The Ethical Case for Making Better People* (Princeton: Princeton University Press, 2007), 57.

3. I. Kirsch et al., "Initial Severity and Antidepressant Benefits: A Meta-Analysis of Data Submitted to the Food and Drug Administration," *PLoS Medicine* 5(2) (2008) e45, and J. Fournier et al., "Antidepressant Drug Effects and Depression Severity," *Journal of the American Medical Association* 303 (2010): 47–53.

permitted for competent adults, but those who choose to enhance need to be informed that doing so may involve physiological and psychological risks. They also need to take responsibility for any medical costs.

Smarter than Smart

In early 2008, the journal *Nature* published the results of an informal survey of its readers.[4] The survey was motivated by a report from cognitive neuroscientists Barbara Sahakian and Sharon Morein-Zamir of Cambridge University that many of their colleagues had used certain drugs to enhance their focus, concentration, and memory.[5] The most commonly used drugs were methylphenidate, modafinil, and propranolol. One in five of the 1,400 readers who responded to the online poll said that they had taken these drugs for the nonmedical purposes just mentioned. One third purchased the drugs over the Internet, bypassing medical practitioners. Based on government data published in 2007, 1.6 million people in the United States had used prescription stimulants for nonmedical purposes in the previous year.[6] Some of the demand is driven by clever marketing strategies by pharmaceutical companies, who stand to reap huge financial benefits from these drugs. But many people use the drugs to perform better cognitively and to gain a competitive edge over others. The use of these drugs to enhance cognitive functions is likely to increase.

Empirical studies suggest that methylphenidate enhances cognitive functions related to working memory. The data from these studies indicate that methylphenidate has mild neuroenhancing effects on these functions. Subjects with a lower baseline of working memory benefit more from this drug; those with a higher baseline benefit less.[7] In some instances, the latter experience impairment in some cognitive functions after taking the drug.[8] Children with ADHD tend to do better academically when taking methylphenidate and other stimulant medications than

---

4. B. Maher, "Poll Results: Look Who's Doping," *Nature* 452 (2008): 674–675.
5. "Professor's Little Helper," *Nature* 450 (2007): 1157–1159. See also Sahakian and Morein-Zamir, "Neuroethical Issues in Cognitive Enhancement," *Journal of Psychopharmacology*, published online March 8, 2010. Cognitive enhancement is not new, since generations of students and others have used stimulants for the same reasons mentioned here.
6. Cited by T. Wilens et al., "Misuse and Diversion of Stimulants Prescribed for ADHD: A Systematic Review of the Literature," *Journal of the American Academy of Child and Adolescent Psychiatry* 47 (2008): 21–31. Racine discusses the social dimensions of cognitive enhancement in *Pragmatic Neuroethics*, Chapter 6.
7. R. de Jongh et al., "Botox for the Brain: Enhancement of Cognition, Mood and Pro-Social Behavior and Blunting of Unwanted Memories," *Neuroscience and Behavioral Reviews* 32 (2008): 760–776. The authors cite many studies showing the effects of cognitive enhancement in this article. The findings in these studies that the effects of enhancement are weaker in those with higher cognitive capacities and stronger in those with lower cognitive capacities confirm the findings in an earlier report by M. Farah et al., "Neurocognitive Enhancement: What Can We Do and What Should We Do?" *Nature Reviews Neuroscience* 5 (2004): 421–425.
8. de Jongh et al., 763, 768.

those with the same disorder who do not take the medications.[9] But there is no conclusive evidence that these drugs would improve the academic performance of children who do not have the disorder. Methylphenidate appears to produce an inverted dose–response curve, with moderate doses improving performance and higher doses impairing or not affecting performance. Higher levels of the neurotransmitters dopamine and norepinephrine do not always improve cognitive functions and may interfere with them. Other studies suggest that methylphenidate enhances executive functions on novel tasks but impairs these functions on tasks that have been learned.[10] The data from these studies help to restrain the tendency to make exaggerated claims about the effects of these drugs in the brain. Insofar as methylphenidate enhances some functions and impairs others, there are cognitive trade-offs that one would have to weigh in considering whether to use this drug.

One study comparing cognitive responses from older and younger subjects suggests that a broad attention span and less focus on a specific task may make a person more able to transfer information from one situation to another. This can facilitate creative thinking and more effective problem solving.[11] Increasing the ability to concentrate on a narrow set of facts might reduce a person's ability to generalize, as is the case among many individuals with autism spectrum disorders. This is significant when considering that the results of this and other methylphenidate studies indicate that the drug can enhance cognitive stability at the cost of a decreased capacity to flexibly alter behavior and adapt to changing circumstances. If the drug enhances some cognitive capacities but impairs others, then one can legitimately ask in what sense it can be described as a "smart" drug.[12] One concern about this drug is that selective chronic stimulation of neurotransmitter systems in the prefrontal cortex might come at the cost of creativity and other noncognitive capacities mediated by the temporal and parietal lobes. This concern is based partly on evidence showing that some people with injuries to and less activity in the frontal lobes develop creative interests correlating with greater activity in posterior regions of the brain.[13] Yet the findings of a preliminary study of the effects of dextroamphetamine (Adderall) on creativity are consistent with its effects on cognition. Whether the drug influences convergent creative thought appears to depend on the baseline creativity of the individual. Those in the higher range of the normal distribution may

9. R. Scheffler et al., "Positive Association between Attention-Deficit/Hyperactivity Disorder Medication Use and Academic Achievement during Elementary School," *Pediatrics* 123 (2009): 1273–1279.
10. R. Elliott et al., "Effects of Methylphenidate on Spatial Working Memory and Planning in Healthy Young Adults," *Psychopharmacology* 131 (1997): 196–206, cited in de Jongh et al., 764.
11. S. Carson et al, "Decreased Latent Inhibition Is Associated with Increased Creative Achievement in High-Functioning Individuals," *Journal of Personality and Social Psychology* 85 (2003): 499–506. The authors note an association between creative thinking and early stages of mental illness. However, any creative benefit from mental illness would be outweighed or cancelled as the illness progressed to a full-blown psychopathology. This occurs in frontotemporal dementia, as I point out in Chapter 1.
12. S. Rose, "How Smart Are Smart Drugs?" *The Lancet* 372 (2008): 198–199.
13. As I mention in Chapter 1, and in note 11 above.

be unaffected or impaired, while those in the lower range may experience enhanced creativity.[14]

Some have raised the possibility of using certain drugs to enhance cognitive and affective capacities in a way that would enhance moral sensitivity.[15] They could make us more responsive to the needs and interests of others and thereby reduce harmful behavior. These effects could also mean that those with enhanced moral capacities could be held to a higher standard of moral responsibility for their actions and omissions. In Chapter 3, I briefly discussed the proposal that certain drugs be given to psychopaths to make them more responsive to moral reasons and modify their behavior so that it would conform to social norms. The plausibility of this proposal rests on the idea that their capacity to respond to moral reasons is outside the normal range of distribution among persons. Just as those with a lower baseline of cognitive and creative functions may benefit from cognition-enhancing drugs, those with a diminished capacity for moral sensitivity may benefit from drugs that increased this capacity.

Consistent with the data on cognitive and creative enhancement, however, there is no compelling evidence that people whose mental capacities fall within the normal range would develop a stronger sense of moral sensitivity from taking psychotropic drugs. The drugs would likely have a marginal positive effect, or no effect at all. People who used them would not become hyperresponsible. It is unclear what it would mean for a person with enhanced cognitive and affective capacities to be more responsible than one with normal capacities. Even if the drugs made a person capable of responding strongly rather than moderately to reasons for or against actions, it would not justify holding that person to a higher standard of responsibility if he or she performed or failed to perform them. Responsibility can be a matter of degree, though this pertains to the negative conditions of coercion, compulsion, and constraint. One can be more or less responsible depending on the extent to which any of these three conditions obtains. There is no gradation of responsibility in the opposite direction, when one is not affected by any of the negative conditions. Some persons may be more responsible than others because of certain roles. Administrators or CEOs are more responsible than other employees for the operation of an institution or organization because of their position of authority. But the greater degree of responsibility is a function of their role rather than any differences between their mental capacities and those of other people.

There is an asymmetry between negative and positive aspects of responsibility. One can be less responsible if the relevant mental capacities are impaired, but not more responsible if they are enhanced. Strong reasons-responsiveness would not be an aggravating factor. The standard of moderate reasons-responsiveness for holding people responsible for their actions would likely not change. This casts doubt on any practical normative implications of enhancement. Even if

---

14. M. Farah et al., "When We Enhance Cognition with Adderall, Do We Sacrifice Creativity? A Preliminary Study," *Psychopharmacology* 202 (2009): 541–547.

15. For example, T. Douglas, "Moral Enhancement," *Journal of Applied Philosophy* 25 (2008): 228–245, and N. Vincent, "Enhancing Responsibility," in Vincent, ed., *Legal Responsibility and Neuroscience* (Oxford: Oxford University Press, 2012), Chapter 12.

a person's capacity to respond to reasons were strengthened, it is unlikely that this would result in raising the reasonable person standard in the criminal law. Conceivably, this standard could be raised to a higher level if enough people took drugs to strengthen their moral sensitivity. If everyone did this, then eventually the higher level of sensitivity might become the norm. Everyone could be held to the same higher standard of moral and legal responsibility. The more probable scenario of a small percentage of people engaging in this type of enhancement would not change the existing standard, which is based on the mental capacities of the general population.

We can distinguish the *degree* of responsibility from the *content* of responsibility, the things for which we are responsible. Cognitive enhancement might increase the content of responsibility. Suppose that modafinil enabled surgeons to remain alert longer and perform more surgeries within a given period of time. Would they be responsible for performing more surgeries? Fair ascriptions of responsibility depend on reasonable expectations about what we can and should do. One can question whether it is reasonable to expect surgeons to push the limit of the number of surgeries they could competently perform. Expectations could increase along with the capacities enhanced by modafinil or other drugs. But there are physical and cognitive limits to what surgeons can do, and expectations must align with these limits to be reasonable. Pushing these limits too far could increase the risk of harm to patients and result in more claims of negligence. The brain is capable of holding and processing a limited amount of information. Being more alert would not increase this capacity. It is also questionable whether third parties would have the authority to override a surgeon's professional autonomy to refuse to cognitively enhance him or herself in order to perform more surgeries, quite apart from considerations of putting patients at increased risk. Responsibility for actions presupposes autonomy in performing them. Yet here we have the counterintuitive situation where the content of one's responsibility expanded while one's autonomy contracted.

If a surgeon freely decided to take modafinil in order to perform more surgeries, then he or she would be responsible for them. The content of responsibility would align with autonomy. Still, enhanced alertness and attention would not likely change the surgeon's intentions and responsiveness to reasons in a way that would increase the extent to which he or she was responsible for his or her actions. The quality of the surgeon's mental states would not be substantially different. The surgeon would be responsible for performing more surgeries, but not more responsible for performing them. An increase in the content of responsibility would not entail an increase in the degree of responsibility.

Safety issues concerning methylphenidate include its potential adverse effects on the central nervous system and possibly other systems in the body. This drug is a CNS stimulant and dopamine reuptake inhibitor. In brains with normal levels of dopamine, methylphenidate increases levels of this neurotransmitter. This may cause dopamine dysregulation in the reward system in mesolimbic and mesoaccumbens pathways and lead to cognitive and conative pathologies such as addiction. This has occurred in some patients taking dopamine agonists for Parkinson's disease, where an activated reward system can interfere with the deliberative and inhibitory functions of the prefrontal cortex. The drugs can overcompensate for dopamine depletion in the basal ganglia and other regions implicated in the disease. Any adverse effects from using methylphenidate for enhancement would be less acceptable than similar effects from its therapeutic use on the grounds that enhancement is not medically indicated. This could influence reasons for imposing limits on physicians in prescribing the drug for this purpose. It would be difficult to control any adverse effects of this or similar drugs, though, since many individuals can purchase them over the Internet or from drugstores and thus outside of the physician–patient relationship.

Modafinil inhibits norepinephrine reuptake in the brain. More precisely, it activates dopamine, which then activates norepinephrine and histamine in a process that blocks the hypothalamus from promoting sleep. Alternatively, it has been suggested that modafinil blocks the release of the inhibitory neurotransmitter gamma-aminobutyric acid (GABA). One fMRI study showed increased activity of the drug in the locus coeruleus region of the brains of human subjects.[16] This neural effect may enable some to become more focused and alert. In a different study of healthy young human volunteers, 100- to 200-mg doses of modafinil improved attention and alertness, as well as spatial planning and visual pattern recognition memory.[17] These functions improve decision making by enabling careful evaluation of a problem before initiating a response. As with the studies on methylphenidate, the effects of modafinil on working memory were most pronounced in subjects with lower cognitive capacities. It improved accuracy in a sustained attention task for those with a lower (but still above-average) IQ and lower baseline of working memory.[18] Those with a higher IQ and a higher baseline of working memory were either unaffected or worse in performing this and other tasks while on modafinil. Thus, the enhancing effects of modafinil are limited to certain cognitive functions, can vary among people, and may not always be beneficial.

In general, cognition-enhancing drugs have two main features. First, they show an inverted dose–response curve: lower doses tend to improve and higher doses tend to impair or not affect performance; they could be toxic as well. Second, the effects of the drugs depend on a person's working memory: those with a lower baseline tend to benefit more, while those with a higher baseline tend to benefit less.

Occasional use of modafinil may not pose any risks. A lower dose (100 mg) of modafinil increased anxiety and aggressive mood in some individuals participating in one study, and these effects resolved when the dose was increased (200 mg).[19] But chronic use of the drug could pose risks. For example, if one used modafinil repeatedly to forego sleep to remain alert and attentive over long periods, then

---

16. M. Minzenberg et al., "Modafinil Shifts Human Locus Coeruleus to Low-Tonic, High-Phasic Activity during Functional MRI," *Science* 322 (2008): 1700–1702.
17. U. Muller et al., "Effects of Modafinil on Working Memory Processes in Humans," *Psychopharmacology* 177 (2004): 161–169.
18. D. Randall et al., "Cognitive Effects of Modafinil in Student Volunteers May Depend on IQ," *Pharmacology, Biochemistry and Behavior* 82 (2005): 133–139. De Jongh et al. cite earlier studies testing the effects of these drugs in "Botox for the Brain.".
19. D. Randall et al., "Modafinil Affects Mood, but not Cognitive Function, in Healthy Young Volunteers,"*Psychopharmacology* 18 (2003): 163–173.

prolonged sleep deprivation could be a risk factor for metabolic and endocrine disorders such as obesity and diabetes, as well as cardiovascular disease. These conditions are more common among the chronically sleep-deprived. Being alert and attentive for short periods when we need to perform a demanding cognitive task can be adaptive. Yet being constantly alert and attentive could cause hyperactivation of the stress response and disturb the feedback loop that sustains balance between the stress and relaxation responses in the sympathetic and parasympathetic arms of the autonomic nervous system. This imbalance could be one cause of the metabolic and endocrine disorders just mentioned. Alterations between sleep and attention are adaptations to the demands of the environment. If the brain senses that constant attention is a sign of constant demand, then this could overload it. Unnecessary wakefulness can be more of a problem than unnecessary sleep. Constant manipulation of sleep–wake cycles may cause dysregulation because the perceived demands of the moment—studying for exams, completing grant applications—may not align with more serious demands from the environment. These could be some effects of chronic use of the drug.

There are established contraindications for modafinil. It should be used with caution in patients with a history of stroke or cardiovascular disease. Its possible side effects are similar to those of other stimulants. Some individuals taking these drugs experience confusion, ataxia, hyperglycemia, paresthesias, dyspnea, and other symptoms. Results from a recent study measuring the acute effects of modafinil at therapeutic doses between 200 and 400 mg showed that the drug can increase dopamine beyond normal levels in the nucleus accumbens and other regions of the brain.[20] One concern is that chronic use of modafinil could dysregulate the dopamine reward system and lead to addictive behavior. This is similar to the potential adverse effects of methylphenidate mentioned earlier. The results of the modafinil study underscore the need for awareness of potential chronic abuse of the drug as a cognitive enhancer. As a matter of autonomy, a competent individual should have the right to take modafinil to enhance attention and alertness if he or she so desires. However, one's prudential reasons for taking it should include knowledge of these contraindications and a careful weighing of its potential benefits and risks. Because the drug may be purchased from sources other than a physician, information about adverse effects may not always be readily available or accurate. It would be up to individuals to inform themselves of these risks.

A more general concern is that chronic use of any psychotropic drug can alter the biochemistry of the brain, which has to adjust to changes in the availability of neurotransmitters. Withdrawing an antidepressant or anxiolytic, for example, requires that the brain readjust to new levels of these chemicals, which depends on such factors as the half-life of the drug. It can be difficult for many people to wean antidepressants and especially benzodiazepines, which often involve significant withdrawal symptoms. It is one thing for a person to go through this process when the drug is taken to control the symptoms of a psychiatric disorder. It is quite

---

20. N. Volkow et al., "Effects of Modafinil on Dopamine and Dopamine Transporters in the Male Human Brain," *Journal of the American Medical Association* 301 (2009): 1148–1154.

another thing to go through it when there is no disorder. The fact that changes in the brain from psychotropic drugs are not always salutary or benign cannot be ignored.

Let us assume that cognition-enhancing drugs would be safe. Would they give some people a competitive advantage over others? Would the advantage be unfair if the drugs were expensive and not affordable for everyone? The answer to both questions depends on how effective the drugs are. A controlled study comparing two groups of students taking methylphenidate or a placebo before the SAT could determine whether the drug was effective in raising test scores. Similarly, a controlled study comparing two groups of airline pilots taking modafinil or a placebo could determine whether the drug was effective in helping them to stay more alert during long flights. There are different cognitive capacities and considerable variation in the extent to which people possess and exercise them. Controlling for these differences in a single study would be difficult. It would also be difficult to control for the influence of affective states and environmental factors on these capacities. Suppose that cognition-enhancing drugs were decisively shown to be effective in improving a range of cognitive functions. Presumably, people would take these drugs to become more competitive in gaining positional goods like a more elite education and more lucrative jobs. Yet there are many factors other than cognitive capacity that are necessary for one to achieve goals involving competition with others. Some people may put more effort into exercising this capacity than others, and environmental factors often provide the opportunities one needs to exercise it. More effective execution of tasks associated with working memory may be necessary but not sufficient to achieve desired goals. Because of this, and because competition is a zero–sum game, a drug that enabled one to get a perfect score on the SAT would not be enough for admission to Harvard.

Some might claim that unequal access to cognition-enhancing drugs due to cost or availability would be unfair to those who could not afford or obtain them. If the drugs were not prohibitively expensive, then the use of them by some might still put social pressure on others to use them just to keep up with fellow students, colleagues, and co-workers. Employers might pressure employees to take methylphenidate or modafinil to enhance their efficiency and productivity. This already occurs to some extent in the military. Some employees might decline to use them because of concern about the safety of the drugs or the deleterious effects of working longer hours on their bodies and brains. If the drugs were effective in the relevant respects, then those who declined to take them might put themselves at a competitive disadvantage compared with peers who took them; it might even jeopardize their jobs. This assumes that the drugs would have only positive effects on the brain and body. It may be true for short-term use; but it cannot be assumed for long-term use. If chronic use of the drugs resulted in cognitive or physical impairment, then the employees who used them, and the employers who encouraged their use, would not be better off. Adverse effects of the drugs might result in reduced productivity and possibly also disability claims by employees, resulting in negative financial and legal consequences for employers.

More importantly, claims about social pressure or competitive disadvantage generally are not supported by the empirical evidence of the effects of methylphenidate, modafinil, and other similarly acting drugs. If a line of work requires a fairly high level of cognitive skills, then there will not be a significant difference among employees in their possession and exercise of these skills. Given that the effects of the drugs diminish as the cognitive baseline increases, and that most or all employees would have roughly the same high baseline, any enhancing effects of the drugs would probably be minimal. They would not make some employees much better off than others. Even if one claimed that differences between people's natural cognitive functions above a high baseline were morally significant, there would be no unfair advantage if some used cognition-enhancing drugs. Marginal enhancing effects of the drugs above the baseline would mean that there would not be a significant difference in cognitive functions between those who used the drugs and those who did not. Therefore, there would be no reason for some to feel coerced to take the drugs. Nor would there be any reason for those who declined to take methylphenidate or modafinil to claim that it would be unfair to them if their peers used these drugs. The latter may decide to work longer hours; but many people do this independently of whether they take cognitive enhancers. Besides, working longer would not automatically result in work of higher quality. Drugs enabling an accountant or law clerk to stay focused longer would not necessarily incline them to work longer. Whether or not one decided to put in more hours would depend not only on the effects of the drugs but also on one's motivation and assessment of the personal benefits and costs.

Matters might be different in companies with tasks involving a greater range of cognitive skills. Employees with a significantly lower cognitive baseline might be expected to take the drugs to perform better. They could become a vulnerable group within the company or organization and could be treated unfairly because the expectation would apply only to them and not also to their higher-performing peers. They might feel coerced to take the drugs, especially if retaining their jobs depended on greater productivity. Even here, though, a realistic assessment of the extent to which the drugs could enhance cognitive functions would be necessary to test these claims. It would also be necessary to assess the extent to which factors external to the brain influence how people develop and exercise cognitive functions.

Another way in which pharmacological agents could enhance cognitive functions would be to increase one's choices. For a person with a lower cognitive baseline, an enhanced capacity to process information could strengthen the perception of options open to that person when acting. This could enable a person to make more rational decisions that were in his or her short- and long-term best interests. But more choices would not necessarily be advantageous for a person. Having options is crucial for making decisions that contribute to one's well-being. Beyond a certain point, though, an increasing number of options could interfere with the ability to process only so much information at a given time. We choose and act effectively within certain self-imposed constraints regarding time and information. The constraints may also be shaped unconsciously by the fact that the brain can hold a limited amount of data. Having or perceiving many choices at one time may increase the burden of processing information. It could impair the ability to make decisions and promote indecisiveness. In many situations, fewer rather than more choices may be optimal for making rational decisions. Having many choices could also increase the perception of opportunity costs and cause one to dwell on the many lost opportunities entailed by every decision.[21] For people with a higher or lower baseline of cognitive functioning, increasing the range of choices might not be better and could be worse for them. In some cases, more choices can exacerbate pathological conditions. People with generalized anxiety/panic disorder who perceive stimuli as threatening may have difficulty making decisions when more information is available to them. They may feel overwhelmed by too many choices and effectively lose their ability to act. A drug that made one perceive more choices might not be enhancing but disabling. Paradoxically, a person whose cognitive functions were impaired by a psychiatric disorder could become even more impaired from taking a drug that "enhanced" cognition.

Among U.S. college students, one study showed that 6.9 percent of this population used prescription stimulants such as methylphenidate and dextroamphetamine to increase alertness and concentration while studying.[22] Interestingly, the use of these stimulants was higher among students who earned lower grade-point averages. It is not known whether this last fact is a function of mechanisms in the brain, mental effort, social environment, or a combination of all of these factors. Nor is it known exactly how each of these factors influences the others. This problem is similar to that of trying to control for factors other than drugs in a study testing their effects on SAT scores. Psychopharmacologist Reinoud de Jongh and coauthors from the Netherlands state: "High expectations regarding the effects of enhancement drugs are not warranted. However, societal pressure may occur with respect to drugs that are ineffective or only slightly effective simply because people believe these drugs improve performance, as the illicit use of methylphenidate and modafinil shows. Creating realistic expectations appears to be very hard to accomplish."[23] Coercion can result from unreasonable expectations imposed by some on others. If everyone were suitably informed of the generally modest effects of these drugs on cognition, then expectations about these effects would adjust accordingly. Consequently, the probability of real or perceived coercion or unfairness would diminish.

Legal theorist Reinhard Merkel and colleagues from an interdisciplinary European group of researchers argue that cognitive enhancement should not be publicly funded because it falls outside the responsibility of health care professionals, which is to prevent and treat disease.[24] But if those who could benefit from enhancement cannot afford the drugs and are worse off than those with superior

---

21. S. Nagel discusses this issue in "Too Much of a Good Thing? Enhancement and the Burden of Self-Determination," *Neuroethics* 3 (2) (2010): 109–119.

22. S. McCabe et al., "Non-Medical Use of Prescription Stimulants among US College Students: Prevalence and Correlates from a National Survey," *Addiction* 100 (2005): 96–106.

23. "Botox for the Brain," 771–772. See also M. Schermer et al., "The Future of Psychopharmacological Enhancements: Expectations and Policies," *Neuroethics* 2(2) (2009): 75–87. More recent findings confirm the conclusion that expectations regarding the effectiveness of these drugs exceed their actual effects, as reported by D. Repantis et al., "Modafinil and Methylphenidate for Neuroenhancement in Healthy Individuals: A Systematic Review," *Pharmacological Research* 62 (2010): 187–206.

24. *Intervening in the Brain*, 297, 327–328.

cognitive skills, then would this not be unfair to them? A response to this question turns on the distinction between absolute and comparative senses of "worse off." The first sense pertains to how two groups fare with respect to an absolute measure of overall cognitive function. The second sense pertains to how one group fares relative to the other regarding this same function. Fairness consists in meeting claims in proportion to their strength, where the strength of a claim depends on the degree of need. A fair distribution of any good will give greater weight to the claims of those with greater needs. It would be unfair not to meet the claims of those with greater needs and provide them with the good if they cannot obtain it on their own. The good in question is cognition-enhancing drugs. Crucially, claims to receive this good have moral weight when the need is defined in absolute rather than comparative terms. If it is unfair that some do not have access to these drugs because they cannot afford them, then it is because they fall below an absolute level of adequate cognitive function and need to be raised to this level. Even if one group has a comparatively lower functional capacity than another and can benefit in a way that will make them equal to the other group, not having access to the drugs will not be unfair to them if they fall above the level of adequate cognitive function. The moral force of their claim to have access to the drugs depends on how they fare with respect to an absolute cognitive scale, not on how they compare with those who are cognitively better-off.[25]

In principle, it would be unfair not to make the drugs available to those with a low absolute level of cognitive function if they could benefit from them. The goal would be to ensure equal opportunity for all people to realize their cognitive potential. Given that the positive effects of the drugs diminish beyond a certain point, providing these drugs to the cognitively worse off could help to level the social playing field. The moral reasons for providing the drugs would depend on the extent to which the worse off benefited from them. These reasons could also change the terms of the debate, since intervention for those falling below the level of adequate cognitive function would not be enhancement but therapy. Providing drugs to all who could benefit from them would be prohibitively expensive for state or federal programs to subsidize and thus not likely to occur. If there were such programs and allocation decisions had to be made, then higher priority should be given to those who would benefit more and be raised to the level of adequate functioning, and lower priority to those who would benefit less and remain below this level. Otherwise, the allocation would result in a net loss rather than a net benefit.

Merkel et al. argue that there should be a clear distinction between treatment and enhancement at the macro level of health resource allocation. They draw this distinction in terms of what it would take to restore normal cognitive functioning or raise it above a normal level.[26] On this view, those who fell below this level and could have their function raised to it would be entitled to treatment and covered by the health care system. The strength of a claim to treatment would depend not only

---

25. Frankfurt defends this view in "Equality as a Moral Ideal," in *The Importance of What We Care About*, 77–92. Frankfurt's main point is that sufficiency, not equality, is what matters morally.

26. *Intervening in the Brain*, 327.

on the degree of impaired function but also on the likelihood of achieving normal function. Those with a lower functional level would have a weaker claim if they benefited only marginally from the drugs.[27] Those who were above the level of normal function could not reasonably expect the health care system to cover the drugs' cost. Merkel's group acknowledges that, for some conditions, treatment may shade into enhancement.[28] When the boundary between treatment and enhancement is blurred, and it is unclear whether a condition meets diagnostic criteria, it is permissible for a physician to prescribe a drug if it benefits a patient and does not expose him or her to risk.[29] But most, if not all, psychotropic drugs entail some risk, regardless of the severity of the condition for which they are prescribed.

Consider a psychiatric condition described as maladaptive but not pathological. One may have mild to moderate impulsivity, which interferes with making rational choices in some situations. It impairs only some of the person's cognitive functions. If a physician prescribes a psychotropic drug to modulate the person's impulses, then his or her obligation to inform the person of any potential harmful effects of the drug is as strong as it would be in a case of severe impulsivity or compulsion. Some would say that the potential of these effects and the likely modest benefit of a drug for a mild disorder might not indicate a favorable benefit–risk ratio. This could be a reason against prescribing the drug. Similar remarks apply to the case of a person with mild depression bordering on a diagnosis of dysthymia. Here, too, prescribing an antidepressant to elevate the person's mood would have to be weighed against the side effects of the drug. Responses to the question of whether a psychotropic drug may or should not be prescribed in these cases will vary according to physicians' judgments of their patients' symptoms.

Some might insist that, by definition, enhancement means improving normal functions and thus does not fall within the goals of medicine. This objection may lose some of its force when we acknowledge that many people purchase these drugs outside of the doctor–patient relationship. But if doctors prescribe drugs for conditions falling in a gray area of the continuum from therapy to enhancement, there should be an acceptable benefit–risk ratio. If there is a risk of adverse effects in the CNS and other systems in the body, and if the benefits are modest, then there is no justification for prescribing them. Even if this ratio were favorable for the patient, prescribing drugs to produce effects that fall somewhere between therapy and enhancement could reinforce the medicalization of conditions that do not

---

27. In *A Theory of Justice* (Cambridge, MA: Harvard University Press, 1971), J. Rawls says that the only admissible inequalities are those that benefit the least advantaged members of society. This is known as the "difference principle" (71 ff). One can question whether a marginal benefit of an expensive good to the worst off would support giving absolute priority to them. For discussion of this issue, see T. Nagel, *Equality and Partiality* (Oxford: Oxford University Press, 1991), and D. Parfit, "Equality or Priority?" in M. Clayton and A. Williams, eds., *The Ideal of Equality* (New York: St. Martin's Press, 2000), 81–125.
28. *Intervening in the Brain*, 328.
29. See Schermer et al., "The Future of Psychopharmacological Enhancements," and M. Synofzik, "Ethically Justified, Clinically Applicable Criteria for Physician Decision-Making in Psychopharmacological Enhancement," *Neuroethics* 2(2) (2009): 89–102.

involve any significant mental or physical dysfunction and impose no significant limitations on people's lives.

Despite their objection to public funding of enhancement, Merkel et al. argue that there is no justification for prohibiting individuals from using enhancing drugs if they so choose.[30] Taking these drugs to improve cognitive capacities should be allowed, provided that individuals pay for them and take responsibility for any resulting costs. This position reflects a libertarian view whereby individuals have the right to do what they want to their brains, provided that they do not thereby harm others. Merkel et al. describe two senses of social cost. The first sense pertains to the idea that an increase in the incidence of enhancement might exacerbate social inequality. They claim that this could be controlled or mitigated by political and legal institutions.[31] But this claim seems inconsistent with their libertarian claim that individuals should not have their choice to enhance constrained by any form of paternalistic intervention. Taking responsibility for the consequences of these choices should not entail losing the right to enhance if social inequality is the outcome of many people exercising this right. In fact, one can question the point about social inequality. Insofar as the group with the highest level of cognitive function would benefit only marginally from the drugs, enhancement would probably not increase social inequality. This claim acknowledges that factors in addition to cognitive capacity can affect social standing. The second sense of social cost pertains to health care expenditures resulting from any adverse effects of the drugs.[32] Assuming that individuals taking these drugs are competent enough to know that these effects may occur, they should be responsible for the medical costs of any treatment and not pass them on to others in the health care system.

Although there are risks with any chronic use of drugs targeting the brain, the effects of long-term use of drugs to enhance cognition are not known. Competent individuals should be allowed to take enhancing drugs with the awareness that chronic use of these drugs entails some risk. One may question whether a marginal benefit for those with normal brain function could justify any risk in taking cognition-enhancing drugs. But until the effects are known, and unless the probability and magnitude of any harm from taking these drugs is significant, there is no reason to invoke a precautionary principle to limit or prohibit their use among adults. Indeed, one could argue that there is an evolutionary advantage in taking risks with cognition-enhancing drugs. This may enable us to adapt faster to environmental changes that could adversely affect us. If we do not take any risks of this sort in improving our traits, then we will not move forward but become more vulnerable to natural forces beyond our control.

A group of neuroscientists and ethicists has formulated a set of recommendations based on the presumption that mentally competent adults should be able to engage in cognitive enhancement using drugs.[33] These recommendations include

---

30. *Intervening in the Brain*, 329.
31. *Ibid*, 363.
32. *Ibid.*, 363.
33. H. Greely et al., "Towards Responsible Use of Cognitive-Enhancing Drugs by the Healthy," *Nature* 456 (2008): 702–705.

an evidence-based approach to the evaluation of risks and benefits and enforceable policies concerning the use of cognition-enhancing drugs to support fairness, protect individuals from coercion, and minimize enhancement-related socioeconomic disparities. The general goal is to maximize benefit and minimize harm. Assessments by regulatory bodies of the risks associated with these drugs will determine whether these recommendations translate into policy. Something akin to a precautionary principle may be appropriate regarding cognitive enhancement in children, however. There may be compelling reasons against using psychoactive drugs in children with normal cognitive functions because of the potential to alter neural pathways in their developing brains. By encouraging the use of drugs that can alter their brains and influence their behavior, parents might be harming them by failing to respect their right to an open future. I will defend this point in the next section.

Keeping One's Cool

Antianxiety medications (anxiolytics) are prescribed and taken for generalized anxiety disorder (GAD). This disorder may manifest in symptoms such as shortness of breath, rapid pulse, and sweating, all of which may occur as part of the body's response to stimuli perceived as stressors. The drugs in this class include benzodiazepines such as diazepam (Valium) and lorazepam (Ativan). They block excess release and overactivity of noradrenaline in the brain through their action on GABA. The beta-adrenergic receptor antagonist, or beta-blocker, propranolol (Inderal) is designed to reduce the cardiovascular excitatory response to adrenaline and noradrenaline. By reducing the response of receptors in the brain to these hormones, propranolol can prevent or attenuate symptoms associated with anxiety. Some musicians and public speakers take this drug to block the body's stress response, reduce stage fright, and improve their musical or oratorical performance in auditions, recitals, concerts, and lectures. Although there is an affective component of fear in anxiety, one's perception of stimuli as stressors also plays an important role in generating this state. Thus it is appropriate to describe the use of antianxiety drugs for this purpose as cognitive enhancement.

It will be instructive to cite the experience of a violinist who has taken a beta-blocker to enhance her musical performance. I will refer to her as "Andrea." In correspondence, she told me that the consensus among musicians is that beta-blockers generally help to control the physical symptoms caused by too much adrenaline. The drugs help to diminish the sensation and conscious awareness of a rapid heartbeat, muscle tension, and other physical symptoms that manifest themselves while playing under pressure. Being conscious of these effects can interfere with one's concentration and impair one's performance. Andrea reported that after taking a beta-blocker, she experienced a slower heart rate and felt calmer and more in control when she practiced at home. She was still nervous during lessons and auditions, but the beta-blocker took the edge off her anxiety when playing the violin in public. Any nervousness was of the good sort, the sort that made her more attentive to what she was doing. She was not nervous to the degree that she could not play at all or could not function normally in daily life. The nervousness was more like how one feels when going on a first date, as distinct from how one feels when riding in a recklessly driven motor vehicle. Andrea admitted that her anxiety before auditions was considerable and that the beta-blocker reduced it and enabled her to play in an unimpaired way.

Although Andrea did not have the same experience, one of her colleagues told her that she felt emotionally detached when taking a beta-blocker before recitals and performances. This effect may not be significant in auditions, which are highly competitive and where there can be intense pressure to be technically perfect. But it may be significant in performance, where sharing music with the audience is an emotional experience. If a performance makes one nervous, then it may do so in a positive way that does not impair but improves one's performance. There may be trade-offs between the physically calming and emotionally blunting effects of these drugs. Anxiety may be preferable to some degree of emotional detachment, though the preference may differ between auditions and performances. Another important factor is that Andrea took atenolol (Tenormin), which, unlike propranolol, does not cross the blood–brain barrier. Because it does not influence the brain, atenolol does not have the psychological effects of propranolol. Equally important, Andrea said that she preferred not to take atenolol because it made her feel dependent on the drug. She hoped to train her body and mind to the point of being able to control any pre-audition or pre-performance anxiety without the need of pharmacological intervention. Cognitive-behavioral therapy could help as well, since it has been effective in treating GAD. If nonpharmacological interventions are not effective, then it seems that beta-blockers are a justifiable intervention to enable musicians or public speakers to prevent or reduce anxiety, maintain control, and perform to their potential.

Philosopher and ethicist Carl Elliott argues that beta-blockers should be seen "not as *improving* someone's skills, but as preventing the effects of anxiety from *interfering* with their skills."[34] This is consistent with the account of Andrea and her experience with atenolol. Elliott says that "taking a beta blocker, in other words, won't turn you into a better violinist, but it will prevent your anxiety from interfering with your public performance."[35] It can "arguably help the best player win."[36] He maintains that beta-blockers used for this purpose should not be thought of as enhancers but as a way of leveling the playing field between the anxiety-ridden and those who are naturally calm. For musicians who experience anxiety that impairs their performance, it can be an equalizing factor by raising them to the performance level of those who do not experience anxiety, at least not in any performance-impairing way. One could argue for the use of beta-blockers to reduce anxiety on grounds of fairness. Assuming that there is a biological cause of anxiety beyond their control, the anxious are worse off than their more relaxed peers through no fault of their own. If one accepts luck egalitarianism, then we should compensate people for conditions that befall them through no fault of their own to make them equal to the

---

34. "In Defense of the Beta Blocker," *The Atlantic Monthly*, August 20, 2008. http://www.theatlantic.com/magazine/archive/2008/08/in-defense-of-the-beta-blocker/696/

35. *Ibid.*

36. *Ibid.*

better off, who are not adversely affected by the same conditions.[37] This would support the idea that the more anxious performers need a beta-blocker or other anti-anxiety drug. Not having access to these drugs would be unfair to them.

The problem with this argument is that those who can benefit from these drugs are worse off than their peers only with respect to one activity. The anxiety-ridden musicians are not worse off in terms of an absolute scale of general cognitive and physical functions. They are above the critical threshold in terms of the total set of these functions. The anxiety that motivated Andrea to use propranolol or atenolol did not put her below the threshold of adequate mental and physical functioning. If it did, then she would fit the criteria of GAD, in which case taking a beta-blocker would not be enhancement but therapy. If one's functions are above the threshold of what is considered adequate, then one does not have an absolute need for the drug. While some musicians might be worse off than their calmer peers, there is no urgent need to raise their level of functioning in absolute terms. Lack of access to the drug would not be unfair to them. On grounds of autonomy, one should have the right to acquire such a drug and take it if one wishes. But such a right should not be construed as a claim on physicians obligating them to prescribe the drug so that one could perform better musically. They might be obligated to prescribe the drug only if the anxiety impaired not just musical performance but a range of cognitive and physical functions in everyday life. Following Elliott, one may question this use of beta-blockers as enhancement. There is no good reason why it should be described as therapy either.

The perception of risk among those who take beta-blockers for anxiety may be one factor in the discussion of fairness. Elliott claims that beta-blockers are "safe, cheap, and their effects wear off in a few hours. So, unlike users of human growth hormones and steroids, users of beta blockers don't have to worry about their heads growing or their testicles shrinking."[38] But a more qualified and accurate statement is that these drugs are *relatively* safe, since they are not without any risks. Propranolol has a half-life of 4–6 hours, which may be relatively short as drugs go but not an insignificant amount of time if the drug remains active in the brain and body. This and other beta-blockers were downgraded in the United Kingdom in 2006 to fourth-line agents for treating hypertension because it was found that they could cause type 2 diabetes. Moreover, adrenaline plays a role in the formation and consolidation of memory. Chronic use of propranolol could interfere with the normal function of adrenaline in brain regions mediating memory. Given its action on hormones and systems in the brain, these and other possible adverse effects of repeatedly using this drug to remain calm cannot be dismissed out of hand. Atenolol would not have any effects on the CNS because it does not penetrate the blood–brain barrier. Yet this drug was one of the beta-blockers identified as having a risk of causing type 2 diabetes. Using atenolol for this purpose would not be entirely risk-free.

---

37. R. Dworkin, "What Is Equality? Part II: Equality of Resources," *Philosophy & Public Affairs* 10 (1981): 283–354, and F. Roemer, "A Pragmatic Theory of Responsibility for the Egalitarian Planner," *Philosophy & Public Affairs* 22 (1993): 146–166.
38. "In Defense of the Beta Blocker."

Among musicians with anxiety who would benefit from a beta-blocker, some may take the drug while others may decline. Like Andrea, the latter may prefer not to be dependent on a drug in order to perform better in auditions, recitals, and concerts. They may also worry about risks in taking the drug on a regular basis. If non-pharmacological treatments failed to prevent the physical symptoms associated with anxiety, then those choosing not to take the drug could put themselves at a competitive disadvantage with other musicians who took it. But if they decided that any benefits were not worth the costs and did not take the drug for this reason, then any inequality would be the result of their decision. Having this choice would give them control of this outcome, and thus it would not be unfair.

Perhaps the main objection to the practice of taking a drug to keep one's cool is that the anxiety at issue does not impair one's capacity to perform a general range of cognitive functions in daily life. Andrea's comment that she did not experience anxiety to the point where she could not function is significant. Musical performance for someone like her is an important component of her life. But impairment caused by the body's response to performing under pressure is not of such a degree as to make it a full-blown anxiety disorder. The difference of degree here is medically and morally significant. Expecting a physician to prescribe propranolol to reduce or prevent anxiety before an audition, recital, or concert would promote the medicalization of a mild or moderate condition.

While competent adults should be allowed to take enhancing drugs, this practice may not be defensible in cases where some individuals make decisions for others. Suppose that a 10-year-old girl is a piano prodigy. Her parents and teachers believe that she is destined for greatness in music. But she becomes anxious before her public performances. As a preventive measure, her parents give her propranolol before she plays. This calms her and ensures a flawless performance in every audition, recital, and concert. Encouraged by her parents, the child identifies with her musical prowess and desires to be a world-class musician. It appears that the child's ability to perform at the highest level will be an essential component of her well-being over the course of her life.[39] Would there be anything objectionable about using propranolol in this case?

There are degrees of decisional capacity, which are not simply a function of age. Yet we can assume that a 10-year-old would not be mature enough to fully comprehend the potential physiological and psychological consequences of chronic use of this or any other drug. She would not have the capacity to make a sufficiently informed decision about whether or not to take it. Her parents would be acting as surrogate decision makers for her. It is significant that she, not her parents, would experience any long-term adverse effects of the drug. This issue needs to be informed by the fact that the brain of a 10-year-old is still labile and very much in the process of development. This is particularly the case with respect to the frontal lobes, which are critical to reasoning and decision making. Repeatedly altering levels of adrenaline, noradrenaline, or other hormones in her brain with a psychoactive drug could influence the development of her brain and modify neural circuits and systems in

---

39. I thank Eugene Bereza for this example.

ways that would not have occurred otherwise. Altering levels of these same hormones with chronic use of atenolol could have adverse effects in her body. For these reasons, the parents' decision to allow her to take either of these drugs would not be justified. This is a decision that she could make on her own once she is competent enough to weigh the potential benefits and risks.

In addition to the safety issue, there is another reason for objecting to the parents' action. If the drug enhances her musical skills, then discontinuing it may foreclose future opportunities for her. Nevertheless, it is possible that by the time she is mature enough to make decisions for herself, she may no longer identify with the desire to be a world-class musician. Even if the possibility of being a great musician were lost, she might be able to accommodate her interests to different opportunities, or develop new interests. By insisting that their daughter take propranolol, the parents may be interfering with her right to an open future, which will only begin to take shape once she is capable of making her own decisions.[40] Only in cases where anxiety significantly limited a child's ability to function in everyday life, and where nonpharmacological therapies had failed, would it be justified for parents to consent to a child's chronic use of propranolol or an anxiolytic. In these cases, the drugs would be used for therapy rather than enhancement.

Some may question the selective concern about the drugs I have discussed. Many people take certain foods or supplements to improve cognitive and affective capacities. Why is there such concern about off-label prescription drugs when food and supplements are taken to produce similar effects? Others may question why some drugs but not others concern us. Why do we not worry as much about the effects of nicotine or alcohol as we do about the effects of modafinil, methylphenidate, or propranolol?

The effects of psychotropic drugs on the brain are more pronounced than the effects of foods and supplements. The fact that a lower dose of an SSRI has more pronounced effects on brain biochemistry and mood than higher doses of St. John's wort or the serotonin precursor tryptophan indicates a significant difference in their effects on the brain. Similarly, methylphenidate, modafinil, and other stimulants such as dextroamphetamine have more pronounced effects on brain biochemistry in sustaining alertness and focus than comparative doses of caffeine, which is the world's most widely used psychoactive substance. The difference between pharmacological agents and food or supplements in their effects on the brain may be one of degree rather than kind. But the difference of degree is significant, which gives us a good reason to be concerned about chronic use of these agents and to ensure that the public is fully informed about their short-term and potential long-term effects on the brain. Regarding the second question, we should be just as concerned about nicotine and alcohol as we are about psychotropic drugs. The effects of nicotine and alcohol on the brain and body may be as harmful to some individuals as the effects of antidepressants and prescribed stimulants. All of these substances should be discussed in the same context of the ratio of benefits to risks for those who use them.

---

40. J. Feinberg, "A Child's Right to an Open Future," in *Freedom and Fulfillment: Philosophical Essays* (Princeton: Princeton University Press, 1992), 76–97.

Long-Term Memory

Since antiquity, humans have been intrigued by the possibility of manipulating memory. In classical mythology, those who drank from or crossed the River Lethe in the underworld would lose all memory of their past existence before reincarnation. Those who drank from the River Mnemosyne would remember everything they experienced. Instead of drinking from or crossing mythical rivers, we now may be able to alter our memory through pharmacological means. Research into the molecular mechanisms of memory has shown promise for interventions in memory systems that could increase our storage and retrieval capacity for long-term memory. These interventions might also prevent the formation of new memories or erase old ones.

Drugs targeting glutamate receptors to expedite the process of long-term potentiation (LTP) may enhance memory consolidation and reconsolidation. LTP stimulates synaptic connections and strengthens signal transmission between neurons. Memory that has been consolidated must be reconsolidated in order not to be removed from long-term storage sites in the cortex. Ampakines are a class of drugs that can enhance the role of LTP in this process by activating glutamate through the AMPA receptor.[41] This promotes better communication between synapses and may increase memory formation and storage. Ampakines have the potential to improve both short- and long-term memory. Other drugs can increase the amount of the transcription factor cyclic AMP response element binding protein (CREB).[42] Like ampakines, drugs targeting CREB may enhance memory by strengthening communication between synapses. Because it would be used by people with normal capacity for memory, this type of enhancement would be different from the therapeutic use of drugs such as the cholinesterase inhibitor donepezil (Aricept) and the glutamate antagonist memantine (Namenda) to retard memory loss in Alzheimer's disease.

Of the drugs designed for enhancing memory, ampakines appear to be the furthest along in development and the most promising. Interestingly, the results of one study using the ampakine farampator (CX-691) in a group of healthy elderly volunteers showed that the drug improved working memory but impaired episodic memory.[43] The effects of ampakines taken over long periods are not well-known because there have not been a sufficient number of longitudinal studies.[44] They would depend on the dose and their half-life. They would also depend on whether the drugs were used intermittently or chronically. Chronic use would probably be needed to produce any effects, and one can reasonably ask how this use might influence different aspects of memory.

---

41. G. Lynch and C. Gall, "Ampakines and the Three-Fold Path to Cognitive Enhancement," *Trends in Neurosciences* 29 (2006): 554–562.
42. T. Tully et al., "Targeting the CREB Pathway for Memory Enhancers," *Nature Reviews: Drug Discovery* 2 (2003): 266–277.
43. E. Wezenberg et al., "Acute Effects of the Ampakine Farampator on Memory and Information Processing in Healthy Elderly Volunteers," *Neuropsychopharmacology* 32 (2007): 1272–1283.
44. See Rose, "How Smart Are Smart Drugs?"

Storing and retrieving more memories of remote facts and events might impair the capacity to process information quickly and execute immediate cognitive tasks. It is unclear how ampakines or other drugs targeting the relevant memory systems could weed out memory of trivial facts from memory of useful facts. It is also unclear whether retrieval of more stored memories would affect the capacity to form new memories. A more specific concern is the effect that tinkering with CREB might have on the binding function of this protein. Binding is a neural selection mechanism preventing information overload in the brain. It does this by letting only a fraction of all sensory data enter conscious awareness. Altering this mechanism could allow too much information into the brain, which could interfere with working memory and the capacity to learn new things.

Neuroscientist Torkel Klingberg argues that we can increase working memory capacity by training our brains to meet its increasing demands in various cognitive tasks.[45] As the demands of working memory in the brain increase, so does the brain's capacity to sustain them. There may be limits to this capacity. While some individuals could handle the increasing demand, others could not. An excess of information at one time could overwhelm their brains, distracting them and impairing their reasoning and decision making. Too much episodic memory may also impair working memory. There are cases of maladaptive and pathological behavior associated with an excess of episodic memory.

Consider the case of 43-year-old Jill Price.[46] At age 14, she noticed that she had exceptional autobiographical memory. Events she had experienced could be recalled in almost perfect detail. Although her memories were beneficial to her when she worked as an administrative assistant at a law firm, most of them were filled with trivial and intrusive details. More significantly, the involuntary nature of her recall put her mind at the will of her memory. Particular memories simply happened to her. Thus it would be inappropriate to describe her condition as an "ability," because much of her recall was beyond her control. In her own words: "I don't make any effort to call memories up; they just fill my mind. In fact, they're not under my conscious control, and as much as I'd like to, I can't stop them."[47] Price describes her autobiographical memories as "a horrible distraction."[48] This type of memory is essential for one to construct a narrative of one's life. But some degree of forgetting is also necessary to project oneself into the future as part of that narrative. This can be a challenge when so much of one's thought consists in recalling the past, as indicated in additional remarks by Price: "Whereas people generally create narratives of their lives that are fashioned by a process of selective remembering and an enormous amount of forgetting, and continuously recrafting that narrative through the course of life, I have not been able to do so."[49] Further, "I've come to

45. *The Overflowing Brain: Information Overload and the Limits of Working Memory* (Oxford: Oxford University Press, 2009).
46. J. Price (with B. Davis), *The Woman Who Can't Forget: A Memoir* (New York: Free Press, 2008).
47. *Ibid.*, 2.
48. *Ibid.*, 38.
49. *Ibid.*, 6.

understand that there is a real value in being able to forget a good deal about our lives." Instead, "I remember all the clutter."[50]

Jill Price was diagnosed with hyperthymestic syndrome. Her condition has also been described as autobiographical memory syndrome, where one recalls in great detail an inordinate number of events from one's past. The excess recall interferes with the ability to focus on the present and imagine the future. It can also cause impairment in other types of memory. Price has a below-normal capacity to memorize facts ("I'm horrible at memorizing"[51]). This suggests that too much recall of memory can interfere with one's capacity to form new memories and process information. Hyperactivity in the parahippocampal gyrus and the anterior region of the prefrontal cortex mediating retrieval of episodic memory might result in decreased activity in ventrolateral and dorsolateral regions of the prefrontal cortex mediating working memory. In normal circumstances there is a balance between the functions of these brain regions ensuring complementarity between these two types of memory. In the case of Jill Price, too much retrieval of long-term memory comes at the cost of impairment in short-term memory.

Memory researchers examined Price and made the diagnosis.[52] The problem is that she cannot turn off retrieval mechanisms in her brain that would ordinarily limit the amount of memory available for recall. The mechanisms of memory reconsolidation in her brain are overactive and do not allow a normal rate of extinction of unnecessary memories. Ordinarily, reconsolidation is an adaptive update mechanism allowing for new information, available at the time of retrieval, to be integrated into the representation of the initial memory. Memories are reconsolidated each time they are retrieved. If memories are not useful for the organism in its interaction with the environment, then they will not be retrieved and eventually will be extinguished from storage sites in the cortex. Constant retrieval reinforces reconsolidation and embeds the memory more firmly in the brain. The result is a maladaptive, if not pathological, condition. Brain scans have shown that the structures mediating Jill Price's episodic memory retrieval are enlarged and hyperactive, which explains her syndrome. This case illustrates that retrieving a considerable volume of memory may be more of a curse than a blessing. It tells us that we should avoid inferring that if a certain amount of memory retrieval is good, then more retrieval is better. As drugs to enhance the neural mechanisms of memory are developed further, great care will have to be taken to ensure that none of these mechanisms becomes hyperactive. Researchers need to ensure an optimal balance between remembering and forgetting. Although hyperthymestic syndrome may be rare, those intent on enhancing memory should look to it as the type of condition they would want to avoid.

There are other critical features of long-term memory involving more than mechanisms of storage and retrieval. It is possible that drugs designed to enhance memory might do more to impair than improve its usefulness and value. A recent

---

50. *Ibid.*, 45.
51. *Ibid.*, 24.
52. E. Parker, L. Cahill, and J. McGaugh, "Case of Unusual Autobiographical Remembering," *Neurocase* 12 (2006): 35–49.

study by neuroscientist Demis Hassabis and colleagues compared people with amnesia caused by bilateral damage to their hippocampi with people whose episodic memory was intact. Whatever episodic memory the amnesiacs retained consisted mainly in recalling isolated trivial details of events.[53] They were unable to express the general meaning of these events because they could not contextualize them as part of a continuous narrative in time and space. Because their prospective memory was impaired as well, they were unable to imagine new experiences. The results of the study by Hassabis et al. support the hypothesis that remembering the past and imagining the future are interrelated mental capacities: one is the mirror image of the other. The fact that none of the amnesiacs was able to capture the gist of the past suggests that what matters is not just *how much* one can recall but also *how* one recalls it. The ability to meaningfully recall the past and anticipate the future appears to depend as much on qualitative as on quantitative aspects of our episodic memory. Hassabis' study suggests that increasing memory might interfere with the capacity to make sense of past experience and simulate future experience. This dual constructive capacity enables us to have a unified set of psychological properties necessary for our experience of persisting through time. While this requires a certain amount of memory storage and retrieval, it is more than a function of how many memories of facts and events our brains can store, or how efficiently they can retrieve them.

As memory researchers Daniel Schacter and Donna Rose Addis point out, "remembering the gist of what happened is an economical way of storing the most important aspects of our experiences without cluttering memory with trivial details."[54] They also note that "information about the past is useful only to the extent that it allows us to anticipate what may happen in the future."[55] Our capacity to learn new things is a function of the meaning we can construct from our experience. Memory is not just a reproduction of the past. In addition to the hippocampus in the temporal lobes, regions in the frontal and parietal lobes are critical to memory. The parietal lobe regulates our orientation to time and space. Together with the temporal and frontal lobes, it provides a holistic representation of the contexts in which we form and meaningfully retrieve memories. The dual capacity to recall the past and imagine the future is critical to the capacity of a human organism to make sense of its interaction with the environment. Storing and retrieving a large number of memories might adversely affect this by leaving us too focused on the past.

Jill Price's hyperthymestic syndrome illustrates that too much storage or retrieval of long-term memory could impair our short-term working memory and our ability to form new memories. Our cognitive capacities could be diminished by our ability to recall more facts and events that had no purpose for us. Constructing a narrative requires the ability to project ourselves into the future, which requires us to forget a considerable amount of information about the past. Memory enhancement could interfere with the need to jettison the excess baggage.

---

53. "Patients with Hippocampal Amnesia Cannot Imagine New Experiences," *Proceedings of the National Academy of Sciences* 104 (2007): 1726–1731.
54. "The Ghosts of Past and Future," *Nature* 445 (2007): 27.
55. *Ibid.*, 27.

Before we pharmacologically tinker with memory systems, we need to consider how this might affect the neurological and mental capacities that mediate the content and meaning of memory.

Therapeutic Forgetting

In Chapter 1, I discussed the possibility that weakening the emotional content of traumatic memories might also weaken the emotional content of positive autobiographical memories. In the United States, the President's Council on Bioethics expressed the more general concern that pharmacological modification of memory could have untoward consequences in our lives.[56] The council worried that blocking or dampening emotionally charged memories could erode much of our moral sensitivity. It could remove psychological constraints on doing things we would not otherwise do. Given the essential role of memory in shaping personal identity and moral responsibility, memory modification could reshape who we are in ways that might not be beneficial or benign.

The Council was concerned not only with manipulating pathological memories, like those in posttraumatic stress disorder, but also unpleasant episodic memories. Such concern would be warranted if memory manipulation caused us to lose the capacity for the moral emotions of shame and regret. These are essential to our capacity to take responsibility for our actions and their consequences, as well as our practices of holding people morally and legally responsible. I stated in Chapter 2 that regret is necessary for the counterfactual reasoning we engage in when considering alternative courses of action and deciding to act. It plays a crucial role in our capacity to respond to prudential and moral reasons for or against different actions. Psychopaths have impaired capacity for empathy and remorse, which partly explains why they do not respond to moral reasons and why they perform actions that harm others. Many of us tend to have weak memories of our moral failures. Drugs might enable us to eradicate these memories. If eradicating the emotional content of an unpleasant memory resulted in the loss of moral emotions, then it could have negative effects on the normative content of one's thought and behavior. It could impair one's capacity to respond to moral reasons.

But there may be some instances in which preventing or erasing an unpleasant memory would benefit a person without weakening the influence of moral emotions on his or her general thought and behavior. Therapeutic forgetting may be defensible in some cases. Suppose that a young academic gives a lecture in which he makes a glaring factual error or fails miserably in responding to questions from the audience. He is embarrassed by the experience and internalizes it to such a degree that it weakens his self-confidence and self-esteem. The memory of this event is not so disturbing that it puts him at risk of developing a psychiatric disorder such as generalized anxiety or major depression. But it has harmful psychological effects nonetheless. Leaving aside questions about selectivity, if a drug could erase

---

56. Staff Working Paper, "Better Memories? The Promise and Perils of Pharmacological Intervention," March 2003. http://www.bioethics.gov/transcripts/mar03.html. See also L. Kass, *Beyond Therapy: Biotechnology and the Pursuit of Happiness* (New York: Harper Collins, 2003).

this episodic memory by interfering with the process of consolidation or reconsolidation, then taking it would eliminate the persistent feeling of embarrassment and insecurity and make the person better off psychologically.[57] Manipulating the memory in this way would not necessarily undermine his capacity for moral emotions and responsiveness to moral reasons. It would not incline him to perform harmful acts that he would not otherwise perform. Erasing this particular memory would not make him fail to respect the rights, interests, and needs of others.

Extinguishing a memory of a wrongful or harmful act that one performed may desensitize one to an appropriate emotional response to future circumstances. In this respect, memory manipulation would be objectionable. But this would not be a likely consequence of erasing an unpleasant memory of an experience in which one did nothing harmful or wrongful. There would be nothing objectionable about therapeutic forgetting that involved deleting one unpleasant episode from one's autobiography. It would not weaken or undermine one's moral sensitivity. Nor would it substantially alter the unity and continuity of the set of life experiences that form one's narrative identity. Erasing the memory would be editing a small part of one's narrative while retaining the integrity of the whole.

This hypothetical case is an example of an intervention that lies in the gray zone on the continuum from therapy to enhancement. In one sense, it can be described as therapy because it prevents psychological harm to the individual. In another sense, it can be described as enhancement because, by eliminating a disturbing memory, it increases the net positive set of memories for the individual. An actual case illustrates how erasing a more disturbing memory may be construed both as therapy and prevention. More importantly, it raises the question of whether it can be ethical for one person to prevent or erase another person's memory. The case was reported in an article published in *Time* magazine on October 15, 2007.[58]

In 1997, orthopedic surgeon Dr. Scott Haig was performing a biopsy on a suspicious-looking lump near the end of a patient's collarbone. The patient consented to receive local rather than general anesthesia for the procedure. Dr. Haig and the patient agreed that some sedation might be given if it became necessary, and an anesthesiologist remained in the surgical suite for this purpose. The surgeon removed the tissue sample and sent it to the hospital pathologist. Over the intercom, Dr. Haig asked the pathologist to discuss the pathology report with him on the phone in a separate room. Saying that he could barely hear Dr. Haig, the pathologist blurted out: "This is a wildly pleomorphic tumor, very anaplastic. I can't tell what cell type it is, but it's really, really bad... cancer." Upon hearing this, the patient, who was not sedated, screamed, "Oh my God, my God! My kids. Then she screamed,"

---

57. In April 2009, the media reported that a drug, ZIP, could edit or erase memories by interfering with the PKMzeta molecule, which plays a role in memory consolidation. But the study showing this effect of ZIP was on rats; no studies of this drug have been conducted on humans.

58. "The Ethics of Erasing a Bad Memory," *Time* (online edition, October 15, 2007), http://www.time.com/time/health/article/0,8599,1671492,00.html. See also the discussion by A. Kolber in "Therapeutic Forgetting: The Legal and Ethical Implications of Memory Dampening," *Vanderbilt Law Review* 59 (2006): 1561–1626.

Oh, my... my arm..." The burning pain in her arm was due to an infusion of propofol administered immediately by the anesthesiologist. This is a white liquid medication that is sometimes called "milk of amnesia." The drug not only induces sedation but also prevents consolidation of memories of events experienced in the last few minutes. It induces short-term anterograde amnesia rather than retrograde amnesia. After the patient woke up, Dr. Haig said that the procedure had gone well but that they would have to wait for the pathology report. The patient had no memory of hearing the pathologist's comment. Dr. Haig admitted in the *Time* article that he did not tell her the whole truth and that, a decade after the event, he still was not sure that he had done the right thing.

At first blush, the surgeon's decision to allow propofol to be given to his patient and the anesthesiologist's action of infusing it into her seem unethical. Because the patient did not consent to receive the drug, the anesthesiologist and surgeon could have been legally charged with battery. They could also be held ethically accountable for failing to respect her right to know what occurred by not informing her after the incident. Before a procedure, a surgeon and patient may discuss the possibility of unanticipated events requiring interventions other than the procedure to which the patient explicitly consents. A patient may implicitly consent to an intervention deemed necessary to prevent any adverse effects of the intended procedure. The patient in this case agreed to receive some sedation, though the presumed purpose of the sedation was to control any pain or discomfort during the surgical procedure. She did not implicitly consent to sedation for the purpose of preventing or erasing a memory.

Dr. Haig's actions can be defended for two reasons. First, he was not withholding medically relevant information from the patient before the procedure. He did not have this information at the time because he could not have foreseen the pathologist blurting out the diagnosis over the intercom. Second, although the propofol infusion was not primarily intended to sedate the patient, it was an intervention necessary to prevent an adverse psychological effect of the pathologist's negligence. It prevented harm to the patient by preventing the retention of a disturbing memory of what the pathologist said. In addition to the suffering she would have to endure from the cancer, a memory of the pathologist's remark on the intercom would only have increased the psychological harm to her.

A more complicated question is whether Dr. Haig was obligated to tell the patient about the pathologist's remark and the propofol infusion after the incident. The malignant tumor was a recurrence of a cancer the patient had some years earlier. She died 6 years after the propofol incident, without Dr. Haig ever telling her about it. Ordinarily, a physician is obligated to disclose a medical error and any corrective measures to a patient when that same physician, or others working under him or her, commits the error and when it results in harm to the patient. Neither of these conditions was present in this case. The error was committed by the pathologist, and Dr. Haig was not obligated to take responsibility for it because the pathologist was not working under his authority. Moreover, the propofol that Dr. Haig allowed to correct the pathologist's error did not cause but prevented harm to the patient. Nevertheless, it was Dr. Haig who allowed the drug infusion. Was he obligated to give her a complete account of what occurred that day despite the fact that she did not ask? One would think that the patient had a right to be informed of the infusion. But informing her immediately after she awoke could have been just as traumatic as not intervening and allowing her to retain the memory. The surgeon could invoke therapeutic privilege to justify withholding the information at that time because of the likelihood that it would harm his patient.

Still, some might argue that she had a right to be informed of the propofol infusion and the reason for it at a later time. This right would be independent of questions about benefit and harm. What is most medically relevant in this case is that the patient be informed of the biopsy and pathology report in a timely manner. Dr. Haig informed her of these once he had the final report. Patients have a right to be informed of all medically relevant information regarding procedures performed on them by physicians, not just any information. Whether Dr. Haig was obligated to inform his patient of the propofol infusion at a later time would depend on whether it was medically relevant at that time. If one answers this question in the affirmative, then he had an obligation to inform her and failed to discharge it. If one answers this question in the negative, then he had the prerogative to inform or not inform her and as such was not obligated to do so. In that case, the answer could be sustained despite Dr. Haig's uncertainty about whether he did the right thing.

Authenticity and Alienation

Another concern about enhancing normal cognitive functions with drugs is that it would undermine our authenticity. According to philosopher Charles Taylor, the moral idea of authenticity emerged at the end of the eighteenth century in Europe. It is up to me as a human being to find my way in the world, to flourish, and be "true to myself. If I am not, I miss the point of my life. I miss what being human is for *me*."[59] Our selves consist of a unified set of embodied mental states that are generated and sustained by normal functions in the brain. We come to have authentic selves by identifying with our mental states. This state of identification results from a process of critical reflection on our desires, beliefs, intentions, and emotions. It is through this reflective self-control that we reinforce these states as the springs of our actions. As discussed in Chapter 2, Frankfurt argues that being a free and authentic agent consists in having the general capacity to control which motivational states issue in our actions. The first-order desires that we execute in our actions should align with our second-order desire to be motivated and act in a certain way.[60] Insofar as agency is a necessary condition of selfhood, being an authentic agent is a necessary condition of having an authentic self.

Altering the process of critical reflection and the mental states that result from it with psychotropic drugs presumably would alienate us from our true selves. We could not identify with these altered states and would not have authentic selves because something alien to us would be the agent of the change. Ethicist Leon Kass

---

59. *The Ethics of Authenticity* (Cambridge, MA: Harvard University Press, 1991), 29. See also E. Parens, "Authenticity and Ambivalence: Toward Understanding the Enhancement Debate," *Hastings Center Report* 35 (3) (2005): 34–41.
60. "Freedom of the Will and the Concept of a Person," and "Identification and Externality."

and other members of the President's Council noted this as a possible consequence of cognitive enhancement: "As the power to transform our native powers increases, both in magnitude and refinement, so does the possibility for 'self-alienation'—for losing, confounding, or abandoning our identity."[61]

It does not necessarily follow that the voluntary use of a drug to enhance cognition would make us inauthentic. If an individual with the capacity for critical self-reflection freely decides to take a cognition-enhancing drug, then he or she is the agent of any change in mental states. The drug is merely the means through which the change is effected. Provided that the individual has the capacity to weigh the reasons for and against enhancement and to act on these reasons, enhancement would not result in an inauthentic or alien self. The same goes for editing or deleting unpleasant memories. If this is what the individual desires, intends, and freely decides to do, then the change is of his or her own doing. Improving one's cognitive functions can be consistent with authenticity by being part of the set of experiences that one wants to have as one's autobiography.

Even if cognitive enhancement disrupted the continuity of one's mental states and resulted in a different self, the capacity to foresee this as the consequence of enhancement would make one responsible for it. Consider Stevenson's tale of Dr. Jekyll and Mr. Hyde. Jekyll transforms himself into the evil Hyde by voluntarily taking a potion. Later, when his curiosity moves him to repeat the experiment, he finds himself the subject of the involuntary mental states that characterize Hyde. Although it is Hyde who commits the evil deeds, Jekyll is responsible for them. He has the capacity to know that they are the likely consequences of his experiment and that he could prevent them by not taking the potion. Foreseeability makes the responsibility transfer from the earlier to the later time. This seems to be the point of Jekyll's admission, when speaking of Hyde that "this too was myself."[62]

Political philosopher Michael Sandel and others have expressed concern about enhancing cognitive and physical functions through pharmacological or other means. There are many ways in which some people may fairly or unfairly gain an advantage over others, quite apart from whether they resort to psychopharmacology. So, one can question the reasons for singling out cognition-enhancing drugs for this purpose. Still, Sandel's main worry about enhancement is not that we would gain an unfair advantage over others with respect to positional goods, but that we would be cheating ourselves.[63] Improving our capacities with drugs, blood doping, or genetic manipulation undermines our sense of excellence. Sandel insists that we should welcome and make the most of the capacities with which we have been endowed, despite their imperfections. Excellence involves availing ourselves of these natural gifts, realizing that much of what happens in life is beyond our control. We should avoid the hubris in trying to gain an illusory sense of control of our lives by manipulating our given mental and physical capacities. Sandel's rejection of enhancement

---

61. *Beyond Therapy*, 294.

62. *Dr. Jekyll and Mr. Hyde, and Other Stories* (New York: Grosset and Dunlap, 1984).

63. *The Case against Perfection: Ethics in the Age of Genetic Engineering* (Cambridge, MA: Harvard University Press, 2007). Kass expresses a similar view in "Ageless Bodies, Happy Souls: Biotechnology and the Pursuit of Perfection," *The New Atlantis* 1 (2003): 9–28.

is driven by the importance he attributes to what he calls "giftedness" and the "unbidden."[64] Many agree with this view and believe that we are giving up something valuable if we do not rely entirely on our natural abilities to achieve our goals. We tend to have a higher opinion of someone who achieves a goal by developing and exercising these abilities than of someone who does this with the help of a drug.

Against Sandel, Harris insists that excellence is not so much a function of our natural endowment as it is of our free choices and capacity to take responsibility for them. Excellence results from effort and practice, which may involve improving on our given traits.[65] For some, accepting these traits as they are may be tantamount to accepting a form of biological determinism. Taking a cognition-enhancing drug may be construed as one component in the process of self-improvement and in this sense can be consistent with excellence. Neuroenhancing agents do not do all of the work for us; they aid us in doing it. Also, Sandel does not appreciate fully the extent of the inequalities in our natural gifts. As an example of natural luck, some people have higher levels of hemoglobin in their red blood cells, which may give them more physical stamina than others and make them more capable of excelling in sports. As another example of natural luck, some people have a higher baseline of working memory and are better at performing cognitive tasks than others because their brains are wired differently. They may have stronger synaptic connections and faster signal transmission between neurons. Enhancement may be a way of enabling those who are less gifted to compete equally with those who are more gifted.

Whether cognition-enhancing drugs improve our performance depends on how we make use of the potential cognitive boost they provide. Separating individual effort from the effects of the drugs may be an oversimplification. Many of our achievements result from the combination of personal effort and enhancement. This includes not only drugs but also private tutors and trainers. The enhancing agent alone will not produce the desired result. A procrastinating student who has to write a research paper overnight for a class the next day has to decide how much time to devote to the research and how much time to write the paper. Modafinil may enable the student to remain awake and methylphenidate may improve the student's ability to focus. But the drugs will not help the student to make this decision. One might become too focused on the research, or on trivial details of the research, and end up failing to submit the paper on time. Caffeine may have the same effect as drugs in producing a positive outcome. Journalist Margaret Talbot writes: "Even with the aid of a neuroenhancer, you still have to write the essay, conceive the screenplay, or finish the grant proposal, and if you can take credit for what you've done on caffeine or nicotine, then you can take credit for work produced on Provigil."[66]

---

64. *The Case against Perfection*, 26–29, 45–46, 86.
65. *Enhancing Evolution*, 109–122. See also the chapters in J. Savulescu and N. Bostrom, eds. *Human Enhancement* (Oxford: Oxford University Press, 2009).
66. "Brain Gain; The Underground World of Neuroenhancing Drugs," *The New Yorker*, April 27, 2009: 32–43, at 40. http://www/newyorker.com/reporting/2009/04/27/090427fa_fact?currentPage=all

As an example of one's effort to improve oneself, taking a cognition-enhancing drug could be a reflection of one's character. It could be part of one's second-order desire to improve one's practical reasoning and decision making. Some may question the type of character that allowed taking enhancing drugs as part of one's effort to improve oneself. But this action would not necessarily be a form of inauthenticity. On the contrary, insofar as one identifies with the desire to enhance cognition and takes responsibility for its consequences, enhancement can be an expression of authenticity. Autonomy is inseparable from authenticity. One should have the right to choose to enhance if it is in one's best interests. Unless the exercise of this right results in harm to others, autonomous individuals should be allowed to enhance their cognitive capacities. Some may be sympathetic to Sandel's objection to the hubristic idea of improving ourselves through psychopharmacology. But this objection does not justify overriding autonomy and prohibiting enhancement. As Harris puts it, "Sandel can have the unbidden and the welcome, but on condition that he will let me and others have access to the bidden."[67]

Conclusion

The use of psychotropic drugs to enhance cognition is likely to increase. Empirical studies have shown that the enhancing effects of methylphenidate, modafinil, and similar drugs are modest for those with a higher cognitive functional baseline and more pronounced for those with a lower baseline. This difference in the effects of the drugs suggests that cognitive enhancement would not exacerbate social inequality. Enhancement would affect only one dimension of our social lives. Social standing and well-being are influenced by many factors in addition to levels of cognitive function.

Beta-blockers can prevent or attenuate the physical and psychological symptoms associated with anxiety and may improve musical and other types of performance in some cases. They may enable musicians plagued by the stress of playing under pressure to perform to their full potential. These drugs can prevent these symptoms from interfering with one's normal ability to perform; or they may enable one to perform better. Yet if these or other drugs are not meant to prevent or treat a psychiatric disorder, then physicians would not be obligated to prescribe them on demand. Although individuals may purchase these drugs from the Internet or other sources, they would not have a right to obtain them from physicians. Prescribing drugs in these cases could contribute to the medicalization of conditions that may involve moderate impairment in specific tasks but do not interfere with the ability to perform a general range of cognitive and physical functions.

Enhancement of mechanisms mediating long-term memory could increase our capacity to recall more facts and events. It could also impair the capacity to process information in short-term, working memory. Attempts to increase our ability to store and retrieve more memories must be sensitive to how we construct meaning from the dual capacity to recall the past and imagine the future, which requires a

---

67. *Enhancing Evolution*, 122.

certain degree of forgetting. Erasing or preventing a memory can be justified in cases where the memory would harm a person who has or would have it. But memory modification would not be justified if it eroded one's capacity for the moral emotions of shame, regret, and remorse. These emotions provide constraints on actions that could be harmful to oneself and others. Contrary to what some bioethicists claim, enhancing memory and other cognitive capacities would not necessarily undermine authenticity or alienate us from our true selves. If a first-order desire to enhance cognitive functions aligns with the second-order desire to improve oneself, then enhancement can be consistent with authenticity.

The long-term effects of chronic use of cognition-enhancing drugs are not known. Empirical data on the effects of the drugs are from short-term studies only, and they do not indicate any serious adverse events. For this reason, a precautionary principle limiting or prohibiting their use is not warranted at this time. The mere potential of adverse events is not enough to justify such a principle. As an expression of autonomy, competent individuals should have the right to use enhancing drugs, provided that they access them on their own, do not pose a risk of harm to others, and take responsibility for the effects of the drugs, including any medical costs. They need to be aware that taking these drugs entails some risk. The most reasonable position is to permit cognitive enhancement but include the warning "User Beware!"

6

Brain Injury and Survival

There is considerable variation in outcomes of severe brain injury resulting from trauma, anoxia, and pathologies such as tumors, strokes, and infections. Some brain-injured individuals become comatose, irreversibly lose all brain functions, and are declared brain-dead. Others may emerge from even prolonged comas with full conscious awareness and many of their physical and cognitive functions intact. But a number of people with these injuries live in disordered states of consciousness and have significant cognitive and physical disabilities. A smaller number retains full consciousness but experiences profound amnesia. These outcomes often involve a substantial change in one's psychological properties before and after an injury. This chapter explores three general questions pertaining to individuals with severe brain injury. The first is metaphysical, while the second and third are ethical: Do individuals with this type of injury survive it? In what sense can they be harmed by the injury? Do interventions aimed at restoring brain function benefit or harm them? How one responds to the second and third questions will depend to a certain extent on how one responds to the first.

After establishing a criterion of survival, I present two actual cases of individuals with severe amnesia resulting from neurosurgery and encephalitis. The amnesia in these cases illustrates the importance of episodic memory for psychological continuity and the experience of persisting through time. I present additional cases in distinguishing coma from the vegetative state (VS) and the minimally conscious state (MCS). These states differ according to the degree of integrated cortical (higher-brain) functioning and the extent of connections between and among the ascending reticular activating system in the brainstem, the thalamus, and the cortex. While there is little or no integrated cortical function and little or no capacity for awareness in the VS, there is integrated but under-sustained cortical function and some degree of awareness in the MCS. This difference underscores the fact that consciousness can be a matter of degree, which complicates the question of survival. I distinguish these two states from locked-in syndrome (LIS). In this syndrome, one retains conscious awareness despite being almost completely paralyzed by an injury to the brainstem that disrupts signals from the cortex to the spinal cord and cranial nerves. Following a discussion of whether individuals in these distinct neurological and psychological states survive their injuries, I consider the respects in which they are harmed by being in these states. I also consider the respects in which interventions designed to restore physical and cognitive functions can benefit or harm them.

Two Distinctions

"Survival" means that an individual continues to exist despite undergoing changes from an earlier to a later time. One can survive as an individual of a certain kind, or as the same individual. In the first case, if the changes involve permanent loss of properties that make an individual a member of a kind, then the individual ceases to exist as one of that kind. In the second case, if the changes involve permanent loss of properties that make one a distinct individual, then the individual ceases to exist as that individual. The metaphysical question of survival in each of these senses hinges on two critical issues: (1) whether one takes us to be essentially human organisms or persons; and (2) whether one adopts numerical identity or narrative identity to track the existence of an individual over time.

If we are essentially human organisms, then we begin to exist when there is a sufficiently integrated set of biological properties to identify each of us as such an organism.[1] This may occur around the later embryonic or early fetal stage of development. We cease to exist when all brain and bodily functions permanently cease. This may occur after the permanent cessation of brain functions. Neurologist Alan Shewmon has shown that some patients who meet criteria of brain death can survive for years as biological organisms with some degree of somatic integration and homeostatic bodily functions intact.[2] So, brain death does not imply the death of a human organism.

If we are essentially persons, then we begin to exist when we develop the capacity for conscious awareness. This occurs when there is a sufficient degree of integrated cerebral cortical function.[3] We cease to exist when we permanently lose the capacity for conscious awareness. This occurs when there is permanent cessation of integrated cortical function. Awareness is mediated not only by the cerebral cortex but also by the thalamus and reticular activating system. Since cortical function is necessary for awareness, permanent loss of function in this region of the brain is sufficient for loss of the awareness essential to personhood. Whether brainstem or somatic functions continue after this point is irrelevant to personhood.

---

1. E. Olson defends this position in *The Human Animal: Personal Identity without Psychology* (Oxford: Oxford University Press, 1997) and *What Are We? A Study in Personal Ontology* (Oxford: Oxford University Press, 2007).
2. "The Brain and Somatic Integration: Insights into the Standard Biological Rationale for Equating `Brain Death' with Death," *Journal of Medicine and Philosophy* 26 (2001): 457–478.
3. J. McMahan defends the view that we are essentially persons, or what he calls "embodied minds" with the capacity for consciousness, in *The Ethics of Killing; Problems at the Margins of Life* (Oxford: Oxford University Press, 2002), 66–94.

Although they overlap through much of the lifespan, a person begins to exist later than and may cease to exist earlier than a human organism, for which consciousness is only a contingent rather than a necessary property. A patient in a permanent vegetative state or irreversible coma who has lost the capacity for conscious awareness but has intact brainstem, cardiocirculatory, and somatic functions continues to exist as a human organism but ceases to exist as a person.

According to numerical identity, x at an earlier time T1 is the same individual as y at a later time T2 just in case x and y have the same basic properties.[4] Numerical identity can be defined as spatiotemporal continuity of the physical body through change. Any changes the individual undergoes are not substantial changes. Numerical identity does not necessarily include any psychological properties and thus is more of a criterion of organisms than persons. It does not admit of degrees; it is all or nothing. An individual at a later time either is or is not numerically identical to an individual at an earlier time.

According to narrative identity, x at T1 is the same individual as y at T2 just in case x and y have the same unified set of psychological characteristics and experiences constituting a distinctive autobiography. Narrative identity presupposes that the episodes in a person's life are continuous and integrated. They have a thematic unity shaped by the values and interests of that person.[5] The meaning of the total set of experiences in the life of a person is more than the sum of its parts. Narrative identity may be a matter of degree, depending on the strength of the connections between and continuity of psychological properties over time. Provided that these properties meet a critical threshold of unity, narrative identity can accommodate some changes in them. Profound amnesia and severe personality change fail to meet the critical threshold because they involve radical psychological disconnectedness and discontinuity between earlier and later times. Personality and memory are both necessary for narrative identity, and thus a substantial alteration of either of these psychological properties can undermine it. Agency is also a necessary property of narrative identity, since whether one can construct a narrative from the episodes in one's life depends on the capacity to plan, undertake, and complete projects over an extended period. Because agency requires the capacity to recall the past and project oneself into the future, agency involves both retrospective and prospective memory.

Following Locke and Derek Parfit, one can say that an individual survives a brain injury as the same person if there is a sufficient degree of connectedness and

---

4. See the papers in J. Perry, ed., *Personal Identity*, 2nd ed. (Berkeley: University of California Press, 2008).

5. In Chapter 1, note 20, I pointed out that M. Schechtman and D. DeGrazia are the main proponents of narrative identity. Schechtman offers an updated account of this conception in "Getting Our Stories Straight," in D. Mathews, H. Bok, and P. Rabins, eds., *Personal Identity and Fractured Selves: Perspectives from Philosophy, Ethics, and Neuroscience* (Baltimore: The Johns Hopkins University Press, 2009), 65–92. In this chapter, Schechtman says: "In the spirit of Locke, I will call the questions of personal identity… questions of *forensic personal identity*…" (68). Our practices of promising, contracting, praising, and blaming are based on this conception.

continuity of that individual's psychological properties before and after the event.[6] Connectedness involves relations between mental states holding over shorter periods, while continuity involves overlapping chains of strong connectedness holding over longer periods. Insofar as these mental states are diachronically unified, narrative identity is grounded in psychological continuity.

The response to the question of whether an individual survives a brain injury depends on which conception of identity one adopts. Recall Phineas Gage from Chapter 2.[7] The iron rod in the railroad accident damaged an area of his frontal lobes. Some of his cognitive capacities were intact following the accident. But he became impulsive and impaired in his capacity for rational and moral decision making. His emotions changed dramatically, and his behavior became erratic. There was such a change in his personality that those who knew him claimed that he was "no longer Gage." By this they did not mean that the post-injury Gage was not numerically identical to the pre-injury Gage. There was enough similarity between his physical properties to be identifiable as the same individual from the earlier to the later time. Instead, they made this claim because of the radical change in the behavioral properties on the basis of which they knew him. His narrative identity changed because of the disconnectedness and discontinuity between the psychological characteristics and experiences that constituted his life before the injury and those that constituted his life after it. In this regard, Gage did not survive his brain injury. We can make this claim even if Gage himself did not experience the change and it was only observed by those who knew him.

If continuity of physical properties alone is sufficient for numerical identity, and if this conception of identity is consistent with the idea that we are human organisms, then an individual could lose all higher-brain functions, become permanently vegetative or comatose, and survive indefinitely as the same individual in this state. Yet it is on the basis of personhood and narrative identity that we are able to value our lives. The capacity for conscious awareness that makes us persons enables us to interact with others. It also enables each of us to integrate our actions and experiences into a meaningful whole. These are not essential properties of human organisms. In light of this, I discuss the metaphysical and ethical aspects of survival of brain injury on the assumptions that we are essentially persons rather than human organisms and that the relevant conception of identity is narrative rather than numerical identity.

Currently, the only medically and legally accepted neurological definition of death is the permanent cessation of all brain functions.[8] Yet the cortical functions

---

6. Locke, *An Essay Concerning Human Understanding*, Book II, Chapter xxvii. Parfit says that what matters in survival is not (numerical) identity, but Relation R, which holds when there is a certain degree of psychological connectedness and continuity. *Reasons and Persons* (Oxford: Clarendon Press, 1984), Part III.

7. See Chapter 2, note 54.

8. This definition has remained unchanged since the *Report of the Ad Hoc Committee of the Harvard Medical School to Examine the Definition of Brain Death*. H. Beecher et al., "A Definition of Irreversible Coma," *Journal of the American Medical Association* 205 (1968): 337–340. See also E. Wijdicks, "The Diagnosis of Brain Death," *New England Journal of*

generating and sustaining the psychological properties necessary for one to be a person and persist as the same person may permanently cease despite intact subcortical and brainstem function. In that case, a person would not survive an injury resulting in this condition, even though he or she would not meet the whole-brain criterion of death. Because personhood and personal identity depend on certain integrated brain functions, and because one can lose these functions and no longer be a person without meeting the standard neurological definition of death, I contrast "survival" with "ceasing to exist" rather than with "death." One ceases to exist as an organism when all brain and bodily functions permanently cease. One ceases to exist as a person when the integrated brain functions supporting conscious awareness permanently cease. Insofar as "brain death" implies permanent cessation of all brain functions, brain death and ceasing to exist as a person are not necessarily co-extensive. Accordingly, my position should not be equated with the view that people go out of existence when they die. A person can go out of existence even when he or she does not meet the whole-brain criterion of death.

Profound Amnesia: H. M. and Clive Wearing

I discussed the different functions of episodic, semantic, working, and procedural memory in Chapters 1, 3, and 5. Amnesia usually affects two types of episodic memory. *Retrograde* amnesia is the inability to recall or retrieve memories that one has already formed. *Anterograde* amnesia is the inability to form new memories. Some regions of the brain are more important than others in generating and sustaining the psychological connectedness and continuity necessary for narrative identity. Even when other brain regions continue to function normally, damage to the hippocampus can extinguish stored memories, disable memory retrieval, and prevent the formation of new memories. It can destroy the episodic memory necessary for the experience of persisting through time and having an autobiography. Hippocampal damage can also affect prospective memory, the ability to plan and project oneself into the future. Cases of profound amnesia are distinct from neurodegenerative diseases such as Alzheimer's disease and frontotemporal dementia. Although Alzheimer's disease and frontotemporal dementia have distinct clinical courses, they are both progressive diseases eventually resulting in significant changes in personality, judgment, and memory. Because these changes are usually gradual, the identities of these individuals are lost gradually and erode over a number of years. In contrast, the loss of identity in profound amnesia occurs in a comparatively shorter period and is due mainly to the loss of episodic memory following brain injury.

Medicine 344 (2001): 1215–1221. In the United Kingdom, permanent cessation of brainstem function is the criterion for brain death. See the Working Group of the Royal College of Physicians, "Criteria for the Diagnosis of Brain Stem Death," *Journal of the Royal College of Physicians of London* 29 (1995): 381–382. The determination of brain death remains controversial, as noted in a 2008 White Paper by the U. S. President's Council on Bioethics, "Controversies in the Determination of Death" (http://www.bioethics.gov/reports/death/determination_of_death_report.pdf).

H. M. (Henry Molaison), who died in December 2008 at age 82, is perhaps the best-known amnesiac.[9] He developed a seizure disorder during childhood. The seizures became more frequent after he was struck to the ground by a bicycle rider in his teens. By the time he was 26 in 1953, the seizures were so severe that he consented to an experimental form of neurosurgery to relieve them. Bilateral surgical removal of both hippocampi and adjacent structures in his medial temporal lobes resolved the seizures but left him with temporally graded retrograde amnesia. H. M. continued to interact with others, and his personality remained unchanged. He retained childhood memories but had difficulty recalling events that occurred during the years immediately preceding the surgery. More significantly, he developed profound anterograde amnesia. He was unable to form new memories and because of this could not construct and sustain an autobiography. Without the hippocampus, new memories cannot be consolidated and stored in the cortex as long-term memories. H. M. retained his working, semantic, and procedural memory, which enabled him to perform daily mental and physical tasks. But he was unable to capture the gist or express the general meaning of the events he could recall. He could not contextualize them as part of a coherent sequence in time and space. H. M. was unable to connect his spare memory of events in the past with his present awareness and could not project himself into the future. Because his brain was unable to consolidate new episodic memories, he would tell and retell the same story within minutes without knowing that he had already told it. For each instance in which he saw the same person or was informed about the same event, it was as if it had occurred for the first time. His verbal responses to the neuroscientists studying his case indicated that, when they examined H. M., it was as though he had never met them before. This was how he experienced these encounters, despite many meetings and exchanges with the same people over months and years.

H. M. lost both retrospective and prospective memory. He lived from one moment to the next, largely confined to the present and unable to construct a narrative and unify his experiences into a meaningful whole. Because he could not project himself into the future, he lost much of his capacity for agency. After his surgery, his life was a fragmented collection of discrete units without any diachronic quality. Others could identify him as the same person from the time of his surgery to his death on the basis of his physical properties, his stable personality, and the behavioral manifestations of his working, semantic, and procedural memory. In these respects, the pre-surgery H. M. was numerically identical to the post-surgery H. M. But his inability to form new episodic memories destroyed psychological continuity between his earlier and later mental states. Indeed, the temporal scope of his attention was so narrow that there was very little, if any, connectedness, between his psychological properties. Working, semantic, and procedural memory are not enough to meet the threshold of psychological continuity necessary for the experience of persisting through time. For those who knew him, his biography was like a book

---

9. W. Scoville and B. Milner, "Loss of Recent Memory after Bilateral Hippocampal Lesions," *Journal of Neurology, Neurosurgery, and Psychiatry* 20 (1957): 11–21. Schacter discusses the case of H. M. in *Searching for Memory*, Chapter 5.

consisting of a disconnected set of sentences repeating themselves. It was not a coherent narrative with a dynamic succession of thematically integrated chapters. If survival is based on narrative identity, and if narrative identity necessarily depends on the capacity to recall the recent and remote past and project oneself into the future, then H. M. did not survive the surgery. He lost his identity, surviving as *a* person, but not as the *same* person.[10]

A similar case of profound amnesia befell British musician and musicologist Clive Wearing. He contracted a herpes encephalitis infection in his brain in 1985, when he was in his mid-40s.[11] The infection destroyed the region of the medial temporal lobes mediating his capacity for episodic memory. His loss of episodic memory was more extreme than that of H. M. Clive developed not only profound anterograde amnesia but also profound retrograde amnesia. This resulted in the deletion of most of the past from his brain and mind. The scope of his short-term memory and attention was also more limited than that of H. M., spanning no more than a few seconds. This made Clive even more of a prisoner of the present than H. M. Since the infection, his life has consisted of very short, disconnected experiences, without any sense of psychological continuity. At home, whenever he sees his wife, he greets her as if she had just arrived. This occurs multiple times throughout each day, though he gradually seems to re-familiarize himself with her. Unfortunately, he has retained enough cognitive ability to infer his amnesia from his experience and is painfully aware of it. As his wife Deborah wrote in a 2005 memoir:

> It was as if every waking moment was the first waking moment. Clive was under the constant impression that he had just emerged from unconsciousness because he had no evidence in his own mind of ever being awake before… "I haven't heard anything, seen anything, touched anything, smelled anything," he would say. "It's like being dead."[12]

Of course, Clive's use of the simile in the last sentence indicates that he was not speaking literally. It is an expression of his experience of being aware of having severe amnesia. It is not to be equated with the state of being dead, which cannot be experienced. Still, his comment indicates the extent to which profound amnesia has harmed him. Clive experiences harm from his awareness of his inability to recall events and people. We cannot experience the loss of additional life years caused by death. But Clive subjectively can feel and suffer from the loss of his memory on a constant basis. This is one case in which retaining consciousness can be worse than losing it. Death can harm us by depriving us of the goods we would have enjoyed

---

10. In *Reasons and Persons*, Parfit says that "to be a person, a being must be self-conscious, aware of its identity and continued existence over time" (202). Although H. M. lacked the experience of persisting through time, he was fully conscious of himself in the present. This is sufficient for one to survive as a person, but not sufficient for one to survive as the same person.

11. O. Sacks discusses this case in "The Abyss: Music and Amnesia," *The New Yorker*, September 24, 2007, 100–111 (http://www.newyorker.com/reporting/2007/09/24/070924fa_fact_Sacks).

12. *Ibid.*, 100.

had we continued to live. The harm may occur even if we cannot experience the loss of these goods. Still, the loss of things we can experience is worse for us than the loss of things we cannot experience. It is because the first but not the second type of loss can cause suffering that a neurological injury with severe psychological symptoms can be worse than death.

Our capacity to anticipate the future depends on our capacity to recall the past. The second is a mirror image of the first. Many with profound amnesia are not only unable to recall the past but also unable to imagine the future. This reinforces the idea that some amnesiacs are stuck in a narrow temporal interval and lose the psychological continuity necessary for survival. In his account of Clive Wearing, neurologist Oliver Sacks writes: "To imagine the future was no more possible for Clive than to remember the past—both were engulfed by the onslaught of amnesia."[13] Clive's experience consists not in persisting through time but only existing at a time in a repeated present.

He has retained three types of memory. His capacity for musical performance is largely intact, indicating that he has procedural memory of how to play the piano. He also has some working memory in being able to process musical and other forms of information for short periods. The emotional memory associated with his relationship with his wife is intact as well. They married before he contracted encephalitis and shared a love of music. Emotionally charged memories may resist erasure from hippocampal injury because memories of fearful or threatening events are critical to survival. For this reason, they are more firmly formed and consolidated in the amygdala than emotionally neutral episodic memories formed and consolidated in the hippocampus. Not all emotionally charged memories are negative; some may be positive. It is possible that Clive's wedding and shared loved of music with his wife were so positively emotionally charged that they have enabled him to retain some nondeclarative memory of them. This emotional memory likely accounts for his ability to continue having an emotional relationship with his wife. He sustains this relationship and experiences a familiarity with her despite the fact that his amnesia makes it difficult for him to recognize and re-identify her each time she appears before him. The regions of the brain mediating his emotional and procedural memory—the amygdala, cerebellum, and striatum—were spared the damage to his hippocampi. Sacks asserts that these intact memory systems confirm Clive's identity.[14] He also suggests that improvement in Clive's mood in the years since the onset of his amnesia may be attributed to the strength of these memories.

Nevertheless, these are unconscious memories and as such lack the subjective quality associated with the conscious awareness of persisting from the past, through the present, to the future. Episodic memories available for conscious recall are necessary for narrative unity and continuity of one's experience. To the extent that this unity and continuity are necessary for one to survive an event as the same person, and Clive Wearing lost them, he did not survive the event of the infection that damaged his brain. The unconscious memory he has retained is one component of his

---

13. "The Abyss," 101.
14. *Ibid.*, 105. See also J. McGaugh, *Memory and Emotion: The Making of Lasting Memories* (New York: Columbia University Press, 2003).

intact numerical identity. It is not sufficient to sustain his narrative identity. One might claim that his capacity for musical performance indicates that he has retained his capacity for agency. Yet if agency involves conscious planning and the execution of conscious intentions in actions, and if musical performance is mainly a function of unconscious procedural memory, then it is questionable whether he has retained a sufficient degree of agency to survive as the same person on this basis. To borrow legal theorist Ronald Dworkin's distinction between critical and experiential interests, Clive's life lacks the temporal scope necessary for critical interests, which consist of the values and commitments one has about one's life as a whole. Critical interests are essential for narrative identity. His life after his hippocampal damage has consisted of experiential interests confined to his immediate thoughts.[15]

The claim that Clive Wearing did not survive his brain injury seems at odds with the claim that he is able to continue his relationship with his wife. Yet the fact that a region of his brain mediating many of the psychological properties associated with this relationship is damaged and that only a region mediating a limited set of these properties is intact suggests that he has not continued this relationship. Instead, it suggests that he has developed a new relationship with her. Some of his cognitive and affective capacities have survived, but not enough to retain the same relationship he had with his wife before the injury. Given the loss of his episodic memory and his ability to imagine the future, he can share only a very limited set of experiences with her. This is consistent with the claim that in this case there are two distinct persons with two distinct narratives before and after the viral infection.

Again, the response to the question of whether a person survives a brain injury depends on which conception of identity one adopts. I have argued that only narrative identity captures the subjective experience of persisting through time, the idea of a unified set of life experiences shaped by one's values and interests, and a meaningful sense of 'survival.' Not all brain-injured individuals develop severe amnesia and lose the unity of their earlier and later mental states. As the cases of H. M. and Clive Wearing illustrate, though, brain injuries damaging the hippocampus and undermining the ability to retain old memories and form new ones can have a devastating effect on the psychological continuity necessary for one to persist as the same person. Unlike numerical identity, narrative identity can be a matter of degree. It can accommodate moderate changes in memory and personality. But the disruption of psychological continuity from the amnesia was so extensive in these two individuals that it caused them to lose this identity and not survive their brain injuries. The loss of narrative identity is based on their first-person experience with profound amnesia and the third-person observations of those who knew them.

Some might claim that H. M. and Clive Wearing did not lose their identities and become distinct persons after their brain injuries. They survived as diminished, disordered, and poorly functioning versions of the same persons who existed before the injuries.[16] But surely one who loses the capacity to recall episodes from one's life and

---

15. *Life's Dominion* (New York: Vintage Books, 1993), 214–215.
16. For example, Perry, "Diminished and Fractured Selves," and S. Barondes, "After Locke: Darwin, Freud, and Psychiatric Assessment," both in Mathews, Bok, and Rabins, 129–162, 165–173.

imagine the future is substantially different from one who previously had these mental capacities. It is unclear in what sense one who undergoes these radical psychological changes could survive as the same person. Ethicist Debra Mathews and coauthors claim that "if an individual cannot construct a single, coherent narrative, with a past, present, and future that are continuous and related… a different person may come to exist within a given human body."[17] The claim that a person is harmed usually presupposes a comparison of two states of affairs in which the same person exists. The person is worse off in one state of affairs than the other, which assumes the retention of identity. Yet both H. M. and Clive Wearing were harmed by the fact that their amnesia destroyed their narrative identity and thwarted their interest in maintaining it. Their brain injuries and resulting amnesia foreclosed future opportunities and stripped them of their agency and capacity for critical interests. They were harmed by the loss of episodic memory as an essential component of their mental life.

Chronic Disorders of Consciousness

Unlike the cases of amnesia just discussed, many individuals fall into unconscious states or altered states of consciousness after severe brain injury. There are seven neurological states that need to be distinguished: full consciousness; coma; brain death; the persistent VS; the MCS; the permanent VS; and LIS.[18] Consciousness is divided into two basic components: arousal (wakefulness or vigilance) and awareness of self and one's surroundings. The first component refers to a *state* of consciousness; the second refers to the *content* of consciousness, what one is conscious *of*.[19] The latter is necessary for a person to interact with other persons and includes what I have called phenomenal consciousness. In a normal conscious state, there is widespread integrated function in the cerebral cortex sustained by projections from the central thalamus, certain brainstem nuclei, and the brainstem ascending reticular activating system. These structures of the brainstem are necessary for arousal and contribute to the cortical activation necessary for awareness. Arousal consciousness is sustained primarily by the reticular formation, while content consciousness requires the engagement of cortical systems. Although the cerebral cortex is commonly associated with awareness, temporary or permanent functional cessation of the thalamus or reticular formation results in loss of awareness. The integrity of these cortical and subcortical regions and functions can be a matter of degree, which corresponds to the seven neurological states at issue.

---

17. "Introduction," *Personal Identity and Fractured Selves*, 5.
18. S. Laureys, A. Owen, and N. Schiff draw these distinctions and discuss their neurological significance in "Brain Function in Coma, Vegetative State, and Related Disorders," *The Lancet: Neurology* 3 (2004): 537–546. See also J. Bernat and D. Rottenberg, "Conscious Awareness in PVS and MCS: The Borderlands of Neurology," *Neurology* 68 (2007): 885–886, J. Fins, "Rethinking Disorders of Consciousness: New Research and its Implications," *Hastings Center Report* 35 (2) (2005): 22–24, and Racine, *Pragmatic Neuroethics*, Chapters 7 and 8.
19. As noted by Zeman, "Does Consciousness Spring from the Brain?" 301.

Coma is characterized by absence of consciousness in the form of complete unresponsiveness.[20] This may involve temporary or permanent disruption or cessation of thalamic–cortical connections, cortical function, and function of the reticular formation. Chronic coma is a relatively rare state. Some comatose patients regain full consciousness, usually within 2 to 4 weeks of the brain insult. This recovery may occur later as well. Others eventually lose all brain functions and become brain-dead. Still other patients may progress from a coma to a VS, where they are awake but unaware of themselves and their surroundings. This may be described as a state of wakeful unconsciousness. Many neurologists consider a persistent VS to have become a permanent VS 3 months after an anoxic brain injury or 12 months after a traumatic injury, including hemorrhagic stroke[21] This classification means that they effectively have no chance of regaining any capacity for awareness. It is supported by studies showing that there have been no instances of vegetative patients improving to awareness during a five-year observation period. All of the patients in these studies either died or remained in the vegetative state.[22]

Not all patients in a persistent VS progress to a permanent VS. A few patients with traumatic brain injury may emerge from the VS and recover full consciousness, cognitive ability, and functional independence. A greater number may progress to an MCS, in which they have a minimal degree of awareness of their surroundings. The MCS has also been called the minimally responsive state. It consists of profound unresponsiveness despite intermittent evidence of awareness. [23] Why some individuals remain in a VS indefinitely, progress to an MCS, or recover a greater degree of consciousness may be explained by differences in integration and activation of intralaminar thalamic nuclei (collections of neurons), thalamic–cortical projections, and cortical functions.[24] These functions are active but under-sustained in the MCS. The greater the integration of these brain features, the greater the probability of recovery of consciousness. The type of brain injury can also influence the probability of recovery. There is a greater degree of cerebral metabolic

20. See F. Plum, "Coma and Related Global Disturbances of the Human Conscious State," in A. Peters and E. Jones, eds., *Cerebral Cortex* (New York: Plenum Press, 1991), 359–425. What has come to be known as the Glasgow Coma Scale was formulated by G. Teasdale and B. Jennett, "Assessment of Coma and Impaired Consciousness: A Practical Scale," *The Lancet* 303 (1974): 81–84. Wijdicks et al. formulate an updated and more refined coma scale in "Validation of a New Coma Scale: the FOUR Scale," *Annals of Neurology* 58 (2005): 589–593. "FOUR" stands for "full outline of unconscious response."
21. Multi-Society Task Force on PVS, "Medical Aspects of the Persistent Vegetative State," *New England Journal of Medicine* 330 (1994): 1499–1508.
22. A.Estraneo et al., "Late Recovery after Traumatic, Anoxic, or Hemorrhagic Long-Lasting Vegetative State," *Neurology* 75 (2010): 239-245, J. Luaute et al., "Long-Term Outcomes of Chronic Minimally Conscious and Vegetative States," *Neurology* 75 (2010): 246–252, and Bernat, "The Natural History of Chronic Disorders of Consciousness," *Neurology* 75 (2010): 206–207.
23. J. Giacino et al., "The Minimally Conscious State: Definition and Diagnostic Criteria" *Neurology* 58 (2002): 349–353.
24. H. Di et al., "Neuroimaging Activation Studies in the Vegetative State: Predictors of Recovery?" *Clinical Medicine* 8 (2008): 502–507.

activity in patients with traumatic injury than in those with anoxic injury, and this activity may indicate potential for improvement in their neurological state. Another potential indicator of recovery from the MCS is trace conditioning of the eye-blink response, which is a form of associative learning.[25] Some integration of cortical and subcortical functions may be enough to enable one to have a limited degree of conscious awareness of oneself and one's immediate environment. Emergence from the MCS is defined by the ability to communicate and use objects functionally.

LIS (*coma vigilante*) involves consciousness with almost total paralysis.[26] Eye or eyelid movements are often the only voluntary movements and the only means of communication. LIS is usually caused by a lesion in the ventral pons of the brainstem resulting from stroke or trauma. It can also be caused by extensive demyelination in the brainstem. In the VS, there is little or no integrated cortical function but brainstem function. In LIS, there is integrated cortical function but little or no function in damaged sections of the brainstem. Crucially, the upper brainstem activating system and sensory pathways are spared, and the patient is awake, aware, and able to feel. Because locked-in patients are fully conscious, LIS is not accurately described as a disorder of consciousness. It is a conscious state involving a disorder in which the cortex is denied its peripheral connections to the body.

If having the capacity for consciousness means having the capacity for both wakefulness and awareness, then the MCS is the only truly chronic disordered conscious state among those I have listed. Epilepsy is also a chronic disorder of consciousness that can result from brain injury or other causes. Seizures can cause loss of awareness.[27] Except in severe forms of epilepsy, though, the intermittent occurrence of seizures distinguishes this condition from the more persistent symptoms of the other conditions in terms of their medical, metaphysical, and ethical significance.

Individuals in a persistent VS may retain some capacity for awareness, but this could only be known post hoc if they progress to the MCS. Brain imaging has helped to clarify the diagnosis of brain function and distinguish these neurological states following brain injury. Imaging can show that patients in this state retain the physiological substrate that sustains the capacity to perform cognitive tasks. This cannot be shown by clinical examination of their behavior. Magnetoencephalography (MEG) measures the magnetic fields generated by electrical activity, PET measures glucose metabolism and blood flow, and fMRI measures blood flow in cortical and subcortical regions of the brain. The neurological states just described correspond to greater or lesser degrees of brain activity as measured by these techniques.

---

25. T. Bekinschtein, "Classical Conditioning in the Vegetative and Minimally Conscious State," *Nature Neuroscience* 12 (2009): 1343–1349.

26. E. Smith and M. Dehaney, "Locked-In Syndrome," *British Medical Journal* 330 (2005): 406–409, and N. Chisholm and G. Gillett, "The Patient's Journey: Living with Locked-In Syndrome," *British Medical Journal* 331 (2005): 94–97.

27. Penfield states: "During epileptic interference with the function of gray matter… consciousness vanishes, and with it goes the direction and planning of behavior. The mind goes out of action and comes into action with the normal functioning of this mechanism." *The Mystery of Mind*, 47.

The MCS correlates with limited integrated activity in the cortex and limited active connections between the thalamus and cortex. Both of these properties are absent in the VS. There is much more integrated cortical activity and a much greater degree of consciousness—indeed full consciousness—in LIS than in the MCS.

If personhood is defined in terms of the capacity for conscious awareness, then patients in a permanent VS no longer exist as persons. They continue to exist as human organisms because they have enough intact brainstem, cardiocirculatory, and somatic functions to remain alive in a biological sense. The fact that vegetative patients are wakeful is not crucial to this classification. Because persistently vegetative individuals may progress to the MCS, they may retain some capacity for awareness and survive as persons, at least for a limited period of time. They would pass through a temporary state of unconsciousness. More precisely, they would pass through a period of arousal without awareness. But if they did not become fully conscious or did not progress to the MCS within 3 months of an anoxic injury or 12 months of a traumatic injury, then they would not survive as persons. Beyond this point, they likely would have permanently lost the capacity for awareness. This assumes that brain imaging can confirm this assessment within the critical period of time. Some minimally conscious patients may emerge from this state and regain a considerable degree of consciousness and physical and cognitive functions, while others may remain in a permanent MCS. It is important to emphasize that consciousness is not always an all-or-nothing phenomenon but may come in degrees, and what degree is sufficient for personhood is not always clear. A disordered or altered state of consciousness results from injury to brain systems that mediate awareness, which in turn alters the informational or representational relationship between the organism and the external world. The world is not misrepresented, but incompletely represented.[28]

What degree of consciousness is sufficient for one to continue to exist as a person? Could a patient survive as a person in a permanent MCS? This would depend on what one includes among the defining properties of consciousness. If one includes only arousal and minimal awareness of self and surroundings, then it might be plausible to say that the patient survives as a person. But if one includes the ability to meaningfully interact with others, which minimally conscious patients lack, then they do not survive as persons in a permanent MCS. Only emergence from this state is consistent with personal survival.

One challenge in using brain imaging to diagnose altered or disordered states of consciousness is that consciousness cannot be measured objectively. Neurologist Steven Laureys states that "in contrast to [whole] brain death... neuroimaging and electrophysiology cannot, at present, determine human consciousness. Therefore, no accurate anatomical criteria can be defined for a higher-brain formulation of death."[29] The interpretation of the extent of integrated brain activity from imaging is ambiguous. Imaging does not provide unequivocal proof of consciousness. In particular, fMRI may not be suitable as a marker of consciousness in patients

---

28. A. Revonsuo et al., "What Is an Altered State of Consciousness?" *Philosophical Psychology* 22 (2009): 187–204.
29. "Death, Unconsciousness, and the Brain," *Nature Reviews Neuroscience* 6 (2005): 899–909, at 904.

with anoxic brain injury because of the global inability of the brain to modulate blood flow following this type of injury.

This does not mean that it is impossible to know whether an individual is or is not conscious, or whether one has permanently lost the capacity for consciousness. Consciousness cannot be "seen" on brain images, and thus neither consciousness nor personhood can be inferred directly from images of brain activation. Yet whether a patient is conscious to any degree may be inferred indirectly from combining MEG, PET, and fMRI measures of function in thalamic–cortical pathways with behavioral features based on neurological examination. When these measures and features are accurately assessed, they may enable neuroscientists to make a valid inference from them to consciousness. Imaging does not capture the content of consciousness but is an indicator of the neurological activity that sustains the capacity for consciousness. By themselves, imaging and clinical examination are imperfect diagnostic measures and may result in mistaking one neurological state for another. In LIS, near-total paralysis may lead some clinicians to mistakenly judge that an individual in this state is persistently or permanently comatose. This shows the limitations of behavioral observation in diagnosing this particular state.

The most difficult challenge is distinguishing between the VS and the MCS. The rate of misdiagnosis of disorders of consciousness is approximately 40 percent. A 23-year-old woman in the United Kingdom had been diagnosed as being in a VS in 2006 following a traumatic brain injury. Images taken of her brain by cognitive neuroscientist Adrian Owen five months after the injury showed much more integrated brain activity than had been previously thought.[30] When asked to imagine herself playing tennis or moving around her home, she activated areas in her primary auditory cortex and motor cortex in a manner indistinguishable from healthy volunteers undergoing the same type of imaging. These indications suggest that she was not in a VS but instead an MCS, with some degree of consciousness and cognitive and physical functions and limited ability to interact with others.[31] This brain activity would have been absent if she were in a VS. During the five months between the time of her injury and the time when images were taken of her brain, she progressed from a persistent VS to an MCS. Her personhood was intact, albeit in a minimal sense.

Arkansas resident Terry Wallis was believed to be in a permanent VS following a coma resulting from a motor vehicle accident in 1984. It became clear that the diagnosis was incorrect when he began speaking and interacting with his family

---

30. Owen et al., "Detecting Awareness in the Vegetative State," *Science* 313 (2006): 1402, and A. Owen and M. Coleman, "Functional Neuroimaging of the Vegetative State," *Nature Reviews Neuroscience* 9 (2008): 235–243.

31. G. Gillett has informed me that Owen's patient may have been in a locked-in rather than a minimally conscious state. As noted above, misdiagnosis of neurological states is not rare. In a widely reported case, Belgian Rom Houben was misdiagnosed as vegetative for 23 years when in fact he had locked-in syndrome. See K. Connolly," Trapped in His Own Body for 23 Years—The Coma Victim Who Screamed Untreated," *The Guardian*, November 23, 2009. http://www.guardian.co.uk/world/2009/nov/23/man-trapped-coma-23-years

in 2003.[32] He remained in an MCS for 19 years, retaining his capacity for consciousness and personhood throughout this period. Commenting on the difficulty of distinguishing the VS from the MCS, physician and ethicist Joseph Fins and neurologist Nicholas Schiff write: "It is not true that the patient is either in an immutable state of permanent unconsciousness or has a heart-wrenchingly normal inner life. In fact, what we must confront is a scale of important gradations—most of which are yet to be discovered and described... Right now the images of gray matter are but shades of gray."[33] Although they are still imperfect measures of the capacity for consciousness, the use of imaging and clinical examination as complementary diagnostic tools has made diagnostic mistakes about consciousness less likely. In fact, it is because of this complementary approach to assessing disorders of consciousness that the MCS has only recently become a diagnostic category. The cases of Adrian Owen's patient and Terry Wallis demonstrate that a correct diagnosis of a disordered neurological state can be made only after detailed and repeated examinations.

The critical metaphysical question for survival is not so much whether the individual retains a sufficient degree of consciousness to remain *a* person. The question is whether the individual retains a sufficient degree of psychological connectedness and continuity before and after a brain injury to remain the *same* person. Simply being conscious and continuing to exist as a person does not make a narrative, as the cases of H. M. and Clive Wearing illustrate. Similar remarks apply to those emerging from an MCS and regaining a greater degree of consciousness. If surviving as the same person requires narrative identity, then there would have to be at least a moderate degree of connectedness and continuity between a person's earlier and later psychological properties. The unity of experience necessary for a thematically integrated narrative would require fairly strong links between memory of personal episodes in the past, present intentions and actions, and imagined future actions.

Individuals in LIS meet these criteria. Although they are locked into their paralyzed bodies and are severely limited in their physical functions, they are fully conscious and retain most if not all of their cognitive functions. This may be sufficient for a robust sense of agency to construct or continue a narrative extending from the time before the brain injury to some time after it. The best example of this is Jean-Dominique Bauby, the former editor-in-chief of the French magazine *Elle*. He suffered a brainstem stroke in 1995 and fell into a LIS shortly thereafter. While in this state, he was able to communicate by blinking his left eyelid. The combination of his mental act of intending to communicate his thoughts and the execution of this intention in the physical act of blinking his eyelid was enough for him to write a book about his experience, which was published shortly before his death in 1997.[34] Bauby underwent significant neurological and physical changes from the

32. As reported by B. Carey, "Mute 19 Years, He Helps Reveal Brain's Mysteries," *New York Times,* July 4, 2006 (http://www.nytimes.com/2006/07/04/health/psychology/04coma.html).

33. "Shades of Gray: New Insights into the Vegetative State," *Hastings Center Report* 36(6) (2006): 9.

34. *The Diving Bell and the Butterfly: A Memoir of Life in Death* (New York: A. A. Knopf,

stroke. But the fact that he literally constructed a narrative of his experience shows that he had and displayed enough psychological continuity and agency between the time of the stroke and the time of his death to survive as the same person during that period. The extreme paralysis of Bauby's LIS does not mean that he survived for two years as a disembodied person. The paralysis may have altered the content of his perception to some extent, but the functions of systems internal to his body were largely intact. The connections between these systems and his cerebral cortex, as well as the psychological states influenced by these connections, were also intact. So he retained a mind–body relation and remained very much an embodied person while in the LIS. Unlike Bauby, some locked-in patients survive for years in this state.

Owen's patient emerged from the MCS with too limited a set of cognitive functions to retain or regain psychological continuity from her pre-injury to her post-injury experience. If she were in a permanent MCS, then she would not be able to actualize the capacity for the mental processes necessary to ground the uni-fied experience of persistence. If she were in an LIS, then she would not have lost this capacity because she would have retained full consciousness despite her injury. A presumed capacity that is never actualized may not be a capacity at all. Yet unless imaging or other diagnostic techniques could determine that she was in a perma-nent MCS, whether she survived as the same person would remain an open ques-tion. The MCS itself would not rule out the possibility of further recovery of cognitive functions. Such recovery may enable one to restore or resume rather than lose the thematic unity of one's mental life disrupted by the injury. Intuitively, there would be a limit to the duration of an MCS for one to survive as the same person, since an indefinite state of minimal consciousness seems too weak a basis for the relevant senses of identity and survival.

The duration of Terry Wallis's MCS and the extent of his neurological and psychological recovery seem to challenge this intuition. Images of Wallis's brain have shown new neural connections in the midline cerebellum, an area involved in motor control.[35] There are also indications of new neural connections in the path-way linking the thalamus and the cortex, which is critical for consciousness and cognitive functions. Axons in Wallis's brain have been growing and forming new connections. This is an example of the brain's plasticity, its ability to allow intact regions to bypass injured ones and devise new ways of connecting axons. The process of growing and forming new neural connections occurs slowly and may explain why Wallis's recovery has extended to almost 30 years. Some reports have suggested that Wallis has recovered some memories of events before his accident and that he has been laying down new memories. However, he has commented to his family that he has no real sense of time. This may simply mean that his temporal perception is impaired, not that he has lost his experience of persisting through time. This point may be supported by reports of his increasing ability to retrieve episodic memories of events that occurred before his injury.

1997). See also Chisholm and Gillett, "The Patient's Journey."
35. H. Voss et al., "Possible Axonal Regrowth in Late Recovery from the Minimally Con-scious State," *Journal of Clinical Investigation* 116 (2006): 2005–2011.

More recent reports indicate that Wallis has not made any further recovery.[36] The critical question is whether he has retained enough episodic memory, agency, and psychological continuity for him to have survived the brain injury as the same person. If only a moderate degree of psychological continuity is necessary for one to retain one's narrative identity and survive, then Wallis's recovery seems enough for him to meet this threshold and to have survived as the same person despite the changes to his brain and mind between 1984 and 2011. But if his memory and cognitive functions are significantly impaired, then one can question whether he meets the threshold. As in the cases of H.M. and Clive Wearing, if he cannot construct a narrative in which his experience of past, present, and future events is continuous and unified, then it may be plausible to say that his identity has been permanently destroyed. If the relevant conception of personal identity is narrative and not just numerical identity, then the Terry Wallis who exists in 2011 is a different person from the Terry Wallis who existed in 1984.

The extent of physical, cognitive, and affective disability from brain injury influences how family and friends of brain-injured individuals respond to the question of survival. A 38-year-old American man who had been in an MCS for six years following an assault recovered some physical and cognitive functions with the help of deep-brain stimulation administered over a 12-month period between 2006 and 2007.[37] He currently still has significant physical and cognitive impairment. It was with reference to this that his mother, in an interview with the CBS program "60 Minutes," commented that she doubted that she would ever "have him back."[38] This is similar to the comment made by those familiar with Phineas Gage who said that he was "no longer Gage" after his brain injury. Some might claim that these two individuals were numerically identical to their earlier selves. But comments from those who knew them suggested that they did not survive their injuries as the same persons because of psychological disconnectedness and discontinuity before and after their brain trauma.

Evaluating Survival

From the argument that narrative identity is the only plausible conception of identity for personal survival, one might conclude that survival is good for persons and those familiar with them. To test this idea, consider the following hypothetical example from Gillett:

> Barry and Alice's three-year-old son, Jeff, is terminally brain-injured by a car and expected to die within 24 hours. But a new experimental treatment promoting the reconstruction of injured nerve pathways is suggested. Even though there are psychological differences between the treated individual and his pre-injury self so that

---

36. See Carey, "Mute 19 Years."
37. N. Schiff et al., "Behavioral Improvement with Thalamic Stimulation after Severe Traumatic Brain Injury," *Nature* 448 (2007): 600–603.
38. A. Cooper, "Awakening," CBS "60 Minutes," November 21, 2007 (http://www. tv.com/6ominutes/november-21-2007-awakening.html).

cognitive skills must be relearned, any memory traces (crucially dependent on the integrated function of the central nervous system) are lost, and temperament may differ, in successful cases, his parents are overjoyed at their child's recovery (despite the treatment taking six months).[39]

Given the difference in mental states between the pre-injury Jeff and the post-injury Jeff, Gillett asks whether the parents are making a metaphysical mistake in thinking that the recovered Jeff is the same person as the Jeff who existed before the accident. Gillett rejects a narrow psychological reductionism and relies on a holistic notion of identity involving more than psychology to argue that they are not mistaken in thinking that he is the same person.

The parents might not be making a metaphysical mistake in believing that the brain-reconstructed Jeff is identical to the pre-injury Jeff. Yet this would be the case only if they were basing their belief on numerical rather than narrative identity. Three years is too short a period of time to establish the requisite psychological connectedness and continuity for a personal narrative. Three-year-old Jeff lacked a sufficient set of beliefs, intentions, and memories to form a unified story of his life. The changes in his mental states from the brain injury did not disrupt connectedness or continuity because these states were not sufficiently integrated at the time of the injury. The brain reconstruction that prevented his death enabled Jeff to survive as a person. But it would be inappropriate to ask whether he survived the reconstruction as the same person, since there were no adequate criteria for personal identity at that time. The brain-reconstructed Jeff would be identical to the pre-injury Jeff in only a numerical and not a narrative sense. This is unlike the case of the 38-year-old MCS patient, who was old enough to have established a unified set of psychological properties, and for the continuity of these properties to be disrupted by his injury. Even if he recovered some physical and cognitive functions, the changes in his mental states were substantial enough to imply that he did not survive as the same person.

These considerations suggest that age may be a critical factor in questions about survival and how we evaluate it. If Jeff's parents had reason to be overjoyed at his recovery, then it was not because he remained the same person, but because his survival as a person gave him the opportunity to develop a narrative over the course of his life. Given Jeff's age, he lacked the psychological capacity to develop a critical interest in continuing to live. Insofar as harm consists in the thwarting of critical interests, and he was too young to have these interests, death would not have harmed him. Surviving at age 3 would not benefit him either because he would not have any critical interests to be satisfied. Any benefit would come only after developing a set of interests at a later age. The 38-year-old brain-injured MCS patient was harmed by the loss of many of his physical and mental capacities from his injury. The change in identity could harm him by thwarting the critical interests associated with his former self. He could be harmed further by the pain caused by his injury and the suffering caused by any awareness of what he had lost.

We can get a better sense of the value individuals with brain injuries attach to survival by considering therapeutic brain interventions that result in radical changes

---

39. *Subjectivity and Being Somebody*, 49.

in memory and personality. Consider an example from Jeff McMahan, which he calls "The Cure":

> Imagine that you are twenty years old and are diagnosed with a disease that, if untreated, invariably causes death... within five years. There is a treatment that reliably cures the disease but also, as a side-effect, causes total retrograde amnesia and radical personality changes. Long-term studies of others who have had the treatment show that they almost always go on to have long and happy lives, though these lives are informed by desires that differ profoundly from those that the person had prior to treatment.[40]

Because the connections between the pre- and post-treatment mental states would be weak and the patient would effectively cease to exist, McMahan says that it would make sense to refuse the treatment. The assumption that the person who exists after such a treatment would be identical to the person who undergoes it grounds the latter's prudential concern for the post-treatment future. If the upshot of the treatment is that these two persons are not identical, then there is no reason to have the treatment, since it will destroy any psychological relation between them. If the prognosis was that the five years between diagnosis and death contained good quality of life for the patient, then refusing treatment could still be a rational choice for him. Surviving the additional five years would be better than ceasing to exist as the same person from the psychological changes resulting from the treatment. On the other hand, if the disease rapidly progressed and resulted in death within 6 months, then there would be no decisive reason to have or refuse the treatment. The person would soon go out of existence in either case. Given the patient's interest in retaining his identity, there would be no metaphysically or prudentially significant difference between dying from the disease and losing his memory and personality traits. There would be no intrinsic value in survival associated with numerical identity.

In a variant of McMahan's example, suppose that the patient did not have a terminal disease but an extremely painful condition. A treatment could control or cure the condition and eliminate the pain; but it would cause the same total retrograde amnesia and radical personality changes. If the pain was unremitting and severely affected the patient's quality of life, then at least some individuals in this situation might choose the treatment knowing that they would lose their narrative identity as a result of it. After suffering from the condition, they might rationally conclude that pain relief that altered identity was preferable to surviving as the same person with unremitting pain. Individuals faced with this situation would have to weigh life with pain and intact identity against life without pain and altered identity. The overriding concern would be pain relief. Arguably, a life of extreme pain with little or no quality for a person is a life with no value. Survival might not have much or any value for a person if it means living in constant pain. Indeed, it could have considerable disvalue for that person.

This example brings us back to the case of H.M. When the hippocampi were bilaterally removed from his brain to control his seizures, his neurosurgeon did not

---

40. *The Ethics of Killing*, 77.

foresee the profound amnesia that would result from the surgery. If the procedure were performed today, MRI-guided stereotactic neurosurgery would minimize the probability and magnitude of brain damage. Nevertheless, if the patient knew that there was a risk of amnesia and personality change from a surgery with a high probability of controlling a severe seizure disorder, it might be rational for the patient to choose the surgery. The disability and suffering the patient experienced from the seizures might be bad enough to justify the risk of a change in identity. If retaining the same set of psychological properties meant a continuation of the seizures, then surviving as the same person might not be valuable to him. Some might claim that he could not benefit from it if he did not remain the same person. Even if he became a different person as a side effect of the treatment, it would satisfy the interest he had in not having seizures. The neurosurgery would benefit him when the seizures stopped or were significantly reduced. It would prevent further harm to him by preventing further seizures that would have affected the same person. These examples show that survival as such does not have intrinsic or prudential value for a person whose identity undergoes substantial change. Survival is not necessarily beneficial and may be harmful in some instances.

Why Consciousness Might Not Always Be Good

Many people assume that recovery of any degree of consciousness following a severe brain injury is beneficial for a patient. A greater degree of recovery of awareness implies a greater benefit. This way of thinking largely motivates the argument for using certain drugs and deep-brain stimulation as therapy for patients in an MCS. It also motivates arguments for continuing life support for these patients, which is necessary for them to receive any therapeutic interventions. Yet there are cases where conscious awareness may not be beneficial but harmful to an individual. What matters for the patient is not the state of consciousness (arousal), but the content of consciousness (awareness). Consciousness as such has no value. It can enable the organism to control its immediate environment. But this assumes that the organism has certain cognitive and physical capacities in addition to arousal and awareness. If the content of consciousness includes awareness of cognitive and physical disability, then it may lead to pain and suffering for a person. Recovering consciousness may result in harm, and recovering a greater degree of consciousness may result in greater harm.

Diagnostic clarity in distinguishing neurological states following brain injury is critical to preventing harm. A mistaken diagnosis of a patient as permanently vegetative rather than minimally conscious could lead to the withdrawal of hydration, nutrition, or other forms of life support. By causing the patient's death, this would preclude therapeutic interventions that might restore a greater degree of consciousness and recovery of some physical and cognitive functions.[41] In addition to deep-brain stimulation of the thalamus, which can activate regions of the cerebral cortex in some MCS patients, beneficial interventions for the MCS and LIS might

---

41. As Fins argues in "Constructing an Ethical Stereotaxy for Severe Brain Injury: Balancing Risks, Benefits, and Access," *Nature Reviews Neuroscience* 4 (2003): 323–327.

include brain–computer interface devices (BCIs). Electrodes implanted in the scalp, or chips implanted in the brain, can detect activity in the motor cortex associated with the intention to move. The signals from the motor cortex are then sent to a computer that executes the intention in the bodily movement through a robotic device. Actions based on a mistaken diagnosis could defeat the individual's interest in realizing this types of recovery. Such mistakes could have especially disastrous consequences for patients with LIS. They may have an interest in staying alive and regaining physical functions yet have the horrifying experience of being conscious of withdrawal of life support without being able to express their objection to this act.

One might question whether patients in an MCS have a sufficient degree of consciousness to generate and sustain an interest in continuing to live. If they do, then it could prohibit withdrawal of interventions necessary to sustain their lives. Yet it is not clear that minimal consciousness is enough to ground such an interest. If a patient in an MCS is capable of having an interest, then it may just as well be in withdrawing life-sustaining care. Some authors have argued that evidence of consciousness from neuroimaging may provide reasons both for and against continuing to keep severely brain-injured patients alive.[42] Keeping them alive could lead to interventions that might restore a greater degree of consciousness. Yet findings from studies suggest that cases of recovery from a VS to an MCS are rare.[43] There are no cases in which an individual in an MCS has had meaningful recovery of consciousness and cognitive and physical functions to pre-injury levels.

In two studies cited earlier in this chapter, one-third of the patients in the MCS improved after more than one year, though they remained severely or completely disabled.[44] These facts raise serious questions about the presumed potential efficacy of interventions aimed at restoring critical functions. The hypnotic drug zolpidem (Ambien) has induced or increased arousal in a small number of patients in the vegetative state; but it has not restored awareness.[45] If this drug or deep-brain stimulation can increase arousal but not also awareness, then it is unclear in what sense it can benefit a wakefully unconscious patient. Increasing arousal by itself does not make a vegetative patient any better off. Zolpidem has also been used on a 44-year-old man who had been in an MCS for 4 years after a traumatic brain injury resulting

---

42. For example, D. Wilkinson et al., "Functional Neuroimaging and Withdrawal of Life-Sustaining Treatment from Vegetative Patients," *Journal of Medical Ethics* 35 (2009): 508–511.

43. H. Di et al., "Cerebral Response to Patient's Own Name in the Vegetative and Minimally Conscious States," *Neurology* 68 (2007): 895–899; Di et al., "Neuroimaging Activation Studies in the Vegetative State"; and J. Fins et al., "Neuroimaging and Disorders of Consciousness: Envisioning an Ethical Research Agenda," *American Journal of Bioethics—AJOB Neuroscience* 8(9) (2008): 3–12.

44. Estraneo et al., "Late Recovery after Traumatic, Anoxic, or Hemorrhagic Long-Lasting Vegetative State," and Luaute et al., "Long-Term Outcomes of Chronic Minimally Conscious and Vegetative States."

45. B.Du et al., "Induced Arousal Following Zolpidem Treatment in a Vegetative State after Brain Injury in 7 Cases: Analysis Using Visual Single Photon Emission Computerized Tomography and Digitized Cerebral State Monitor," *Neural Regeneration Research* 3 (2008): 94–96.

from an automobile accident. Assessment with a number of tests showed that his cognitive and physical scores were no better and in fact worse with the drug than without it.[46] Zolpidem has increased awareness in a small number of minimally conscious patients. But its overall benefit remains questionable.

Chronic pain is a common complication of traumatic brain injury.[47] A recent PET study of minimally conscious patients suggests that they experience pain and suffering.[48] Consciousness involves at least minimal sentience and the capacity to suffer. The suffering of these patients is made worse by the fact that many of them are unable to report this experience to physicians treating them. Physician and ethicist Dominic Wilkinson and coauthors argue: "If such patients suffer, they can be harmed by continuing treatment; there may be stronger reasons in terms of non-maleficence and the best interests of the patient to allow them to die. This must be balanced against the possibility of having positive experiences, and the greater uncertainty about prognosis for such patients compared with those in a permanent vegetative state."[49] If the probability of significant physical and cognitive recovery for these patients is low, and if they can experience pain and suffering, then the reasons for discontinuing life-sustaining treatment and allowing them to die may be stronger than the reasons for keeping them alive and pharmacologically or surgically manipulating their brains. This is one situation in which the content of the patient's consciousness would make continued conscious life worse for that patient.

One problem with this claim is that it is difficult to know the wishes of these patients. BCIs and similar technologies may allow some locked-in patients to communicate their thoughts to a limited extent. But this is possible because they can process information and have the mental capacity to competently express their wishes. MCS patients might not have the capacity to operate a BCI device. More importantly, the limited consciousness of these patients suggests that they would not have the cognitive capacity to adequately consider the reasons for or against life-sustaining treatment. An advance directive might not be very helpful either. Most of the conditions for which people do not want life-sustaining care are terminal or irreversible, such as the permanent VS. The MCS does not fall within this category because theoretically it allows the possibility of recovery. In formulating an advance directive when their physical and cognitive functions were intact, few people would consider whether they should have or forego interventions if they were to fall into a minimally conscious state.

In a study conducted by researchers in the United Kingdom and Belgium involving 54 patients with disorders of consciousness, 5 were able to modulate brain

---

46. R. Singh et al., "Zolpidem in a Minimally Conscious State," *Brain Injury* 22 (2008): 103–106.

47. D. Nampiaparampil, "Prevalence of Chronic Pain after Traumatic Brain Injury: A Systematic Review," *Journal of the American Medical Association* 300 (2008): 711–719.

48. M. Boly et al., "Perception of Pain in the Minimally Conscious State with PET Activation: an Observational Study," *The Lancet Neurology* 7 (2008): 1013–1020.

49. "Functional Neuroimaging and Withdrawal of Life-Sustaining Treatment from Vegetative Patients," at 509–510. G. Kahane and J. Savulescu make the same point in "Brain Damage and the Moral Significance of Consciousness," *Journal of Medicine and Philosophy* 34 (2009): 6–26.

activity in response to mental imagery tasks.[50] One patient was able to give "yes" or "no" answers to simple questions. This suggested the possibility of communication with patients who appear unresponsive. But the fact that only 1 of 54 patients was able to do this indicates that it is rare for a minimally conscious patient to respond in this way. Even if there are more patients among the global MCS population who can do this, the responses are not indicative of decisional capacity regarding treatment. Limited awareness of one's self and surroundings is not enough for one to have this capacity. So, physicians and families need to be cautious in asking communicative MCS patients which treatments they would want. Some of these patients might respond "yes" to the question, "Do you want to stop the treatments keeping you alive?" Given their limited cognitive capacities, this response alone would not meet criteria of consent or assent. A surrogate might in principle give proxy consent to withdraw life-sustaining treatment on the patient's behalf. This would be permissible if the patient clearly stated at an earlier time that he or she would not want to be kept alive in a disordered neurological condition corresponding to the MCS. Lacking such a directive, physicians and surrogates would have no indication of the patient's wishes as to whether life-sustaining or restorative interventions should be initiated, continued, or withdrawn.

Because they have lost the ability to express their wishes, there will always be uncertainty about which actions would be in an MCS patient's best interests. Some patients may have a categorical desire to continue living, while others may judge that poor quality of life with cognitive and physical disability would make continued life not worth living. Cognitive neuroscientist Robert Knight spells out the problem as follows:

> It is not clear if the key issue is "consciousness" or the clinical experience of these patients per long-term recovery of "meaningful" life. Of course, "meaningful" is as poorly defined as "consciousness" and herein lies the quandary. This conundrum stresses the pre-injury intention of the patient to live in a VS or MCS. Some might opt for any "life," but most would not enjoy the prison of VS or MCS. Without knowing ante-injury, it is hard to make the right clinical call.[51]

The experience of pain and suffering and the low probability of meaningful recovery from the MCS could provide a reason for withdrawing care and letting the patient die. Families will more likely insist on continued care than withdrawal of care when brain imaging and clinical assessments reveal some degree of mental life in these patients. This is because of the intrinsic value many attach to mental life. They often insist on continued care for VS patients because they misinterpret wakefulness, movement, visual tracking, and reflexes as signs of mentality. Neurologist Allan Ropper notes that "it will always be more difficult to prove the lack of a mental

50. M. Monti et al., "Willful Modulation of Brain Activity in Disorders of Consciousness," *New England Journal of Medicine* 362 (2010): 579–589.
51. "Consciousness Unchained: Ethical Issues and the Vegetative and Minimally Conscious State," *American Journal of Bioethics—AJOB Neuroscience* 8(9) (2008): 1–2.

life than to demonstrate its presence."[52] Brain activity as such is not always evidence of consciousness. But the more important point here is that even when there is conclusive evidence of mental life in a patient, this is not necessarily good for the patient and can be bad for him or her. The main ethical issue is not that one condition may be misdiagnosed as another. Instead, the issue is whether continued life is in the best interests of any patient with a chronic disorder of consciousness, since available data indicate that all of these disorders involve a poor prognosis and poor quality of life.

One who survives a brain injury as the same person could be harmed through awareness of the difference between one's cognitive capacities before and after the injury. This could occur if the brain injury caused one to have cognitive disabilities. It could cause one to suffer even if the injury did not result in any pain. The harm would pertain not only to the effects of the injury but also to interventions that allowed one to emerge from a coma, VS, or MCS and survive with impaired quality of life. For some, continued life with cognitive disability would not be worth living. Survival would not benefit them.

Suppose that life-sustaining and additional therapeutic treatments restored full conscious awareness to a mathematician with a traumatic brain injury. Suppose further that only some of his cognitive capacities were restored. The injury affected the region of his prefrontal cortex mediating working memory, which caused him great difficulty in processing numbers and doing other mathematical tasks. This forced him to lose an academic position and give up his career as a mathematician. His awareness that he had significant cognitive impairment and could no longer perform many of the cognitive tasks he performed so well before the injury caused him to suffer and experience poor quality of life. Or suppose that a singer sustained an injury to her medial temporal lobes and prefrontal cortex. Although treatments enabled her to recover full consciousness, they could not reverse the anterograde and retrograde amnesia that caused her great difficulty in learning new lyrics, recalling old lyrics, and following harmony and melody. This forced her to abandon her singing career and caused her to suffer and experience poor quality of life as well.

In both instances, these individuals would be aware of their impairments and of the difference between their current cognitive disability and their cognitive ability prior to the brain injury. This outcome could harm them by defeating their interest in wanting and expecting at least a moderately high level of cognitive functioning, one that was not significantly different from their pre-injury level. The harm would be especially serious given that their particular impairments and lost capacities were essential to the livelihood of each of these individuals. Improvement in neurological functions associated with consciousness, without similar improvement in neurological functions associated with particular cognitive functions, could make them worse off rather than better off. We can make this same claim if deep-brain stimulation could generate awareness in vegetative patients. One could argue that not being aware of cognitive impairments would be preferable to being aware of them. This would occur in cases where there was considerable disparity between one's

---

52. *"Cogito Ergo Sum* by MRI," *New England Journal of Medicine* 362 (2010): 648–649, at 649.

general set of cognitive capacities before and after a brain injury. Patients with poor quality of life might judge that interventions necessary to keep them alive while they were comatose, vegetative, or minimally conscious should have been withdrawn. They might judge that they should have been allowed to die while in the disordered conscious state, on the grounds that having to live with significant cognitive and physical disabilities, and being aware of them, is worse than death.

Not all individuals with brain injuries who lose many physical or cognitive functions would make this judgment. The content of Bauby's book, *The Diving Bell and the Butterfly*, indicates that he had some positive experiences while in LIS. He and others with his condition would say that continued life was valuable for them, and that interventions that enabled them to remain alive benefited them and thus were justified. There is, however, at least one important difference between Bauby's condition and the condition of the individuals in my hypothetical examples. As much as Bauby was physically limited by being locked into his body, he did not suffer from cognitive impairment. For many people, cognitive disability can be just as important to quality of life as physical disability. Also, we cannot assume that Bauby would have had positive experiences if he had remained locked-in for many years.

Adverse psychological effects of interventions targeting or affecting the brain are not limited to individuals with brain injuries. A substantial number of patients discharged from intensive care units have permanent or long-term cognitive and physical disabilities.[53] These may be the result of primary or secondary trauma or anoxia. The disabilities may also be among the effects of mechanical ventilation and other life-sustaining interventions given to patients while they are critically ill. These long-term outcomes underscore the need for reassessment of short-term interventions that may save patients' lives at the cost of poor quality of life following discharge. At the same time, they underscore the need to assess how patients adjust to disabilities. They require more careful long-term prediction of outcomes of critical interventions for different conditions. This may provide a clear sense of whether critical medical interventions offer a net benefit to patients and are in their best interests. The same considerations should apply to life-sustaining and therapeutic treatments for brain-injured patients.

More empirical studies on quality of life following brain injury would not likely provide a single positive or negative picture. There would be considerable variation among individuals in how they adjusted to cognitive and physical impairments from brain injuries. It could not be predicted how these individuals would respond to their altered neurological and psychological states. Quality of life can be measured to some extent objectively on the basis of interviews with patients in clinical observation. These measures can assess the extent of cognitive and physical functions, as well as patients' psychological responses to them. But there is an irreducibly subjective aspect to quality of life that cannot be captured by objective measures. The experience of living with physical and mental impairment cannot be generalized because it is unique to the individual. Thus the question of whether it

---

53. See, for example, F. Garcia-Lizana et al., "Long-Term Outcome in ICU Patients: What about Quality of Life?" *Intensive Care Medicine* 8 (2003): 1286–1293.

is worth continuing a life with these impairments does not have a definitive answer but is case-sensitive.

Fins points out that some people with brain injuries may be able "to accommodate their expectations to their altered abilities."[54] He gives the hypothetical example of a physician who sustains an injury to her frontal lobe. In relearning how to sequence daily tasks, she becomes an accomplished abstract artist. This is due to the release of previously inhibited creative impulses from her injury, which resulted in increased activity in posterior regions of her brain. The physician and others like her may be able to turn something devastating into something positive. They may be able to discover "a new self while recalling a lost identity."[55]

I do not take Fins to be claiming that the physician's autobiography has substantially changed and that she has created a narrative completely unrelated to the one she created prior to her injury. Otherwise, 'she' would refer to a different person. Instead, I assume that Fins means only that some of her cognitive and affective capacities have changed and that she is now constructing a new chapter in her life that is thematically related to her narrative up to the time of her injury. Many people tend to revert to their mean level of satisfaction after a period of time following a serious illness or injury. We cannot assume that their psychological response to altered physical, cognitive, and affective states is always negative. But we cannot assume that it is always positive either. American champion endurance athlete Barbara Warren broke her neck in a cycling accident while competing in a triathlon in August 2008. She was paralyzed from the neck down and needed a ventilator to breathe. Three days later, she signaled by blinking her eyes that she wanted the ventilator turned off, and she died shortly thereafter. In giving Warren's reasons for dying, a friend said that "no athlete would like to have a life with only their eyes talking."[56] How one responds to a sudden-onset or prolonged cognitive or physical disability may be a function of its severity. The response may also be strongly influenced by one's pre-injury abilities. Not everyone is able or willing to accommodate their expectations to altered physical or cognitive states.

Discovering a new self would be more difficult the more a person identified with particular cognitive or physical abilities lost through a brain or spinal cord injury. It would depend on the extent to which these abilities figured in the livelihood and well-being of the person. Fins says that cognitive impairments from brain injury are highly individual rather than generic and are "superimposed on each patient's personal psychology and past."[57] The person could be harmed by the combination of the memory of what it was like to have these abilities and the awareness of having lost them. This is illustrated by the hypothetical examples of the mathematician and singer, and the actual example of Barbara Warren. By causing a person to lose an ability that made life meaningful for him or her, a brain or spinal cord

---

54. "Rethinking Disorders of Consciousness," 24.

55. *Ibid.*, 24.

56. B. Webber, "Barbara Warren, Winner of Endurance Competitions, Dies at 65," *New York Times*, August 29, 2008 (http://www.nytimes.com/2008/08/30/sports/othersports/30warren. html).

57. "Rethinking Disorders of Consciousness," 24.

injury would be a serious harm to that person. It would be a greater harm if one were aware of and suffered from the loss than if one were not aware of it. Because experienced harms are worse than non-experienced ones, an individual who recovered enough consciousness to be aware of newly acquired disabilities would be harmed to a greater extent than one who remained unconscious and unaware of them. Recovery of consciousness might not be good and could be bad for a person.

A neurological improvement in a patient's brain following injury does not necessarily translate into an improvement in the patient's psychology and quality of life. Restoration of some neurological functions may not always benefit individuals emerging from disordered conscious states. Whether one benefits from or is harmed by treatments for brain injury will depend on the degree of one's conscious awareness, which cognitive and physical functions were lost or restored, and the extent to which one adjusts to altered neurological, physical, and mental functions.

Conclusion

I have used narrative rather than numerical identity to ground a meaningful sense of personal survival. Particular regions of the brain are essential to the capacity for consciousness and personhood. They are also essential to the capacity to experience events in one's life in a thematically unified way. By generating and sustaining the neurological functions mediating these psychological capacities, a considerable degree of integrated activity in the cerebral cortex and projections to it from the thalamus and ascending reticular activating system are necessary for one to survive as a person and as the same person from an earlier to a later time. This is despite the fact that the only medically and legally accepted neurological definition of death is based on the permanent cessation of all brain functions. This definition is inadequate for a discussion of survival because it applies only to humans as biological organisms, not to persons as beings with the capacity for conscious awareness. Persons cease to exist when they permanently lose integrated cortical functions, even if they retain subcortical and brainstem functions. They may survive as human organisms, but not as individuals who could benefit from or be harmed by actions or events affecting their bodies in such a state. Some may survive as persons but not as the same persons because of discontinuity between mental states before and after a brain injury. Those who survive a brain injury with their identity intact may be harmed by physical and cognitive disability and awareness of what they have lost.

The combination of electrical and magnetic brain imaging and clinical examination has improved the diagnosis of different neurological disorders. It has enabled cognitive and clinical neuroscientists to identify states that may allow for partial or full recovery of consciousness and cognitive and physical functions. This has significant implications for the question of harm, since mistaking an MCS or LIS patient for one in a coma or permanent VS could result in withdrawing life-support and precluding therapeutic interventions. On the other hand, maintaining life-support and activating neural networks could harm some brain-injured patients. What matters is not the state of consciousness but the content of consciousness, and this content may have value or disvalue for a patient. I gave examples where awareness of cognitive disabilities following brain injury could harm patients. Survival may not always be in one's best interests. If a harmful outcome of survival could be predicted when a patient was in a severely disordered conscious state, then there might be grounds for withdrawing life-sustaining care and letting the patient die.

The high incidence of misdiagnosis of patients with chronic disorders of consciousness shows the uncertainty in determining whether or to what extent patients are conscious or retain the capacity for consciousness. Further refinement in imaging and clinical observation will reduce the incidence of these mistakes. Yet even the most sophisticated brain imaging techniques cannot resolve philosophical questions about the sorts of beings we are and which conception of identity we should adopt. These techniques will inform but not determine how one responds to questions about survival, benefit, and harm in cases of severe brain injury. Neurological and philosophical analysis and discussion are needed to adequately address and resolve these questions.

7

Stimulating Brains, Altering Minds

Electrical and magnetic stimulation of the brain has been effective in treating some neurological and psychiatric disorders and has shown therapeutic potential for treating others. This includes techniques such as electroconvulsive therapy (ECT), transcranial magnetic stimulation (TMS), transcranial direct current stimulation, vagus nerve stimulation, and deep-brain stimulation (DBS). ECT has been used to treat severe cases of depression and bipolar disorder. Although the side effect of memory impairment remains a persistent problem, the safety of this technique has improved over the years. TMS involves delivering a localized magnetic pulse to the cortex through coils placed on the scalp. The pulse is delivered over a longer period in the repetitive version of the technique (rTMS). Vagus nerve stimulation involves stimulating the left vagus nerve in the neck with a series of electrical pulses generated by a device implanted in the chest or collarbone. TMS and vagus nerve stimulation have ameliorated symptoms in some patients with depression, stroke, and epilepsy, though questions remain about their general safety and efficacy. Transcranial direct current stimulation has improved recognition memory performance in some patients with Alzheimer's disease.

DBS is the most widely used brain-stimulating technique. Electrodes are surgically implanted in a particular brain region using stereotactic methods. They are connected by wires to a battery-driven pulse generator implanted near the collarbone that can be switched on and off. Activation of the electrodes stimulates a targeted area of the brain. The area may be directly or indirectly associated with a symptom or set of symptoms. Most neurological and psychiatric disorders involve dysregulation in both cortical and subcortical regions of the brain. The effects of TMS are limited because it stimulates only the cortex, and the strength of the magnetic field it generates falls off sharply beyond a few centimeters from the stimulated site. DBS is superior to TMS and other techniques because of its modulating effects on many brain regions.

Neurosurgeon Alim-Louis Benabid performed the first implant of a DBS system as part of a clinical trial in France in 1987. Ten years later, a high-frequency thalamic stimulating system was used as an alternative to thalamotomy to control the disabling tremors in a patient with Parkinson's disease. Since then, stimulation of two structures in the basal ganglia, the globus pallidus interna and the subthalamic nucleus, has restored a significant degree of motor control in many patients in advanced stages of the disease. DBS was approved by the U.S Food and Drug Administration (FDA) in 1997 as a treatment for Parkinson's and essential tremor. In 2003, the FDA approved this technique for primary dystonia. DBS has also been used to treat chronic pain, obsessive-compulsive disorder (OCD), major depressive disorder (MDD), Tourette syndrome, cerebral palsy, obesity, addiction, early-stage Alzheimer's, and the minimally conscious state.[1] Approximately 75,000 patients globally have been treated with this technique. Although DBS involves more risks than noninvasive forms of brain stimulation, it avoids the risks in ablative neurosurgery, where the effects of removing brain tissue can be permanent. Unlike surgical lesions made to correct dysfunctional brain circuits, DBS is adjustable and its effects are reversible. The stimulation parameters can be changed, the device can be turned off, or the implanted electrodes can be surgically removed from the brain. Depending on the disorder and its symptoms, the stimulator can be activated continuously or intermittently. Nevertheless, because DBS is brain-invasive and involves risks, it likely will continue to be offered only to patients with conditions that have not responded to nonsurgical treatments.

The purpose of DBS is to modulate underactive or overactive neural circuits mediating motor functions and mental states associated with conation, cognition, and emotion. The stimulated site in the brain is often an area where some circuits project to others. DBS can restore or improve physical and mental functions lost from or impaired by neurological and psychiatric disorders. Many researchers and clinicians refer to DBS as 'neuromodulation' rather than 'neurostimulation.' But because the goal and the means through which the goal is achieved are closely related, the two terms can be used interchangeably.

Unlike structural neurosurgery to resect a tumor or clip an aneurysm, DBS can be described as functional neurosurgery for diseases of the brain and mind. Although the main problem with Parkinson's is motor control, many patients with this disease experience cognitive and affective symptoms as well. For this and other reasons, many clinical neuroscientists do not strictly distinguish neurological and psychiatric disorders but classify them under the single category of

---

1. Benabid, considered by many to be the father of DBS, outlines and discusses potential future uses of this technique in "What the Future Holds for Deep-Brain Stimulation," *Expert Review of Medical Devices* 4 (2007): 895–903. See also Benabid, "Deep-Brain Stimulation for Parkinson's Disease," *Current Opinion in Neurobiology* 13 (2003): 696–706. B. Kuehn discusses some uses of DBS in "Scientists Probe Deep Brain Stimulation: Some Promise for Brain Injury, Psychiatric Illness," *Journal of the American Medical Association* 298 (2007): 2249–2251. For the results of a study showing that DBS was safe and could improve memory in the early stages of Alzheimer's, see A. Laxton et al., "A Phase I Trial of Deep-Brain Stimulation of Memory Circuits in Alzheimer's Disease," *Annals of Neurology* 68 (2010), published online August 4.

neuropsychiatric disorders.[2] DBS can be life-transforming for many patients, resolving debilitating symptoms and enabling them to regain control of their lives. Yet its effects may include alteration of a range of mental states critical to thought, personality, and behavior. These effects can harm patients. They can also disrupt the integrity and continuity of the psychological properties that constitute personal identity. In these cases, DBS may cause symptoms that patients cannot control. Merkel and coauthors point out that "practically no intervention in the structure or functioning of the human brain can be undertaken in complete certainty that it will not affect mental processes, some of which may come to play a key role in a person's self-concept."[3] This uncertainty reflects the fact that it is not known exactly how electrical or magnetic stimulation alters brain activity. It is not known which targets in the brain are optimal for modulating dysfunctional neural and mental processes. Nor is it known at what frequency the stimulation should be delivered to produce its effects, which can vary among patients with the same disorder. Electrical stimulation of the brain could reshape synaptic connectivity and permanently alter neural circuits in ways that may or may not be salutary for a patient's state of mind.

In this chapter, I focus on the effects of DBS on the brain and mind and how they influence decisions by physicians and patients to initiate, forego, continue, or discontinue this treatment for neurological and psychiatric disorders. I present four cases involving four distinct disorders to generate and frame discussion of the psychological, metaphysical, and ethical issues surrounding the technique. The discussion of all these cases is grounded in the following questions: Are patients with neurological and psychiatric disorders able to give fully informed consent to this intervention in their brains? How do patients and their physicians weigh the potential benefit against the potential harm of DBS? How much risk of alteration of one's thought and personality with this technique is consistent with a patient's rational choice to initiate or continue DBS? Is it permissible for surrogates to give proxy consent to DBS for patients who lack the cognitive capacity to consent on their own? Discussion of these questions will lead to the general conclusion that what counts as success in DBS is not only how it modulates brain function but also whether it improves the patient's quality of life.

Neurological Disorders: Parkinson's Disease

DBS has been successful in controlling motor symptoms associated with advanced forms of Parkinson's disease. The characteristic symptoms are rigidity, tremor, and bradykinesia. This last symptom involves a lack of spontaneous movement and a slowing of movement. Parkinson's is the second most common neurodegenerative disorder (after Alzheimer's disease). One million people in the United States already have the disease, and 60,000 new cases are diagnosed every year. DBS is now

---

2. In "A New Intellectual Framework for Psychiatry," Kandel predicted "a new level of cooperation between neurology and psychiatry. This cooperation is likely to have its greatest impact on patients for whom these two aspects—neurological and psychiatric—overlap" (467).

3. Merkel et al., *Intervening in the Brain*, 6.

considered standard of care for treating Parkinson's in many medical centers. It can enable patients to have more control of their condition and their lives. This is not only because the device can improve motor function, but also because patients can operate the device on their own outside of a clinical setting. For some patients, the procedure has a more favorable benefit–risk ratio and is thus preferable to drugs such as dopamine agonists, which can cause addiction and other types of impulsive and compulsive behavior.[4] The drugs can overcompensate for degeneration of dopaminergic neurons in the substantia nigra, which has been implicated as one cause of the disease. This may occur through activation of circuits regulating the reward system in the brain. Other drugs, such as levodopa, can control motor symptoms but cause motor fluctuations, dystonia, and impair some forms of learning.

DBS may be too costly for some health care systems to provide the technique to all patients who could benefit from it. The implant costs approximately US $50,000, and the expensive batteries need to be replaced every two years. This second problem could be resolved by periodically re-charging the batteries. Leaving cost aside, there are significant risks associated with DBS. A recent randomized controlled clinical trial of this technique for Parkinson's showed significant improvement in motor functions but also a number of adverse neurological and psychiatric events, including one death secondary to intracerebral hemorrhage.[5] Earlier, I said that the effects of DBS are reversible; but this claim needs qualification. The technique may produce positive effects by reshaping synaptic connectivity. However, this same reshaping could permanently alter neural circuits and have long-term adverse neurological and psychological effects that may not be reversible. Neuroplasticity may enable the brain to correct or compensate for some of these effects, though this would depend on the age of the patient and particular features of his or her brain. Still, any question about risk must be weighed against the fact that dysfunction in synaptic connectivity is part of the pathophysiology of Parkinson's and other neurological and psychiatric disorders. Whether altering this connectivity is beneficial or harmful depends on its effects on a person's body and mind.

In some patients, this technique has caused symptoms similar to those associated with dopamine agonists. They became impulsive, displaying impairment in their capacity for decision making.[6] One explanation for the impulsive behavior is

---

4. M. Dodd et al., "Pathological Gambling Caused by Drugs Used to Treat Parkinson Disease," *Archives of Neurology* 62 (2005): 579–583.
5. F. Weaver et al., "Bilateral Deep-Brain Stimulation vs. Best Medical Therapy for Patients with Advanced Parkinson Disease," *Journal of the American Medical Association* 301 (2009): 63–73. The risk of intracerebral hemorrhage from electrode implantation is 3 to 4 percent, with 1 percent of patients experiencing permanent physical, cognitive, and affective deficits.
6. M. Frank et al., "Hold Your Horses: Impulsivity, Deep-Brain Stimulation, and Medication in Parkinsonism," *Science* 318 (2007): 1309–1312. Also, S. Piasecki and J. Jefferson, "Psychiatric Complications of Deep-Brain Stimulation for Parkinson's Disease," *Journal of Clinical Psychiatry* 65 (2004): 845–849. However, a different study showed that stimulation of the subthalamic nucleus was relatively safe from a cognitive standpoint, with only transient impairment in frontal-executive functions. R. Zangaglia et al., "Deep-Brain

that stimulation of the subthalamic nucleus (STN) activates the reward circuit in mesoaccumbens and mesolimbic dopamine pathways. Because of its projections to the prefrontal cortex, activation of this circuit can interfere with prefrontal regulation of executive functions. The STN consists of circuits regulating motor, cognitive, and affective functions, and the last of these involves part of the limbic system. Implanting and stimulating electrodes near the limbic circuit may alter mood. This may explain why some patients receiving DBS for Parkinson's regain motor control but develop psychiatric symptoms such as hypomania, mania, and psychosis. These are examples of the trade-offs between physiological benefit and potential psychological harm in treating Parkinson's with this technique. More selective placement of the electrodes and adjustment of the stimulation parameters may resolve some of these problems.

Because not all patients benefit from DBS, and because the adverse effects of the technique on the mind can be significant, there must be careful screening and selection of patients as suitable candidates for it. A full complement of medical professionals should be involved in this process. These would include a neurosurgeon, psychiatrist, neurologist, device programmer, and anesthesiologist directly involved in the procedure, as well as a psychologist, social worker, and the family to explore the potential physiological and psychological impact of the procedure for the patient. A complete explanation of the procedure's potential benefits and risks is required. This involves not only discussing whether to offer the procedure, but also monitoring its effects in determining whether it should be continued once initiated.[7] The justification for medical professionals to offer DBS for this disorder depends on a favorable assessment of benefit and risk. Ultimately, though, it is the mentally competent patient who has to decide whether the effects of DBS would be acceptable and whether he or she should have it. Even so, these actions will not guarantee a successful outcome in all cases because the effects of DBS are variable and not predictable across patients.

On one level, the patient's decision to undergo DBS hinges on a comparison between the physical benefit of motor control and the potential psychological harm of changes in the patient's personality and behavior. On a deeper level, the decision hinges on a question involving a comparison between two psychological states: whether the suffering from loss of motor control is worse than potential changes in other states of mind. The key factor is the patient's quality of life and whether DBS yields a net benefit in this respect. Some patients with a movement disorder, such as Parkinson's or dystonia, who experience depression as a side effect of DBS may not

Stimulation and Cognitive Functions in Parkinson's Disease: A Three-Year Controlled Study," *Movement Disorders* 24 (2009): 1621–1628.

7. See the discussion of the ethical and legal issues regarding the use of DBS for Parkinson's and other neurological and psychiatric disorders by R. de Bie and colleagues of the Benelux Neuromodulation Society, "Ethical and Legal Aspects of Neuromodulation: On the Road to Guidelines," *Neuromodulation* 10 (2007): 177–185. Also, P. Rabins et al., "Scientific and Ethical Issues Related to Deep-Brain Stimulation for Disorders of Mood, Behavior, and Thought," *Archives of General Psychiatry* 66 (2009): 931–937.

judge that they have benefited from the procedure. This is despite the fact that restoration of motor control would be considered a success by any objective measure. The medical trade-offs between positive physical and negative cognitive or affective effects of drugs versus electrical stimulation also involve ethical trade-offs between different types and degrees of psychological harm. Not all uses of DBS for movement disorders result in adverse neurological or psychiatric events. But studies indicate that the risk of these effects is clinically significant and thus worthy of concern.

We can gain insight into the problem of trade-offs by considering a case of a 59-year-old male patient from the Netherlands who began receiving stimulation of the subthalamic nucleus to relieve severe motor symptoms from advanced Parkinson's.[8] He was later admitted to a psychiatric hospital for a manic state resulting from the stimulation. A mood stabilizer failed to control his psychiatric symptoms, which included megalomania and chaotic behavior that resulted in serious financial debts. He became mentally incapacitated. Adjustment of the stimulator resolved the mania and restored his capacity for insight and rational judgment. But this came at the cost of an exacerbation of his motor symptoms, which were so severe that the patient became bedridden. The mania returned soon after restimulation. This left him and his health care providers with a choice between two equally undesirable actions: to admit the patient to a nursing home because of a severe physical disability, despite intact cognitive and affective functions; or to admit the patient to a chronic psychiatric ward for mania, despite restoration of good motor function.

Although DBS produced the desired effect of motor control, it radically altered the patient's state of mind. When his brain was not being stimulated, he had no mania or symptoms of any psychiatric disorder. He was deemed to have enough capacity to understand the information his physicians gave him about his condition and the proposed therapy, and to make a voluntary decision to have or forego it on the basis of this information.[9] He was able to give informed consent and chose the second action. In accord with his expressed wish, he was legally committed to a chronic ward in a regional psychiatric hospital. The patient made this choice on

---

8. A. Leentjens et al., "Manipulation of Mental Competence: An Ethical Problem in a Case of Electrical Stimulation of the Subthalamic Nucleus for Severe Parkinson's Disease," *Nederlands Tijdschrift voor Geneeskunde* 148 (2004): 1394–1398.

9. A. Jonsen, M. Siegler, and W. Winslade distinguish the ethical determination of decisional capacity from the legal determination of competency in *Clinical Ethics: A Practical Approach to Ethical Decisions in Clinical Medicine*, 6th ed. (New York: McGraw-Hill, 2006), 60–61. Decisional capacity can come in degrees, which may be a reflection of different degrees of neurological function or dysfunction. Competency does not come in degrees: one either has or lacks it. Not everyone agrees with this distinction. T. Grisso and P. Appelbaum assert that "when clinicians determine that a patient lacks decision-making capacity, the practical consequences may be the same as those attending a legal determination of incompetence." *Assessing Competence to Consent to Treatment: A Guide for Physicians and Other Health Professionals* (New York: Oxford University Press, 1998), 11. See also T. Beauchamp and J. Childress, *Principles of Biomedical Ethics*, 6th ed. (New York; Oxford University Press, 2009), 111.

quality-of-life grounds. For him, loss of motor control was worse than being in a manic state. He chose to continue DBS because the net benefit of being on the stimulator was greater than being off it. Or more accurately, the net harm of stimulation was less than the net harm of stopping it. It was the lesser of two evils.

This case raises three main questions. First, by choosing an option that would leave him in a manic and thus mentally incapacitated state, would he be losing his ability to decide to continue or discontinue stimulation? Second, given that his choice would radically alter his state of mind, should this influence the decision of the medical team to continue stimulating his brain? Third, if his thought and behavior and thus his identity changed as a result of brain stimulation, then how could he benefit from it? Each of these ethical questions hinges on the trade-offs between positive and negative physiological and psychological effects of a medically indicated treatment.

The patient's decision seems similar in some respects to an advance directive. This is a legal document in which a person expresses wishes regarding subsequent decisions about medical treatment that will have to be made when he or she is no longer capable of making them. This occurs most commonly in cases of dementia such as Alzheimer's disease and usually pertains to end-of-life care. The ethical and legal force of the directive extends from the earlier to the later time. Individuals with decisional capacity are able to consider the interests they will have over the course of their lives. They can foresee that their bodies and minds will deteriorate over time and know which medical interventions would be consistent with their interests. Formulating an advance directive gives one control of one's life by constraining or enabling actions by others that can affect one when one is no longer capable of making informed decisions about medical interventions.

What is at issue here is different from the loss of decisional capacity in a typical advance directive in at least two respects. First, the loss of decisional capacity associated with the mania was not a subsequent development but occurred soon after the activation and reactivation of the stimulator. When the stimulator was turned off, the patient was capable of foreseeing the consequence of reactivating it. He freely and knowingly chose the option that made him lose decisional capacity and his agency. Although he regained motor control, he lost the cognitive and volitional capacity necessary for him to choose which actions to perform. Agency consists not only of the unconscious ability to move the body but also the conscious ability to form and execute plans of action. The rapid loss of agency distinguishes this case from the more gradual loss of agency in dementias such as Alzheimer's, where it can be difficult to know at what point one loses decisional capacity. Second, unlike the demented patient, whose condition is irreversible, this patient's mental incompetence might have been reversible because the mania might have resolved by turning off the stimulator or more careful adjustment of its parameters.

The Parkinson's patient's decision to keep the stimulator on should not be understood as a Ulysses contract, where one freely decides to bind oneself to a future condition as stipulated in the contract. This is a type of advance directive where one directs others to ignore one's future wishes or orders until a specified condition is satisfied. In psychiatry, such a contract can preauthorize involuntary commitment of a patient who becomes symptomatic at a later time. While the Parkinson's patient's decision had the effect of binding him to a state of mental incapacity and commitment to a psychiatric ward, this was not his intention in opting for stimulation. After the first course of stimulation, the mania was an unwanted but known side effect of the realization of his intention to relieve the suffering he experienced from his loss of motor control. By constraining any subsequent capacity to choose, the patient's decision precluded the possibility of changing his mind. We assume that medical treatments promote physical and mental autonomy and improve the patient's quality of life. Yet in this case DBS made the patient lose his autonomy and capacity to choose to have or forego this or other treatments for his disease.

Although the patient exercised his autonomy in consenting to continue DBS for his disease, he did not have to be so constrained by his decision. Before initiating the procedure, the medical team caring for this patient was obligated to discuss options that would not foreclose future possibilities that might benefit him. More careful adjustment of the stimulation settings might resolve the mania and sustain motor control. Given this possibility, his physicians would also be obligated to revisit the question of whether to continue or discontinue DBS for his condition. This would mean turning off the stimulator so that his decisional capacity could be restored. The patient and his physicians could then discuss treatment options. Safer and equally effective noninvasive treatments for Parkinson's might have developed since he first underwent DBS. In this way, the medical team would be providing conditions allowing the patient the fullest expression of his autonomy in consenting to or refusing an intervention in line with his all-things-considered best interests.

This assumes that turning off the stimulator would automatically restore the patient's capacity to make an informed decision about continuing or discontinuing treatment. Yet it is possible that progression of the disease would result in the loss of this capacity. It is also possible that untoward effects of stimulation on neural circuits mediating cognition and mood would impair his judgment. The impairment could be caused by heightened dopaminergic effects or increased levels of other neurotransmitters. In any case, psychiatric complications could cause the patient to lose the capacity necessary to agree to or refuse continued stimulation. So, turning off the stimulator would not necessarily allow him to reconsider his earlier decision. An additional complication is that, in many cases of Parkinson's, subtle changes in cognition and personality precede the motor symptoms and may impair the patient's decision making. These changes occur not only in Parkinson's but also in other neurodegenerative diseases such as Huntington's, amyotrophic lateral sclerosis, and Alzheimer's. They are more common when these diseases are associated with frontotemporal dementia. As noted, the basal ganglia have a role in cognition and emotion as well as motor control. Recent research suggests that Parkinson's has an extensive pathology that involves not just dysregulation of dopamine and but also of other neurotransmitters associated with psychiatric symptoms.[10] These may include acetylcholine and noradrenaline. The disease may impair the patient's capacity to

---

10. E. Elgh et al., "Cognitive Function in Early Parkinson's Disease: A Population-Based Study," *European Journal of Neurology* 16 (2009): 1278–1284. Also, H.J. Freund et al., "Cognitive Functions in a Patient with Parkinson-Dementia Syndrome Undergoing Deep-Brain Stimulation," *Archives of Neurology* 66 (2009): 781–785.

consent to DBS in the first place. Still, any questions about the patient's decisional capacity could be answered by psychiatric and neurological assessment of the patient's cognitive functions.

The risks in DBS indicate that candidates for the procedure should display a high degree of decisional capacity to give informed consent to it. If the patient loses decisional capacity, then in rare cases a surrogate might be permitted to consent to continue stimulation on his behalf. Because the Parkinson's patient clearly stated at an earlier time that he preferred motor control to cognitive and affective control, the action that ensured motor control is what he would have wanted and in his best interests. But the treating team and the surrogate would have to carefully discuss the reasons for and against continued stimulation on the patient. It would depend on a patient's physical and mental conditions. Insofar as the patient retains some understanding of these conditions, he or she should participate in these discussions and assent to the decision made for him or her. There may be cases where this treatment could be given to a patient who was unable to assent. A person with cerebral palsy may lack the capacity to have even a minimal understanding of DBS. The technique might be given if it could benefit that person. Nevertheless, this would be permissible only with an understanding of the safety and efficacy of DBS for this condition. It would be difficult to justify offering it as a one-off innovative procedure.

The psychological continuity in virtue of which one persists as the same individual can accommodate some degree of change in one's mental states. But how much change in these states can an individual undergo and remain the same person? How much disruption of psychological continuity can one's narrative accommodate without it threatening the integrity of the whole? There is a critical threshold of continuity and narrative integrity that can tolerate only so much alteration of the psyche without substantially altering the identity of the person.[11] Gradual changes in mental states are more likely to allow one to retain the necessary continuity and integrity and remain above the threshold. This may not be the case when these changes involve a sudden radical disruption between earlier and later mental states. The DBS-induced mania seems to put the Parkinson's patient below the threshold. When a medical procedure relieves physical symptoms, can it be justified if it effectively turns one into a different person?

The metaphysical question of the identity of a person must be addressed together with the normative question of what benefits or harms the person. The main question is whether the treatment results in a net benefit or net harm for the Parkinson's patient. For him, altering a self to reduce suffering is preferable to retaining a self with continued suffering. To be sure, not every patient would have this same preference. Freud had a painful oral cancer for many years that required a series of mouth and jaw operations. He refused to take anything stronger than aspirin until the very end, reportedly saying: "I prefer to think in torment than not to be able to think clearly." He preferred the tormented lucidity in retaining full consciousness and his mental faculties to comfortable but muddled consciousness.

---

11. See the discussion of these questions by Merkel et al. in *Intervening in the Brain*, Chapter 5.

Retaining a state of mind that allowed him to remain aware of his surroundings and to interact with others was more important than relief of his suffering with narcotics, which would have altered these states.[12] The contrast between Freud and the Parkinson's patient illustrates that weighing the positive and negative effects of a drug or procedure on the mind can be quite different from one person to the next.

One might question how a person can benefit from a treatment if his or her identity changes as a result of it. If an intervention controls or cures symptoms and thereby ameliorates pain and suffering, then it benefits the person. This presupposes that the person is the same before and after treatment. Yet the effects of DBS on the Parkinson's patient seem to substantially alter his personality and his identity. His manic state may not entail a complete disruption of psychological continuity, though. Mania alone would not necessarily preclude his capacity to recall what it was like to lose motor control and to experience the positive effect of restoring this control. In spite of the change from a non-manic to a manic state, there may be enough psychological continuity for him to retain a weaker yet sufficient sense of narrative identity to remain the same person. Even if there is a substantial change in his identity following the brain stimulation, the moment he experiences relief from his suffering is enough to plausibly say that he benefits from it. The stimulation satisfies his interest in being free from suffering, and for him this is more important than retaining an identity associated with loss of motor control. This evaluation stands in contrast to the one McMahan makes regarding the hypothetical patient who declines a curative but identity-altering treatment, as discussed in Chapter 6.

In its recommendations, the Benelux Neuromodulation Society has said that DBS of the subthalamic nucleus for Parkinson's disease "should not be abandoned because of potential risks for behavior and cognition. For the time being, extensive preoperative psychiatric and neuropsychological screening and special attention for cognitive and behavioral changes during follow-up seems to be warranted."[13] The discussion of the Parkinson's patient indicates that some individuals with neurological disorders desire symptom relief to such a degree that changes to some of their mental states would be an acceptable price to pay for it. This may be perceived as desperation motivating their decision. But decisions perceived as desperate do not necessarily indicate that a patient lacks decisional capacity or is making an irrational choice. If the upshot of discussion of treatment options by the patient and the medical team is that the net benefit of DBS outweighs the net harm for him, then the decision to continue stimulation can be in the patent's best interests and thus ethically justified. These issues did not arise in the case at hand because the patient died from a cause unrelated to DBS one year after admission to the psychiatric ward. Nevertheless, the case illustrates how adverse psychiatric effects of the technique can complicate assumptions about decisional capacity and consent, as well as assessments of benefit and harm.

---

12. J. Griffin cites and discusses the psychological and moral implications of Freud's statement in *Well-Being: Its Meaning, Measurement, Moral Importance* (Oxford: Clarendon Press, 1986), 8.

13. de Bie et al., "Ethical and Legal Aspects of Neuromodulation," 182.

The discussion raises the more general question of what counts as a successful application of DBS. This would depend on whether it achieved reasonable therapeutic goals and resulted in an improvement in the patient's quality of life. Because the therapeutic goal was controlling his motor symptoms, and DBS achieved this goal, the intervention was a success. More accurately, given the side effect of the mania, it was a qualified success for the patient. It improved his quality of life with respect to his physical symptoms but worsened it with respect to his psychological symptoms. For many Parkinson's patients, DBS can control motor symptoms with few or no adverse effects on cognition or mood. In these cases, the technique is an unqualified success. Yet, patients who experience depression or other psychological symptoms as a side effect of DBS may not judge that they have benefited from it, despite restoration of motor control. A successful application of DBS depends not just on whether it achieves the therapeutic goals of the researcher or clinician. It also depends on how it affects the patient, both neurologically and psychologically.

We can get a better sense of the ethical issues surrounding the question of the success of DBS when it is raised in the context of a different neurological disorder. DBS has been used on a more limited basis for refractory epilepsy. It may be indicated for patients who are not candidates for conventional neurosurgery because the seizures are multifocal.[14] Stimulation of the anterior thalamic nucleus may reduce the frequency of seizures. Remission of all or most of them would clearly count as a success by any measure. Some practitioners would consider a 50 percent reduction a mark of success. Depending on the frequency of seizures before DBS, reducing them by half may translate into a significant improvement in a patient's quality of life. Even a more limited reduction in seizures through DBS could benefit a patient with severe epilepsy. This may be interpreted more favorably when comparing the risks of DBS with the greater risks of neurosurgery in resecting part of the hippocampus or other structures identified as the source of the disorder.

When DBS is used for epilepsy or other conditions, there may be different measures of success between practitioners and patients. This is important for informed consent, since data from clinical trials and innovative applications may be interpreted more positively by physicians than by patients. Practitioners may be biased in their belief about the efficacy of DBS. At the same time, a patient desiring symptom relief will put more weight on positive than negative data about the procedure. To minimize bias from practitioners and unreasonable therapeutic expectations from patients, the team evaluating candidates for DBS should include professionals such as social workers and psychiatric consultants who do not have a vested interest in DBS and are not directly involved in implanting and stimulating the device. Given the risk of significant adverse physiological and psychological effects from DBS, in principle there should be a higher standard of success than there is for anticonvulsant drugs or TMS, both of which entail fewer risks because they are noninvasive. Still, a reasonable standard of success for both practitioners

---

14. S. J. Nagel and I. Najm, "Deep Brain Stimulation for Epilepsy," *Neuromodulation* 12 (2009): 270–280.

and patients should allow for less than complete remission of symptoms when the condition is severe and has not responded to other treatments.

DBS can modulate dysfunctional brain circuits and improve psychiatric symptoms for patients with treatment-resistant obsessive-compulsive disorder and major depression. Like Parkinson's, stimulation of the brain may result in subtle and, in some cases, radical changes in the thought and behavior of these patients. Unlike Parkinson's, these disorders involve more severe cognitive and affective impairment, which may interfere with the capacity to consent to DBS. Also, unlike Parkinson's, any trade-off for these patients is not between physical and psychological states, but between different types of psychological states. It will be helpful to discuss whether patients with OCD and MDD can consent to DBS and to further explore the question of how much risk would be rational for patients with these disorders to take in order to control their symptoms.

Psychiatric Disorders: Obsessive-Compulsive Disorder

The first psychiatric disorder to be treated with DBS was OCD. Results of a pilot study conducted by Swiss and Belgian researchers published in 1999 showed positive results in three of four patients with the disorder.[15] The electrodes were implanted in the anterior limbs of the internal capsule. In the 12 years that it has been used, an increasing number of people have received DBS for OCD. The technique is considered in cases where patients have severe symptoms that have failed to respond to pharmacological and cognitive-behavioral therapies. A recent review indicated that more than one third of those with the disorder who were treated with DBS went into remission, and roughly two thirds were living independently.[16] In February 2009, the FDA granted a Humanitarian Device Exemption for the use of DBS to treat OCD, the first such approval for a psychiatric disorder in the United States. A Humanitarian Device Exemption is a form of limited approval for treating conditions affecting fewer than 4,000 people per year when no other effective treatment is available. This will help to make DBS more accessible and affordable for patients with this disorder.

OCD is characterized by obsessions or compulsions, or both. Obsessions are recurrent and persistent intrusive thoughts, impulses, or images. Compulsions are repetitive behaviors that a person feels driven to perform in response to an obsession or rigid application of rules. Individuals with OCD feel that they must think certain thoughts or do certain things. They do not want to have these mental states and often fight against them. It is as though these states were alien to their true selves. Constant awareness of this disorder and one's response to it can lead to other

---

15. B. Nuttin et al., "Long-Term Electrical Capsular Stimulation in Patients with Obsessive-Compulsive Disorder," *Neurosurgery* 52 (2003): 1263–1274.
16. G. Miller, "Rewiring Faulty Circuits in the Brain," *Science* 323 (2009): 1554–1556. Results of a recent major study of the technique for OCD have been published by B. Greenberg et al., "Deep-Brain Stimulation of the Ventral Internal Capsule/Ventral Striatum for Obsessive-Compulsive Disorder: Worldwide Experience," *Molecular Psychiatry* 15 (2010): 64–79.

psychiatric disorders such as anxiety and depression. One hypothesis for the etiology of this disorder is that the obsessions and compulsions are due to a dysfunctional anterior cingulate gyrus, which regulates cognitive and affective processing in its function as a major pathway between the prefrontal cortex and limbic structures such as the amygdala. Another hypothesis is that the disorder results from dysfunction in the internal capsule. Electrical stimulation of these brain structures can modulate critical neural circuits and reduce the frequency of the obsessions and compulsions.

DBS is an alternative to the ablative procedures of capsulotomy and cingulotomy, which have been treatments of last resort for patients with OCD.[17] These interventions involve making small lesions in the internal capsule and anterior cingulate. They are still performed on a relatively small number of patients, many of whom may not be candidates for DBS. Cingulotomy is the more common of the two procedures. Gamma ventral capsulotomy may be safer than electrolytic capsulotomy because it removes targeted tissue using a "knife" consisting of beams of gamma radiation without intracranial surgery. There have been cases of cysts associated with the radiation developing in the brain. Overall, though, the gamma version of capsulotomy entails less risk of intracerebral hemorrhage, edema, and infection than the electrolytic version. The safety and efficacy of this procedure will not be known until the first ongoing controlled study of it has been completed.[18] In some respects, ablative neurosurgery is preferable to DBS for refractory OCD. As a one-off procedure, it is much less expensive and involves less follow-up than DBS. Patients who undergo lesioning do not require life-long commitment to program the stimulator, repair hardware failures, or change batteries. Lesioning is thus less burdensome for both patients and providers. By eliminating the source of the disorder, lesioning may seem as effective as DBS in controlling and possibly eliminating the obsessions and compulsions.

Still, the irreversibility of lesions is a major drawback of ablative neurosurgery. Even in gamma knife surgery, removing a small amount of brain tissue could result in permanent neurological and psychological sequelae. It is not known how long it would take for the brain to adjust to these changes, if at all. A recent study evaluating the long-term safety and efficacy of conventional capsulotomy in 25 patients who had this procedure from 1988 to 2000 at the Karolinska Institute showed that it effectively reduced symptoms associated with OCD.[19] But half of the patients developed apathy and poor self-control. More brain tissue was removed in the Karolinska procedure than in other procedures performed at other centers. Smaller lesions may have better results. Significantly, the researchers concluded that capsulotomy entails substantial risk of adverse effects and that the risk is greater than previously thought. Because these effects are associated with the removal of brain tissue, they cannot be

---

17. See J. Fins et al., "Psychosurgery: Avoiding an Ethical Redux while Advancing a Therapeutic Future," *Neurosurgery* 59 (2006): 713–716.
18. I have been informed of this by psychiatrist B. Greenberg, one of the investigators in the study.
19. C. Ruck et al., "Capsulotomy for Obsessive-Compulsive Disorder: Long-Term Follow-Up of 25 Patients," *Archives of General Psychiatry* 65 (2008): 914–922.

resolved as they might be in DBS by changing the stimulation parameters or removing the electrodes. Another ethical concern about lesioning as a one-off procedure that is less expensive and involves less follow-up than DBS is that these factors may unduly influence a patient's perception of risk. They may incline a patient to choose ablative neurosurgery over neurostimulation without a careful assessment of the risks of the procedure. Combined with desperation for relief of symptoms, the patient might not adequately consider potentially permanent untoward consequences of lesioning.

The mixed outcomes and irreversibility of lesioning raise questions about the efficacy and especially safety of this procedure as a treatment for psychiatric disorders. They suggest that the benefit–risk ratio of lesioning may not be better but worse than that of DBS for OCD. These considerations indicate that DBS should be among the inclusionary criteria for cingulotomy and capsulotomy, which should be treatments of last resort. It is possible that long-term studies of gamma ventral capsulotomy, or other forms of gamma psychiatric neurosurgery, will show that the procedure is as safe as and more effective than DBS for diseases of the mind. But current data are not positive enough to support this position. Because the effects of electrolytic or gamma lesions can be irreversible, physicians offering lesioning for a psychiatric disorder have an absolute obligation to discuss all potential benefits and risks of the procedure with patients. For the same reason, a patient who is a candidate for the procedure must demonstrate a high degree of decisional capacity in assessing the potential benefits and risks to consent to it. DBS is generally safer than lesioning for OCD because it does not remove any brain tissue and modulates brain activity in a more flexible manner. It is also safer than lesioning because many of its adverse effects are reversible.

For the majority of patients with this and other psychiatric disorders, the extent of symptom reduction with DBS is no better than 50 percent. An expert consensus panel on treatments for OCD in the late 1990s concluded that a full response was defined as at least a 35 percent reduction in symptoms. A partial response was defined as a 25 percent reduction.[20] These figures might not suggest a significant therapeutic effect. But whether the definition of a full or partial response translates into an improvement in the patient's quality of life depends on the frequency and degree of symptoms before treatment. It also depends on the extent of improvement in the patient's ability to function on a daily basis after treatment. There have been serious neurological and psychological outcomes of DBS for OCD, some of which might not be reversible. Findings from one randomized controlled study indicated that stimulation of the subthalamic nucleus could reduce the symptoms of OCD. But of the eight patients in the active arm of the study, one experienced an intracerebral hemorrhage, two had infections, and others experienced 23 adverse events associated with mood.[21] Most of the psychiatric symptoms involved hypomania. Again, these symptoms probably resulted from activation of the limbic circuit of

---

20. "Treatment of Obsessive-Compulsive Disorder," *Journal of Clinical Psychiatry* 58 (1997), Supplement 4: 2–75.
21. L. Mallet et al., "Subthalamic Nucleus Stimulation in Severe Obsessive-Compulsive Disorder," *New England Journal of Medicine* 359 (2008): 2121–2134.

the STN. Physical, cognitive, and affective symptoms caused by the intracerebral hemorrhage may not be reversible. Also, it is unclear whether discontinuing stimulation would reverse all unintended psychological effects. Altered affective states may not be as serious as intracerebral hemorrhage. But they are clinically significant and need to be considered by physicians and patients in providing and undergoing DBS for OCD. It may achieve the goal of reducing symptoms associated with one disorder only to cause other symptoms. This may reduce the net benefit and may result in net harm for some patients.

Unlike Parkinson's, where the stimulator has to be turned on in continuous cycles for motor control, the desired effect in OCD can be produced by activating the device intermittently. Yet even intermittent activation can result in disturbing psychological effects. These effects may take weeks or months to appear when using DBS for OCD, where the response is slower than it is for movement disorders such as Parkinson's. The same guidelines adopted for the use of DBS for Parkinson's should be in place for the use of the procedure for OCD. This would require that a multidisciplinary medical team assess the patient's suitability for DBS and monitor his or her condition over time. It would also involve assessment of the patient's capacity to consent to the implantation and activation of the electrodes in his or her brain. This capacity may or may not be impaired by the abnormal cognitive and affective processes behind the obsessions and compulsions.

Decisional capacity can come in degrees.[22] Given that the risks in DBS are significant, an individual should show a high degree of capacity and should be able to carefully weigh the reasons for and against the procedure to consent to it. Although there are important differences between Parkinson's and OCD, electrical brain stimulation for the second disorder raises the same ethical questions as it does for the first. Assuming that the patient is deemed to have sufficient decisional capacity, how much risk of untoward psychological effects from a treatment is acceptable when that treatment is the only way to relieve the obsessions and compulsions? Would some cognitive or emotional effects be more or less acceptable than others for the individual who is a candidate for DBS? From the perspective of the treating team, to what extent should the risk of these effects influence the justification for providing this treatment to the patient?

To discuss these questions, it is instructive to cite a 2005 interview of a patient following successful DBS for severe OCD.[23] Before the procedure, the patient was unable to work and had received other therapies for 20 years with little benefit.

---

22. P. Appelbaum, "Assessment of Patients' Competence to Consent to Treatment," *New England Journal of Medicine* 357 (2007): 1834–1840. As pointed out in note 9, Appelbaum takes competence to be practically equivalent to decisional capacity.

23. This interview is cited and discussed by Merkel et al. in *Intervening in the Brain*, 181 ff. This and other cases suggest that DBS may give new meaning to the expression, "left to one's own devices."

Question 1: How severe was your disease before the operation?
Answer: I surely would have committed suicide if the surgery [implantation and stimulation of the electrodes] hadn't taken place.
Question 2: Do you think the surgery has changed anything?
Answer: After surgery, there was a major change in my life. I can enjoy life again, which was impossible before. My compulsions and obsessions are greatly reduced. They do not bother me so much anymore and I can now live with them. I am neither depressed nor anxious anymore.
Question 3: Would you advise anyone else, who has the same degree of illness as you, to have the surgery?
Answer: Yes, without any doubt.
Question 4: Don't you find it an ethical problem that an artificial stimulating device rules your life and makes you feel better?
Answer: I don't see the ethical problem. It makes me feel better and I like to be better. If this is an ethical problem, then any medical treatment to improve the condition of a patient is an ethical problem.

The patient's responses to all four questions give no indication that he lacked the capacity to understand the procedure and consider the potential benefits and risks of DBS. His comment that he was depressed and anxious before the procedure does not necessarily mean that these mental states undermined his capacity to weigh reasons for and against stimulating his brain. Moderate depression does not preclude one from making informed decisions about medical treatment.[24] Nor does the admission that he would have committed suicide imply that he was so desperate for relief that his decision to undergo the procedure was not a rational one. Suicide may be a rational choice for a person if the pain or suffering caused by a condition makes continued life worse than death. There is an affective component to decisional capacity, but there is no evidence that moderate affective impairment undermines this capacity. Still, one might claim that the compulsions would render the patient incapable of making a rational decision about DBS. Experiencing compulsions for a number of hours each day would appear to undermine the cognitive functions necessary for consent. In addition, desperation for symptom relief and unreasonable hope that DBS would result in a complete remission of symptoms may unduly influence the patient's perception of risk. This may not be as great a concern as perception of risk in a one-off ablative neurosurgical procedure for OCD, but it is a concern nonetheless. These issues highlight the need for a psychiatric determination that the patient has sufficient capacity to consider the possible outcomes of DBS before consenting to it.

Admittedly, there are limitations to using the content of an interview conducted after the procedure to infer that a patient had enough decisional capacity to consent to it. But these limitations do not imply that the patient in question lacked this capacity. The patient's comments that his obsessions and compulsions were greatly reduced by the procedure and that he could live with them indicate less than a

---

24. Appelbaum, "Assessment of Patients' Competence to Consent to Treatment."

complete remission of symptoms. His further comment that they did not bother him so much anymore suggests that he was pleased with the outcome and had reasonable expectations about the therapeutic potential of DBS. From discussion with the medical team, his knowledge that DBS had been used successfully to treat other individuals with severe OCD would help to make it a viable therapeutic option and thus a rational choice for him. This, in addition to his knowledge that the stimulation settings could be changed if he experienced adverse effects, could attenuate any feeling of desperation or anxiety. In light of these considerations, we can conclude that he had enough capacity to make a free and informed decision to undergo DBS. Although the fact that he had the disorder indicated that some of the neural circuits mediating some of his cognitive capacities were dysfunctional, other circuits mediating other cognitive capacities were intact. Also, his comment that he felt better after the procedure clearly indicates that DBS benefited him by improving his quality of life. He was better off than before, and in this respect the technique could be considered a success. This is consistent with the consensus among psychiatrists that a 35 percent reduction of symptoms of OCD is considered a full response.

Contrary to what the interviewer suggested, the stimulation was not something that controlled the patient's life but a necessary means through which he could regain control of it. OCD had taken away control of his life; DBS restored it. What are alien to the patient are not the electrodes or the electrical stimulation, but the obsessions and compulsions. In many respects, DBS should not be treated differently from other interventions for other serious medical conditions. DBS has been described as a pacemaker for the brain. It is analogous to a pacemaker for the heart to maintain normal cardiac function for people with rhythm abnormalities. The use of DBS to maintain brain function may not be fundamentally different from the use of insulin enabling diabetics to control blood glucose levels and other endocrine and organ functions. Among other things, this intervention enables them to prevent the adverse psychological effects associated with hyperglycemia and hypoglycemia. The purpose of any intervention in the central nervous, cardiovascular, or endocrine system is to restore the normal functioning of these systems when they have become dysfunctional. What is critical to one's identity is not whether one has a stimulating device in one's brain but how the device affects one's mental states. Although the device can alter how the brain generates and sustains these states, it is not the device but conscious desires, beliefs, intentions, emotions, and memories that constitute one's identity.

Some might claim that the stimulating device is critical to identity because of the way it can directly modulate neural and mental processes. Moreover, a person's identification with the device may be reinforced by concern that it could malfunction inside his or her brain. Yet this mental state is not fundamentally different from people's concern that an implanted cardiac defibrillator, cardiac pacemaker, or ventricular assist device could malfunction inside their bodies. Nor is it fundamentally different from the beliefs and emotions of people with type-1 diabetes who need access to insulin, or those in chronic kidney failure who need access to dialysis machines. These devices, substances, and machines do not influence mental states as directly as a brain-stimulating device. Nevertheless, fear of malfunction or lack of access to them can have as strong an impact on a person's psyche.

Constant awareness that critical bodily functions depend on them involves some of the beliefs and emotions that constitute identity. Indeed, the link between these interventions and identity may be stronger than that between DBS and identity, given the knowledge that people can or will die if their hearts stop beating, if they develop diabetic ketoacidosis, or if they have fatal uremia. Fractured defibrillator wires have caused at least 13 deaths in the United States. Apart from rare instances of intracerebral hemorrhage resulting from implanting electrodes in the brain, the risks associated with deep-brain stimulation generally are not life-threatening. So, even if a stimulating device in one's brain strongly influences one's identity, having other devices or substances in one's body, or being connected to a machine, can have just as much influence one's identity.

Reshaping synaptic connectivity through DBS by itself is medically and morally neutral. What matters is whether it can modulate the particular mental states associated with the disorder, and whether or how it alters normal mental states. If the mental states mediated by the patient's existing synaptic connectivity are pathological, then there are good reasons to reshape it. If DBS can reshape synaptic connectivity in a way that resolves or reduces symptoms while preventing or minimizing changes to normal mental states, then it is a medically and morally justified treatment.

The patient's response to Question 1 underscores the importance of quality of life in his decision to undergo DBS. It suggests that he was willing to take some risk of unwanted side effects for the sake of alleviating the severe symptoms of the disorder, which weakened his interest in continuing to live. Because he would have committed suicide without DBS, he was rational in choosing to have the technique, despite the risks it entailed. But *how much* risk would be rational for him to take and acceptable to the physicians treating him? And *which* effects would be acceptable? Mild memory impairment or mild personality changes might be acceptable for both parties. Profound amnesia, mania, severe depression, or radical personality changes might not be, though this would depend on whether or to what extent these effects were reversible. It would also depend on the comparative values the patient attached to personality, memory, and other mental capacities and traits. The extent of these changes could be minimized or reversed by monitoring the patient and adjusting the stimulator or removing the electrodes. Any normative assessment of personality changes that would or would not be acceptable would have to be weighed against the deleterious influence of his obsessions and compulsions on his quality of life. Because different patients may weigh these trade-offs differently, this assessment cannot be generalized but must be case-sensitive. The treating team would be obligated to disclose and discuss data from previous applications of DBS for OCD and the potential positive and negative cognitive and affective outcomes before administering the procedure. As a critical component of this discussion, the team would be obligated to inform the patient that improvement or impairment of cognitive or affective capacities from DBS cannot be predicted in each case. Insofar as his choice to have the procedure followed a careful weighing of the potential benefits and risks, it would not be compelled by the condition it treated but a voluntary choice.

Concern about altered cognition and affect notwithstanding, all of this has to be considered in light of the fact that OCD is a psychopathology that causes considerable suffering. The obsessions and compulsions that make up a significant part of the psyche of patients with OCD are not mental states with which they identify.

Our selves are constituted by mental states that have undergone a process of critical reflection and self-identification.[25] Because the symptoms of psychiatric disorders such as OCD can undermine the capacity to engage in this process, they can be alien to our true selves. The disunity of mental states in these psychopathologies can disrupt the identities of the people who have them. Relieving their symptoms can restore the unity of one's mental states, the integrity of the self, and thus one's identity. Addressing the question of whether DBS would alter the personality of his patient, "Herr Z," psychiatrist Michael Schormann commented: "Patients don't see their obsessions as part of their personality. They see them as something imposed on them, that they yearn to be rid of."[26]

Neurologist Matthis Synofzik and psychiatrist Thomas Schlaepfer point out that "the ethically decisive question is not whether DBS alters personality or not, but whether it does so in *a good or bad way* from the patient's very own perspective."[27] This suggests that objective measures of success based on the extent to which dysfunctional brain circuits have been modulated do not determine whether DBS benefits a patient. Even if researchers and clinicians achieve their therapeutic goals in using the technique to control certain symptoms, this alone does not indicate that the patient is better off as a result of it. Objective measures cannot capture the patient's subjective experience before, during, and after neuromodulation. Synofzik and Schlaepfer further note: "To provide an actual *benefit* to the individual patient, however, DBS must not only be effective, i.e., improve scores in OCD or MD [major depression] rating scales, but also demonstrate that these abstract improvements indeed are associated with an actual improvement of the individual patient's abilities to achieve *personally valuable goals*, i.e., goals that are valuable in light of his or her individual psychosocial situation and on the basis of his or her particular individual evaluative concept of a good life."[28] This position does not imply brain–mind dualism. It implies that the patient's mental states necessarily depend on but involve more than and are not reducible to the neurological states altered by DBS.

A major problem with DBS is that there is no way of knowing which adverse effects of this intervention would be temporary or permanent. It is not known which effects would resolve or persist. The probability of memory impairment, mania, or personality changes may be low. Yet it is the magnitude of harm to the psyche, if the probability were actualized, that generates the ethical concern. It is possible that the procedure would control one set of symptoms only to generate a different set of symptoms. Given the risk of suicide in the OCD patient interviewed, though, the potential benefit of DBS for him would outweigh the risk. We cannot assume that the technique would result in a complete remission of symptoms for every patient. Nevertheless, an improvement in the patient's quality of life with a corresponding reduction in the risk of suicide would suggest a favorable benefit–harm

25. See Frankfurt, "Identification and Externality."
26. Cited by A. Abbott, "Deep in Thought," *Nature* 436 (2005): 18–19, at 19.
27. "Stimulating Personality: Ethical Concern for Deep Brain Stimulation in Psychiatric Patients and for Enhancement Purposes," *Biotechnology Journal* 3 (2008): 1511–1520, at 1514.
28. *Ibid.*, 1514–1515.

calculus and justify the treatment. We can make this claim even if the technique yields no more than a 50 percent reduction in symptoms and has the potential to generate some adverse effects. It could meet a reasonable standard of success, all things considered. By reducing symptoms, it could restore some degree of autonomy to the patient by enabling him to have more control of his behavior. Also, by offering what may be the only remaining potentially beneficial option to the patient and by monitoring any adverse effects of DBS, this intervention would be consistent with the treating team's obligations of beneficence and nonmaleficence to him.

Psychiatric Disorders: Major Depressive Disorder

A study published in 2005 showed that DBS modulated hyperactivity in the subgenual cingulate region of the brain and produced clinical benefit in six patients with major depressive disorder who failed to respond to all other treatments.[29] There were lingering questions about the efficacy of DBS for depression in this study because it did not test the experimental treatment against a placebo. Moreover, the number of subjects in the study may have been too small to draw any definitive conclusions about its clinical significance. In a more recent study published in 2008, 12 of 20 severely depressed patients undergoing DBS targeting the subcallosal cingulate gyrus had significant improvement in their symptoms, effectively going into remission for one year.[30] Another study published in the same year showed that stimulation of an underactive nucleus accumbens relieved anhedonia in some patients with refractory depression with no side effects.[31] Although each of these studies shows that modulating a particular neural circuit may relieve a particular symptom or set of symptoms, collectively they suggest that depression involves a number of neural circuits. As in cases of Parkinson's disease and OCD, the results also indicate that the effects of DBS depend on whether the targeted brain regions are overactive or underactive.

To say that depressed patients *feel* better after DBS does not always mean that they *are* better. Overstimulation of circuits in the reward system may produce hypomania or mania in some patients. These states may seem preferable to anhedonia, since feelings such as euphoria intuitively are more desirable than the inability to experience pleasure. But the fact that the Dutch Parkinson's patient's irrational behavior during his manic phase harmed him clearly shows that hypomania and especially mania are not beneficial states.

Neuroscientists have a better understanding of the neural circuitry underlying Parkinson's and OCD than the circuitry underlying depression. There is also greater variation in symptoms among people with depression than those with other neurological and psychiatric disorders. The changes induced by stimulating the brains of

---

29. H. Mayberg et al., "Deep-Brain Stimulation for Treatment-Resistant Depression," *Neuron* 45 (2005): 651–660.

30. A. Lozano et al., "Subcallosal Cingulate Gyrus Deep Brain-Stimulation for Treatment-Resistant Depression," *Biological Psychiatry* 64 (2008): 461–467.

31. T. Schlaepfer et al., "Deep-Brain Stimulation to Reward Circuitry Alleviates Anhedonia in Refractory Major Depression," *Neuropsychopharmacology* 33 (2008): 368–377.

depressed patients are poorly understood and may produce different effects among them. Adjusting the stimulation parameters to reverse any untoward effects is not a simple action. Drugs have only a dosage parameter. Stimulating devices have five parameters: the intensity of the stimulation, its frequency, the duration of each pulse, the intervals between pulses, and the site being stimulated. All of these factors make it more difficult to assess short- and long-term effects of stimulating the brain to relieve the symptoms of depression. In addition, given the extent of the placebo response in treatments for depression, placebo-controlled studies may be necessary to firmly establish the efficacy of DBS for this disorder. These would be ethically controversial because of the deception and risk entailed by sham surgical procedures.

DBS for major depression raises ethical questions similar to those I raised in discussing Parkinson's and OCD. Does an individual with moderately severe to severe depression and some cognitive impairment have the decisional capacity to consent to the procedure?[32] To what degree of risk would the clinicians treating the patient be permitted to expose him or her? Would it be rational for the patient to expose him or herself to this risk? In cases where a patient lacks sufficient decisional capacity to consent, could a surrogate consent to the implantation and stimulation of the device on the patient's behalf? I will address these questions by presenting and discussing a fictionalized version of an actual case using DBS as an innovative treatment for depression at Vancouver General Hospital.

H. G. is a 37-year-old woman. Seven years ago, she was diagnosed with major depressive disorder on the basis of sleep disturbance, extreme fatigue, inability to concentrate, impeded initiative, and low mood, which included suicidal ideation.[33] She had attempted suicide on two occasions. Her psychiatrist prescribed three different selective serotonin reuptake inhibitors (SSRIs), none of which had any beneficial effect. Some had adverse effects. During this time, she had a number of sessions of cognitive-behavioral therapy in combination with pharmacotherapy. These had no positive effect either. Different combinations of tricyclic antidepressants were tried as well, to no avail. H. G. then underwent a series of ECT sessions. This relieved some of her symptoms, especially the dark moods. But she experienced some retrograde amnesia and rebound depression a month after the last ECT session. Desperate for relief from her symptoms, H. G. learned that a psychiatrist at a local medical center, Dr. Y, had performed DBS as an innovative treatment for depression. Having exhausted all other treatment options, H.G.'s psychiatrist referred her to Dr. Y. for medical consultation.

Dr. Y explained that he had performed DBS on two patients with major depression in the last year. He noted that while it was too soon to determine that the treatment was clearly safe and effective, the two patients reported relief of symptoms and

32. L. Dunn et al., "Ethical Issues in Deep-Brain Stimulation Research for Treatment-Resistant Depression: Focus on Risk and Consent," *AJOB Neuroscience*, published online September 24, 2010.

33. *Diagnostic and Statistical Manual of Mental Disorders* (DSM-IV-TR), 369–376. Also, the draft of *DSM-5: The Future of Psychiatric Diagnosis* (forthcoming 2013), http://www.dsm5.org/Pages/RecentUpdates.aspx. In addition, R. H. Belmaker and G. Agam, "Major Depressive Disorder," *New England Journal of Medicine* 358 (2008): 55–68.

no adverse effects. The inclusionary criteria were that patients must have had major depressive disorder for at least five years, persistent severe symptoms, and no other available treatments had been effective. Patients must have failed to respond to antidepressant and cognitive-behavioral therapy, as well as ECT. DBS would be offered to patients with this disorder as a treatment of last resort. Dr. Y explained that the risks of implanting the electrodes in H. G.'s subgenual cingulate included edema, infection, and intracerebral hemorrhage. The risks associated with activation of the device included seizures from malfunctioning electrodes, hypomania, mania, amplification of the effects of antidepressants, and rebound depression during periods when the device was not activated. Overall, these risks are greater than those associated with ECT. While ECT may cause some amnesia, and while premature discontinuation of the technique may increase the probability of relapse, it does not involve surgical intervention in the brain. Dr. Y also noted that DBS had caused impulsive behavior in some patients receiving DBS for Parkinson's disease. But he pointed out that any untoward effects of the procedure could be reversed by changing the settings of the electrodes and the stimulator.

The electrodes would be implanted and activated in a medical clinic at the hospital by Dr. Y. and other staff, including a neurosurgeon, neurologist, and anesthesiologist. The treatment would consist of monitored activation for two hours each week for two months, after which the patient's condition would be re-evaluated. Because there were questions about whether H. G.'s depression impaired her decisional capacity, and because the innovative nature of the treatment made it impossible to predict any short- or long-term neurological and psychological sequelae of stimulating her brain, Dr. Y. pointed out that an ethics consultation and approval would be necessary before they could proceed. The ethics committee, H. G., her family, and the physicians treating her would discuss her capacity to consent to the intervention and its potential benefits and risks.

The severity of her symptoms might suggest that her affective state would interfere with her cognitive capacity to make an informed decision about medical treatment. Presumably, this would make her unable to consent to DBS. As discussed in Chapters 2 and 4, Damasio has argued that affective and cognitive capacities are interdependent and together are necessary for reasoning and decision making.[34] Impairment in one of these capacities could mean impairment in the other. Still, the effects of depression on reasoning are measured in degrees rather than in absolute terms. H. G.'s affective state might not be so severe that it undermined her decisional capacity. This could be determined on the basis of behavioral criteria on clinical examination. From the fact that one has a mood disorder, it does not follow that one cannot rationally decide to act in one's best interests. Depression as such does not necessarily undermine decisional capacity. What is necessary in this case is that H. G. has *enough* decisional capacity to understand the reasons for and against DBS for her condition. If a psychiatrist determines that her depression slightly impairs but does not undermine her ability to understand what the procedure

---

34. "Neuroscience and Ethics: Intersections," and *Descartes' Error*.

entails, and that what she understands is sufficient to establish the requisite degree of mental capacity, then she can consent to the treatment.

One might again raise the issue of desperation in challenging the claim that H. G. is competent enough to understand the risks of DBS before deciding to have the treatment. She may agree to undergo the implantation and stimulation of the device out of a desperate desire for relief from her symptoms. This could impair her ability to carefully weigh the risks. Yet, as noted in the Parkinson's and OCD cases, desperation itself is not a sign of irrationality or lack of decisional capacity. Although some might associate desperation with an unreasonable perception of risk, the risks of DBS would be acceptable given the certainty of continued suffering, the potential for suicide without the treatment, and the potential of the technique to benefit her. This assessment would be based in part on the positive results of the technique in Dr. Y's two previous patients, as well as the results from studies completed in the last five years at other medical centers. Given the severity of H. G.'s condition, the fact that all other treatment options had been exhausted, and the potential benefit of DBS, it would be medically and ethically justified for Dr. Y to provide it and for H. G. to receive it. It would be consistent with the physician's duty of care to his patient and in her best interests. A successful outcome of DBS for major depression theoretically should involve roughly a 50 percent reduction in symptoms. This may not seem a high standard of success, at least not one measured in terms of a complete remission of symptoms. But it is a reasonable standard of success. As with other neuropsychiatric disorders, a critical factor in these assessments is that it is difficult to predict what the outcome of the procedure will be for each patient. This complicates the informed consent process. Nevertheless, practitioners informing patients of DBS as a therapeutic option for depression are obligated to include this uncertainty in presenting this information.

Another concern about using DBS for H. G.'s depression is that it could result in substantial changes to the mental states constituting her personality. It could result in an altered self. This concern would be warranted if the alteration involved deleterious effects on her normal mental states and caused her psychological harm. Significantly, H. G.'s depression is a manifestation of a dysfunctional brain and disordered mind that already have caused her considerable harm. The purpose of the intervention is to alter her brain so that it and her mind can be restored to a functional and ordered state. Altering mental states to relieve suffering is preferable to retaining mental states causing suffering. Like the cases of the Parkinson's and OCD patients, the metaphysical question of whether an intervention in the brain changes the identity of the person must be considered together with the normative question of whether the person benefits from or is harmed by it. The dysfunctional state of the brain and mind causing H. G.'s depression is not a state with which she identifies. Altering some of her psychological properties is necessary to produce the desired result and restore the integrity of her self.

If assessment of her mental state determined that H. G. lacked sufficient decisional capacity to consent to DBS, then a family member or other surrogate might consent to the treatment on her behalf. Although substitute decision making in this situation would be rare, it could be permissible on the grounds that DBS was in H. G.'s best interests and is what she would have chosen if she were competent to consent on her own. Still, proxy consent to a medical intervention is ethically weightier than standard consent because the decision is not being made by the patient but for her. It is also weightier because of the potential harmful neurological and psychological consequences of this intervention in her brain. Proxy consent would be permissible if H. G.'s quality of life was poor and the technique would ameliorate at least some of her symptoms. Assuming that H. G. retained some degree of cognitive capacity, she should participate in the discussion about DBS and assent to the decision to offer it for her condition. The fact that the decision to accept or forego the treatment is not made by the patient makes it imperative that proxy consent consist in a deliberative process of dialogue between and among the medical team, the substitute decision maker, and the patient.

Merkel and colleagues say that we should be more concerned about brain interventions resulting in subtle changes in the psyche and personality than more radical changes. They claim that focusing on the latter distracts us from what is more likely to occur.[35] Yet most people are more concerned about the possibility of radical changes in personality and behavior resulting from these interventions. As with Parkinson's and OCD, these changes may occur in some patients undergoing DBS for major depression. Potential and actual changes to a patient's psychology can influence decisions about whether to initiate, forego, continue, or discontinue this treatment. Patients with this and other serious disorders of the mind, and medical teams treating them, need to weigh the risks *with* DBS against poor quality of life and the risk of suicide *without* DBS.

DBS has also been used to restore a greater degree of conscious awareness and cognitive and physical functioning in a small number of patients in the minimally conscious state (MCS). Questions about benefit and harm for these patients are different in important respects from those that figured in the discussion of Parkinson's, OCD, and major depression because of the distinctive features of the MCS. I will now explore the ethical implications of using DBS for patients who fall within this neurological category.

Neurological Disorders: The Minimally Conscious State

In Chapter 6, I discussed the differences between the persistent and permanent vegetative state, as well as the MCS. Specifically, I discussed how these states figure in the idea of survival. Although they require different forms of life-sustaining care, some patients may emerge from an MCS and regain a greater degree of consciousness without any intervention. Others may regain a greater degree of consciousness and cognitive and physical ability through different interventions, one of which is DBS. Electrical stimulation of the central thalamus may restore some physical and cognitive capacities that have been disrupted by brain injury.[36] This is because the thalamus has extensive projections to the basal ganglia and cortex, and stimulating the thalamus may in turn activate subcortical and cortical circuits mediating motor

---

35. *Intervening in the Brain*, 284.
36. See Fins, "Constructing an Ethical Stereotaxy."

function and awareness. Neurostimulation for the MCS is still an area of investigation and not yet a viable therapy. The technique is much more innovative for this condition than it is for Parkinson's or other neuropsychiatric disorders because it has been performed on a much smaller number of patients. Questions remain about its safety and efficacy. Still, DBS holds promise for improving or restoring physical and cognitive capacities in patients with chronic disorders of consciousness resulting from brain anoxia and especially traumatic brain injury.

This brain intervention raises three ethical questions: Although their neurological state precludes the capacity to consent, do patients in an MCS have enough mental capacity to assent to DBS? Could surrogates consent to DBS on behalf of the patient? Does the potential benefit of this intervention outweigh the potential harm?

I have noted difficulties in knowing which interventions a minimally conscious patient would want. The capacity to respond to questions with "yes" and "no" answers is not indicative of the decisional capacity necessary to consent to treatment. Minimal communicative ability also makes it questionable whether minimally conscious patients could assent to DBS. They probably would not be able to participate in discussion of the reasons for or against the treatment. A surrogate must have a clear sense of what a patient wants in order to give proxy consent to DBS. Yet the patient's wishes may be unknown. The fact that DBS is a new area of investigation for the MCS presents an additional problem for proxy consent. Without data on outcomes from a sufficient number of patients in clinical trials, investigators would not have a sound understanding of the benefits and risks and would not be able to adequately inform surrogates of them. They should have this information in order to consent to DBS for a minimally conscious patient, as well as the understanding that the intervention is experimental. What might justify proxy consent would be an estimation of the probability of some degree of recovery on the basis of imaging using fMRI and MEG.[37] Patients with more integrated cortical function, more intact thalamic-cortical connections, and more intact intralaminar thalamic nuclei would have a greater chance of recovery. These features could also justify investigators' use of the technique on grounds of beneficence. Still, thus far there have been no indications of any patients having any meaningful recovery from the MCS.

In a case mentioned in Chapter 6, researchers from three American sites reported that continued DBS over a six-month period for a 38-year-old assault victim in an MCS restored greater limb control, oral feeding, and some cognitive functions.[38] These outcomes suggest that the technique has been a success. Yet, it is unclear how many patients in an MCS from a traumatic brain injury would benefit from DBS, or to what extent they would benefit from it.[39] Even if this technique resulted in improvement or restoration of some neurological functions, it would not

---

37. See Jonsen, Siegler, and Winslade, *Clinical Ethics*, 88–91, and Beauchamp and Childress, *Principles of Biomedical Ethics*, Chapter 3.
38. N. Schiff et al., "Behavior Improvements with Thalamic Stimulation after Severe Traumatic Brain Injury."
39. One pharmacological intervention that has been used to try to induce a greater degree of awareness in the MCS is zolpidem. I cited the discouraging results from one study using this drug in Chapter 6, note 46.

necessarily result in improvement or restoration of all critical physical and cognitive functions. One's state of mind and quality of life would determine whether this technique benefited or harmed one. Because these psychological factors can vary among patients, questions about benefit and harm have to be considered on a case-by-case basis.

What is critical in assessing whether DBS could benefit a minimally conscious patient is *which* cognitive and physical functions and *how much* of these functions the technique could restore. If DBS could restore a patient to full consciousness and full cognitive and physical functioning, then clearly the procedure and the clinicians or researchers using it would benefit the patient. Significant but less than complete recovery could also make the patient better off. In these instances, a surrogate consenting to the procedure for the patient would be acting in the patient's best interests. In addition, it could result in benefits to caregivers and society if the patient were less disabled. Recovery of consciousness and cognitive and physical capacities following brain injury is often a matter of degree and may fall anywhere along a spectrum of these capacities. But I have noted above and in Chapter 6 that available data from studies of minimally conscious patients indicate that they have a poor prognosis and poor quality of life. In principle, patients in an MCS should have access to therapeutic interventions.[40] These include not only interventions to keep them alive, but also those like DBS that may improve their physical and cognitive functions. However, physicians and especially families need to be disabused of any unreasonable expectations of what this technique can do for these patients.[41] Selection of patients with more integrated thalamic-cortical activity may promote positive outcomes. But no one can predict what the neurological and psychological effects of neurostimulation will be for each patient who undergoes it.

Neurostimulation might enable some patients to progress from a nonfunctional or minimally functional part to a moderately or highly functional part of the neurological spectrum. Whether a patient benefited from or was harmed by the technique would depend not only on neurological improvement, but also on how any corresponding increase in awareness and cognitive functions aligned with that neurological improvement. It is not just third-person assessments of improved cognitive and physical functions that matter in determining net benefit, but also the first-person experience of the individual who must live with these functions. They may be significantly impaired, and the individual may be aware of the difference in his or her cognitive and physical abilities and disabilities before and after a brain injury. The technique could have the unwitting effect of causing the patient to suffer from his or her awareness of being disabled and of what he or she had lost as a result of the brain injury. This could be the outcome of DBS on such brain-injured patients as the hypothetical mathematician and singer that I discussed in Chapter 6. The harm associated with conscious awareness of one's cognitive and physical impairments

---

40. Fins argues along these lines in "Constructing an Ethical Stereotaxy." See also Schiff, Giacino, and Fins, "Deep-Brain Stimulation, Neuroethics, and the Minimally Conscious State," *Archives of Neurology* 66 (2009): 697–702.
41. Schlaepfer and Fins note the problem of bias in reporting only positive results of DBS in "Deep Brain Stimulation and the Neuroethics of Responsible Publishing," *Journal of the American Medical Association* 303 (2010): 775–776.

might be enough to cancel any cognitive and physical benefits. Becoming more conscious could defeat the therapeutic purpose of the intervention. On the other hand, an individual with recovery of some but not all cognitive and physical functions might not focus on the impairments but on the functions that enable him or her to interact with others and the world in a positive, life-affirming way.

As in the other disorders I have discussed, an acceptable standard of success for DBS would be one in which the technique achieved reasonable therapeutic goals and improved the MCS patient's quality of life. It should promote patient autonomy and meet criteria of beneficence and nonmaleficence. Given the concerns I have raised about the potential outcomes of stimulating the brains of MCS patients, one can question whether this intervention can meet this standard. It is not known how often DBS would have to be repeated to activate and reactivate neural networks and sustain a certain degree of cortical activity. This is a reflection of the complexity of the central nervous system and how it responds to injury. Some individuals may have more integrated thalamic-cortical activity than others and have better prospects of regaining a broader range of neurological functions that would ensure a good, or at least minimally decent, quality of life. Yet it is precisely the uncertainty of these outcomes, and the probability that not all of them would involve a net benefit to patients, that should give researchers and clinicians pause in considering the use of DBS to restore neurological functions in MCS patients.

Because there are no conclusive data to support a definitive positive or negative assessment of DBS for the MCS, these are open questions for debate. Inducing a neurological improvement with neurostimulation would not necessarily induce a net psychological benefit for a brain-injured patient. This is a critical inference that we could not draw without a qualitative assessment of the patient's psychological state following the procedure. Reports from doctors caring for the 38-year-old man in the MCS who underwent DBS in 2006 and 2007 indicate that he is still unable to say what he thinks about the procedure and is unable to describe his own conscious state. These are not necessarily indications of poor quality of life; but they are not indications of good quality of life either. Further improvement in his physical and cognitive functions would be necessary for a positive assessment of his overall neurological and mental condition.

The FDA has approved DBS as an experimental intervention for a small number of additional patients in the MCS.[42] Data from these cases will help to clarify the prognosis and probability of recovery of physical and cognitive functions in these patients. This will provide critical information on whether there would be a favorable ratio of benefits to risks of DBS for patients in an MCS, which cannot be derived from only a few case histories. Discussion of the ethical issues raised by neurostimulation for patients in an MCS or other disordered neurological states is to some extent speculative. Yet the innovative and experimental use of DBS for this condition generates an obligation of clinical neuroscientists to carefully consider how individuals with severe brain injuries might benefit from or be harmed by this intervention in the brain. By addressing these issues, researchers, clinicians, and ethicists together can establish a framework for determining when, and on which patients, this technique should or should not be used.

---

42. As noted by Kuehn, "Scientists Probe Deep-Brain Stimulation," 2251.

Conclusion

DBS can control and relieve physical and psychological symptoms of a number of neurological and psychiatric disorders that have not responded to other therapies. While DBS is now considered standard treatment for Parkinson's disease, it is being used increasingly for other neurological and psychiatric disorders on an experimental and innovative basis. More randomized controlled studies will yield a clearer picture of its therapeutic potential for these disorders. Closed-loop devices that can be activated or turned off in response to symptoms will improve its safety and efficacy. These devices will enable patients and practitioners to have more control of these symptoms. Diffusion tractotomy can help to identify areas of the brain that would respond to stimulation. This procedure uses brain imaging to trace fiber bundles associated with brain pathology. On this basis, researchers and clinicians can better inform patients with these disorders, or surrogate decision makers, of the relative benefits and risks.

DBS can reshape synaptic connectivity in ways that may be either beneficial or harmful. The technique may effectively treat symptoms associated with a neurological or psychiatric disorder, only to cause other symptoms that are not predictable. Medical teams need to inform candidate patients of the uncertainty of these outcomes of DBS. But it is the suitably informed and competent patient who has to decide whether the trade-offs in any given treatment would be acceptable and whether he or she should have or continue to have it. In the foreseeable future, DBS may be used to enhance mood in healthy people by activating circuits in the brain's reward system, such as the nucleus accumbens. This will require discussion of whether there are optimal levels of mood, and whether it is permissible to expose healthy people to the risks associated with DBS so that they can be happier. Assuming that the electrodes and stimulator were implanted safely, the justification of mood enhancement would depend mainly on whether it overstimulated the reward system and impaired people's capacity to reason and make decisions.

The success of DBS depends not only on the extent to which it modulates dysfunctional neural circuits, but also on how it affects a person's body and mind and whether it improves his or her quality of life. In many cases, neuromodulation results in physical and psychological improvement. This is not always the case, however, because some patients experience adverse effects from this technique. Such effects suggest that not all patients undergoing DBS are able to regain complete or even moderate control of their symptoms and lives. Symptom relief may cause personality changes in some patients and unanticipated negative consequences for their families. To the extent that DBS improves a patient's quality of life, it promotes the autonomy of the patient and is consistent with providers' obligations of nonmaleficence and beneficence. Those with diseases of the brain and mind should not be deprived of DBS or other standard, experimental, and innovative therapies. In some psychiatric disorders, these therapies can liberate patients from profound mental paralysis. At the same time, DBS should not create unreasonable expectations in patients or providers. It should not generate hope that is disproportionate to the probability and extent of benefit. Improving the safety and efficacy of DBS will continue to be a challenge for researchers and clinicians using this treatment for an increasing number of neurological and psychiatric disorders.

8

Regenerating the Brain

Cellular and molecular replacement therapy for the brain has the potential to treat neurodegenerative disorders such as Parkinson's, Huntington's, and Alzheimer's disease, as well as traumatic brain injury and stroke. It may also be possible for this therapy to slow the progression of dementias in addition to Alzheimer's. Implantation or injection of fetal, embryonic, and adult stem cells, genes, and trophic factors that could integrate into diseased regions of the brain could replace lost neurons and restore function in dysfunctional neural circuits. Deep-brain stimulation might also induce neurogenesis, though the evidence for this is based on only a few applications and thus is very preliminary. The goal of these interventions is fundamentally different from brain-computer interface systems, which do not restore brain function but bypass brain and CNS dysfunction. Neural cell replacement can be described as a form of regenerative medicine for the brain. Regenerative medicine "aims to provide the elements required for in vivo repair, to design replacements that seamlessly interact with the living body, and to stimulate the body's intrinsic capacities to regenerate."[1] Genetically reprogramming the body's own cells can revitalize damaged tissues and organs, or grow new ones. If the success of stem-cell therapy in regenerating tissue and cells in the heart and other organs could be replicated in the brain, then it could ameliorate the suffering of millions of people with neurodegenerative diseases and extend and improve the quality of their lives.

The first instance of cellular intervention in the human brain was the autologous transplantation of grafts from the adrenal medulla into the striatum of four people with Parkinson's disease in the 1980s.[2] Because the cells were taken from the patient's

---

1. H. Greenwood and A. Daar, "Regenerative Medicine," in *The Cambridge Textbook of Bioethics* (New York: Cambridge University Press, 2008), 153–158, at 153.
2. E.-O. Backlund et al., "Transplantation of Adrenal Medullary Tissue to Striatum in Parkinsonism: First Clinical Trials," *Journal of Neurosurgery* 62 (1985): 169–173. I. Madrazo et al., "Open Microsurgical Autograft of Adrenal Medulla to the Right Caudate Nucleus

own body, the donor was the same individual as the recipient. The aim of the procedure was to replace the dopaminergic neurons that had been lost through the disease. There appeared to be some improvement in some patients 6 months after the surgery; but there were no sustained positive effects. Autopsies revealed that the adrenal medulla graft did not survive for very long. Around the same time, Swedish doctors began transplanting cells from the substantia nigra of fetal brains into the striatum of a different group of Parkinson's patients.[3] The initial results were generally positive, and by 1997 approximately 200 people globally had undergone the treatment. But the long-term effects of this procedure were highly variable. Some patients experienced symptom relief; for others, many of the symptoms associated with Parkinson's returned. Specifically, dyskinesias occurred in approximately 15 percent of the transplant recipients. Many patients experienced adverse cognitive and affective symptoms as well. The results of trials transplanting and injecting fetal cells into the dorsal striatum of people with Huntington's disease have not been very encouraging either.[4] These outcomes show that neural cell replacement therapy has not lived up to its promise.

Safety and efficacy issues remain to be worked out through more preclinical and clinical trials. The main challenge is striking the right balance between growth-promoting and growth-inhibiting factors.[5] Researchers have to find ways of coaxing implanted or injected cells to differentiate and functionally integrate into targeted brain regions. They also have to prevent the cells from proliferating along unpredictable pathways and causing tumors or otherwise adversely affecting healthy brain tissue. This could result in neurological and psychiatric dysfunction, which in some cases may be worse for a patient than the disease being treated. It is unclear whether

in Two Patients with Intractable Parkinson's Disease," *New England Journal of Medicine* 316 (1987): 831–834.

3. O. Lindvall et al., "Grafts of Fetal Dopamine Neurons Survive and Improve Motor Function in Parkinson's Disease," *Science* 247 (1990): 574–577.

4. S. Dunnett and A. Rosser, "Cell Transplantation for Huntington's Disease: Should We Continue?" *Brain Research Bulletin* 72 (2007): 132–147. More positive results have been reported by A. Bachoud-Levi et al., "Effect of Foetal Neural Transplants in Patients with Huntington's Disease 6 Years after Surgery: A Long-Term Follow-Up Study," *The Lancet Neurology* 5 (2006): 303–309. Compare this with the results reported by C. W. Olanow, et al., "A Double-Blind Controlled Trial of Bilateral Fetal Nigral Transplantation in Parkinson's Disease," *Annals of Neurology* 54 (2003): 403–414.

5. See the discussions by D. Swaab, "Developments in Neuroscience: Where Have We Been? Where Are We Going?" and G. Boer, "Transplantation and Xenotransplantation: Ethics of Cell Therapy in the Brain Revisited," both in J. Giordano and B. Gordijn, eds., *Scientific and Philosophical Perspectives in Neuroethics* (Cambridge: Cambridge University Press, 2010), 1–36, 190–215. Also, R. Sabetrasekh et al., "Current Views of the Embryonic and Neural Stem Cell: Cell Replacement or Molecular Repair?" N. Christophersen et al., "Developing Novel Cell Sources for Transplantation in Parkinson's Disease," and C. Kelly, S. Dunnett, and A. Rosser, "Cell-Based Therapy for Huntington's Disease," all in C. Sanberg and P. Sanberg, eds., *Cell Therapy, Stem Cells, and Brain Repair* (Totowa, NJ: Humana Press, 2006), 1–30, 31–59, 83–115.

neural cell replacement will become a viable therapy for a significant number of patients. Major obstacles must be overcome for it to achieve this goal.

In this chapter, I describe different types of cellular and molecular therapy for neurodegenerative diseases. I explore their regenerative potential and point out their limitations. In many of these diseases, the underlying pathophysiology may preclude long-term positive effects. I note the differences between tissue, cell, and organ replacement in the body and tissue and cell replacement in the brain. Restoration of tissue, cells, and organs in the body could extend our lives. Yet without a corresponding restoration of tissue and cells in the brain, there could be a mismatch between our physical and mental capacities as we live longer. A longer life may not be a better life. It could also result in intergenerational unfairness, where children of parents with extended lives would be unduly burdened by having to care for them in a prolonged process of cognitive decline. I then speculate on the possibility that safe and effective neural cell replacement might enable people to retain their physical and cognitive capacities indefinitely. This could increase competition for social goods between the young and old. Cell replacement therapy that ensured an extended period of mental vitality could also have interesting psychological consequences for personal identity and the extent to which we could sustain our desires and interests into the future.

Regenerative Neural Therapies

There are five main sources of neural regeneration: fetal stem cells, embryonic stem cells, adult stem cells, xenotransplantation, and viral-vector-delivered neurotrophic factors and genes. Fetal stem cells are a good source for neural restoration because they are multipotent and can be manipulated to differentiate into a number of cell types, including neural cells. This was the type of cell used in the Swedish Parkinson's trial and in the Huntington's trials. Yet the use of fetal cells raises the ethical concern of aborting fetuses from which the cells are derived. This concern is noteworthy given that four to six fetuses are necessary to implant an adequate supply of tissue and cells in the brain of one patient. It is questionable whether there would be enough fetal tissue to treat all of the patients needing therapy.

Embryonic stem cells are more desirable in terms of their regenerative potential because they are pluripotent, or capable of differentiating into virtually any cell type. Because of this property, they might be more likely to promote cell growth, functional integration, and neural regeneration in diseased brains. At the same time, their proliferative potential could lead to the growth of teratomas, which are germ-cell–derived tumors.[6] These result from cells growing in areas of the body and brain where they were not designed to grow. If implanted in the brain in an undifferentiated state, these cells could cause significant damage to healthy brain tissue. It is with embryonic stem cells that striking the right balance between promoting differentiation

---

6. As noted by Christophersen et al., "Developing Novel Cell Sources for Transplantation in Parkinson's Disease," and by T. Asano et al., "In Vivo Tumor Formation from Primate Embryonic Stem Cells," *Methods in Molecular Biology* 329 (2006): 459–467.

and controlling proliferation is most challenging. The same ethical and supply issues that beset the use of fetal stem cells also beset the use of embryonic stem cells. They would be derived from pre-implantation human embryos. Many claim that the creation and destruction of embryos for this purpose is a violation of the sanctity of human life. Leaving this ethical issue aside, cells from four to six embryos would be needed for each patient. There would not be enough embryos for all of the candidates for neural cell therapy. Thus, neither fetal nor embryonic stem cells would be an adequate source of the needed cells. Also, these cells would have to be harvested and implanted at the right stage of development. Otherwise, they could become immunogenic and trigger an adverse immune response in the recipient. This would require immunosuppression to protect recipients from graft rejection and put them at risk of infection. Induced pluripotent stem cells may sidestep some of these problems and give researchers more control of differentiation. These are adult somatic cells from the skin and other organs that have been genetically reprogrammed into an embryonic stem-cell-like state. But it is not known whether they would integrate more effectively than other types of stem cells into diseased regions of the brain. More controlled trials using these cells in patients are needed to clarify this.

Adult stem cells have several advantages over fetal and embryonic stem cells. Because they are derived from a person's own body rather than from aborted fetuses or preimplantation embryos, they would not raise any ethical concerns. In addition, they could be the source of neural autografts, where the patient would donate his or her own cells. This would avoid the problem of graft rejection and thus obviate the need for immunosuppression. It would also avoid the potential problem of viruses being passed from graft to host. Research has shown that adult stem cells are more versatile than previously thought. As induced pluripotent stem cells, they could be dedifferentiated and become a number of cell types, including neural cells. In fact, neural stem cells are found in adult brain tissue. If researchers could manipulate these cells in the right way, then they could differentiate directly into new neurons, astrocytes, and oligodendrocytes. Still, adult stem cells do not have the same growth potential as fetal or embryonic stem cells and thus may not stimulate neural regeneration to the same extent as these other types. Although studies involving animal models have shown positive results, thus far there is no evidence that neural stem cells would restore function in diseased human brains. If their regenerative potential were realized, then they would have to differentiate into the right proportion of neurons, astrocytes, and oligodendrocytes so as not to result in uncontrolled growth and tumors. Overall, adult stem cells would probably be safer than other types of stem cells but not necessarily more effective in regenerating brain cells.

Xenotransplants would solve the supply problem. An unlimited amount of cells could be derived from fetal porcine (pig) tissue and transplanted into diseased brain regions.[7] Pigs can produce litters of 5 to 10, or more, at a time. They reach reproductive maturity within 6 months, and sows are ready to mate every 3 weeks. Yet there is no indication that porcine cells would survive longer in the human brain and

7. R. Barker, A. Kendall, and H. Widner, "Neural Tissue Xenotransplantation: What Is Needed Prior to Clinical Trials in Parkinson's Disease?" *Cell Transplantation* 9 (2000): 235–246.

promote neural growth any better than other cells. More importantly, the need for immunosuppression and the risk of animal-to-human virus transmission would likely outweigh the potential benefit of these cells in promoting neural regeneration. Immunosuppression would make people more susceptible to infectious diseases. Those receiving pig cells would have to be monitored for infection much more intensively than recipients of cells from human sources. There is also an ethical issue with xenotransplantation itself, since some animal rights activists would object to creating and destroying pig fetuses for this purpose.

In open-label trials, glial cell line-derived neurotrophic factor (GDNF) was injected into the putamen of some Parkinson's patients.[8] These patients showed improvement in motor function after one year. Trophic factors can prevent or delay further deterioration of neurons. As with other neuroregenerative therapies, however, the long-term outcomes have been variable and not positive enough to consider GDNF a successful treatment. For people with hereditary conditions such as Huntington's disease, cell therapy may not produce any benefit. Instead, genes that might correct the protein dysfunction responsible for the disease could be delivered through a viral vector and injected into the striatum.[9] As a form of molecular rather than cellular replacement, gene therapy could release protein compounds that might stop or slow the degeneration of neurons in Huntington's and other diseases. But, like cellular replacement, gene therapy would have to be targeted precisely to prevent growth factors from proliferating in nontargeted healthy brain regions.[10] The gene products would have to differentiate into the specific phenotype needed to replace the lost cells and restore neural function.

Safety and Efficacy

Although I have cited a number of limitations in neural regeneration, there are two major concerns that are especially significant. The primary concern is safety, given the risk that transplanted or injected cells could proliferate out of control and cause tumors in the brain. A particular concern is that cell proliferation causing dysfunction in previously unaffected areas of the brain could have deleterious effects on the mind. These interventions target the subcortical basal ganglia. Some of the component structures in this region have circuits regulating not only motor but also cognitive and affective functions. These circuits may project to cortical and limbic areas mediating these same functions. Stem cells or trophic factors gone awry or even slightly misplaced could alter neural circuitry and in turn personality, mood,

8. J. Korecka, J. Verhaagen, and E. Hol, "Cell Replacement and Gene Therapy Strategies for Parkinson's and Alzheimer's Disease," *Regenerative Medicine* 2 (2007): 425–446.

9. Cited by Dunnett and Rosser, "Cell Transplantation for Huntington's Disease."

10. As noted by Sabetrasekh et al., "Current Views of the Embryonic and Neural Stem Cell"; Christophersen et al., "Developing Novel Cell Sources for Transplantation in Parkinson's Disease"; Kelly, Dunnett, and Rosser, "Cell-Based Therapy for Huntington's Disease"; Korecka, Verhaagen, and Hol, "Cell Replacement and Gene Therapy Strategies for Parkinson's and Alzheimer's Disease"; Swaab, "Developments is Neuroscience"; and Boer, "Transplantation and Xenotransplantation."

and thought. This could occur if cells implanted in the striatum to control a motor disorder unexpectedly migrated to circuits in limbic or cortical regions. As discussed in Chapter 7, some of these circuits have been implicated in the impulse and mood disorders induced by dopamine agonists and DBS in some Parkinson's and OCD patients. The fact that the ventral striatum has limbic connections may facilitate the unintended migration of cells that could affect circuits regulating mood. Kidney, liver, and other types of organ transplantation entail some risk of morbidity and mortality. But this risk may be less significant than the risk of neural transplantation altering not only physical function but also mental states, especially if this alteration were permanent. The concern is not about having foreign cells implanted in one's brain, but adverse effects of uncontrolled growth of these cells on the brain and mind.

Because the brain generates and sustains the mind, implanting or injecting cells in subcortical regions must be done with precision so as not to cause significant changes in cortical and limbic regions regulating cognition and mood. If a neurodegenerative disorder already manifests in cognitive and mood disturbances, then the intervention must not exacerbate them. Drugs such as dopamine agonists or DBS can be discontinued to reverse any sequelae they may cause in patients with Parkinson's disease or other neuropsychiatric disorders. Any adverse effects of cells implanted in the brain cannot be reversed so easily. They may even be irreversible. Although neuroplasticity declines as we age, the brain can adjust to changes in its structure and function over much of our lives. Yet if rogue cells or genes remain active and proliferate uncontrollably, then it can be extremely difficult to stop the cascade of adverse events in the brain. Neuroscientist Gerard Boer explains that "cell implantation cannot be undone, only destroyed, and not without consequences for the intact neighboring tissue (perhaps only minimally in the case of implants of encapsulated cells for a molecular treatment)."[11] He also notes that, before implantation, cells can be injected with the thymidine kinase (HSV-tk) gene. This would make the cells susceptible to ganciclovir, an antiviral drug used to treat or prevent cytomegalovirus infections. This drug could kill rogue implanted cells but would also trigger an inflammatory response to remove the cell debris.[12] Inflammation in the brain would introduce another pathological process. Implanted cells should stimulate enough neurogenesis to restore function in affected areas of the brain. But they must not stimulate so much growth that the cells cause dysfunction in areas that are structurally and functionally intact. Again, this underscores the problem of balancing growth-promoting and growth-inhibiting factors in the brain.

Not all of the results of neural cell therapy have been negative. In addition to the patients in the Parkinson's trials who regained some degree of motor function from fetal cell implants, some patients have benefited from cell therapy for spinal cord injuries. Portuguese neurologist Carlos Lima has used adult stem cells in olfactory mucosal autografts to restore function in a number of patients with

---

11. "Transplantation and Xenotransplantation," 203.

12. *Ibid.*, 203, n. 3.

these injuries.[13] Stem cells differentiating into oligodendrocytes may be able to grow new nerve connections in damaged spinal cords. Still, the brain is a more complex component of the central nervous system than the spinal cord, and any positive or negative results from one might not be generalized to the other. Some neural stem-cell experiments have gone badly awry with disastrous results. In one case, an Israeli boy received intracerebellar and intrathecal injections of human fetal neural stem cells as a treatment for ataxia-telangiectasia at a Moscow clinic when he was 9, 10, and 12 years old. This is a rare autosomal recessive disorder that causes neurodegeneration and impaired immunity. It is usually fatal in the second or third decade of life. Four years after the first injection, he developed a multifocal brain tumor from the transplanted cells, which was confirmed from tests of the tumor tissue.[14] This case is important because the tumor was not the result of pathology from an existing disease but of the new cells. The proposed therapy not only did not control the progression of his disease but created a new pathology. An intervention designed to benefit him instead harmed him over and above the harm he already experienced from the ataxia.

Some might argue that the irreversibility of neurodegenerative diseases and lack of treatment options can justify experimental neural stem-cell transplantation in individuals who have these diseases. But the risk associated with uncontrolled growth factors is significant, as the case just described illustrates. Harmful effects may occur not only in innovative uses but in controlled experimental trials as well. Most adverse events in Parkinson's trials involving implanted fetal neural cells have been linked to the disease rather than the new cells. Nevertheless, the long-term benefits of implanted cells are not clear enough to decisively outweigh the risk of brain tumors, edema, infection, intracerebral hemorrhage, and an immune response resulting in graft rejection. The suffering they have to endure, the lack of treatment options, and the irreversible course of neurodegenerative diseases make these patients a vulnerable group. From the researchers' perspective, these patients may be good subjects to test the safety and efficacy of an experimental procedure with therapeutic potential. From the patients' perspective, participation as subjects in a restorative neurosurgery trial is an expression of their autonomy and of what they judge to be in their best interests. It could also be their only opportunity to possibly control the progression of their diseases and alleviate their symptoms, or at least contribute to research that may achieve these goals for others. However, as in cases of patients with severe psychiatric disorders, candidates for neural stem-cell therapy may be desperate for symptom relief. This may unduly influence their perception of risk, making them give insufficient thought to the potential adverse effects. It may impair their capacity to consent to the procedure. Cognitive impairment associated with a neurodegenerative disease could affect this capacity as well, though it would

---

13. "Olfactory Mucosa Autografts in Human Spinal Cord Injury: A Pilot Clinical Study," *Journal of Spinal Cord Medicine* 29 (2006): 191–203. Also, A. Mackay-Sim et al., "Autologous Olfactory Ensheathing Cell Transplantation in Human Paraplegia: A 3-Year Clinical Trial," *Brain* 131 (2008): 2376–2386.
14. N. Amariglio et al., "Donor-Derived Brain Tumor Following Neural Stem-Cell Transplantation in an Ataxia-Telangiectasia Patient," *PLoS Medicine* 6(2) (2009): e1000029.

not necessarily interfere with decision making at an early stage of the disease. Patients would have to be assessed by psychiatrists to confirm that they had this capacity. In addition, researchers must ensure that these patient-subjects are not exposed to an unreasonable level of risk before performing this neurosurgical procedure on them. What constitutes a reasonable level of risk can be determined only by results from a sufficient number of controlled clinical trials.

The second concern about neural regeneration pertains to efficacy. Replacement and restoration of neurons and neural circuits may not alter the underlying disease process of neurodegenerative disorders. In that case, any benefits of the therapy would only be short-lived for most patients. Some Parkinson's patients in two uncontrolled fetal-nigral transplant trials in Sweden in the 1990s had sustained improvement in motor function up to 14 years following the transplant. As noted, though, others experienced dyskinesias and other harmful effects associated with the disease. The brain of one patient with grafted embryonic-nigral cells was found to have Lewy bodies.[15] These are clumps of abnormal proteins responsible for the dementia that develops in later stages of Parkinson's. The problem is not one of implanted cells damaging nontargeted brain regions but the progressive course of the disease itself. Tissue and cells grafted into the striatum would be subject to the same degeneration as host dopamine neurons in the substantia nigra. Parkinson's disease involves an extensive pathology than includes more than just dopamine-producing cells in this subcortical region. Other neurotransmitter systems and the autonomic nervous system are involved as well. It is not clear whether all neural grafts would have the same fate. The Lewy-body finding suggests that any type of neural graft would be affected by the ongoing disease process. In fact, the same outcome has occurred in some patients receiving fetal neural tissue transplants in the striatum for Huntington's disease. The transplanted tissue not only failed to slow disease progression but also underwent degeneration similar to the pathological changes of the disorder.[16]

Restoring or ameliorating motor, cognitive, and affective capacities likely requires more than implanting a small cluster of cells in a single region of the brain. It requires interventions consisting of larger groups of cells to restore function in wider neural networks mediating these capacities. This highlights a critical difference between cell replacement in the brain and replacement or regeneration of other organs through stem-cell therapy or tissue engineering. A transplanted kidney, one with tissue regenerated from a patient's own genetically modified stem cells, or kidney grafts engineered from an extracellular matrix could restore renal function. In contrast, the implantation or injection of a small set of neural stem cells in one region of the brain cannot completely replace lost neurons necessary to sustain physical and mental functions. Because these neurons are not restricted to one brain region but are distributed across neural networks, the targeted area for neural

---

15. J. Kordower et al., "Lewy Body-Like Pathology in Long-Term Embryonic Nigral Transplants in Parkinson's Disease," *Nature Medicine* 14 (2008): 504–506.

16. F. Cicchetti et al., "Neural Transplants in Patients with Huntington's Disease Undergo Disease-Like Degeneration," *Proceedings of the National Academy of Sciences* 106 (2009): 12483–12488.

cell therapy is not self-contained. Unlike the kidney, liver, or heart, the brain is a structurally and functionally heterogeneous organ consisting of multiple systems mediating a range of physical and mental capacities. Many of these capacities depend on interacting brain regions. Adding small neural cell masses to a specific region of the brain would at best restore only a subset of the physical and mental capacities that decline in neurodegenerative diseases. As Boer points out: "Neuronal networks altered by neural disease, and subsequently structurally or functionally changed by the implantation of a minute volume of neural or non-neural cells, will never fully restore CNS morphology in the way that one can completely rebuild an old house."[17]

The striatum is the largest component of the basal ganglia. Restorative dopaminergic cells would have to be implanted or injected through a number of trajectories to functionally integrate into this structure. Neurosurgeons performing this procedure may not be able to target all of these trajectories and cover all of the dopamine-depleted striatum. Parkinson's and Huntington's diseases are not limited to the basal ganglia but extend to cortical areas mediating cognition. This explains the dementia in advanced stages of these diseases. In brains where the pathology extends over multiple brain regions, implanting or injecting cells into the striatum alone may be equivalent to pouring buckets of water on a forest fire. To make matters worse, inadvertently injecting cells into trajectories involving cortical and limbic circuits could cause or exacerbate cognitive and affective dysfunction.

It is possible that patients who have had better outcomes of neural cell therapy have less extensive brain pathology than those who have not fared so well. There may be different subtypes of Parkinson's that could explain the variability of outcomes. It is also likely that those with less favorable results are at a more advanced stage of the disease. This suggests that earlier intervention could restore a greater degree of motor and cognitive function and possibly decelerate the disease process. By the time symptoms appear in neurodegenerative diseases, dopaminergic and other neurons are substantially depleted in the brain. PET scans can reveal early signs of neural degeneration that might be stopped or reversed by cell therapy. Testing of cerebrospinal fluid (CSF) can identify biomarkers of these diseases and predict who would develop them. These tests can show early signs of abnormal amounts of the amyloid beta (A-beta) protein associated with the characteristic plaques in Alzheimer's disease. They can also reveal early abnormalities in the tau protein associated with the neurofibrillary tangles in this same disease.[18] Because there are no effective drugs for Alzheimer's, information about these biomarkers would not necessarily benefit individuals who have them. The information could allow them to plan the rest of their lives more prudently. It could also harm them by generating the belief or knowledge that they will develop the disease. It is not yet known what level of amyloid or tau in the CSF is a sign of pathology. Nor is it known whether every person with some amyloid plaques or neurofibrillary tangles

---

17. "Transplantation and Xenotransplantation," 210.
18. R. Petersen and J. Trojanowski, "Use of Alzheimer Disease Biomarkers," *Journal of the American Medical Association* 302 (2009): 436–437. Also, G. De Meyer et al., "Diagnosis-Independent Alzheimer Disease Biomarker Signature in Cognitively Normal Elderly People," *Archives of Neurology* 67 (2010): 949–956.

will develop the disease during their lifetime. These features may be only indirectly related to Alzheimer's

For the purpose of cell replacement therapy, biomarkers of any neurodegenerative disease would not be very helpful if the pathology is diffuse and involves multiple brain regions. It might not be feasible to implant cells in many regions, both because of limited availability of the cells and because of the risk of uncontrolled growth factors damaging healthy brain tissue. Even if adult stem cells could functionally integrate into the affected areas, the underlying disease process could negate any short-term positive effects, as the case of the Parkinson's patient with Lewy bodies illustrates. As an alternative to neural transplantation, cultivated cells could be delivered on microchips implanted in the brain. But a different means of delivering the cells would not necessarily make them any more effective in reversing the pathophysiology of the disease.

Parkinson's has been considered the most promising candidate for neural cell replacement therapy. Yet the issues I have discussed indicate that this procedure is not a cure for and does not control the progression and symptoms of Parkinson's in most cases. They also cast doubt on the idea that this intervention offers a greater benefit than and is thus superior to DBS as a treatment for the disease. Restorative neurosurgery using stem cells may be preferable to DBS in treating neurodegenerative diseases because it may not involve as much monitoring and may be less expensive on the whole. But this possibility is not very appealing if the procedure is not safer and more effective than DBS. Significantly, the Michael J. Fox Foundation for Parkinson's Research has tempered its views on the promise of stem cell therapy. They are now focusing more on drug development than on stem cell research.[19] Neurologist C. Warren Olanow, who has conducted fetal-nigral transplant trials involving patients with Parkinson's, contends that "the near-term future of cell and gene therapies based on dopamine restoration doesn't look particularly promising."[20] Because the same problems that beset neural cell therapy for Parkinson's would beset restorative neurosurgery for other neurodegenerative diseases, there are reasons to be skeptical of its potential to control and ameliorate symptoms of these diseases.

All of these concerns underscore the need for more preclinical studies and controlled clinical trials to determine the safety and efficacy of neural cell and molecular therapies. Until a sufficient number of trials have been conducted, and until there is long-term follow-up of a sufficient number of research subjects, it will remain an open question whether restorative neurosurgery can be medically and ethically justified. This pertains to whether this procedure is superior to other therapies in controlling the progression of neurodegenerative diseases and to whether it is consistent with patient autonomy and researchers' obligations of beneficence and nonmaleficence.[21]

19. The Foundation's CEO, Katie Hood, has said that she has "not totally lost hope in cell replacement, but I just don't think it's a near-term hope." Cited by C. Holden, "Fetal Cells Again?" *Science* 326 (2009): 358–359, at 359.
20. *Ibid.*, 359.
21. Boer discusses these ethical issues in "Transplantation and Xenotransplantation," 199–210.

In 2012, the European Commission will sponsor a preliminary safety trial in which Parkinson's patients will receive transplanted cells from the brains of 6- to 9-week-old fetuses. This will be followed by a double-blind placebo-controlled clinical trial in centers in Europe and North America.[22] Subjects in the control arm of this trial will receive sham surgery. Incisions will be made through the skull; but no active cells will be grafted into the brain. This will determine whether improvement in motor and other functions is nothing more than a placebo response or a sign that the implanted cells have functionally integrated into the affected brain regions. Many object to sham surgery on the grounds that it involves deception and exposes subjects to an unacceptable risk of edema, hemorrhage, and infection related to the incisions. If the deception includes giving subjects cyclosporine to prevent rejection of "transplanted" cells, then they may be at risk of infection from immunosuppression. These concerns notwithstanding, placebo-controlled trials may be necessary to know whether neural cell replacement therapy is superior to existing treatments for Parkinson's and possibly other neurodegenerative diseases.[23] Trials testing the safety of implanting stem cells into the brains of people with traumatic brain injury are underway at a number of centers. These would lead to trials testing the efficacy of the intervention to determine whether this would be a viable therapy for this condition. But it will be some time before there are safe and effective cellular and molecular therapies for brain disorders in general.

A Body–Brain Problem

Dementia is a progressive loss of cognitive functions. Alzheimer's disease, dementia with Lewy bodies, and cerebral vascular disease are the most common forms. The most prevalent of these by far is Alzheimer's. More than 35 million people worldwide—5.5 million in the United States alone—have this disease.[24] The number of people with Alzheimer's will increase exponentially over the next 25 years. Death usually occurs within 3 to 9 years after diagnosis, though the disease may extend over a longer period. The principal risk factor for Alzheimer's is age, with the incidence of the disease doubling every 5 years after age 65.[25] Aging itself is not a disease; but the neural degeneration resulting in dementia is the by-product of the aging process. As more humans live longer, health care systems in particular and societies in

---

22. Holden, "Fetal Cells Again?" 358–359.
23. For discussion of the ethics of using sham surgery in these trials, see W. Dekkers and G. Boer, "Sham Surgery in Patients with Parkinson's Disease: Is it Morally Acceptable?" *Journal of Medical Ethics* 27 (2001): 151-156, and Boer, "Restorative Therapies for Parkinson's Disease: Ethical Issues," in P. Brundin and C. W. Olanow, eds., *Restorative Therapies for Parkinson's Disease* (New York: Springer, 2006), 12–49.
24. H. Querfurth and F. LaFeria, "Alzheimer's Disease," *New England Journal of Medicine* 362 (2010): 329–344.
25. T. Montine and E. Larson, "Late-Life Dementias: Does This Unyielding Global Challenge Require a Broader View?" *Journal of the American Medical Association* 302 (2009): 2593–2594.

general may be overwhelmed by having to deal with so many people living with dementia and depending on others for care.

It is important to emphasize that thus far no drugs have been able to prevent or control the progression of Alzheimer's. The cholinesterase inhibitor donepezil and the glutamate antagonist memantine have shown only marginal benefit is slowing cognitive decline in some patients with dementia.[26] In March 2010, the pharmaceutical companies Pfizer and Medivation announced that a late-stage clinical trial testing the antihistamine latrepirdine (Dimebon) showed that it was no more effective than a placebo in treating Alzheimer's symptoms. Eli Lilly announced in August of the same year that it had halted development of the gamma secretase inhibitor LY-450139 (Semagacestat). Two late-stage clinical trials showed that the drug did not slow the progression of the disease and resulted in more rapid cognitive decline in research subjects. In light of these failures, one idea is that cellular or molecular interventions might have the potential to delay the onset of or slow the neural degeneration in Alzheimer's. This would reduce the harm the disease causes to patients and their caregivers. It would also have obvious social benefits. People could have more productive and independent lives without having to undergo a prolonged period of physical and mental decline. There has been at least one Phase 1 trial where nerve growth factor as a form of gene therapy was implanted in the forebrain of 8 subjects with mild Alzheimer's disease.[27] Clinical trials have been conducted in Europe to test the safety of the AD02 vaccine, which is designed to prevent the accumulation of A-beta in the brain. Phase II trials testing the efficacy of this vaccine are in progress, and results should be available by 2012. Proving that these agents are safe is a major hurdle to clear, however, since a significant number of patients in a preliminary study developed brain inflammation after being inoculated with a different vaccine. More advanced-phase trials are needed to determine whether the interventions I have considered would be both safe and effective.

The idea that Alzheimer's and other late-life dementias associated with aging might be slowed or even reversed through neural restoration or regeneration is still an unrealized possibility. Nevertheless, it is instructive to explore the social and psychological consequences of two hypothetical states of affairs. In the first, cellular or molecular therapy results in regeneration of the body but not of the brain. In the second, therapy results in regeneration of both the body and the brain. To frame discussion of these possibilities, it will be helpful to describe four scenarios in biogerontology:[28] prolonged senescence, compressed morbidity, decelerated aging,

---

26. The authors of a recent study testing memantine state that the drug "might be beneficial" for the treatment for two types of dementia. This is hardly indicative of any actual efficacy. D. Aarsland et al, "Memantine in Patients with Parkinson's Disease Dementia or Dementia with Lewy Bodies: A Double-Blind, Placebo-Controlled, Multicentre Trial," *The Lancet Neurology* 8 (2009): 613–618.

27. M. Tuszynski et al., "A Phase I Clinical Trial of Nerve Growth Factor Gene Therapy for Alzheimer Disease," *Nature Medicine* 11 (2005): 551–555.

28. E. Juengst et al., "Biogerontology, 'Anti-Aging Medicine,' and the Challenges of Human Enhancement," *Hastings Center Report* 33(4) (2003): 21–30.

and arrested aging. Senescence is the process through which cells stop dividing and all biological functions decline and gradually cease. Prolonged senescence would involve lives in which the degenerative physical and mental effects of aging extended over a number of years. Compressed morbidity would shorten the length of time between the onset of aging-related disease and death. It would allow us to have relatively long lives free of chronic disease and disability and to die quickly from an acute condition such as pneumonia. Compressed morbidity might involve accelerated aging, but only for a brief period before death. Decelerated aging would retard but not prevent senescence. Through cellular or molecular interventions, it would postpone the onset and slow the progression of degenerative diseases. This would result in a moderate extension of the human lifespan. Arrested aging would involve complete control of the aging process and could prevent most of its deleterious effects. It could neutralize the effects of senescence by continuously repairing damage to and restoring function in cells, tissue, and organs. Arrested aging could result in a substantial extension of the human lifespan. Unlike decelerated aging, arrested aging would not involve cell and tissue regeneration but genetic manipulation of the mechanisms regulating senescence.

Some researchers believe that manipulation of telomeres and the enzyme telomerase, which controls cell division, could arrest aging and extend the human lifespan many years beyond the current norm. But others are skeptical that altering telomerase could achieve this goal. The increasing incidence of global morbidity and premature mortality associated with diabetes and hypertension is one reason for this skepticism, since sustained activity of telomerase may not be able to neutralize the effects of these diseases on the body and brain. I will not assess the arguments for these opposing positions here.[29]

Prolonged senescence would be the least desirable of the four scenarios because it would involve a long period of physical and cognitive decline before death. This is the process that regenerative medicine for the body and brain aims to prevent. Arrested aging would be the most desirable scenario because it would ensure healthy bodies and brains for many years and extend the lifespan indefinitely. Compressed morbidity arguably would be the second most desirable scenario because it would limit the duration of physical and mental degeneration. Controlling the length of time between disease onset and death would be difficult to achieve, however, given the number of biological and environmental factors in the disease process. Decelerated aging is the most plausible of the four scenarios because stem cells and engineered tissue can already regenerate organs and in this respect slow the aging process.

Ideally, embryonic, fetal, induced pluripotent, or adult stem cells could be implanted in affected regions of people's brains at an early stage of Alzheimer's. This might compensate for cell death in these regions and delay the physical and cognitive decline of the disease. As such, it would be a form of decelerated aging. This would be a challenge because multiple brain regions are implicated in

---

29. For discussion, see T. Kirkwood, *Time of Our Lives: The Science of Human Aging* (Oxford: Oxford University Press, 2001), and "A Systematic Look at an Old Problem," *Nature* 451 (2008): 644–647. Also, S. J. Olshansky and B. Carnes, *The Quest for Immortality: Science at the Frontiers of Aging* (New York: W. W. Norton: 2001).

Alzheimer's, and cells would have to be implanted or injected into not one but several regions. A greater challenge would be to reverse or even slow the underlying pathology of the disease itself. Researchers at Harvard University recently found correlations between genes associated with Alzheimer's and genes associated with the innate immune system. This system is critical for the brain to resist life-threatening pathogens, since antibodies from the adaptive immune system cannot penetrate the blood–brain barrier. The researchers found a strong connection between A-beta and a protein of the innate immune system, LL-37.[30] People whose brains make low levels of LL-37 are at an increased risk of infection. The hypothesis drawn from these findings is that A-beta levels rise and plaques in the brain develop as a consequence of the inflammation resulting from LL-37's response to infection, or the brain's response to perceived infections.

It is not known whether A-beta accumulation in the brain is the cause or effect of inflammation, or the effect of other factors such as genetics. Cell death in Alzheimer's may also be linked to abnormalities in insulin signaling. The findings of the Harvard group suggest that the plaques are the effect of inflammation. They may be the by-product of mechanisms of the innate immune system in the brain. This is consistent with the hypothesis that inflammation resulting in atherosclerotic plaques in coronary and carotid arteries is a consequence of the body's response to infection. Alzheimer's may be an unfortunate but natural consequence of the brain being protected from infectious agents over the course of our lives.

This hypothesis about the pathophysiology of Alzheimer's may be explained in terms of the theory of antagonistic pleiotropy.[31] According to this theory, natural selection favors genes exhibiting beneficial effects on human organisms earlier in life at the cost of detrimental effects later in life. Antagonistic pleiotropy is the foundation of evolutionary medicine, which understands the body and its responses to pathogens as a set of compromises that have evolved over time. A gene or genes protecting us from some diseases early in life can make us susceptible to other diseases as we age. Specifically, the gene coding for the LL-37 protein may prevent or minimize the effects of infection in the brain. But any inflammation occurring as a by-product of its response to pathogens can have deleterious effects in the brain and central nervous system. Apart from the heritable early-onset form of the disease, Alzheimer's and other late-life dementias may be the result of a repeated inflammatory response that protects us from life-threatening pathogens but also causes neural degeneration.

Natural selection favors this trade-off by limiting the number of genetic mutations that can accumulate in cells through reproductive years. This period may be extended to allow for the nurturing of offspring so that they can reach reproductive age and transmit their genes to the next generation. But natural selection does not limit mutations beyond this period. By that time, there is no longer any evolutionary reason to limit mutations causing diseases. There are many examples of

30. S. Soscia et al., "The Alzheimer's Disease-Associated Amyloid-Beta Protein Is an Antimicrobial Peptide," *PLoS ONE* 5(3) (2010): e9505.
31. G. Williams, "Pleiotropy, Natural Selection, and the Evolution of Senescence," *Evolution* 11 (1957): 398–411.

genetically controlled physiological processes that illustrate this point. High circulating levels of estrogen in women and testosterone in men promote fitness earlier in life by increasing body mass and enabling fertility. But they may increase the risk of breast, ovarian, and prostate cancer later in life. Another example is immune-mediated inflammatory responses preventing infection but increasing the risk of cardiovascular disease and stroke. Cancer too may be a consequence of design limitations that characterize evolutionary processes. If Alzheimer's fits this model, then most of us may be doomed to this and other dementias if we live long enough.

This raises the question of whether neural cell grafting could decelerate the neural degeneration resulting in Alzheimer's. The underlying disease process itself may not be reversible. In that case, neural cell transplantation would have at best only temporary positive effects. A more effective intervention would be a drug or vaccine that would modulate the activity of LL-37 so that it limited inflammation, but not so much that it impaired the innate immune system's ability to kill pathogens. This might control the extent of A-beta accumulation in the brain, or other biological factors that cause the disease. Striking the right balance here would be similar in some respects to striking the right balance between the differentiation and proliferation of neural stem cells. Even if this were possible, there are no studies underway to test whether proteins regulating brain function could be altered in this way.

Tissue engineering could allow kidneys, livers, hearts, pancreatic islet cells, cartilage, and bones to be grown in culture and transplanted into the body to restore functions lost through diseases such as hypertension, diabetes, hepatitis, and osteoarthritis. Induced pluripotent stem cells could regenerate tissue in damaged organs and avoid allograft rejection in solid-organ transplantation. But the diffuse pathology of Alzheimer's and other neurodegenerative diseases makes a corresponding replacement of brain tissue and cells less likely. The brain and central nervous system are much more structurally and functionally complex than other organs and systems. This complexity would make it difficult to slow the progression of neurodegenerative diseases. Gene therapy delivering growth factors and normally functioning proteins could conceivably counteract the negative neural effects associated with A-beta. Yet this might not be effective if the plaques and dementia associated with the accumulation of this protein are by-products of protective processes in the brain. Antagonistic pleiotropy might preclude any potential of this intervention to decelerate neural death. Unless LL-37 or similar proteins could be genetically modified in just the right way, the cost of less of this protein and less A-beta might be infections that would accelerate neurodegeneration faster than Alzheimer's and kill us sooner.

If regeneration of bodily functions were not matched by regeneration of brain functions, then people would retain physical vigor over a longer period but undergo cognitive decline and develop dementia over many years. This would result in an undesirable trade-off between increased quantity and decreased quality of life, given the difference between physical function and mental dysfunction. There would be decelerated aging of the body but prolonged senescence of the brain. A longer life with such disparity between the body and the brain would be worse than a shorter life in which one's physical and cognitive functions declined at roughly the same rate. For many people, their minds would have died while their bodies remained alive.

Social philosopher Francis Fukuyama describes this physical–mental mismatch in regenerative medicine as a "national nursing home scenario, in which people routinely live to be 150 but spend the last fifty years in a state of child-like dependence on caretakers."[32] He further says that "stem-cell research might yield new ways to grow body parts... But without a parallel cure for Alzheimer's disease, this wonderful new technology would do no more than allow more people to persist in vegetative states for years longer than is currently possible."[33] If regenerated body parts could not be matched by regeneration of the brain, then the prospect of even moderate life extension would not be so appealing. Fukuyama's point is not that people who retain physical functions but lose cognitive functions would fit the diagnostic category of the vegetative state. His point is that their neurological decline and severely impaired mental capacity would for practical purposes put them in such a state. Some gerontologists have described dementia as a terminal condition.[34] As such, it is not likely that those with dementia would live for 50 years after diagnosis. Still, Fukuyama effectively makes the point that even a moderate extension of life in which cognitive functions did not align with physical functions would have disturbing implications. These would go beyond the actual burdens suffered by demented patients and their caregivers.

Intergenerational Problems

Many people would choose regenerative therapies for cells and tissue damaged from type 1 diabetes, kidney, liver, and heart disease, as well as osteoarthritis even if there were no equally effective therapies for dementia. While they were still capable of assessing benefits and risks and of making informed decisions about medical care, they would rationally choose therapies that would improve their physical functions and quality of life for an extended period. They would not give much thought to any deterioration in mental functions that would come later. As their brains aged, eventually they would go into cognitive decline.

An extended period of cognitive decline accompanying an extended period of physical function would further strain already limited health resources. Health care systems would have to use a disproportionate amount of these resources for long-term care of cognitively impaired patients. The medical needs of the younger population might not be met because of the needs of the older population. To be sure, the old and young have different medical needs. Still, the increasing incidence and ramifications of prolonged dementia might force health care systems to give priority to managing dementia over programs that would benefit a substantial percentage of the population. It could limit the ability of these systems to provide immunizations, antibiotics, and other interventions necessary to prevent infectious diseases in children and enable them to have a normal lifespan. It could also limit

---

32. *Our Posthuman Future: Consequences of the Biotechnology Revolution* (New York: Farrar, Straus and Giroux, 2002), 69.
33. *Ibid.*, 69.
34. S. Mitchell et al., "The Clinical Course of Advanced Dementia," *New England Journal of Medicine* 361 (2009): 1529–1538.

the ability to pay for screening programs to prevent cancer and other diseases that afflict many people in the prime of life.

Children of parents in prolonged cognitive decline would bear a large portion of the burden of caring for them. Their own medical needs may go unmet, and they would have to sacrifice interests and projects integral to having a life of their own. To cite Fukuyama again, the increasing incidence of prolonged dementia would create a "novel situation in which individuals approaching retirement age today find their own choices constrained by the fact that they still have an elderly parent alive and dependent on them for care."[35] With people now living longer, an increasing number of caregivers are older and have chronic illnesses of their own. In addition to constraining life choices, increasing the lifespan and the period of cognitive decline of the old would have harmful effects on caregivers' health.

Suppose that the biological problems associated with neural cell replacement could be resolved and researchers could design therapies that would decelerate neural degeneration. People's mental capacities would align with their physical capacities. This would probably result in a reduction in health care costs by providing protection against diseases for which aging is a risk factor.[36] But there may be other costs. A moderate or more substantial extension of the lifespan for a healthy older generation could still be unfair to the younger generation. The birth rate in developing countries has been steadily declining. This is especially the case in continental European countries such as Germany and Italy. Among other things, this demographic fact has widened the ratio of retirees to workers. Smaller families result in fewer people available to pay for the social safety net. The solvency of entitlement programs such as public pensions and health insurance for retirees depends on productivity, inflation, birth rates, and how long beneficiaries live. A scenario in which the number of retirees far exceeded the number of workers, and where people lived longer between retirement and death, would threaten the sustainability of these programs. Younger workers would be burdened with substantial payroll taxes to keep them solvent. These programs operate on a "pay-as-you-go" basis. Retired beneficiaries of social security paid their fair share into them during their working years. In the past, however, most people did not live long beyond retirement age. Therapies that could regenerate the body and possibly also the brain would enable people to live well beyond this age, and many people would spend a greater portion of their lives as beneficiaries of entitlements. The first generation to have an extended lifespan would not have paid the same amount in payroll taxes that younger workers would have to pay to sustain public pensions.

Neural cell regeneration for all neurodegenerative diseases would be expensive and not a sustainable area of public health funding. If people paid for it on their own, then arguably they should not be eligible for publicly funded entitlement programs during the extended period of their lives. With an increasing portion of

---

35. *Our Posthuman Future*, 68.

36. P. Kapahi and J. Vijg, "Aging—Lost in Translation?" *New England Journal of Medicine* 361 (2009): 2669–2670.

younger workers' incomes taken to sustain these programs, they might not have the financial capacity to choose the same regenerative life-extending technology that their elders had chosen. Assuming that body and brain restoration was safe and effective, this would be one more instance in which the young would have their choices constrained. In the unlikely scenario where neural regeneration was publicly funded and nonworking people who availed themselves of it received benefits for many years, entitlement programs would be bankrupt by the time younger workers retired. For all of these reasons, neural regeneration for older people would be unfair to younger people.

One proposed solution to this problem is to require people with extended lives of good physical and mental health to continue working past the current minimum retirement age. Germany and Denmark have increased from 65 to 67 the age when one can benefit from the public pension system. This idea has been met by stiff opposition is some countries. A plan to raise the minimum retirement age from 60 to 62 in France triggered widespread protests in 2010. There are at least two reasons why there would be strong resistance to attempts to further increase the retirement age in an extended lifespan. First, many people dread their jobs and look forward to the day when they can retire. In many cases, this day cannot come soon enough. Some find their work meaningful and would want to continue working indefinitely; but this is more likely the exception rather than the rule. Many would prefer to spend the remainder of their lives free from the restrictions and demands of formal employment. Second, most people would not be able to do sustained productive and meaningful work beyond a certain age if cognitive decline were only decelerated and not arrested. A society in which many people lived considerably longer than 80 years could generate intractable intergenerational problems. It would increase competition for scarce public goods and force difficult decisions regarding the allocation of these goods.

Psychological Possibilities

Let us leave the social problems aside and focus on the possible psychological consequences of neural cell replacement therapy. Although the potential to decelerate neural degeneration may not be realized in the foreseeable future, we can imagine what our individual lives would be like if this therapy could substantially extend them. Neural regeneration that decelerated cognitive aging could have interesting implications for personal identity. If a person at age 50 decided to undergo neural cell replacement to retain his or her cognitive capacities to age 100, then this would not likely have any substantial effects on psychological connectedness and continuity. The connections between the person's desires and intentions, their realization in actions, and the memory of these mental states and actions could hold over this period of time. The person would retain his or her narrative identity. But if body and brain regeneration allowed one to live for 150 years or more, then it is not clear that one could retain the unity of one's mental states and actions for a single life narrative. Our ability to learn new things and project ourselves into the future requires a certain degree of forgetting. As one lived further into the future, one's ability to plan and undertake new projects would involve forgetting an increasing number of experiences from one's past. Beyond a certain point, one would begin a distinct narrative consisting of a distinct set of experiences. One would continue to exist as the same organism with the same integrated set of biological properties but would become a different person. There would be a mismatch between biological and psychological lives.

One might ask whether it would be a rational choice for a 50-year-old to undergo a neuroregenerative procedure with this outcome. This question is similar in some respects to the question raised by McMahan in the example of "The Cure" that I cited in Chapter 6. If an intervention in my brain would eventually make me become a different person, then on what prudential grounds would I choose to have it? The person at 50 would be psychologically connected to the person at 100, and the person at 100 would be psychologically connected to the person at 150. But there would be only weak connections between the 50-year-old and the 150-year-old. They might be too weak for narrative identity to hold from the earlier to the later time. Yet when I undergo a process that will substantially extend my physical and mental life, I assume that I will continue to exist as the same person for the duration of that life.

Some people might not have a strong interest in retaining their narrative identity. They may welcome the opportunity to allow a new narrative to develop as part of an expansive view of humanity in which there is no strict separation of selves. Also, some people may want to develop a completely new set of interests and plans in the further future, in which case they would not want to retain their current interests and plans for too long. There are limits to our capacity to imagine the experiences we might have in the future. Given limited information, choices that are rational or irrational depend on situations that cannot obtain too far from the present. So, it might be neither rational nor irrational to receive a therapy that would substantially extend our lives with physical and cognitive capacities intact, despite weak psychological connectedness and continuity between earlier and later stages. Provided that the therapy was safe and had no untoward effects, it would not be irresponsible to have it.

Harris doubts that a substantially longer lifespan would undermine personal identity. Even so, he says that "personal identity is not required for a coherent desire for indefinite survival."[37] It is worth quoting him at greater length:

> Suppose "Methuselah" has three identities, A, B, and C, descending vertically into the future and that C can remember nothing of A's life. But suppose the following is also true: A will want to be B, who will remember being A; B will want to become C, who will remember being B but possibly not remember being A. It is not irrational for A to want to be B and not irrational for A to want to be B partly because he or she knows that B will be able to look forward to being C, even though by the time she is C she won't remember being A. Thus, even if personal identity in some strict sense fails over time because of the loss in continuity of memory, it is not clear that a sufficiently powerful motivation for physical longevity

---

37. *Enhancing Evolution*, 65.

fails with personal identity. This would remain true however many selves "Methuselah" turns out to be.[38]

An extended lifespan could result in or exacerbate overpopulation and increase competition for resources. Harris has an interesting reply to this worry. He points out that a multiplication of selves in the same body would "involve the creation of extra individuals without the necessity of creating the extra bodies and the extra resources those bodies would consume, or the extra opportunities or space those extra bodies would require."[39] This would be "ecologically sound, environmentally friendly, and population efficient."[40] The divergence of biological and psychological lives with increased longevity would not necessarily be negative. Nevertheless, how this scenario affected opportunities and competition for limited resources would depend on the birth rate and how many bodies were already in existence. It would also depend on the extent to which these bodies retained their cognitive and physical functions while they existed.

Kass and others have discussed the value of a lifespan with symbolically equal stages of childhood, youth, adulthood, and old age. There is a natural contour of a life shaped by definite temporal boundaries. The psychological connections between the intentions, actions, and memories that unify our past and future from the present and make each life an integrated whole are influenced by these boundaries. Kass asserts that "the 'lived time' of our natural lives has a trajectory and a shape, its meaning derived in part from the fact that we live as links in the chain of generations."[41] He worries that regenerative medicine that decelerated aging could lengthen the lifespan in a way that would disrupt its natural trajectory. It would cause an imbalance between the last stage of life and the preceding three.

A life with a disproportionately long last stage would not necessarily be bad for people. On the contrary, for those who retained physical and mental vigor for many years, a longer life would intuitively be better than a shorter one. It could significantly increase one's lifetime well-being by promoting the satisfaction of a greater number of desires and interests. Evolutionary biologist David Gems comments on this possibility: "Depending partly on whether one retained the mental plasticity of youth as one aged and on whether one opted for an open-ended life plan, extending a life has the potential to improve it."[42] Such a life might enable people to pursue a series of rewarding projects or careers that would not be available to them in a normal lifespan.

Kass' concern about altering the contour of a life presupposes a conception of life viewed as a whole from the outside. Viewed from the inside, though, the idea of a disproportionately long last stage of life would not necessarily have any adverse psychological effects and could enable us to have more fulfilling lives. Although a

---

38. *Ibid.*, 65.
39. *Ibid.*, 67.
40. *Ibid.*, 67.
41. "Ageless Bodies, Happy Souls," 13.
42. "Is More Life Always Better? The New Biology of Aging and the Meaning of Life," *Hastings Center Report* 33(4) (2003): 31–39, at 38.

final stage of life that was considerably longer than earlier stages might weaken the psychological connections between these stages, the connections holding between our mental states in earlier and later parts of the last stage could be unified enough to form a self-contained narrative. One's subjective sense of time would not fundamentally change, since one would continue to imagine, plan, and act within the same temporal horizon toward the future. The horizon would move along with the person as he or she persisted further into the future.

The narrative in an extended last stage of life may be distinct from the narrative in the earlier stages of our lives. But it could contain enough projects and achievements to make its author glad that an ancestor to which he or she was only weakly related underwent neural cell regeneration. Since one's memory of events in the remote past would naturally fade in any case, and since one's attention would be more focused on the period between the present and the future than between the present and the past, forgetting earlier parts of one's life and leaving that narrative behind would not obviously be bad for one. A longer narrative of one person is not intrinsically better than shorter narratives of several persons. Multiple narratives would involve a more diverse set of desires and interests and could result in greater well-being than a single narrative. On the other hand, a substantially longer life in which remote memories faded could undermine one of the valuable aspects of memory. The ability to recall the past can provide us with opportunities to make amends for regretful choices. Many of these choices are made in adolescence and early adulthood. Memory allows for insight and moral growth that only come through years of experience and reflection. The inability to recall mistakes much earlier in life could weaken these rational and moral capacities.

If neural regeneration sustained our cognitive functions indefinitely, then would we sustain our interest in completing existing projects and undertaking new ones? Would there be a point beyond which we would lose this interest? Would our lives become devoid of meaning and degenerate into a state of boredom? This is the fate of Elina Makropulos, the 342-year-old character in Karel Capek's play, "The Makropulos Secret," after taking an elixir to extend her life. In a classic paper, philosopher Bernard Williams cites this character in discussing the question of whether immortality would be a state of terminal boredom.[43] The core of Williams' discussion is the distinction between conditional and categorical desires. Conditional desires are conditional upon being alive. They do not provide reasons for continuing to live or having a longer life. Categorical desires are not conditional upon being alive but provide reasons for continuing to live. For example, one may desire to do volunteer work after retirement to make the remainder of one's life meaningful. But this desire would not provide a reason to stay alive and therefore would be a conditional desire. In contrast, if one is engaged in medical research and has an intense desire to find a cure for a neurodegenerative disease, then this desire may give one a reason to stay alive. It would be a categorical desire.

Desires to initiate, engage in, and complete a series of projects in an extended life could be categorical rather than conditional. They might not be contingent

---

43. "The Makropulos Case: Reflections on the Tedium of Immortality," in Williams, *Problems of the Self* (Cambridge: Cambridge University Press, 1973), 82–100.

simply on remaining alive. These desires might motivate one to undergo neural regeneration in order to retain one's cognitive capacities well beyond the current norm. This assumes that one will have categorical desires as long as one exists, and that these desires will sustain an indefinite series of projects. But it is possible that these desires could weaken over time. We may be biologically programmed to have categorical desires and reasons to remain alive for only so many years. There may be limits to these desires and our imagination of future possibilities that are beyond our cognition. Whether there is a limit on categorical desires and imagination is speculative and an open question. Suppose that there were no such limit. In that case, the value of sustained cognitive capacity would still depend on opportunities for meaningful activity and the nature of human relations. It would also depend on how much pain and suffering we would experience in our lives. A sobering note is that decelerated aging would only postpone and not prevent or reverse the cognitive decline that would eventually occur in an extended life. Compressed morbidity could limit the duration of this decline. But it would be difficult to biologically control the amount of time between the onset of dementia and death.

Would a substantially longer life alter our conception of human nature?[44] The length of the human lifespan is not fixed but malleable. While it has increased significantly over the last two centuries, our understanding of what it means to be human or a person has not changed. A lifespan made considerably longer through body and brain regeneration would be unique in the sense that the last stage of life would be considerably longer than earlier stages. The most notable effects of decelerated aging would occur in what we currently describe as late adulthood, when most people decline mentally and physically. But there is no reason why postponing the period when we begin to decline would change our cognitive and emotional understanding of humanity. Our minds would adjust to a longer life that was not substantially different in other respects from a shorter life. There would still be enough general agreement about what it means to be human. Yet if we retained physical vigor for many years, only to experience a long period of cognitive decline, then this might cause us to rethink this issue. A world in which our biological life far outlasted our psychological life could influence the debate on whether we are essentially persons or organisms and fundamentally change how we define ourselves. This would not be a function of the length of life as such, or whether the last stage was much longer than earlier stages. Rather, it would depend on the extent to which our mental capacities aligned with our physical capacities over the entire lifespan.

Conclusion

Stem cell therapies have the potential to regenerate or replace damaged tissue and cells and thereby restore and sustain bodily functions. Indeed, this potential has already been realized in a number of cases. Tissue engineering using different types

---

44. Kass and Fukuyama would probably answer this question affirmatively, hence their worries about a "posthuman" future.

of stem cells or extracellular matrices can grow organs, bones, and other body parts that will enable people to live longer, more productive, and independent lives. It is in this respect that regenerative therapy could revolutionize medicine.

It is possible that cells transplanted or injected into the brain will decelerate or even prevent neurodegenerative diseases such as Parkinson's and Huntington's. Regenerative therapy might also ameliorate the effects of stroke and spinal cord injury. It would be especially beneficial to the millions of people who develop Alzheimer's and other dementias, as well as to the caregivers and health care systems that have to bear the emotional and financial costs of these diseases. But the structural and functional differences between the body and the brain raise serious questions about whether bodily regeneration could be replicated in neural regeneration. Unlike a kidney, liver, or heart, the brain is a heterogeneous organ consisting of multiple systems mediating a number of physical and mental functions. Because many of these systems project to others, the salutary effects of replacement cells targeting one region of the brain may be limited. There could also be deleterious effects on functionally intact neural networks if implanted cells unexpectedly migrated to them. Researchers must strike a delicate balance between growth-promoting and growth-inhibiting factors. They must regulate these factors so that the cells differentiate and functionally integrate into affected brain regions without proliferating out of control along unpredictable pathways. Even cells that differentiate as planned might have only short-term positive effects and not reverse the underlying pathophysiology of neurodegenerative diseases.

People with these diseases should have the opportunity to participate in clinical trials testing these interventions. But because they are a vulnerable group with conditions that have not responded to other treatments, they cannot be exposed to undue risk for the sake of testing the efficacy of experimental procedures. In some cases, these procedures can harm them further by causing pathologies in addition to those they already have. Results from embryonic and fetal stem-cell transplants for Parkinson's over the past 25 years have not been encouraging on the whole and provide grounds for skepticism. More clinical trials are needed to establish the long-term safety and efficacy of neural cell regeneration. Until a sufficient number of these trials have been completed, there is a critical need for researchers and the media to be cautious in making claims about the potential of neural cell replacement and to distinguish reasonable hope from hype.

The difference between the success of cell therapy to regenerate the body and the failure of cell therapy to regenerate the brain could have disturbing consequences. People could have extended lives with their physical capacities intact, only to undergo a prolonged period of cognitive decline. A longer life would not be better but worse than a shorter life. This could also result in a number of intergenerational problems. The young could have their choices constrained by having to care for the old for a considerable period. If neural cell replacement could decelerate neural degeneration and enable us to retain cognitive and physical functions for an extended period, then it could benefit us by enabling us to plan, undertake, and complete a number of projects for a longer time. It may alter narrative identity in ways that may be welcome without fundamentally changing human nature. Still, a longer life with physical and mental capacities intact could involve a number of conflicts between the young and old. Neural regeneration is a possibility that may or may not be realized for a significant number of people in the future. But it is a possibility worth considering, given the increasing incidence of neurodegenerative diseases as we live longer and the increasing ability of neuroscience to alter the brain and mind.

References

Aarsland, D., et al. 2009. "Memantine in Patients with Parkinson's Disease Dementia or Dementia with Lewy Bodies: A Double-Blind, Placebo-Controlled, Multicentre Trial." *The Lancet Neurology* 8: 613–618.

Abbott, A. 2005. "Deep in Thought." *Nature* 436: 18–19.

Aharoni, E., et al. 2008. "Can Neurological Evidence Help Courts Assess Criminal Responsibility? Lessons from Law and Neuroscience." *Annals of the New York Academy of Sciences* 1124: 145–160.

Amariglio, N., et al. 2009. "Donor-Derived Brain Tumor Following Neural Stem-Cell Transplantation in an Ataxia-Telangiectasia Patient." *PLoS Medicine* 6(2): e1000029.

American Psychiatric Association. 2000. *Diagnostic and Statistical Manual of Mental Disorders*, 4th edition, text revision, *DSM-IV-TR*. Washington, DC: American Psychiatric Association.

American Psychiatric Association. 2013. *DSM-5: The Future of Psychiatric Diagnosis*. http://www.dsm5.org/Pages/RecentUpdates.aspx.

Appelbaum, P. 1998. "Ought We to Require Emotional Capacity as Part of Decisional Competence?" *Kennedy Institute of Ethics Journal* 8: 371–387.

Appelbaum, P. 2006. "Insanity, Guilty Minds, and Psychiatric Testimony." *Psychiatric Services* 57: 1370–1372.

Appelbaum, P. 2007. "Assessment of Patients' Competence to Consent to Treatment." *New England Journal of Medicine* 357: 1834–1840.

Appelbaum, P. 2009. "Through a Glass Darkly: Functional Neuroimaging Evidence Enters the Courtroom." *Psychiatric Services* 60: 21–23.

Appiah, K. A. 2008. *Experiments in Ethics*. Cambridge, MA: Harvard University Press.

Aristotle. 1984. *Nicomachean Ethics*, trans. and ed. J. Barnes. Princeton: Princeton University Press.

Asano, T., et al. 2006: "In Vivo Tumor Formation from Primate Embryonic Stem Cells." *Methods in Molecular Biology* 329: 459–467.

Bachoud-Levi, A., et al. 2006. "Effect of Foetal Neural Transplants in Patients with Huntington's Diseases 6 years after Surgery: A Long-Term Follow-Up Study." *The Lancet Neurology* 5: 303–309.

Backlund, E.-O., et al. 1985. "Transplantation of Adrenal Medullary Tissue to Striatum in Parkinsonism: First Clinical Trials." *Journal of Neurosurgery* 62: 169–173.

Baer, J., Kaufman, J., and Baumeister, R., eds. 2008. *Are We Free? Psychology and Free Will.* Oxford: Oxford University Press.

Barker, R., Kendall, A., and Widner, H. 2000. "Neural Tissue Xenotransplantation: What Is Needed Prior to Clinical Trials in Parkinson's Disease?" *Cell Transplantation* 9: 235–246.

Baron-Cohen, S. 2005. "Autism — 'Autos': Literally, A Total Focus on the Self?" In Feinberg and Keenan, 166–180.

Barondes, S. 2009. "After Locke: Darwin, Freud, and Psychiatric Assessment." In Mathews, Bok, and Rabins, 156–173.

Batts, S. 2009. "Brain Lesions and their Implications for Criminal Responsibility." *Behavioral Sciences & the Law* 27: 261–272.

Bauby, J.-D. 1997. *The Diving Bell and the Butterfly: A Memoir of Life in Death.* New York: A. A. Knopf.

Beauchamp, T., and Childress, J. 2009. *Principles of Biomedical Ethics*, 6th ed. New York: Oxford University Press.

Beauregard, M. 2007. "Mind Really Does Matter: Evidence from Neuroimaging Studies of Emotional Self-Regulation, Psychotherapy, and Placebo Effect." *Progress in Neurobiology* 81: 218–236.

Bechara, A., and Vander Linden, M. 2005. "Decision-Making and Impulse Control after Frontal Lobe Injuries." *Current Opinion in Neurology* 18: 784–790.

Bechara, A., et al. 1994. "Insensitivity to Future Consequences Following Damage to Human Prefrontal Cortex." *Cognition* 50: 7–15.

Beecher, H., et al. 1968. Report of the Ad Hoc Committee of the Harvard Medical School to Examine the Definition of Brain Death. "A Definition of Irreversible Coma." *Journal of the American Medical Association* 205: 337–340.

Bekinschtein, T. 2009. "Classical Conditioning in the Vegetative and Minimally Conscious State." *Nature Neuroscience* 12: 1343–1349.

Bell, E. 2009. "Neuroimmunology: Finding a Way into the Brain." *Nature Reviews Immunology* 9: 386.

Belmaker, R., and Agam, G. 2008. "Major Depressive Disorder." *New England Journal of Medicine* 358: 55–68.

Benabid, A.-L. 2003. "Deep-Brain Stimulation for Parkinson's Disease." *Current Opinion in Neurobiology* 13: 696–706.

Benabid, A.-L. 2007. "What the Future Holds for Deep-Brain Stimulation." *Expert Review of Medical Devices* 4: 895–903.

Benedetti, F. 2009. *Placebo Effects: Understanding the Mechanisms in Health and Disease.* Oxford: Oxford University Press.

Bennett, M. R., and Hacker, P. M. S. 2003. *Philosophical Foundations of Neuroscience.* Malden, MA: Blackwell.

Berker, S. 2009. "The Normative Insignificance of Neuroscience." *Philosophy & Public Affairs* 37: 293–325.

Berkowitz, L. 1993. *Aggression: Its Causes, Consequences, and Control.* Philadelphia: Temple University Press.

Bernat, J. 2010. "The Natural History of Chronic Disorders of Consciousness." *Neurology* 75: 206–207.

Bernat, J., and Rottenberg, D. 2007. "Conscious Awareness in PVS and MCS: The Borderlands of Neurology." *Neurology* 68: 885–886.

Bernet, W., et al. 2007. "Bad Nature, Bad Nurture, and Testimony Regarding MAOA and SLC6A4 Genotyping at Murder Trials." *Journal of Forensic Science* 52: 1362–1371.

Bickle, J. 2003. *Philosophy and Neuroscience: A Ruthlessly Reductive Account.* Amsterdam: Kluwer.

Blair, R. J. R. 2003. "Neurobiological Basis of Psychopathy." *British Journal of Psychiatry* 182: 5–7.

Blair, R. J. R. 2007. "Aggression, Psychopathy, and Free Will from a Cognitive Neuroscience Perspective." *Behavioral Sciences & the Law* 25: 321–331.

Blair, R. J. R. 2008. "The Cognitive Neuroscience of Psychopathy and Implications for Judgments of Responsibility." *Neuroethics* 1 (3): 149–157.

Blair, R. J. R., Mitchell, D., and Blair, K. 2005. *The Psychopath: Emotion and the Brain.* Malden, MA: Blackwell.

Boer, G. 2006. "Restorative Therapies for Parkinson's Disease: Ethical Issues." In Brundin and Olanow, 12–49.

Boer, G. 2010. "Transplantation and Xenotransplantation: Ethics of Cell Therapy in the Brain Revisited." In Giordano and Gordijn, 190–215.

Boly, M., et al. 2008. "Perception of Pain in the Minimally Conscious State with PET Activation: An Observational Study." *The Lancet Neurology* 7: 1013–1020.

Bratman, M. 1987. *Intention, Plans, and Practical Reason.* Cambridge, MA: Harvard University Press.

Brentano, F. 1973. *Psychology from an Empirical Standpoint*, trans. T. Rancurello, D. Terrell, and L. McAllister. Atlantic Highlands, NJ: Humanities Press.

Brodmann, K. 1994. *Localization in the Cerebral Cortex*, trans. L. Garey. London: Smith-Gordon.

Brundin, P., and Olanow, C. W., eds. 2006. *Restorative Therapies for Parkinson's Disease.* New York: Springer.

Buckholtz, J., et al. 2010. "Mesolimbic Dopamine Reward System Hypersensitivity in Individuals with Psychopathic Traits." *Nature Neuroscience* 13: 419–421.

Bunge, S., and Wallis, J., eds. 2008. *Neuroscience of Rule-Guided Behavior.* Oxford: Oxford University Press.

Burns, J., and Swerdlaw, R. 2003. "Right Orbitofrontal Tumor with Pedophilia Symptom and Constructional Apraxia." *Archives of Neurology* 62: 437–440.

Cacioppo, J., et al. 2003. "Just Because You're Imaging the Brain Doesn't Mean that You Can Stop Using Your Head: A Primer and Set of First Principles." *Journal of Personality and Social Psychology* 85: 650–661.

Canadian Medical Association. 2008. 8th Annual National Report Card on Health Care. http://www.cma.ca/report-card/august2008.html.

Carey, B. 2006. "Mute 19 Years, He Helps Reveal Brain's Mysteries." *New York Times*, July 4. http://www.nytimes.com/2006/07/04/health/psychology/04coma.html

Carson, S., et al. 2003. "Decreased Latent Inhibition Is Associated with Increased Creative Achievement in High-Functioning Individuals." *Journal of Personality and Social Psychology* 85: 499–506.

Cashmore, A. 2010. "The Lucretian Swerve: The Biological Basis of Human Behavior and the Criminal Justice System." *Proceedings of the National Academy of Sciences* 107: 4499–4504.

Caspi, A., et al. 2002. "Role of Genotype in the Cycle of Violence in Maltreated Children." *Science* 297: 851–854.

Changeux, J.-P. 1997. *Neuronal Man: The Biology of Mind*, trans. L. Garey. Princeton: Princeton University Press.

Chisholm, N., and Gillett, G. 2005. "The Patient's Journey: Living with Locked-In Syndrome." *British Medical Journal* 331: 94–97.

Christensen, A.-L., Goldberg, E., and Bougakov, D., eds. 2009. *Luria's Legacy in the 21st Century*. New York: Oxford University Press.

Christophersen, N., et al. 2006. "Developing Novel Cell Sources for Transplantation in Parkinson's Disease." In Sanberg and Sanberg, 31–59.

Churchland, P. 1995. *The Engine of Reason, the Seat of the Soul*. Cambridge, MA: MIT Press.

Churchland, P.-S. 2002. *Brain-Wise: Studies in Neurophilosophy*. Cambridge, MA: MIT Press.

Cicchetti, F., et al. 2009. "Neural Transplants in Patients with Huntington's Disease Undergo Disease-Like Degeneration." *Proceedings of the National Academy of Sciences* 106: 12483–12488.

Cima, M., Tonnaer, F., and Hauser, M. 2010. "Psychopaths Know Right from Wrong but Don't Care." *Social Cognitive and Affective Neuroscience* 5: 59–67.

Clark, A. 1997. *Being There: Putting Brain, Body, and World Together Again*. Cambridge, MA: MIT Press.

Clark, A. 2008. *Supersizing the Mind: Embodiment, Action, and Cognitive Extension*. Oxford: Oxford University Press.

Clark, A., and Chalmers, D. 1998. "The Extended Mind." *Analysis* 58: 7–19.

Clarke, R. 2003. *Libertarian Accounts of Free Will*. New York: Oxford University Press.

Clayton, M., and Williams, A., eds. 2000. *The Ideal of Equality*. New York: St. Martin's Press.

Cleckley, H. 1967. *The Mask of Sanity*, 2nd ed. St. Louis: Mosby.

Cooks, D., Forth, A., and Hare, R., eds. 1998. *Psychopathy: Theory, Research, and Implications for Society*. Dordrecht: Kluwer.

Cooper, A. 2007. "Awakening." CBS "60 Minutes," November 21. http://www.tv.com/60minutes/november-21-2007-awakening.html

Connolly, K. 2009. "Trapped in His Own Body for 23 Years—The Coma Victim Who Screamed Unheard." *The Guardian*, November 23. http://www.guardian.co.uk/world/2009/nov/23/man-trapped-coma-23-years.

Crick, F. 1994. *The Astonishing Hypothesis: The Scientific Search for the Soul*. New York: Scribner's.

Csernansky, J., et al. 2006. "Plasma Cortisol and Progression of Dementia in Subjects with Alzheimer-Type Dementia." *American Journal of Psychiatry* 163: 2164–2169.

Damasio, A. 1994. *Descartes' Error: Emotion, Reason, and the Human Brain*. New York: Grosset/Putnam.

Damasio, A. 1999. *The Feeling of What Happens: Body and Emotion in the Making of Consciousness*. Orlando, FL: Harcourt Brace.

Damasio, A. 2000. "A Neural Basis for Sociopathy." *Archives of General Psychiatry* 57: 128–129.

Damasio, A. 2002. "The Neural Basis of Social Behavior." In Marcus, 18–22.

Damasio, A. 2007. "Neuroscience and Ethics—Intersections." *American Journal of Bioethics—AJOB Neuroscience* 7 (1): 3–7.

Damasio, H., et al. 1994. "The Return of Phineas Gage: The Skull of a Famous Patient Yields Clues about the Brain." *Science* 264: 1102–1108.

Dantzer, R., et al. 2008. "From Inflammation to Sickness and Depression: When the Immune System Subjugates the Brain." *Nature Reviews Neuroscience* 9: 46–56.

Davidson, R. 2000. "Dysfunction in the Neural Circuitry of Emotion Regulation—A Possible Prelude to Violence." *Science* 289: 591–594.

De Bie, R., et al. 2007. "Ethical and Legal Aspects of Neuromodulation: On the Road to Guidelines." *Neuromodulation* 10: 177–185.

Decety, J., and Ickes, W., eds. 2009. *The Social Neuroscience of Empathy*. Cambridge, MA: MIT Press.

DeGrazia, D. 2005. *Human Identity and Bioethics*. New York: Cambridge University Press.

De Jongh, R., et al. 2008. "Botox for the Brain: Enhancement of Cognition, Mood, and Pro-Social Behavior and Blunting of Unwanted Memories." *Neuroscience and Behavioral Reviews* 32: 760–776.

Dekkers, W., and Boer, G. 2001. "Sham Surgery in Patients with Parkinson's Disease: Is it Morally Acceptable?" *Journal of Medical Ethics* 27: 151–156.

De Meyer, G., et al. 2010. "Diagnosis-Independent Alzheimer Disease Biomarker Signature in Cognitively Normal Elderly People." *Archives of Neurology* 67: 949–956.

Dennett, D. 1991. *Consciousness Explained*. Boston: Little Brown.

Di, H., et al. 2007. "Cerebral Response to Patient's Own Name in the Vegetative and Minimally Conscious States." *Neurology* 68: 895–899.

Di, H., et al. 2008. "Neuroimaging Activation Studies in the Vegetative State: Predictors of Recovery?" *Clinical Medicine* 8: 502–507.

Dodd, M., et al. 2005. "Pathological Gambling Caused by Drugs to Treat Parkinson Disease." *Archives of Neurology* 62: 579–583.

Douglas, T. 2008. "Moral Enhancement." *Journal of Applied Philosophy* 25: 228–245.

Dresser, R. 2008. "Neuroscience's Uncertain Threat to Criminal Law." *Hastings Center Report* 38 (6): 9–10.

Du, B., et al. 2008. "Induced Arousal Following Zolpidem Treatment in a Vegetative State after Brain Injury in 7 Cases: Analysis Using Single Photon Emission Computerized Tomography and Digitized Monitor." *Neural Regeneration Research* 3: 94–96.

Duff, R. A. 1990. *Intention, Agency, and Criminal Liability: Philosophy of Action and the Criminal Law*. Oxford: Blackwell.

Dunn, L., et al. 2010. "Ethical Issues in Deep-Brain Stimulation Research for Treatment-Resistant Depression: Focus on Risk and Consent." *AJOB Neuroscience*, published online September 24.

Dunnett, S., and Rosser, A. 2007. "Cell Transplantation for Huntington's Disease: Should We Continue?" *Brain Research Bulletin* 72: 132–147.

Dworkin, R. 1981. "What Is Equality? Part II: Equality of Resources." *Philosophy & Public Affairs* 10: 283–354.

Dworkin, R. 1993. *Life's Dominion*. New York: Vintage Books.

Eastman, N., and Campbell, C. 2006. "Neuroscience and Legal Determination of Criminal Responsibility." *Nature Reviews Neuroscience* 7: 311–318.

Elgh, E., et al. 2009. "Cognitive Function in Early Parkinson's Disease: A Population-Based Study." *European Journal of Neurology* 16: 1278–1284.

Elliott, C. 2008. "In Defense of the Beta Blocker." *The Atlantic Monthly*, August 20. http://www.theatlantic.com/magazine/archive/2008/08/in-defense-of-the-beta-blocker/696/

Elliott, R., et al. 1997. "Effects of Methylphenidate on Spatial Working Memory and Planning in Healthy Young Adults." *Psychopharmacology*: 131: 196–206.

Estraneo, A., et al. 2010. "Late Recovery after Traumatic, Anoxic, or Hemorrhagic Long-Lasting Vegetative State." *Neurology* 75: 239–245.

Expert Consensus Panel for Obsessive-Compulsive Disorder. 1997. "Treatment of Obsessive-Compulsive Disorder." *Journal of Clinical Psychiatry* 58: Supplement 4: 2–75.

Farah, M. (ed.). 2010. *Neuroethics: An Introduction with Readings*. Cambridge, MA: MIT Press.

Farah, M. 2005. "Neuroethics: The Practical and the Philosophical." *Trends in Cognitive Sciences* 9: 34–40.

Farah, M., and Murphy, N. 2009. "Neuroscience and the Soul." *Science* 323: 1168.

Farah, M., et al. 2004. "Neurocognitive Enhancement: What Can We Do and What Should We Do?" *Nature Reviews Neuroscience* 5: 421–425.

Farah, M., et al. 2008. "Brain Imaging and Brain Privacy: A Realistic Concern?" *Journal of Cognitive Neuroscience* 21: 119–127.

Farah, M. et al. 2009. "When We Enhance Cognition with Adderall, Do We Sacrifice Creativity? A Preliminary Study." *Psychopharmacology* 202: 541–547.

Feinberg, J. 1992. *Freedom and Fulfillment: Philosophical Essays*. Princeton: Princeton University Press.

Feinberg, T., and Keenan, J. eds. 2005. *The Lost Self: Pathologies of the Brain and Identity*. New York: Oxford University Press.

Feresin, E. 2009. "Lighter Sentence for Murderer with 'Bad Genes.'" *Nature*, published online October 30. http://www.nature.com/new/2009/091030/full/news.2009.html

Fine, C., and Kennett, J. 2004. "Mental Impairment, Moral Understanding, and Criminal Responsibility: Psychopathy and the Purposes of Punishment." *International Journal of Law and Psychiatry* 27: 425–443.

Fins, J. 2003. "Constructing an Ethical Stereotaxy for Severe Brain Injury: Balancing Risks, Benefits, and Access." *Nature Reviews Neuroscience* 4: 323–327.

Fins, J. 2005. "Rethinking Disorders of Consciousness: New Research and its Implications." *Hastings Center Report* 35 (2): 22–24.

Fins, J., and Schiff, N. 2006. "Shades of Gray: New Insights into the Vegetative State." *Hastings Center Report* 36 (6): 9.

Fins, J., et al. 2006. "Psychosurgery: Avoiding an Ethical Redux While Advancing a Therapeutic Future." *Neurosurgery* 59: 713–716.

Fins, J., et al. 2008. "Neuroimaging and Disorders of Consciousness: Envisioning an Ethical Research Agenda." *American Journal of Bioethics—AJOB Neuroscience* 8 (9): 3–12.

Fischer, J. M., and Ravizza, M. 1998. *Responsibility and Control: A Theory of Moral Responsibility*. New York: Cambridge University Press.

Foot, P. 2002. *Virtues and Vices: And Other Essays in Moral Philosophy*. Oxford: Oxford University Press.

Fournier, J., et al. 2010. "Antidepressant Drug Effects and Depression Severity." *Journal of the American Medical Association* 303: 47–53.

Frank, M., et al. 2007. "Hold Your Horses: Impulsivity, Deep-Brain Stimulation, and Medication in Parkinsonism." *Science* 318: 1309–1312.

Frankfurt, H. 1988. *The Importance of What We Care About*. New York: Cambridge University Press.

Freund, H.-J., et al. 2009. "Cognitive Functions in a Patient with Parkinson-Dementia Syndrome Undergoing Deep-Brain Stimulation." *Archives of Neurology* 66: 781–785.

Fuchs, T. 2003. "The Challenge of Neuroscience: Psychiatry and Phenomenology Today." *Psychopathology* 35: 319–326.

Fuchs, T. 2004. "Neurobiology and Psychotherapy: An Emerging Dialogue." *Current Opinion in Psychiatry* 17: 479–485.

Fuchs, T. 2007. "Mind, Brain, and Life: A Phenomenological View on Embodied Cognitive Neuroscience." Unpublished paper presented at a neurophilosophy symposium in Munich, September 20.

Fuchs, T. 2008. *Das Gehirn—Ein Beziehungsorgan*. Berlin: Springer.

Fuchs, T., and Schlimme, J. 2009. "Embodiment and Psychopathology: A Phenomenological Perspective." *Current Opinion in Psychiatry* 22: 570–575.

Fukuyama, F. 2002. *Our Posthuman Future: Consequences of the Biotechnology Revolution*. New York: Farrar, Straus and Giroux.

Gallagher, S. 2005. *How the Body Shapes the Mind*. Oxford: Clarendon Press.

Garcia-Lizana, F., et al. 2003. "Long-Term Outcome in ICU Patients: What about Quality of Life?" *Intensive Care Medicine* 8: 1286–1293.

Garland, B., ed. 2004. *Neuroscience and the Law: Brain, Mind, and the Scales of Justice*. New York: Dana Press.

Garland, B., and Glimcher, P. 2006. "Cognitive Neuroscience and the Law." *Current Opinion in Neurobiology* 16: 130–134.

Gems, D. 2003. "Is More Life Always Better? The New Biology of Aging and the Meaning of Life." *Hastings Center Report* 33(4): 31–39.

Giacino, J., et al. 2002. "The Minimally Conscious State: Definition and Diagnostic Criteria." *Neurology* 58: 349–353.

Gillett, G. 2008. *Subjectivity and Being Somebody: Human Identity and Neuroethics*. Exeter: Imprint Academic.

Gillett, G. 2009. "Intention, Autonomy, and Brain Events." *Bioethics* 23: 330–339.

Giordano, J., and Gordijn, B., eds. 2010. *Scientific and Philosophical Perspectives in Neuroethics*. Cambridge: Cambridge University Press.

Glenn, A., and Raine, A. 2009. "Psychopathy and Instrumental Aggression: Evolutionary, Neurobiological, and Legal Perspectives." *International Journal of Law and Psychiatry* 32: 253–258.

Glenn, A., Raine, A., and Schug, R. 2009. "The Neural Correlates of Moral Decision-Making in Psychopathy." *Molecular Psychiatry* 14: 5–6.

Glover, J. 1977. *Causing Death and Saving Lives*. New York: Penguin.

Goldapple, K., et al. 2004. "Modulation of Cortical-Limbic Pathways in Major Depression: Treatment-Specific Effects of Cognitive Behavior Therapy." *Archives of General Psychiatry* 61: 34–41.

Graham v. Florida. 2010. 560 U.S.

Greely, H., et al. 2008: "Towards Responsible Use of Cognitive-Enhancing Drugs by the Healthy." *Nature* 456: 702–705.

Greenberg, B., et al. 2010. "Deep-Brain Stimulation of the Ventral Internal Capsule/Ventral Striatum for Obsessive-Compulsive Disorder." *Molecular Psychiatry* 15: 64–79.

Greene, J. 2003. "From Neural 'Is' to Moral 'Ought': What Are the Moral Implications of Neuroscientific Moral Psychology?" *Nature Reviews Neuroscience* 4: 847–850.

Greene, J. 2007. "Why Are VMPFC Patients More Utilitarian? A Dual-Process Theory of Moral Judgment Explains." *Trends in Cognitive Sciences* 11: 322–333.

Greene, J. 2008. "The Secret Joke of Kant's Soul." In Sinnott-Armstrong, 35–79.

Greene, J., and Haidt, J. 2002. "How (and Where) Does Moral Judgment Work?" *Trends in Cognitive Sciences* 6: 517–523.

Greene, J., and Cohen. J. 2004. "For the Law, Neuroscience Changes Nothing and Everything." *Philosophical Transactions of the Royal Society of London* 359: 1175–1785.

Greene, J., et al. 2001. "An fMRI Investigation of Emotional Engagement in Moral Judgment." *Science* 293: 2105–2108.

Greene, J., et al. 2004. "The Neural Bases of Cognitive Conflict and Control in Moral Judgment." *Neuron* 44: 389–400.

Greene, J., et al. 2008. "Cognitive Load Selectively Interferes with Utilitarian Moral Judgment." *Cognition* 107: 1144–1154.

Greene, J., et al. 2009. "Pushing Moral Buttons: The Interaction between Personal Force and Intention in Moral Judgment." *Cognition* 111: 364–371.

Greenwood, H., and Daar, A. 2008. "Regenerative Medicine." In *The Cambridge Textbook of Bioethics*. New York: Cambridge University Press, 153–158.

Griffin, J. 1986. *Well-Being: Its Meaning, Measurement, and Moral Importance*. Oxford: Clarendon Press.

Grisso, T., and Appelbaum, P. 1998. *Assessing Competence to Consent to Treatment: A Guide for Physicians and Other Health Professionals*. New York: Oxford University Press.

Haggard, P. 2005. "Conscious Intention and Motor Cognition." *Trends in Cognitive Sciences* 9: 290–295.

Haggard, P. 2008. "Human Volition: Towards a Neuroscience of Will." *Nature Reviews Neuroscience* 9: 934–946.

Haidt, J. 2001. "The Emotional Dog and its Rational Tail. A Social Intuitionist Approach to Moral Judgment." *Psychological Review* 108: 814–834.

Haig, S. 2007. "The Ethics of Erasing a Bad Memory." *Time*, October 15. http://www.time.com/time/health/article/0.8599.1671492.00.html

Haji, I. 2010. "Psychopathy, Ethical Perception, and Moral Culpability." *Neuroethics* 3(2): 135–150.

Hare, R. 1993. *Without Empathy: The Strange World of the Psychopaths among Us*. New York: Pocket Books.

Hare, R. 1998. "Psychopaths and their Nature." In Millon et al., 188–212.

Hare, R. 2003. *The Hare Psychopathy Checklist*, 2nd ed. Toronto: Multi-Health Systems.

Harenski, C., et al. 2010. "A Functional Imaging Investigation of Moral Deliberation and Moral Intuition." *NeuroImage* 49: 2707–2716.

Harris, J. 2007. *Enhancing Evolution: The Ethical Case for Making Better People*. Princeton: Princeton University Press.

Hart, H. L. A. 1968. *Punishment and Responsibility*. Oxford: Clarendon Press.

Hartocollis, A. 2007. "In Support of Sex Attacker's Insanity Plea, A Look at his Brain." *New York Times*, May 11. http://www.nytimes.com/2007/05/11/nyregion/11fake/html

Hartocollis, A. 2007. "Attack not Disputed in Trial, Just Intent of the Attacker." *New York Times* May 23. http://www.nytimes.com/2007/05/23fake.html.

Hassabis, D., et al. 2007. "Patients with Hippocampal Amnesia Cannot Imagine New Experiences." *Proceedings of the National Academy of Sciences* 104: 1726–1731.

Haynes, J.-D. 2010. "Beyond Libet: Long-Term Prediction of Free Choices from Neuroimaging Signals." In Sinnott-Armstrong and Nadel, Chapter 8.

Haynes, J.-D., et al. 2007. "Reading Hidden Intentions in the Human Brain." *Current Biology* 17: 323–328.

Hippocrates. 1981 *On the Sacred Disease*. Cited in Spillane.

Holden, C. 2009. "Fetal Cells Again?" *Science* 326: 358–359.

Hume, D. 1978. *A Treatise of Human Nature*, ed. P. H. Nidditch. Oxford: Clarendon Press.

Husserl, E. 1966. *The Phenomenology of Internal Time Consciousness*, trans. J. Churchill. Bloomington, IN: Indiana University Press.

Husserl, E. 1970. *Logical Investigations*, trans. J. Findlay. London: Routledge.

Insel, T., and Wang, P. 2010. "Rethinking Mental Illness." *Journal of the American Medical Association* 303: 1970–1971.

Jonsen, A., Siegler, M., and Winslade, W. 2006. *Clinical Ethics: A Practical Approach to Ethical Decisions in Clinical Medicine*, 6th ed. New York: McGraw-Hill.

Juengst, E. 1998. "What Does Enhancement Mean?". In Parens, 29–47.

Juengst, E., et al. 2003. "Biogerontology, 'Anti-Aging Medicine,' and the Challenges of Human Enhancement." *Hastings Center Report* 33(4): 21–30.

Kahane, G., and Savulescu, J. 2009. "Brain Damage and the Moral Significance of Consciousness." *Journal of Medicine and Philosophy* 34: 6–26.

Kalivas, P., and Volkow, N. 2005. "The Neural Basis of Addiction." *American Journal of Psychiatry* 162: 1403–1413.

Kamm, F. M. 2007. *Intricate Ethics: Rights, Responsibilities, and Permissible Harm*. Oxford: Oxford University Press.

Kamm, F. M. 2009. "Neuroscience and Moral Reasoning: A Note on Recent Research." *Philosophy & Public Affairs* 37: 330–345.

Kandel, E. 1998. "A New Intellectual Framework for Psychiatry." *American Journal of Psychiatry* 155: 457–469.

Kane, R. 1996. *The Significance of Free Will*. New York: Oxford University Press.

Kant, I. 1998. *Groundwork of the Metaphysics of Morals*, trans. and ed. M. Gregor. New York: Cambridge University Press.

Kapahi, P., and Vijg, J. 2009. "Aging—Lost in Translation?" *New England Journal of Medicine* 361: 2669–2670.

Kass, L. 2003. *Beyond Therapy: Biotechnology and the Pursuit of Happiness*. New York: Harper Collins.

Kass, L. 2003. "Ageless Bodies, Happy Souls: Biotechnology and the Pursuit of Perfection." *The New Atlantis* 1: 9–28.

Kelly, C., Dunnett, S., and Rosser, A. 2006. "Cell-Based Therapy for Huntington's Disease." In Sanberg and Sanberg, 83–115.

Kessler, R., et al. 2008. "Individual and Societal Effects of Mental Disorders on Earnings in the United States: Results from the National Comorbidity Survey Replication." *American Journal of Psychiatry* 165: 703–711.

Kiehl, K., et al. 2001. "Limbic Abnormalities in Affective Processing by Criminal Psychopaths as Revealed by Functional Magnetic Resonance Imaging." *Biological Psychiatry* 50: 677–684.

Kim, J. 2006. "Emergence: Core Ideas and Issues." *Synthese* 151: 547–559.

Kindt, M., et al. 2009. "Beyond Extinction: Erasing Human Fear Responses and Preventing the Return of Fear." *Nature Neuroscience* 12: 256–258.

Kirkwood, T. 2001. *Time of Our Lives: The Science of Human Aging*. Oxford: Oxford University Press.

Kirkwood, T. 2008. "A Systematic Look at an Old Problem." *Nature* 451: 644–647.

Kirsch, I., et al. 2008. "Initial Severity and Antidepressant Benefits: A Meta-Analysis of Data Submitted to the Food and Drug Administration." *PLoS Medicine* 5(1): e45.

Klingberg, T. 2009. *The Overflowing Brain: Information Overload and the Limits of Working Memory*. Oxford: Oxford University Press.

Knabb, J., et al. 2009. "Neuroscience, Moral Reasoning, and the Law." *Behavioral Sciences & the Law* 27: 219–236.

Knight, R. 2008. "Consciousness Unchained: Ethical Issues and the Vegetative and Minimally Conscious State." *American Journal of Bioethics—AJOB Neuroscience* 8(9): 1–2.

Koenigs, M., et al. 2007. "Damage to the Prefrontal Cortex Increases Utilitarian Moral Judgments." *Nature* 446: 908–911.

Kolber, A. 2006. "Therapeutic Forgetting: The Legal and Ethical Implications of Memory Dampening." *Vanderbilt Law Review* 59: 1561–1626.

Koob, G., and Volkow, N. 2010. "Neurocircuitry of Addiction." *Neuropsychopharmacology* 35: 217–238.

Kordower, J., et al. 2008. "Lewy-Body-Like Pathology in Long-Term Embryonic Nigral Transplants in Parkinson's Disease." *Nature Medicine* 14: 504–506.

Korecka, J., Verhaagen, J., and Hol, E. 2007. "Cell Replacement and Gene Therapy Strategies for Parkinson's and Alzheimer's Disease." *Regenerative Medicine* 2: 425–446.

Kuehn, B. 2007. "Scientists Probe Deep-Brain Stimulation: Some Promise for Brain Injury, Psychiatric Illness." *Journal of the American Medical Association* 298: 2249–2251.

LaBar, K., and Cabeza, R. 2006. "Cognitive Neuroscience of Emotional Memory." *Nature Reviews Neuroscience* 7: 54–64.

Laureys, S. 2005. "Death, Unconsciousness, and the Brain." *Nature Reviews Neuroscience* 6: 899–909.

Laureys, S., Owen, A., and Schiff, N. 2004. "Brain Function in Coma, Vegetative State, and Related Disorders." *The Lancet Neurology* 3: 537–546.

Laxton, A., et al. 2010. "A Phase I Trial of Deep-Brain Stimulation of Memory Circuits in Alzheimer's Disease." *Annals of Neurology* 68, published online August 4.

LeDoux, J. 1996. *The Emotional Brain*. New York: Simon and Schuster.

LeDoux, J. 2002. *Synaptic Self: How Our Brains Become Who We Are*. New York: Viking.

Leentjens, A., et al. 2004. "Manipulation of Mental Competence: An Ethical Problem in a Case of Electrical Stimulation of the Subthalamic Nucleus for Severe Parkinson's Disease." *Nederlands Tijdschrift voor Geneeskunde* 148: 1394–1398.

Levy, N. 2007. "Rethinking Neuroethics in the Light of the Extended Mind Thesis." *American Journal of Bioethics—AJOB Neuroscience* 7(9): 3–11.

Levy, N. 2007. "The Responsibility of the Psychopath Revisited." *Philosophy, Psychiatry & Psychology* 14: 129–138.

Levy, N. 2007. *Neuroethics: Challenges for the 21st Century*. Cambridge: Cambridge University Press.

Lewontin, R. 2000. *The Triple Helix: Gene, Organism, and Environment*. Cambridge, MA: Harvard University Press.

Libet, B. 1985. "Unconscious Cerebral Initiative and the Role of Conscious Will in Voluntary Action." *Behavioral and Brain Sciences* 8: 529–566.

Libet, B. 2001. "Consciousness, Free Action, and the Brain." *Journal of Consciousness Studies* 8: 59–65.

Libet, B. 2004. *Mind Time: The Temporal Factor in Consciousness*. Cambridge, MA: Harvard University Press.

Libet, B. 2010. "Do We Have Free Will?" In Sinnott-Armstrong and Nadel, Chapter 1.

Lima, C., et al. 2006. "Olfactory Mucosa Autografts in Human Spinal Cord Injury: A Pilot Clinical Study." *Journal of Spinal Cord Medicine* 29: 181–203.

Lindvall, O., et al. 1990. "Grafts of Fetal Dopamine Neurons Survive and Improve Motor Function in Parkinson's Disease." *Science* 247: 574–577.

Locke, J. 1975. *An Essay Concerning Human Understanding*, ed. P. H. Nidditch. Oxford: Clarendon Press.

Lozano, A., et al. 2008. "Subcallosal Cingulate Gyrus Deep-Brain Stimulation for Treatment-Resistant Depression." *Biological Psychiatry* 64: 461–467.

Luaute, J., et al. 2010. "Long-Term Outcomes of Chronic Minimally Conscious and Vegetative States." *Neurology* 75: 246–252.

Luria, A. R. 1973. *The Working Brain: An Introduction to Neuropsychology*, trans. B. Haigh. Cambridge, MA: Harvard University Press.

Luria, A. R. 1987. *The Man with a Shattered World: The History of a Brain Wound*, trans. L. Solotaroff. Cambridge, MA: Harvard University Press.

Lynch, G., and Gall, C. 2006. "Ampakines and the Three-Fold Path to Cognitive Enhancement." *Trends in Neurosciences* 29: 554–562.

Mackay-Sim, A., et al. 2008. "Autologous Olfactory Ensheathing Cell Transplantation in Human Paraplegia: A 3-Year Clinical Trial." *Brain* 131: 2376–2386.

Madrazo, I., et al. 1987. "Open Microsurgical Autograft of Adrenal Medulla to the Right Caudate Nucleus in Two Patients with Intractable Parkinson's Disease." *New England Journal of Medicine* 316: 831–834.

Maher, B. 2008. "Poll Results: Look Who's Doping." *Nature* 452: 674–675.

Mallet, L., et al. 2008. "Subthalamic Nucleus Stimulation in Severe Obsessive-Compulsive Disorder." *New England Journal of Medicine* 359: 2121–2134.

March, J., et al. 2007. "The Treatment of Adolescents with Depression Study (TADS)." *Archives of General Psychiatry* 64: 1132–1143.

Marcus, S., ed. 2002. *Neuroethics: Mapping the Field*. New York: Dana Press.

Mathers, C., and Loncar, D. 2006. "Projection of Global Mortality and Burden of Disease from 2002 to 2030." *PLoS Medicine* 3(2): e442.

Mathews, D., Bok, H., and Rabins, P., eds. 2009. *Personal Identity and Fractured Selves*. Baltimore: The Johns Hopkins University Press.

Mayberg, H., et al. 2005. "Deep-Brain Stimulation for Treatment-Resistant Depression." *Neuron* 45: 651–660.

McCabe, S., et al. 2005. "Non-Medical Use of Prescription Stimulants among US College Students: Prevalence and Correlates from a National Survey." *Addiction* 100: 96–106.

McGaugh, J. 2003. *Memory and Emotion: The Making of Lasting Memories*. New York: Columbia University Press.

McGaugh, J. 2004. "The Amygdala Modulates the Consolidation of Memories of Emotionally Arousing Experiences." *Annual Review of Neuroscience* 27: 1–28.

McGaugh, J. 2006. "Make Mild Moments Memorable: Add a Little Arousal." *Trends in Cognitive Sciences* 10: 345–347.

McMahan, J. 2002. *The Ethics of Killing; Problems at the Margins of Life*. Oxford: Oxford University Press.

McSherry, B. 2004. "Criminal Responsibility, Fleeting States of Mental Impairment, and the Power of Self-Control." *International Journal of Law and Psychiatry* 27: 224–257.

M'Naghten's Case. 1843. 8 Eng. Rep. 718, 722. Cited in the Report of the Committee on Mentally Abnormal Offenders. London: Her Majesty's Stationery Office, 1975, 217.

Medford, N., et al. 2005. "Emotional Memory: Separating Content and Context." *Psychiatric Research: Neuroimaging* 138: 247–258.

Mele, A. 2006. *Free Will and Luck*. New York: Oxford University Press.

Mele, A. 2008. "Recent Work on Free Will and Science." *American Philosophical Quarterly* 45: 107–130.

Mele, A. 2009. *Effective Intentions: The Power of Conscious Will*. New York: Oxford University Press.

Mele, A. 2010. "Libet on Free Will, Readiness Potentials, Decisions, and Awareness." In Sinnott-Armstrong and Nadel, Chapter 3.

Menary, R., ed. 2010. *The Extended Mind*. Cambridge, MA: MIT Press.

Merkel, R., et al. 2007. *Intervening in the Brain: Changing Psyche and Society*. Berlin and Heidelberg: Springer.

Merleau-Ponty, M. 2002. *Phenomenology of Perception*, trans. C. Smith. London: Routledge.

Meyers, D. 2002. *Intuition: Its Powers and Perils*. New Haven: Yale University Press.

Miller, B., and Hou, C. 2004. "Portraits of Artists: Emergence of Visual Creativity in Dementia." *Archives of Neurology* 61: 841–844.

Miller, G. 2009. "Rewiring Faulty Circuits in the Brain." *Science* 323: 1554–1556.

Miller, G. 2009. "fMRI Evidence Used in Murder Sentencing." *ScienceInsider* November 23. http://blogs.sciencemag.org/scienceinsider/2009/11/fmri-evidence-u.html.

Miller, G. 2010. "Beyond DSM: Seeking a Brain-Based Classification of Mental Illness." *Science* 327: 1437.

Millon, T., et al., eds. 1998. *Psychopathy: Antisocial, Criminal, and Violent Behavior*. New York: Guilford Press.

Minsky, M. 1986. *The Society of Mind*. New York: Simon and Schuster.

Minzenberg, M., et al. 2008. "Modafinil Shifts Locus Coeruleus to Low-Tonic, High-Phasic Activity during Functional MRI." *Science* 322: 1700–1702.

Mitchell, S., et al. 2009. "The Clinical Course of Advanced Dementia." *New England Journal of Medicine* 361: 1529–1538.

Mobbs, D., et al. 2007 "Law, Responsibility, and the Brain." *PLoS Biology* 5(4): e103.

Model Penal Code. 1985. Official Draft and Commentaries. Philadelphia: American Law Institute.

Moll, J., and Oliveira-Souza, R. 2007. "Moral Judgments, Emotions, and the Utilitarian Brain." *Trends in Cognitive Sciences* 11: 319–321.

Monti, M., et al. 2010. "Willful Modulation of Brain Activity in Disorders of Consciousness." *New England Journal of Medicine* 362: 579–589.

Montine, T., and Larson, E. 2009. "Late-Life Dementias: Does This Unyielding Global Challenge Require a Broader View?" *Journal of the American Medical Association* 302: 2593–2594.

Moore, M. 2009. *Causation and Responsibility*. New York: Oxford University Press.

Morse, S. 2004. "New Neuroscience, Old Problems." In Garland, 157–198.

Morse, S. 2006. "Brain Overclaim Syndrome and Criminal Responsibility: A Diagnostic Note." *Ohio State Journal of Criminal Law* 3: 397–412.

Morse, S. 2008. "Psychopathy and Criminal Responsibility." *Neuroethics* 1(3): 205–212.

Muller, U., et al. 2004. "Effects of Modafinil on Working Memory Processes in Humans." *Psychopharmacology* 177: 161–169.

Multi-Society Task Force on PVS. 1994. "Medical Aspects of the Persistent Vegetative State." *New England Journal of Medicine* 330: 1499–1508.

Nagel, S. 2010. "Too Much of a Good Thing? Enhancement and the Burden of Self-Determination." *Neuroethics* 3 (2): 109–119.

Nagel, S. J., and Najm, I. 2009. "Deep-Brain Stimulation for Epilepsy." *Neuromodulation* 12: 270–280.

Nagel, T. 1991. *Equality and Partiality*. Oxford: Oxford University Press.

Nahmias, E., et al. 2005. "Surveying Freedom: Folk Intuitions about Free Will and Moral Responsibility." *Philosophical Psychology* 18: 561–584.

Nampiaparampil, D. 2008. "Prevalence of Chronic Pain after Traumatic Brain Injury: A Systematic Review." *Journal of the American Medical Association* 300: 711–719.

Nesse, R. 2000. "Is Depression an Adaptation?" *Archives of General Psychiatry* 57: 14–20.

Nesse, R. 2009. "Explaining Depression: Neuroscience Is not Enough, Evolution Is Essential." In Pariante et al., 17–36.

Newman, J. 1998. "Psychopathic Behavior: An Information Processing Perspective." In Cooks, Forth, and Hare, 81–104.

Noe, A. 2009. *Out of Our Heads: Why You Are not Your Brain, and Other Lessons from the Biology of Consciousness*. New York: Hill and Wang.

Nordenfelt, L. 2007. *Rationality and Compulsion: Applying Action Theory to Psychiatry*. Oxford: Oxford University Press.

Northoff, G. 2009. "What Is Neuroethics? Empirical and Theoretical Neuroethics." *Current Opinion in Psychiatry* 22: 565–569.

Nuttin, B., et al. 2003. "Long-Term Electrical Capsular Stimulation in Patients with Obsessive-Compulsive Disorder." *Neurosurgery* 52: 1263–1274.

Olanow, C. W., et al. 2003. "A Double-Blind Controlled Trial of Bilateral Fetal Nigral Transplantation in Parkinson's Disease." *Annals of Neurology* 54: 403–414.

Olshansky, S. J., and Carnes, B. 2001. *The Quest for Immortality: Science at the Frontiers of Aging*. New York: W. W. Norton.

Olson, E. 1997. *The Human Animal: Personal Identity without Psychology*. Oxford: Oxford University Press.

Olson, E. 2007. *What Are We? A Study in Personal Ontology*. Oxford: Oxford University Press.

Owen, A., and Coleman, M. 2008. "Functional Neuroimaging of the Vegetative State." *Nature Reviews Neuroscience* 9: 235–243.

Owen, A., et al. 2006. "Detecting Awareness in the Vegetative State." *Science* 313: 1402.

Pallanti, S. 2008. "Transcultural Observations of Obsessive-Compulsive Disorder." *American Journal of Psychiatry* 165: 169–170.

Pampallona, S., et al. 2004. "Combined Pharmacotherapy and Psychological Treatment for Depression: A Systematic Review." *Archives of General Psychiatry* 61: 714–719.

Pardo, M., and Patterson, D. 2010. "Minds, Brains, and Norms." *Neuroethics*, published online June 19.

Parens, E., ed. 1998. *Enhancing Human Traits: Ethical and Social Implications*. Washington, DC: Georgetown University Press.

Parens, E. 2005. "Authenticity and Ambivalence: Toward Understanding the Enhancement Debate." *Hastings Center Report* 35(3): 34–41.

Parfit, D. 1984. *Reasons and Persons*. Oxford: Clarendon Press.

Parfit, D. 2000. "Equality or Priority?" In Clayton and Williams, 81–125.

Pariante, C., et al., eds. 2009. *Understanding Depression: A Translational Approach*. Oxford: Oxford University Press.

Parker, E., Cahill, L., and McGaugh, J. 2006. "Case of Unusual Autobiographical Remembering." *Neurocase* 12: 35–49.

Penfield, W. 1952. "Memory Mechanisms."*Archives of Neurology and Psychiatry* 67: 178–198.

Penfield, W. 1975. *The Mystery of the Mind: A Critical Study of Consciousness and the Human Brain*. Princeton: Princeton University Press.

Pereboom, D. 2001. *Living without Free Will*. New York: Cambridge University Press.

Perry, J., ed. 2008. *Personal Identity*, 2nd ed. Berkeley: University of California Press.

Perry, J. 2009. "Diminished and Fractured Selves." In Mathews, Bok, and Rabins, 129–162.

Peters, A., and Jones, E., eds. 1991. *Cerebral Cortex*. New York: Plenum Press.

Petersen, R., and Trojanowski, J. 2009. "Use of Alzheimer Disease Biomarkers." *Journal of the American Medical Association* 302: 436–437.

Piasecki, S., and Jefferson, J. 2004. "Psychiatric Complications of Deep-Brain Stimulation for Parkinson's Disease." *Journal of Clinical Psychiatry* 65: 845–849.

Pitman, R., et al. 2002. "Pilot Study of Secondary Prevention of Posttraumatic Stress Disorder with Propranolol." *Biological Psychiatry* 51: 189–192.

Plum, F. 1991. "Coma and Related Global Disturbances of the Human Conscious State." In Peters and Jones, 359–425.

President's Council on Bioethics. 2003. Staff Working Paper, "Better Memories? The Promise and Perils of Pharmacological Intervention." http://www.bioethics.gov/transcripts/mar03.html

President's Council on Bioethics. 2008. White Paper. "Controversies in the Determination of Death." http://www.bioethics.gov/reports/death/determination_of_death_report.pdf

Price, J. (with Davis, B.). 2008. *The Woman Who Can't Forget*. New York: Free Press.

Putnam, H. 1981. *Reason, Truth, and History*. New York: Cambridge University Press.

Querfurth, H., and LaFeria, F. 2010. "Alzheimer's Disease." *New England Journal of Medicine* 362: 329–344.

Rabins, P., et al. 2009. "Scientific and Ethical Issues Related to Deep-Brain Stimulation for Disorders of Mood, Behavior, and Thought." *Archives of General Psychiatry* 66: 931–937.

Racine, E. 2010. *Pragmatic Neuroethics: Improving Treatment and Understanding of the Mind-Brain* Cambridge, MA: MIT Press.

Raichle, M. 2006. "Neuroimaging." *Cerebrum* 9, January. http://www.dana.org/printerfriendly.aspx?id=4224

Raine, A., et al. 1998. "Reduced Prefrontal and Increased Subcortical Brain Functioning Assessed Using Positron Emission Tomography in Predatory and Affective Murderers." *Behavioral Sciences & the Law* 16: 319–332.

Raison, C. L., et al. 2006. "Cytokines and the Blues: Inflammation and the Pathogenesis of Depression." *Trends in Immunology* 27: 24–31.

Randall, D., et al. 2003. "Modafinil Affects Mood, but not Cognitive Function, in Healthy Young Volunteers." *Psychopharmacology* 18: 163–173.

Randall, D., et al. 2005. "Cognitive Effects of Modafinil in Student Volunteers May Depend on IQ." *Pharmacology, Biochemistry, and Behavior* 82: 133–139.

Rawls, J. 1971. *A Theory of Justice.* Cambridge, MA: Harvard University Press.

Relkin, N., et al. 1996. "Impulsive Homicide Associated with an Arachnoid Cyst and Unilateral Frontotemporal Cerebral Dysfunction." *Seminars in Clinical Neuropsychiatry* 1: 172–183.

Repantis, D., et al. 2010. "Modafinil and Methylphenidate for Neuroenhancement in Healthy Individuals: A Systematic Review." *Pharmacological Research* 62: 187–206.

Report of the Committee on Mentally Abnormal Offenders. 1975. London: Her Majesty's Stationery Office.

Revonsuo, A., et al. 2009. "What Is an Altered State of Consciousness?" *Philosophical Psychology* 22: 187–204.

Rissman, J., Greely, H., and Wagner, A. 2010. "Detecting Individual Memories through the Neural Decoding of Memory States and Past Experience." *Proceedings of the National Academy of Sciences*, published online April 12.

Roediger, H., et al. 2008. "Free Will and Control of Action." In Baer, Kaufman, and Baumeister, 205–225.

Roemer, J. 1993. "A Pragmatic Theory of Responsibility for the Egalitarian Planner." *Philosophy & Public Affairs* 22: 146–166.

Roozendaal, B., et al. 2008. "Adrenal Stress Hormones, Amygdala Activation, and Memory for Emotionally Arousing Experiences." *Progress in Brain Research* 167: 79–97.

Roper v. Simmons. 2005. 543 U.S. 551.

Ropper, A. 2010. "*Cogito Ergo Sum* by MRI." *New England Journal of Medicine* 362: 648–649.

Rose, S. 2005. *The Future of the Brain: The Promise and Perils of Tomorrow's Neuroscience.* Oxford: Oxford University Press.

Rose, S. 2008. "How Smart Are Smart Drugs?" *The Lancet* 372:198–199.

Roskies, A. 2002. "Neuroethics for the New Millennium." *Neuron* 35: 21–23.

Roskies, A. 2006. "Neuroscientific Challenges to Free Will and Responsibility." *Trends in Cognitive Sciences* 10: 419–423.

Roskies, A. 2010. "Why Libet's Studies Don't Pose a Threat to Free Will." In Sinnott-Armstrong and Nadel, Chapter 2.

Ruck, C., et al. 2008. "Capsulotomy for Obsessive-Compulsive Disorder: Long-Term Follow-Up of 25 Patients." *Archives of General Psychiatry.* 65: 914–922.

Sabetrasekh, R., et al. 2006. "Current Views of the Embryonic and Neural Stem Cell: Cell Replacement or Molecular Repair?" In Sanberg and Sanberg, 1–30.

Sacks, O. 2007. "The Abyss: Music and Amnesia." *The New Yorker*, September 24. http://www.newyorker.com/reporting/2007/09/24/070924fa_fact_Sacks

Sadler, J. 2009. "Stigma, Conscience, and Science in Psychiatry: Past, Present, and Future." *Academic Medicine* 84: 413–417.

Sahakian, B., and Morein-Zamir, S. 2007. "Professor's Little Helper." *Nature* 450: 1157–1159.

Sahakian, B., and Morein-Zamir, S. 2010. "Neuroethical Issues in Cognitive Enhancement." *Journal of Psychopharmacology*, published online March 8.

Sanberg, C., and Sanberg, P., eds. 2006. *Cell Therapy, Stem Cells, and Brain Repair.* Totowa, NJ: Humana Press.

Sandel, M. 2007. *The Case against Perfection: Ethics in the Age of Genetic Engineering.* Cambridge, MA: Harvard University Press.

Sapolsky, R. 1992. *Stress, the Aging Brain, and the Mechanisms of Neuron Death.* Cambridge, MA: MIT Press.

Sapolsky, R. 2004. "The Frontal Cortex and the Criminal Justice System." *Philosophical Transactions of the Royal Society of London* 359: 1787–1796.

Savulescu, J., and Bostrom, N., eds. 2009. *Human Enhancement.* Oxford: Oxford.University Press.

Scanlon, T. 1998. *What We Owe to Each Other.* Cambridge, MA: Harvard University Press.

Schacter, D. 1996. *Searching for Memory: The Brain, the Mind, and the Past.* New York: Basic Books.

Schacter, D., and Tulving, E., eds. 1994. *Memory Systems.* Cambridge, MA: MIT Press.

Schacter, D., and Scarry, E., eds. 2000. *Memory, Brain, and Belief.* Cambridge: MA: Harvard University Press.

Schacter, D., and Addis, D. R. 2007. "The Ghosts of Past and Future." *Nature* 445: 27.

Schechtman, M. 1997. *The Constitution of Selves.* Ithaca, NY: Cornell University Press.

Schechtman, M. 2009. "Getting Our Stories Straight." In Mathews, Bok, and Rabins, 65–92.

Scheffler, R., et al. 2009. "Positive Association between Attention-Deficit/Hyperactivity Disorder Medication Use and Academic Achievement during Elementary School." *Pediatrics* 123: 1273–1279.

Schermer, M., et al. 2009. "The Future of Psychopharmacological Enhancements: Expectations and Policies." *Neuroethics* 2(2): 75–87.

Schiff, N., Giacino, J., and Fins. J. 2009. "Deep-Brain Stimulation, Neuroethics, and the Minimally Conscious State." *Archives of Neurology* 66: 697–702.

Schiff, N., et al. 2007. "Behavioral Improvement with Thalamic Stimulation after Severe Traumatic Brain Injury." *Nature* 448: 600–603.

Schiller, D., et al. 2010. "Preventing the Return of Fear in Humans Using Reconsolidation Update Mechanisms." *Nature* 463: 49–53.

Schlaepfer, T., and Fins, J. 2010. "Deep-Brain Stimulation and the Neuroethics of Responsible Publishing." *Journal of the American Medical Association* 303: 775–776.

Schlaepfer, T., et al. 2008. "Deep-Brain Stimulation to Reward Circuitry Alleviates Anhedonia in Refractory Major Depression." *Neuropsychopharmacology* 33: 368–377.

Schmidtz, D. and Brennan, J., 2010. *A Brief History of Liberty.* Malden, MA: Wiley-Blackwell.

Scoville, W., and Milner, B. 1957. "Loss of Recent Memory after Bilateral Hippocampal Lesions." *Journal of Neurology, Neurosurgery, and Psychiatry* 20: 11–21.

Sexton v. State. 2000. 775 So. 2d. 923, Fla.

Sherwin, B. 2006. "Estrogen and Cognitive Aging in Women." *Neuroscience* 138: 1021–1026.

Shewmon, A. 2001. "The Brain and Somatic Integration: Insights into the Standard Biological Rationale for Equating 'Brain Death' With Death." *Journal of Medicine and Philosophy* 26: 457–478.

Singer, P. 2005. "Ethics and Intuitions." *The Journal of Ethics* 9: 331–352.

Singh, R., et al. 2008. "Zolpidem in a Minimally Conscious State." *Brain Injury* 22: 103–106.

Sinnott-Armstrong, W., ed. 2008. *Moral Psychology, Volume 3: The Neuroscience of Morality: Emotion, Brain Disorders, and Development.* Cambridge, MA: MIT Press.

Sinnott-Armstrong, W., and Nadel, L., eds. 2010. *Conscious Will and Responsibility: A Tribute to Benjamin Libet.* New York: Oxford University Press,.

Sinnott-Armstrong, W., et al. 2009. "Brain Images as Legal Evidence." *Episteme* 5: 359–373.

Smith, E., and Dehaney, M. 2005. "Locked-In Syndrome." *British Medical Journal* 330: 406–409.

Soscia, S., et al. 2010. "The Alzheimer's Disease-Associated Amyloid-Beta Protein Is an Antimicrobial Peptide." *PLoS ONE* 5(3): e9505.

Spence, S. 2008. "Can Pharmacology Help Enhance Human Morality?" *British Journal of Psychiatry* 193: 179–180.

Spence, S. 2009. *The Actor's Brain: Exploring the Cognitive Neuroscience of Free Will.* Oxford: Oxford University Press.

Spillane, J. 1981. *The Doctrine of the Nerves.* Oxford: Oxford University Press.

Stevenson, R. L. 1984. *Dr. Jekyll and Mr. Hyde, and Other Stories.* New York: Grosset and Dunlap.

Strawson, G. 1994: "The Impossibility of Moral Responsibility." *Philosophical Studies* 75: 5–24.

Swaab, D. 2010. "Developments in Neuroscience: Where Have We Been? Where Are We Going?" In Giordano and Gordijn, 1–36.

Synofzik, M. 2009. "Ethically Justified, Clinically Applicable Criteria for Physician Decision-Making in Psychopharmacological Enhancement." *Neuroethics* 2(2): 89–102.

Synofzik, M., and Schlaepfer, T. 2008. "Stimulating Personality: Ethical Concern for Deep-Brain Stimulation in Psychiatric Patients and for Enhancement Purposes." *Biotechnology Journal* 3: 1511–1520.

Talbot, M. 2009. "Brain Gain: The Underground World of Neuroenhancing Drugs." *The New Yorker,* April 27. http://www.newyorker.com/reporting/2009/04/27/090427fa_fact?currentPage=all

Tallis, R. 2004. "Trying to Find Consciousness in the Brain." *Brain* 127: 2558–2563.

Taurek, J. 1977. "Should the Numbers Count?" *Philosophy & Public Affairs* 6: 293–316.

Taylor, C. 1991. *The Ethics of Authenticity.* Cambridge, MA: Harvard University Press.

Teasdale, G., and Jennett, B. 1974. "Assessment of Coma and Impaired Consciousness: A Practical Scale." *The Lancet* 303: 81–84.

Thompson, E. 2007. *Mind in Life: Biology, Phenomenology, and the Sciences of Mind.* Cambridge, MA: Harvard University Press.

Thomson, J. 1976. "Killing, Letting Die, and the Trolley Problem." *The Monist* 59: 204–217.

Thomson, J. 1985. "The Trolley Problem." *Yale Law Journal* 94: 1395–1415.

Thomson, J. 2008. "Turning the Trolley." *Philosophy & Public Affairs* 36: 359–374.

Tully, T., et al. 2003. "Targeting the CREB Pathway for Memory Enhancers." *Nature Reviews Drug Discovery* 2: 266–277.

Tulving, E., and Lepage, M. 2000. "Where in the Brain Is the Awareness of One's Past?" In Schacter and Scarry, 208–228.

Tuszynski, M., et al. 2005. "A Phase I Clinical Trial of Nerve Growth Factor Gene Therapy for Alzheimer Disease." *Nature Medicine* 11: 551–555.

Tversky, A., and Kahneman, D. 1981. "The Framing of Decisions and the Psychology of Choice." *Science* 211: 453–458.

Vincent, N. 2008. "Responsibility, Dysfunction, and Capacity." *Neuroethics* 1(3): 199–204.

Vincent, N. 2012. "Enhancing Responsibility." In Vincent, ed., Chapter 12.

Vincent, N., ed. 2012. *Legal Responsibility and Neuroscience.* Oxford: Oxford University Press.

Viding, E., et al. 2005. "Evidence for Substantial Genetic Risk for Psychopathy in 7-Year-Olds." *Journal of Child Psychology and Psychiatry* 46: 592–597.

Volkow, N., et al. 2009. "Effects of Modafinil on Dopamine and Dopamine Transporters in the Male Human Brain." *Journal of the American Medical Association* 301: 1148–1154.

Voss, H., et al. 2006. "Possible Axonal Regrowth in Late Recovery from the Minimally Conscious State." *Journal of Clinical Investigation* 116: 2005–2011.

Walkup, J. T., et al. 2008. "Cognitive Behavioral Therapy, Sertraline, or a Combination in Childhood Anxiety." *New England Journal of Medicine* 359: 2753–2766.

Watson, G. 2004. *Agency and Answerability*. New York: Oxford University Press.

Weaver, F., et al. 2009. "Bilateral Deep-Brain Stimulation vs. Best Medical Therapy for Patients with Advanced Parkinson Disease." *Journal of the American Medical Association* 301: 63–73.

Webber, B. 2008. "Barbara Warren, Winner of Endurance Competitions, Dies at 65." *New York Times*, August 29. http://www.nytimes.com/2008/08/30/sports/othersports/30warren.html

Wegner, D. 2002. *The Illusion of Conscious Will*. Cambridge, MA: MIT Press.

Wegner, D. 2008. "Self Is Magic." In Baer, Kaufman, and Baumeister, 226–247.

Weisberg, D., et al. 2008. "The Seductive Allure of Neuroscience Explanations." *Journal of Cognitive Neuroscience* 20: 470–477.

Weiskrantz, L., and Davies, M., eds. 2008. *Frontiers of Consciousness*. Oxford: Oxford University Press.

Wexler, B. 2008. *Brain and Culture: Neurobiology, Ideology, and Social Change*. Cambridge, MA: MIT Press.

Wezenberg, E., et al. 2007. "Acute Effects of the Ampakine Farampator on Memory and Information Processing in Healthy Elderly Volunteers." *Neuropsychopharmacology* 32: 1272–1283.

Wijdicks, E. 2001. "The Diagnosis of Brain Death." *New England Journal of Medicine* 344: 1215–1221.

Wijdicks, E., et al. 2005. "Validation of a New Coma Scale: The FOUR Scale." *Annals of Neurology* 58: 589–593.

Wilens, T., et al. 2008. "Misuse and Diversion of Stimulants Prescribed for ADHD: A Systematic Review of the Literature." *Journal of the American Academy of Child and Adolescent Psychiatry* 47: 21–31.

Wilkinson, D., et al. 2009. "Functional Neuroimaging and Withdrawal of Life-Sustaining Treatment from Vegetative Patients." *Journal of Medical Ethics* 35: 508–511.

Williams, B. 1973. *Problems of the Self*. Cambridge: Cambridge University Press.

Williams, B. 1981. *Moral Luck*. Cambridge: Cambridge University Press.

Williams, G. 1957. "Pleiotropy, Natural Selection, and the Evolution of Senescence." *Evolution* 11: 398–411.

Wilson, E. O. 1998. *Consilience: The Unity of Knowledge*. New York: Alfred A. Knopf.

Wittgenstein, L. 1997. *Philosophical Investigations*, 3rd ed., trans. and ed. G. E. M. Anscombe. Cambridge, MA: Blackwell.

Working Group of the Royal College of Physicians. 1995. "Criteria for the Diagnosis of Brain Stem Death." *Journal of the Royal College of Physicians of London* 29: 381–382.

Wrosch, C., and Miller, G. 2009. "Depressive Symptoms Can Be Useful: Self-Regulatory and Emotional Benefits of Dysphoric Mood in Adolescence." *Journal of Personality and Social Psychology* 96: 1181–1190.

Young, L., and Koenigs, M. 2007. "Investigating Emotion in Moral Cognition: A Review of Evidence from Functional Neuroimaging and Neuropsychology." *British Medical Bulletin* 84: 69–79.

Zangaglia, R., et al. 2009. "Deep-Brain Stimulation and Cognitive Functions in Parkinson's Disease: A Three-Year Controlled Study." *Movement Disorders* 24: 1621–1628.

Zeman, A. 2004. *Consciousness; A User's Guide*. New Haven: Yale University Press.

Zeman, A. 2008. "Does Consciousness Spring from the Brain? Dilemmas of Awareness in Practice and in Theory." In Weiskrantz and Davies, 289–321.

Index

CPSIA information can be obtained at www.ICGtesting.com
Printed in the USA
BVOW08s2009180816

459476BV00001B/4/P

9 780199 315796